Lecture Notes in Computer Science   11400

Commenced Publication in 1973
Founding and Former Series Editors:
Gerhard Goos, Juris Hartmanis, and Jan van Leeuwen

More information about this series at http://www.springer.com/series/7407

Joanna Kołodziej · Horacio González-Vélez (Eds.)

High-Performance Modelling and Simulation for Big Data Applications

Selected Results of the COST Action IC1406 cHiPSet

EUROPEAN COOPERATION
IN SCIENCE & TECHNOLOGY

Editors
Joanna Kołodziej
Cracow University of Technology
Cracow, Poland

Horacio González-Vélez
National College of Ireland
Dublin, Ireland

ISSN 0302-9743   ISSN 1611-3349   (electronic)
Lecture Notes in Computer Science
ISBN 978-3-030-16271-9   ISBN 978-3-030-16272-6   (eBook)
https://doi.org/10.1007/978-3-030-16272-6

Library of Congress Control Number: 2019936007

LNCS Sublibrary: SL1 – Theoretical Computer Science and General Issues

Acknowledgement and Disclaimer
This publication is based upon work from the COST Action IC1406 High-Performance Modelling and
Simulation for Big Data Applications (cHiPSet), supported by COST (European Cooperation in Science and
Technology).
The book reflects only the authors' views. Neither the COST Association nor any person acting on its behalf
is responsible for the use, which might be made of the information contained in this publication. The COST
Association is not responsible for external websites or sources referred to in this publication.

This Springer imprint is published by the registered company Springer Nature Switzerland AG
The registered company address is: Gewerbestrasse 11, 6330 Cham, Switzerland

European Cooperation in Science and Technology (COST)

This publication is based upon work from COST Action IC1406 "High-Performance Modelling and Simulation for Big Data Applications (cHiPSet)" supported by COST (European Cooperation in Science and Technology).

COST (European Cooperation in Science and Technology) is a funding agency for research and innovation networks. Our Actions help connect research initiatives across Europe and enable scientists to grow their ideas by sharing them with their peers. This boosts their research, career and innovation.

www.cost.eu

Funded by the Horizon 2020 Framework Programme of the European Union

Preface

Long considered important components of the scientific method, Modelling and Simulation (M–S) have evolved from traditional discrete numerical methods to complex data-intensive continuous analytical optimisations. Resolution, scale, and accuracy have become essential to predict and analyse natural and complex systems in science and engineering. When their level of abstraction rises to have a better discernment of the domain at hand, their computational representation becomes increasingly demanding for computational and data resources. It is not unusual to have models with hundreds of features, conditions, and constraints coupled with complex simulations with large data sets. These complex systems do not easily lend themselves to straightforward modular decompositions that support parallelisation and trivial computational support. They often require a significant amount of computational resources with associated data sets scattered across multiple sources and different geographical locations.

It is then required to have a seamless interaction of large computational resources with M–S in order to store, compute, analyze, and visualize large data sets in science and engineering. To nurture such data-intensive computational M–S, the 4-year cHiPSet Action enabled the cross-pollination of distinct expert communities:

1. High Performance Computing (HPC)
2. Modelling and Simulation (M–S)
3. Domain scientists and practitioners

Funded by the European Commission, cHiPSet has provided a dynamic trans-European forum for their members and distinguished guests to openly discuss novel perspectives and topics of interest for the M–S and HPC communities. Figure 1 presents a schematic representation of cHiPSet.

Structured into 12 complementary chapters, this cHiPSet compendium presents a set of selected case studies related to data-intensive computational M–S in artificial intelligence, bioinformatics, electrical engineering, pharmacology, finance, healthcare, social media, and telecommunications. Its purpose is to illustrate the tangible improvement in the understanding of those domains, which has been faciliated by cHiPSet collaborations. All case studies are co-authored by individuals associated with cHiPSet who have worked together through dedicated meetings, workshops, short-term scientific missions, and summer schools.

– Grelck et al. introduce the overall cHiPSet aims and objectives with special emphasis on how Big Data has both posed a challenge and offered development opportunities for HPC: how to efficiently turn massively large data into valuable information and meaningful knowledge. They also describe how M–S offer suitable abstractions to manage the complexity of analysing Big Data in various scientific and engineering domains.

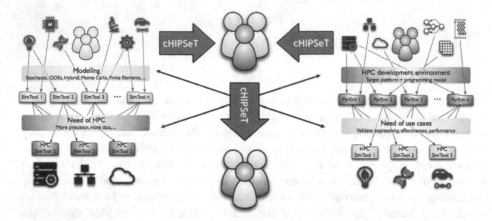

Fig. 1. Schematic representation of the cHiPSet action.

- Larsson et al. describe two classes of algorithms for the numerical solution of large electromagnetic scattering problems and include results for a proof-of-concept parallel implementation. They conclude by providing various perspectives on large-scale simulations that require parallel implementation.
- Rached and Larsson have furnished a survey of currently used parametric and non-parametric methods for the non-statistical estimation of tail distributions and extreme quantiles. They also render some perspectives on how to move forward with non-parametric kernel-based estimation.
- Kilanioti et al. describe why social data streams raise a variety of practical challenges, including the real-time generation of meaningful insights. They present a methodological approach to work with large-scale social media streams in order to efficiently perform content distribution, data diffusion, and data replication.
- Nejkovic et al. look into the forthcoming fifth generation of mobile networks, commonly known as 5G, which will significantly improve the bandwidth, capacity, and reliability of current telecommunication operators. They enumerate some key 5G use cases from home entertainment to product manufacturing and healthcare.
- Brdar et al. focus on location data collected in mobile cellular networks and on how to identify patterns of human activity, interactions, and mobility. They also point out the critical challenges to unlock the value of data coming from mobile cellular networks.
- Vitabile et al. report on recent developments in health monitoring technologies to enable diagnosis and treatment of patients with chronic diseases, older adults, and people with disabilities. They also highlight the value of sensor-supported pervasive healthcare to facilitate independent living and disease management.
- Spolaor et al. enquire into HPC-enabled model reduction techniques to uncover emergent behaviors in complex cellular systems. Their large-scale comprehensive approach aims to improve the understanding of cell behavior using multiple scales of temporal and spatial organisation.

- Olgac et al. survey tools and workflows for cloud-based virtual screening, a data-intensive computational method for rational drug design and development. They explain its relevance to medicinal chemists, pharmacologists, and computational scientists for the discovery and testing of novel pharmaceuticals.
- Kołodziej et al. introduce ultra wide band for wireless body area networks—interconnected structures of nodes attached to a human body, an external base station, and possibly the Internet. Their survey describes cloud-based data storage, security, and analysis in the context of mobile health monitoring.
- Marechal et al. discuss the challenges involved in automatic human emotion recognition. As an evolving area in artificial intelligence, it entails the development of data-driven systems for emotion representation, recognition, and prediction.
- Finally, Zamuda et al. outline the state of the art in forecasting cryptocurrency value by sentiment analysis. Their contribution includes current challenges in the deployment of distributed ledgers (blockchains) and sentiment analysis metrics using large data streams and cloud platforms.

In summary, the cHiPSet COST Action facilitated the exchange of knowledge, experiences, and best practices between individuals with a track record in HPC and domain scientists and engineers. Its tangible collaborative endeavors have arguably enhanced the resolution and accuracy of M–S by deploying smart algorithms and techniques on large-scale infrastructures. The cHiPSet COST Action has contributed toward improving the understanding of natural phenomena and complex systems for European academics and industry practitioners.

This compendium is based on collaborative endeavors partly supported by IC1406 High-Performance Modelling and Simulation for Big Data Applications – cHiPSet (cHiPSet), an Action supported by COST (European Cooperation in Science and Technology) from 2015 to 2019, as part of Horizon 2020—the EU Framework Programme for Research and Innovation.

We are grateful to all the contributors of this book, for their willingness to work on this interdisciplinary book project. We thank the authors for their interesting proposals of the book chapters, their time, efforts, and their research ideas, which makes this volume an interesting complete state-of-the-art monograph of the latest research advances and technology developments on the next generation of distributed and complex HPC M-S in the big data era. We also would like to express our sincere thanks to the reviewers, who helped us ensure the quality of this volume. We gratefully acknowledge their time and valuable remarks and comments.

Our special thanks go to Alfred Hoffmann, Aliaksandr Birukou, Anna Kramer, and all the editorial team of Springer for their patience, valuable editorial assistance, and excellent cooperative collaboration in this book project.

Finally, we would like to send our warmest gratitude to our friends and families for their patience, love, and support in the preparation of this volume.

January 2019

Joanna Kołodziej
Horacio González–Vélez

IC1406 Committee

Action Scientific Officer

Ralph Stübner   Cost Association, Brussels, Belgium

Action Chair

Joanna Kołodziej   Cracow University of Technology, Poland

Action Vice Chair

Horacio González–Vélez   Cloud Competency Centre, National College
                                 of Ireland, Dublin, Ireland

Scientific Coordinator

Clemens Grelck   University of Amsterdam, The Netherlands

Working Group (WG) Leaders

WG1 Leader
Ewa Niewiadomska–   Warsaw University of Technology, Poland
Szynkiewicz

WG2 Leader
Marco Aldinucci   University of Turin, Italy

WG3 Leader
Andrea Bracciali   University of Stirling, UK

WG4 Leader
Elisabeth Larsson   University of Uppsala, Sweden

STSM Coordinator

Juan Carlos Burguillo-Rial   University of Vigo, Spain

TS Coordinator

Ciprian Dobre   University Politehnica of Bucharest, Romania

Dissemination Coordinator

Peter Kilpatrick   Queen's University, Belfast, UK

Industry Collaboration Coordinator

Dave Feenan   Technology Ireland ICT Skillnet, Ireland

Contents

Why High-Performance Modelling and Simulation for Big Data Applications Matters

Clemens Grelck[1]([✉]) [iD], Ewa Niewiadomska-Szynkiewicz[2] [iD],
Marco Aldinucci[3] [iD], Andrea Bracciali[4] [iD], and Elisabeth Larsson[5] [iD]

[1] University of Amsterdam, Amsterdam, Netherlands
c.grelck@uva.nl
[2] Warsaw University of Technology, Warsaw, Poland
ens@ia.pw.edu.pl
[3] University of Turin, Turin, Italy
marco.aldinucci@unito.it
[4] University of Stirling, Stirling, UK
abb@cs.stir.ac.uk
[5] Uppsala University, Uppsala, Sweden
elisabeth.larsson@it.uu.se

Abstract. Modelling and Simulation (M&S) offer adequate abstractions to manage the complexity of analysing big data in scientific and engineering domains. Unfortunately, big data problems are often not easily amenable to efficient and effective use of High Performance Computing (HPC) facilities and technologies. Furthermore, M&S communities typically lack the detailed expertise required to exploit the full potential of HPC solutions while HPC specialists may not be fully aware of specific modelling and simulation requirements and applications.

The COST Action IC1406 *High-Performance Modelling and Simulation for Big Data Applications* has created a strategic framework to foster interaction between M&S experts from various application domains on the one hand and HPC experts on the other hand to develop effective solutions for big data applications. One of the tangible outcomes of the COST Action is a collection of case studies from various computing domains. Each case study brought together both HPC and M&S experts, giving witness of the effective cross-pollination facilitated by the COST Action.

In this introductory article we argue why joining forces between M&S and HPC communities is both timely in the big data era and crucial for success in many application domains. Moreover, we provide an overview on the state of the art in the various research areas concerned.

1 Introduction

The big data era poses a critically difficult challenge for high-performance computing (HPC): how to efficiently turn massively large and often unstructured or

© The Author(s) 2019
J. Kołodziej and H. González-Vélez (Eds.): cHiPSet, LNCS 11400, pp. 1–35, 2019.
https://doi.org/10.1007/978-3-030-16272-6_1

semi-structured data first into valuable information and then into meaningful knowledge. HPC facilities and technologies are effectively required in a rapidly increasing number of data-intensive domains from life and physical sciences to socioeconomic systems. Thus, the big data era likewise offers striking opportunities for HPC to widen its scope and to strengthen its societal and economic impact.

High-performance Computing (HPC) and high throughput computing underpin the large scale processing of grand challenge problems with data-intensive requirements in order to enable complex applications in distinct scientific and technical fields such as high-energy physics, genomics, systems and synthetic biology, industrial automation, social and economic data analytics and medical informatics. This has led to a substantial improvement in the understanding of diverse domains ranging from the evolution of the physical world to human societies. Application performance in HPC systems is nowadays largely dominated by remote and local data movement overhead (network messages, memory and storage accesses). This poses new challenges to HPC modelling and programming languages, which should enhance data locality where possible and enable fast data transition where needed.

When investigating the behaviour and complexity of abstractions for large-scale big data systems, one employs a series of technologies that have their roots in well-funded large compute cluster environments. With the advent of hardware accelerators (GPU, FPGA), pay-by-use cloud services, and the increased performance of general-purpose processors, HPC has become an option for many scientific disciplines.

The COST Action IC1406 *High-Performance Modelling and Simulation for Big Data Applications* facilitates cross-pollination between the HPC community (both developers and users) and M&S disciplines for which the use of HPC facilities, technologies and methodologies still is a novel, if any, phenomenon. Data-intensive domains make the issue of efficiency particularly relevant for problems such as multi-dimensional and multi-level integration and model state explosion. Furthermore, these complex systems do not straightforwardly lend themselves to modular decomposition, a crucial prerequisite for parallelisation, and, hence, HPC support. They often require a significant amount of computational resources with data sets scattered across multiple sources and different geographical locations.

Modelling and Simulation (M&S) are widely considered essential tools in science and engineering to substantiate the prediction and analysis of complex systems and natural phenomena. Modelling has traditionally addressed complexity by raising the level of abstraction and aiming at an essential representation of the domain at hand. This has resulted in a complicated trade-off between accuracy and efficiency. That is to say, the properties of a system can be studied by reproducing (i.e., *simulating*) its behaviour through its abstract representation. Arguably, the context of the application level should be reconsidered. For instance, Monte Carlo simulations must be fed with input data, store intermediate results, and filter and merge output data in an adjusted and reliably robust manner. Thus, M&S approaches are particularly affected by the data deluge phenomenon since they need to use large data sets to enhance resolution and scale and distribute and analyse data in the different phases of the simulation-analysis pipeline.

Both HPC and M&S are well established research areas each by themselves. However, a better integration of the two, aimed at applications from various domains, will bring substantial progress in addressing big data problems.

On the one hand, domain experts need HPC for simulation, modelling, and data analysis, but are often unaware of performance and parallelism exploitation pitfalls in their designs. On the other hand, designers of HPC development tools and systems primarily focus on absolute performance measures, by definition the raison d'être for HPC. However, MIPS, FLOPS, and speedups need not be the only measures. Domain-specific considerations may put some more or even almost all emphasis on other factors, such as usability, productivity, economic cost and time to solution. By further improving collaboration with domain experts HPC architects ought to be able to develop programming models and architectures better tailored to specific problems. Likewise, analysis and validation tools ought to be improved for a better understanding of HPC systems by domain experts.

The COST Action IC1406 *High-Performance Modelling and Simulation for Big Data Applications* is based on the idea that key aspects of HPC-enabled M&S must be jointly addressed by considering the needs and issues posed by the two communities together. When multidimensional, heterogeneous, massive data sets need to be analysed in a specific big data application domain, the methods required to suitably process the data are necessarily determined by the kind of data and analysis to be performed.

Consequently, the features of a programming language, library or execution machinery supporting the efficient implementation of the analysis should not be thought of as independent of the specific data and analysis themselves. Analogously, data characteristics must drive the design and implementation of data storage systems enabling efficient storage, access, and manipulation. Within this vision, the COST Action addresses the specific challenges of both M&S and HPC in a unified way.

The participants of the COST Action jointly work towards a unified framework for the systematic advancement of M&S and big data endeavours supported by leading HPC-enabled models and tools through a coordinated effort of HPC and M&S experts. The main objective is to create a long-lasting, sustainable, reference network of research links between the HPC community on the one hand and the multiple M&S research communities addressing big data problems on the other hand. Such links enable a novel and persisting collaboration framework across HPC and M&S communities, covering both academia and industry across Europe and beyond with a common agenda: turning huge amounts of raw data into useful knowledge.

The remainder of this paper is organised as follows: We first illustrate the background of our work and review the current state of the art in Sect. 2.

Following this introductory part, we have a closer look at the subjects relevant to the four working groups that make up the COST Action IC1406. We focus on *Enabling Infrastructures and Middleware for Big-Data Modelling and Simulation* in Sect. 3, *Parallel Programming Models for Big-Data Modelling and Simulation* in Sect. 4, *HPC-enabled Modelling and Simulation for Life Sciences* in Sect. 5, *HPC-enabled Modelling and Simulation for Socio-Economical and Physical Sciences* in Sect. 6, respectively. Last, but not least, we draw some conclusions in Sect. 7.

2   Background and State of the Art

High-Performance Computing is currently undergoing a major change with *exascale systems* expected for the early 2020s. They will be very different from today's HPC systems and pose a number of technological challenges, from energy consumption to the development of adequate programming models for millions of computing elements. Several current exascale research programmes, therefore, span a 10 to 20-year period. Major experiments depend on HPC for the analysis and interpretation of data and the simulation of models.

Modelling and Simulation have traditionally been used where the complexity of the problem makes more direct analytical approaches unsuitable or impossible. This is particularly true for big data problems where the support of HPC infrastructures and programming models is essential. The design and optimisation of HPC-enabled big data experiments and large scale HPC systems require the realistic description and modelling of the data access patterns, the data flow across the local and wide area networks and the scheduling and workload presented by hundreds of jobs running concurrently and exchanging very large amounts of data. Data-intensive (*big data*) HPC is arguably fundamental to address *grand-challenge* M&S problems.

In fact, several M&S approaches are based on discrete-event frameworks due to their efficiency and scalability. M&S have addressed problems such as scheduling in distributed, heterogeneous environments, economy-driven resource allocation, big data access in distributed environments and more generic HPC concurrent, distributed and cloud architecture. As described in the CERN Big Data HPC infrastructure, stochastic data traffic, management of virtual machines, and job allocation in data centers represent *grand-challenge* HPC-related problems, which require extensive use of M&S and HPC itself. Attempts to describe and analyse hardware, middleware and application co-design, an important development direction for HPC, have been made, but they currently appear too costly. The complexity can be reduced by means of coarse-grained models, which need precise measures of uncertainty and associated errors and statistical inference. Simulations have been run in this context for systems with one million cores. Recent trends aim to empower programmers to more easily control the hardware performance. Examples include the embedding of HPC facilities in standard OS distributions.

From an application perspective, HPC-enabled M&S has started to play a crucial role in a number of diverse knowledge domains. Preliminary proposals with direct porting of existing techniques in HPC (e.g. in climate modelling) and further developments are being sought. In computational electromagnetics modelling problems with up to one billion variables have been addressed with both memory- and CPU-intensive algorithms, solving major longstanding problems. More structured approaches based on pattern-based parallel programming effectively cater for the design and development of parallel pipelines for M&S in systems biology and next generation sequencing [1,2], providing developers with portability across a variety of HPC platforms, like clusters of multi-cores [3,4] as well as cloud infrastructures [5].

However, HPC-enabled M&S has still not reached a fully satisfactory maturity, facing relevant problems in terms of computational efficiency and lack of generality and expressiveness when addressing data-intensive scenarios. The development of new complex HPC-enabled M&S applications requires collaborative efforts from researchers with different domain knowledge and expertise. Since most of these applications belong to domains within the life, social and physical sciences, their mainstream approaches are rooted in non-computational abstractions and they are typically not HPC-enabled.

Recent surveys of the use of HPC in life sciences illustrate possible new scenarios for knowledge extraction and the management of large-scale and heterogeneous data collections with numerous applications in medical informatics. Valuable big data diagnostic applications are being developed with the aim of improving diagnosis by integrating images and large multi-source data sets. These come at the extraordinary price of HPC-level infrastructure and suffer from the lack of standard protocols for big data representation and processing. Once computational results are obtained, large amounts of information need domain-specific validation. For instance, in bio-medical studies, wet-lab validation typically involves additional resource-intensive work that has to be geared towards a statistically significant distilled fragment of the computational results, suitable to confirm the bio-medical hypotheses and compatible with the available resources.

Big data is an emerging paradigm whose size and features are beyond the ability of the current M&S tools [6]. Datasets are heterogeneous, i.e., they are produced by different sources and are of a large size with high in/out rates. big data accessibility and the capability to efficiently bring and combine data together will be extremely valuable. Currently, many HPC-enabled M&S efforts have been proposed in several big data contexts, as diverse as performance evaluation and the management of HPC frameworks, research on blood anti-coagulants, the numerical evaluation of quantum dynamics, computational social network analysis (e.g. the relationship between Internet use and specific emotions, human obesity or happiness) and genomic sequence discovery. Some approaches have been successful, leading to potential industrial impact and supporting experiments that generate petabytes of data, like those performed at CERN for instance.

Furthermore, there are a growing number of new implementations of memory-demanding applications that have not yet been adapted for HPC environments, mainly because of limited communication between field experts and those with suitable skills for the parallel implementation of data-intensive applications. Therefore, another natural objective of our work is to intelligently transfer the heterogeneous workflows in M&S to HPC, which will boost those scientific fields that are essential for both M&S and HPC societies [7]. Benefits will be reciprocal. M&S experts are be supported in their investigations by properly-enabled HPC frameworks, currently sought but missing. HPC architects in turn obtain access to a wealth of application domains by means of which they will better understand the specific requirements of HPC in the big data era. Among others, we aim at the design of improved data-center oriented programming models and frameworks for HPC-enabled M&S.

3   Enabling Infrastructures and Middleware for Big-Data Modelling and Simulation

From the inception of the Internet, one has witnessed an explosive growth in the volume, speed and variety of electronic data created on a daily basis. Raw data currently originates from numerous sources including mobile devices, sensors, instruments (e.g., CERN LHC, MR scanners, etc.), computer files, Internet of Things, governmental/open data archives, system software logs, social networks, commercial datasets, etc. The challenge is how to collect, integrate and store, with less hardware and software requirements, tremendous data sets generated from distributed sources.

The so-called big data problem requires the continuous improvement of servers, storage, and the whole network infrastructure in order to enable the efficient analysis and interpretation of data through on-hand data management applications, e.g. agent-based solutions in Agent Component in Oracle Data Integrator (ODI). The main challenge in big data modelling and simulation is to define a complete framework which includes intelligent management and communication, data fusion, mapping algorithms and protocols. The programming abstractions and data manipulation techniques must, therefore, be designed for (a) the seamless implementation of application solutions with efficient levels of virtualisation of computational resources (communications, storage, and servers) and (b) the effective normalisation and merging of data with dissimilar types into a consistent format (wide class of data services).

Energy-awareness is an important aspect of big data computing and simulation. The goal is to reduce the gap between the capacity provided by distributed computing environments and application requirements, especially during low workload periods. Various efforts are undertaken to develop energy efficient task scheduling and balancing of loads [8–11] and frequency scaling techniques [12–14].

Infrastructure and Middleware for Big Data Processing. Numerous algorithms, computing infrastructures and middleware for HPC and big data processing have been developed during previous decades [15,16]. In general, current middleware for parallel computating focuses on providing powerful mechanisms for managing communication between processors and environments for parallel machines and computer networks. High Performance Fortran (HPF), OpenMP, OpenACC, PVM, and MPI were designed to support communications for scalable applications. The application paradigms were developed to perform calculations on shared memory machines and clusters of machines with distributed memory. However, the easy access to information offered by the internet led to a new idea: extending the connection between computers, so that distributed resources, including computing power, storage, applications, etc. could be accessed as easily as information on web pages. The idea was implemented in many forms, but lately it has grown into three main computing environments: computing clusters, grids and clouds. A survey of software tools for supporting cluster, grid and cloud computing is provided in [15,17,18]. Examples of commonly known kernels for cluster computing are MOSIX [19], OpenSSI [20] and Kerrighed [21]. Uniform interfaces to computing resources in grids and toolkits for building grids (e.g. UNICORE [22] or Globus Toolkit [23]) are described in literature [24,25]. Cloud computing infrastructures consisting of services delivered through common centers and built on servers are discussed in [18].

An alternative to supercomputers and computing clusters the (General-Purpose) Graphics Procession Unit (GPGPU)—is widely used in HPC simulation [26]. Using both CPU and GPU through CUDA or OpenCL many real-world applications can rather easily be implemented and run significantly faster than on multi-processor or multi-core systems.

Tools and Platforms for Big Data Processing. Job scheduling, load balancing and management play a crucial role in HPC and big data simulation [27,28]. TORQUE [29] is a distributed resource manager providing control over batch jobs and distributed compute nodes. Slurm [30] is an open source, fault-tolerant and highly scalable cluster management and job scheduling system for large and small Linux clusters. MapReduce [31] is a framework that simplifies the processing of massive volumes of data through using two subsequent functions, i.e. the Map function that sorts and splits the input data and the Reduce function that is responsible for processing the intermediate output data. Resource management and job scheduling technology like YARN [32] allows multiple data processing engines such as batch processing, real-time streaming, interactive SQL and data science to handle data stored in a single platform. The Apache Hadoop software library [32] supports the distributed, scalable batch processing of large data sets across clusters of computers using a simple programming model. The power of the Hadoop platform is based on the Hadoop Distributed File System (HDFS), a distributed and scalable non-relational database HBase, MapReduce, YARN and many other open source projects. Some of the best-known include: Spark, Pig, Hive, JAQL, Sqoop, Oozie, Mahout, etc. Apache Spark [33], a unified engine for big data processing, provides an alternative to MapReduce that enables workloads to execute in memory, instead of on disk. Thus Spark avoids the resource-intensive disk operations that MapReduce requires. It processes data in RAM utilizing a data model based on the Resilient Distributed Dataset (RDD) abstraction. Apache Storm [34] is a scalable, rapid, fault-tolerant platform for distributed computing that has the advantage of handling real time data processing downloaded from synchronous and asynchronous systems. Apache Flink [35] can be used to batch and stream processing, event-time processing and stateful computations, well-suited for discrete-event simulation.

Platforms for Big Data Visualisation and Machine Learning. Numerous tools for big data analysis, visualisation and machine learning have been made available. RapidMiner Studio [36], Orange [37] and Weka [38] belong to this group. New software applications have been developed for browsing, visualizing, interpreting and analyzing large-scale sequencing data. Some of them have been designed specifically for visualisation of genome sequence assemblies, including Tablet [39]. Other tools, such as BamView [40] have been developed specifically to visualise mapped read alignment data in the context of the reference sequence. Artemis [41] is a freely available integrated platform for visualisation and analysis of large-scale experimental data. The survey of platforms and packages for social network analysis, simulation and visualisation that have wide applications including biology, finance and sociology is presented in [42].

Frameworks for Big Data Systems Simulation. Another issue is concerned with large-scale systems simulation. The combination of efficient and reliable simulation software and purpose-built hardware optimized for simulation workloads is crucial to fully exploit the value of simulation and big data. Synchronous and asynchronous distributed simulation have been one of the options that could improve the scalability of a simulator both in term of application size and execution speed, enabling large scale systems to be simulated in real time [43,44]. ScalaTion [45] provides comprehensive support for discrete-event simulation and big data analytics. A software framework for federated simulation of WSN and mobile ad-hoc networks is presented in [46]. The paper [47] reviews several large-scale military simulations and describes two frameworks for data management based on layered and service oriented architectures. GPU-based simulation platforms are mainly dedicated to massive data processing, e.g. high-performance neural network simulators [48,49], simulation of P systems [50], large-scale volume of data simulation and visualisation [51].

Numerous software platforms have been designed to simulate large-scale distributed data centers and computer networks. JADE [52] is the heterogeneous multiprocessor design simulation environment that allows to simulate network-on-chips, inter-chip networks and intra-rack networks using optical and electrical interconnects. SimGrid [53] can be used to simulate grids, clouds, HPC or P2P systems and evaluate heuristics or prototype applications. CloudSim [54] is one of the most popular open source framework for modeling and simulation of cloud computing infrastructures and services. Multi2Sim [55] is a software platform for simulation of new CPU and GPU technologies.

4 Parallel Programming Models for Big-Data Modelling and Simulation

A core challenge in modelling and simulation is the need to combine software expertise and domain expertise. Even starting from well-defined mathematical models, manual coding is inevitable. When parallel or distributed computing is required, the coding becomes much harder. This may impair time-to-solution, performance, and performance portability across different platforms. These problems have been traditionally addressed by trying to lift software design and development to a higher level of abstraction.

In the domain-specific languages (DSL) approach abstractions aim to provide domain experts with programming primitives that match specific concepts in their domain. Performance and portability issues are ideally moved (with various degrees of effectiveness) to development tools. Examples include Verilog and VHDL hardware description languages, MATLAB for matrix programming, Mathematica and Maxima for symbolic mathematics, etc.

In general-purpose approaches such as model-driven engineering (MDE), general-purpose programming concepts are abstracted into high-level constructs enforcing extra-functional features by design, e.g. compositionality, portability, parallelisability. In this regard, the number and the quality of programming models enabling the high-level management of parallelism have steadily increased and, in some cases, these approaches have become mainstream for a range of HPC, data-intensive and big data workloads: streaming (e.g. Storm [56] and Spark [57]), structured parallel programming and MapReduce [58] (e.g. Hadoop [59], Intel TBB [60], OpenMP [61], MPI [62]), SIMD (e.g. OpenACC [63]). This list can be extended by various academic approaches, including ones proposed and advocated by members of the COST Action (e.g. FastFlow [64,65]), SkePU [66], SaC [67], S-Net [68]).

A sensible result achieved by the working group on *Parallel Programming Models for Big-Data Modelling and Simulation* has been the assessment of the state of the art. A selection of the mainstream approaches in this area are presented in Sect. 4.1, namely Google MapReduce, Apache Spark, Apache Flink, Apache Storm and Apache Beam. In Sect. 4.2 we describe a systematic mapping study, aimed to capture and categorise non-mainstream DSLs.

4.1 Languages and Frameworks for Big Data Analysis

Boosted by big data popularity new languages and frameworks for data analytics are appearing at an increasing pace. Each of them introduces its own concepts and terminology and advocates a (real or alleged) superiority in terms of performance or expressiveness against its predecessors. In this hype, for a user approaching big data analytics (even an educated computer scientist) it is increasingly difficult to retain a clear picture of the programming model underneath these tools and the expressiveness they provide to solve some user-defined problem.

To provide some order in the world of big data processing, a toolkit of models to identify their common features is introduced, starting from data layout.

Data-processing applications are divided into *batch* vs. *stream* processing. Batch programs process one or more *finite* datasets to produce a resulting finite output dataset, whereas stream programs process possibly unbounded sequences of data, called *streams*, in an incremental manner. Operations over streams may also have to respect a total data ordering, for instance to represent time ordering.

The comparison of different languages for big data analytics in terms of the expressiveness of their programming models is a non-trivial exercise. A formalised approach requires to map them onto an unifying (and lower-level) computation model, i.e. the *Dataflow model* [69]. As shown in [70], it is able to capture the distinctive features of all frameworks at all levels of abstraction, from the user-level API to the execution model. In the Dataflow model, applications as a directed graph of actors. In its "modern" macro-data flow version [71], it naturally models independent (thus parallelizable) kernels starting from a graph of true data dependencies, where a kernel's execution is triggered by data availability.

The Dataflow model is expressive enough to describe batch, micro-batch and streaming models that are implemented in most tools for big data processing. Also, the Dataflow model helps in maturing the awareness that many big data analytics tools share almost the same base concepts, differing mostly in their implementation choices. For a complete description of the Dataflow model we refer back to [6,70], where the main features of mainstream languages are presented.

Google MapReduce. Google can be considered the pioneer of big data processing, as the publication of the MapReduce framework paper [72] made this model mainstream. Based on the *map* and *reduce* functions, commonly used in parallel and functional programming [73], MapReduce provides a native key-value model and built-in sorting facilities. These made MapReduce successful for several big data analytics scenarios.

A MapReduce program is built on the following user-defined functions:

1. a `map` function that is independently applied to each item from an input key-value dataset to produce an *intermediate* key-value dataset;
2. a `reduce` function that combines all the intermediate values associated with each key (together with the key itself) into lists of reduced values (one per key);
3. a `partitioner` function that is used while *sorting* the intermediate dataset (i.e., before being reduced), so that the order over the key space is respected within each partition identified by the partitioner.

Parallel Execution. A simple form of data parallelism can be exploited on the flat-map side, by partitioning the input collection into n chunks and having n executors process a chunk. In Dataflow terms this corresponds to a graph with n actors, each processing a token that represents a chunk. Each flat-map executor emits R (i.e. the number of intermediate partitions) chunks, each containing the intermediate key-value pairs mapped to a given partition.

The intermediate chunks are processed by R reduce executors. Each executor:

1. receives n chunks (one from each flat-map executor);
2. merges the chunks into an intermediate partition and partially sorts it based on keys, as discussed above;
3. performs the reduction on a per-key basis.

Finally, a downstream collector gathers R tokens from the reduce executors and merges them into the final result.

A key aspect in the depicted parallelisation is the *shuffle* phase in which data is distributed between flat-map and reduce operators, according to an *all-to-all* communication schema. This poses severe challenges from the implementation perspective.

Run-time Support. The most widespread implementation (i.e. *Hadoop*), is based on a *Master-Workers* approach, in which the master retains the control over the global state of the computation and informs the workers about the tasks to execute.

A cornerstone of Hadoop is its distributed file system (HDFS), which is used to exchange data among workers, in particular upon shuffling. As a key feature HDFS exposes the *locality* for stored data, thus enabling the principle of moving the computation towards the data and to minimise communication. However, disk-based communication leads to performance problems when dealing with iterative computations, such as machine learning algorithms [74].

Apache Spark. *Apache Spark* [75] was proposed to overcome some limitations in Google's MapReduce. Instead of a fixed processing schema, Spark allows datasets to be processed by means of arbitrarily composed primitives, constructing a directed acyclic graph (DAG). Moreover, instead of exclusively relying on disks for communicating data among the processing units, in-memory caching is exploited to boost performance, in particular for iterative processing.

Parallel Execution and Runtime Support. From the application DAG, Spark infers a parallel execution dataflow, in which many parallel instances of actors are created for each function and independent actors are grouped into *stages*. Due to the Spark batch-oriented implementation, each stage that depends on some previous stages has to wait for their completion before execution commences, equivalent to the classical Bulk Synchronous Parallelism (BSP) approach. Thus, a computation proceeds in a series of global *supersteps*, each consisting of:

1. concurrent computation, in which each actor processes its own partition;
2. communication, where actors exchange data between themselves if necessary (the *shuffle* phase);
3. barrier synchronization, where actors wait until all other actors have reached the same barrier.

Similar to the MapReduce implementation, Spark's execution model relies on the master-Workers model: a cluster manager (e.g. YARN) manages resources and supervises the execution of the program. It manages application scheduling to worker nodes, which execute the application logic (the DAG) that has been serialized and sent by the master.

Apache Flink. *Apache Flink* [76] is similar to Spark, in particular from the API standpoint. However, Flink is based on *streaming* as a primary concept, rather than a mere linguistic extension on top of batch processing (as Spark). With the exception of iterative processing, stream parallelism is exploited to avoid expensive synchronizations among successive phases when executing both batch and stream programs.

Parallel Execution and Runtime Support. Flink transforms a JobGraph into an ExecutionGraph, in which the JobVertex contains ExecutionVerteces (actors), one per parallel sub-task. A key difference compared to the Spark execution graph is that, apart from iterative processing (that is still executed under BSP), there is no barrier among actors or verteces. Instead, there is effective pipelining.

Also Flink's execution model relies on the master-workers model: a deployment has at least one job manager process that receives Flink jobs and coordinates checkpointing and recovery. The job manager also schedules work across the task manager processes (i.e. the workers), which usually reside on separate machines and in turn execute the code.

Apache Storm. *Apache Storm* [56,77] is a framework that exclusively targets stream processing. It is perhaps the first widely used large-scale stream processing framework in the open source world. Whereas Spark and Flink are based on a declarative data processing model, i.e., they provide as building blocks data collections and operations on those collections, Storm, in contrast, is based on a "topological" approach in that it provides an API to explicitly build graphs.

Parallel Execution and Runtime Support. At execution level, each actor is replicated to increase the inter-actor parallelism, and each group of replicas corresponds to the Bolt/Spout in the semantics Dataflow. Each of these actors represents independent data-parallel tasks, on which pipeline parallelism is exploited. Eventually, tasks are executed by a master-workers engine, as in the previously discussed frameworks.

Google Cloud Platform and Apache Beam. Google Dataflow SDK [78] is part of the Google Cloud Platform. Google Dataflow supports a simplified pipeline development via Java and Python APIs in the Apache Beam SDK, which provides a set of windowing and session analysis primitives as well as an ecosystem of source and sink connectors. Apache Beam allows the user to create pipelines that are executed by one of Beam's supported distributed processing back-ends, which are called *runners*. Currently, they include, among others, Apache Flink, Apache Spark and Google Cloud Dataflow.

Parallel Execution and Runtime Support. The bounded (or unbounded) nature of a PCollection also affects how data is processed. Bounded PCollections can be processed using batch jobs, that might read the entire data set once and perform processing as a finite job. Unbounded PCollections must be processed using streaming jobs—as the entire collection will never be available for processing at any one time—and bounded subcollections can be obtained through logical finite size windows.

As mentioned, Beam relies on the *runner* specified by the user. When executed, an entity called *Beam Pipeline Runner* (related to execution back-end) translates the data processing pipeline into the API compatible with the selected distributed processing back-end. Hence, it creates an execution graph from the Pipeline, including all the Transforms and processing functions. That graph is then executed using the appropriate distributed processing back-end, becoming an asynchronous job/process on that back-end. Thus, the final parallel execution graph is generated by the back-end.

The parallel execution data flow is similar to the one in Spark and Flink. Parallelism is expressed in terms of data parallelism in Transforms (e.g. ParDo function) and inter-actor parallelism on independent Transforms. In Beam's nomenclature this graph is called the Execution Graph. Similar to Flink pipeline parallelism is exploited among successive actors.

4.2 The Systematic Mapping Study on Parallel Programming Models for Big-Data Modelling and Simulation

A major challenge undertaken within the working group on *Parallel Programming Models for Big-Data Modelling and Simulation* was that of trying to understand and classify the state of the art in this area and to better understand the lines of future development. In order to minimize the bias, given that many Action participants actively design programming models and tools, the working group refined and adopted a systematic methodology to study the state of the art, called systematic mapping study (SMS). The mapping study focused on the main paradigms and properties of programming languages used in high-performance computing for gig data processing.

The SMS started from the definition of a workflow based on the methodology proposed in [79] that is organised in five successive steps:

Research Questions aiming at formulating the research questions the SMS should answer;

Search of Primary Studies aiming at detecting the largest number of primary articles related to the proposed research questions;

Selection of Primary Studies aiming at sieving false positive by a human-driven abstract inspection;

Quality Assessment aiming at validating the fitness of the articles against the aims of the SMS;

Data Extraction and Synthesis which aims at answering each research question for all selected articles.

Specifically, the SMS focused on domain-specific languages and explicitly excluded general-purpose languages, such as C, C++, OpenMP, Fortan, Java, Python, Scala, etc., combined with parallel exploitation libraries, such as MPI.

Quantitatively, in the SMS, the initial literature search resulted in 420 articles; 152 articles were retained for final review after the evaluation of initial search results by domain experts. Results of our mapping study indicate, for instance, that the majority of the used HPC languages in the context of big data are text-based general-purpose programming languages and target the end-user community. To evaluate the outcome of the mapping study, we developed a questionnaire and collected the opinions of domain experts. A comparison of mapping study outcome with opinions of domain experts reveals that the key features of HPC programming languages for big data are portability, performance and usability. We identified the language learning curve and interoperability as the key issues that need more attention in future research.

5   HPC-Enabled Modelling and Simulation for Life Sciences

Life Sciences typically deal with and generate large amounts of data, e.g., the flux of terabytes about genes and their expression produced by state of the art sequencing and microarray equipment, or data relating to the dynamics of cell biochemistry or organ functionality. Some modelling and simulation techniques require the investigation of large numbers of different (virtual) experiments, e.g., those addressing probabilistic, noise and robustness aspects [80–84], or based on statistical approaches. Curation and mining of large, typically multimedia, medical datasets for therapeutic and analytics purposes, are computationally expensive. Recent and future developments, such as personalised medicine need to integrate a mix of genomics, Systems and Synthetic Biology and medical information in a systemic description of a single individual. A surge of large-scale computational needs in these areas spans from the BBMRI (Biobanking and Biomolecular Resources Research Infrastructure) and the flagship effort Human Brain Project, which targets simulating the behaviour of a human brain, to FP7 projects like PD-HUMMODEL and TRANSFORM. In fact, this COST Action integrates well with the goals of the ESFRI Roadmap, promoted by the EC. Requirements go from pure computational efficiency, to large data file management and storage capabilities and vast memory-bound computational power.

This section focuses on the much-needed integration of HPC architects and Life Sciences modellers, with the goal of letting them develop and diffuse a coordinated, mature and productive use of HPC facilities. In order to bridge these two communities, some big data problems, applications and modelling techniques in the broad context of live sciences are discussed. We will consider approaches for modelling healthcare and diseases as well as problems in systems and synthetic biology. We will survey some themes on genomics and metabolic networks, then discuss efficient modelling and learning techniques, and finally consider also the modelling of the management of healthcare.

Healthcare and Disease Modelling. Understanding disease complexity is the definite scientific challenge of the 21st century medicine [85, 86]. Using computational models is the path to a technological medical revolution, where modelling will have a truly catalytic effect in biomedical big data by bridging the large body of knowledge produced by next generation genomic data with the clinical quantities and the functional observable (for instance through self monitor and implantable sensor devices). Biomedicine is essentially a big data field, and modelling is superior to the data-mining correlative approach in transforming data into knowledge.

Taking into account only the DNA sequencing data, its rate of accumulation is much larger than other major generators of big data, such as astronomy, YouTube and Twitter. Recent estimates show that the total amount of sequencing data produced is doubling approximately every seven months. The growth is driven by three main factors:

1. Biomedicine is heavily interdisciplinary and e-Healthcare requires physicians, bioinformaticians, computer scientists and engineers to team up. Although they continuously produce results that are underutilised in medical practice, such interdisciplinarity generates the need for large-scale data integration. Areas such as systems medicine, clinical informatics, systems biology and bioinformatics have large overlaps with classical fields of medicine, and extensively use biological information and computational methods to infer new knowledge towards understanding disease mechanism and diagnosis.
2. Many acute and chronic diseases originate as network diseases. A patient's condition is characterised by multiple, complex and interrelated conditions, disorders or diseases [87, 88]. A state of health can be defined as the capacity of absorbing accidents and showing metabolic flexibility, and is altered by infections and ageing, that cause comorbidities to emerge. Therefore, a good-quality stratification of a patient requires lots of information. The bridge between the characterisation of a disease mechanism and the stratification of a patient would require a data-driven computational model. Current successful approaches focus on resource-intensive hybrid modelling approaches including cellular automata, (stochastic) differential equations and agent-based models. The more effective the diagnostic and prognostic markers are, the less information will be needed to correctly stratify a patient. This aspect makes precision medicine highly computation-resource intensive. In particular, complex disease management is mostly based on electronic health records collection and analysis, which are expensive processes. Analyses are presented in a rather empirical and sometimes simplistic way, completely missing the opportunity of uncovering patterns of predictive relationships and meaningful profiles. Our chances to make the data the drivers of paths to cures for many complex diseases depends in a good percentage on extracting evidences from large-scale electronic records comparison and on models of disease trajectories. The medical approach to comorbidities represents an impressive computational challenge, mainly because of data synergies leading to the integration of heterogeneous sources of information, the definition of deep phenotyping

and markers re-modulation; the establishment of clinical decision support systems. Computational model development is further complicated by aspects of geo-differentiation and ethnic balance, protocols for sharing of digital information, interoperability between different record types (structured and nonstructured) to optimize the process of decision making in an actionable way.

3. A third important factor is the multi-scale nature of the biomedical information. The genome sequence is only the first level of understanding of the human biology. Bioinformatics data resources should be much more populated with longitudinal information gathered at intracellular, cell, intercellular and tissue levels. The longitudinal sampling could happen for important clinical events, such as hospitalisation or routinely perhaps a few times from uterine to elderly age. At the bioinformatics level, genome wide information of all the different levels of biological information will be integrated and this may include: Genomic sequence variations (haplotypes), levels of gene functioning for different tissues and conditions (circadian and longitudinal data) (gene expression), Epigenetic changes for different tissues (methylations and histonic modifications), information on chromatin conformation for different cell types and conditions (FISH, HI-C, 5C, microscopy), protein and metabolites abundances for different cell types and conditions, protein-protein interaction variations (longitudinal data).

For instance by using the Next Generation Sequencing technology approaches cancer clones, subtypes and metastasis could be appropriately traced. Microbiome data (number, type and multi Omics) for different part of the body and different conditions. Furthermore, gut microbiome could be regularly sampled, monitoring the diets and nutritional shifts. This could be of great importance for epigenetic data, which shows alteration with ageing, inflammatory diseases, obesity, cardiovascular and neurodegenerative diseases. Gene expression may vary in relation to the circadian cycle or ageing. Sampling may focus on determining the actual level of inflammation that is related to ageing rate (inflammaging). Large number of high-resolution images of the different parts of the patient's body such as MRI, PET, CT scan, including intravital microscopy techniques, can be used. The images will tend to be progressively enriched with genomics and proteomics data information. A disease first emerges as a dysfunction at the nucleus level, then metabolic and signalling, cell level and is then translated at the tissue level due to a change in the cell response. The tissue level is central to stem cells organisation in maintaining the mechanical properties of the tissue: the current thinking is that the dominant effect of reduced stem cell activity and failing tissue maintenance is due to changes in the niches that support and control stem cell activity. Therefore, tissue modelling can be thought as the missing link between basic research and clinical practice and will require a conceptual framework for an efficient multi-scale analysis between the cell and tissue levels. The cell level will be represented with agent-based or ODE models that will be specifically developed to handle millions of single cells. The tissue level will be represented using image-based finite element modelling (partial differential equation, PDE).

An important example is the bone system which is also related to the immune and endocrine systems. The osteocytes in the bone act as sensitive mechanosensors so they react to microdamages that alter the tension; with their flattened morphology and long processes, they form a sensory network which allows the detection of abnormal strain situations such as generated by microcracks. Normal locomotion is thought to cause microdamage to bone material and, thus, stimulate osteoclasts and osteoblasts to remove and then replace damaged tissue. They can be modelled as agents driven by signals and could reflect concentrations and velocities. Osteocytes are connected to one another and to surface osteoblasts via gap junctions. In general, mechanical forces are experienced by many osteoprogenitor cells which are present in the bone marrow and in the soft mesenchymal tissues subjected to mechanical strain. Dependant on the magnitude of mechanical stress osteoprogenitors differentiate or transdifferentiate into osteoblastlike cells that express characteristic proteins and can form bone matrix. Under physiological mechanical stimuli osteocytes prevent bone resorption by changing the RANKL/osteoprotegerin (OPG) ratio. By communicating these signals to bone lining cells (the second terminally differentiated osteoblast cell type) or secrete factors that recruit osteoclasts, osteocytes initiate the repair of damaged bone. The functional behaviour of bone tissues is primarily described in term of physical quantities such as pressures and forces to reflect deformation, loading, stress, strain, etc. Such quantities, are usually considered to vary across space and time, in a continuous fashion, and can be thus represented using fields, and systems of partial differential equations (PDE). The transition between a continuous representation and a discrete representation makes the coupling of the models across the cell-tissue scale particularly difficult. Conventional homogenisation approaches, frequently used as relation models to link to component models defined at different scales, are computationally resource demanding [89–92].

Modelling Problems in System and Synthetic Biology. Systems Biology approaches and methodologies are also very interesting in Synthetic Biology pipelines: in semi-synthetic minimal cells, for instance, liposomes are synthesized with some metabolic networks entrapped inside [93]. These devices, called protocells, share some properties in common with real biological cells, and can perform some biological action [94]. In wet-lab the problem is which metabolic component to choose, among the several different ones that can perform the same biological action. A combinatorial experimental approach is not affordable, since it requires a lot of time, budget and lab resources. A computational approach, instead, is very useful, as it can score the different hypotheses about the protocell to synthesize, sorting out the best theoretically performing. Along this research line, several papers have been published, based on computer simulation of the metabolic networks entrapped in the protocells [95], to understand the solute distribution and enrichments processes [96, 97] and the energetic balance of complex biological processes like DNA transcription and RNA translation [98].

Genomics. In recent years, thanks to faster and cheaper sequencing machines, a huge amount of whole genomic sequences within the same population has become available (e.g. [99]). Modern genomes analyses workflows have thus to face new challenges to perform functional annotations and comparative analysis, as there is no longer just *a* reference genome, but rather many of them that can have to be used all together as a control sequence. A collection of genomic sequences to be analysed jointly, or to be jointly used as a reference, is called *pangenome* [100]. The reference genome is a representative example of the whole genomic sequence of a species, acting as a control sequence against which fragments of a newly sequenced individual are mapped to be located, or against which another whole genome is compared. A single well annotated reference genome was - and mostly still is - traditionally used as a control sequence, as it could provide a good approximation of any individual genome. However, in loci where polymorphic variations occur (a *polymorphism* is a genetic variation of an individual or a population), such mappings and comparisons are likely to fail: this is where a multiple reference genome—a reference pan-genome—would be a better control [101].

In the data structure literature, several different compressed representations have been considered for sets of similar texts [102,103], as well as algorithmic methods for their investigation [104]. We present here a natural representation of pan-genomes (whole genomes or their fragments): *elastic-degenerate texts*. An *elastic-degenerate text* (*ED-text*) is a sequence compactly representing a multiple alignment of several closely-related sequences: substrings that match exactly are collapsed, while those in positions where the sequences differ (by means of substitutions, insertions, and deletions of substrings) are called *degenerate*, and therein all possible variants observed at that location are listed [105]. Actually, *ED*-texts correspond exactly to the Variant Call Format (.vcf), the *standard* for files storing genomic variations [106]. As an example, consider the following three closely-related sequences, where their similarity is highlighted by their alignment, and where the symbol '−' represents a deletion:

```
CAATGTGTGAC
CAGTCAAT-AC
C--T-ACTGAC
```

These sequences can be compacted into the single *ED*-text:

$$\tilde{T} = \text{C} \cdot \left\{ \begin{array}{c} \text{AA} \\ \text{AG} \\ \varepsilon \end{array} \right\} \cdot \text{T} \cdot \left\{ \begin{array}{c} \text{GTG} \\ \text{CAA} \\ \text{AC} \end{array} \right\} \cdot \text{T} \cdot \left\{ \begin{array}{c} \text{G} \\ \varepsilon \end{array} \right\} \cdot \text{AC} \qquad (1)$$

where ε is the empty string. The *length* n of $\tilde{T}$ is the total number of segments, and its *size* N is the total number of letters, that all belong to an alphabet Σ. Due to biotechnologies limitations, sequencing (that is, giving as input the *in vitro* DNA and getting out an *in silico* text file) can only be done on a genome fragment of limited size. For this reason, before the sequencing process, a genome is actually broken into many fragments of such limited size and then, whenever a reference is available, the resulting *in silico* fragments (named *reads*) are mapped onto it. This mapping is a critical step and there is an ample literature aiming at making as efficient as possible. When the reference is an ED-text, the reads mapping problem translates into the problem of finding all matches of a deterministic pattern P (that is, $P \in \Sigma^*$) in text $\tilde{T}$. We call this the $EDSM$ problem.

In [107] the problem has been solved for the simplest case of ED-text, in which a degenerate segment can only contain single letters. In [108] the problem has been efficiently solved for the more general case of ED-texts introducing (i) an algorithmic framework that has been conserved also by more recent papers, and (ii) adding a very fast bit-vector based version of the same algorithm that requires the pattern to have size no longer than the machine word. In [109] the algorithmic framework has been extended to find *approximate* occurrences of P, under both the Hamming and the edit distance model. In other words, occurrences of P are detected allowing up to a given amount of mismatches (Hamming distance model), or even insertions or deletions (edit distance model). In [110] the bit-vector algorithm of [108] has been extended to work with a *collection* of patterns $P_1, P_2, \ldots, P_h$ rather than a single string P, and in [111] a step of the algorithm presented in [108] has been improved by a factor $\sqrt{|P|}$. Another natural problem that arises is the comparison of two ED-texts and, in particular, whether the sets of strings the actually represent has a non empty intersection. This problem has been efficiently solved in [112] with a linear time algorithm for the case of non-elastic D-texts (a degenerate segment can only contain strings of the same size).

Once that a set of DNA fragments of an individual have been aligned, haplotype phasing is an important problem in the analysis of genomics information. It consists of determining which one of the possible alleles (alternative forms of a gene) each fragment comes from. Haplotype information is relevant to gene regulation, epigenetics, genome-wide association studies, evolutionary and population studies, and the study of mutations. Haplotyping is currently addressed as an optimisation problem aiming at solutions that minimise, for instance, error correction costs, where costs are a measure of the confidence in the accuracy of the information acquired from DNA sequencing. Solutions have typically an exponential computational complexity. WHATSHAP [113] is a framework returning exact solutions to the problem of haplotyping which moves computational complexity from DNA fragment length to fragment overlap, i.e., coverage, and is hence of particular interest when considering sequencing technology's current trends that are producing longer fragments. Nonetheless, the combinatorial nature of the problem makes larger coverages quickly intractable. An interesting experiment, paradigmatic of a HPC-supported modelling solution, is pWHATSHAP [1,114], i.e. a freely-available, multicore parallelisation of WHATSHAP, based on the FastFlow parallel programming framework [65]. This parallel implementation on multi-core architectures allows for a relevant reduction of the execution time for haplotyping, while the provided results enjoy the same high accuracy as that provided by WHATSHAP, which increases with coverage.

Metabolic Network Robustness Analysis. Many functional modules are linked together in a Metabolic Network for reproducing metabolic pathways and describing the entire cellular metabolism of an organism. An enormous interdisciplinary interest has grown for metabolic networks robustness studies in terms of errors and attacks tolerance. Scale-free networks based approaches suggest that metabolic networks are tolerant to errors, but very vulnerable to targeted attacks against highly connected nodes. An integrated approach based on statistical, topological, and functional analysis allows for obtaining a deep knowledge on overall metabolic network robustness. With more details, several software frameworks were developed to model a metabolic network and perform the Topological Analysis, the Flux Balance Analysis, and the Extreme Pathways Analysis over it [115, 116]. The simulation trials have demonstrated that metabolic network robustness is not simply associated to the network local properties (low-connectivity-degree node or high-connectivity-degree node) but also to functional network properties. So, ultra-peripheral non-hub nodes can assume a fundamental role for network survival if they belong to network extreme pathways, while hub nodes can have a limited impact on networks if they can be replaced by alternative nodes and paths [115, 116].

The same approach have been applied as a bio-inspired optimisation method to different application domains. In [117] the use of the previous bio-inspired techniques allows for analysing the structural aspects of a road network, finding its extreme pathways, and outlining the balanced flow combinations. The approach optimises traffic flows over a road network, minimises road congestion and maximises the number of vehicles reaching their destination target. In [118], the bio-inspired methodology has been applied to a class of digital ecosystems based on a scale-free architecture for both maximum information flow and fault/error tolerance detection. Highly connected nodes, inter-module connectors and ultra-peripheral nodes can be identified by evaluating their impact on digital ecosystems behavior and addressing their strengthen, fault tolerance and protection countermeasures.

Modelling Methodologies. The computational analysis of complex biological systems can be hindered by three main factors:

1. modelling the system so that it can be easily understood and analysed by non-expert users is not always possible;
2. When the system is composed of hundreds or thousands of reactions and chemical species, the classic CPU-based simulators could not be appropriate to efficiently derive the behaviour of the system. To overcome these first two limitations, [119] proposes a novel approach that combines the descriptive power of Stochastic Symmetric Nets, a graphical mathematical formalism, with LASSIE, a GPU-powered deterministic simulator that offloads onto the GPU the calculations required to execute many simulations by following both fine-grained and coarse-grained parallelisation strategies. The effectiveness of this approach was showed on a case study aimed at understanding the role of possible malfunctions in the cross-balancing mechanisms that regulate

peripheral tolerance of self-reactive T lymphocytes in case of a relapsing-remitting multiple sclerosis. From our experiments, LASSIE achieves around 97 speed-up with respect to the sequential execution of the same number of simulations;

3. The determination of model structure and model parameters is difficult. Due to economical and technical reasons, only part of these details are well characterised while the rest remains unknown. To deal with this aspect, many parameter estimation and reverse engineering methods were developed. However, these methods often need an amount of experimental data that not always is available.

An alternative approach to deal with situations in which insufficient experimental data hamper the application of PE and RE methods was proposed in [120]. To overcome the lack of information concerning undetermined reactions an empirical biological knowledge was exploited to overcome model indetermination solving an optimisation problem (OP) with an objective function that, similarly to Flux Balance Analysis, is derived from empirical biological knowledge and does not require large amounts of data. The system behaviour is described in detail by a system of ordinary differential equations (ODE) while model indetermination is resolved selecting time-varying coefficients that maximize/minimize the objective function at each ODE integration step. As discussed by the authors, in this context approximation techniques in which OP is not solved at every integration step and/or parallelisation strategies are mandatory to speed-up the solution process.

Learning-Based Modelling Approaches. Some interesting applications in this context are based on the study of integrated biological data and how they are organised in complex systems. In particular, these approaches focus on multi-omic spaces and multi-view analysis. They are very complex applications that require high-throughput analysis based on advanced machine learning (ML) and, more recently, deep learning (DL). One of the several applications in this field is described by Bardozzo et al. [121], where high throughput omic analysis (HTO) is adopted with the aim to the end of describing the antibiotics efficacy with respect to the bacterial adaptive mechanisms. Moreover, a specific survey on HTO is introduced by Suravajhala et al. [122]. Nevertheless, a general survey oriented to high throughput biomedical data analysis with ML and DL is widely described in the work of Serra et al. [123].

Healthcare Management Modelling. Globally healthcare faces many challenges that result in increasing healthcare costs [124] and poor outcomes [125] (morbidity or mortality) depending on the setting and demographic. These challenges have been traced to weak health systems whose symptoms can manifest in: low productivity, poor financial management, inadequate information for decision making, insufficient strategic management, issues with managed care and other systems dynamics [126].

The persistent challenges in the healthcare sector call for urgent review of strategies. Several industry application of operations management have been documented [127]. There has also been diverse application of operations management techniques in several domains including the health sector. While there is still room for health use-case modification, adoption of innovations used in other domains has been slow. A major classification identified resource and facility management, demand forecasting, inventory and supply chain management, and cost measurement as application groupings to prioritise [126].

An area of increasing interest is human resource planning that captures recruitment, rostering, scheduling and management of clinical and non-clinical staff, their retention, training, payment and incentives as well as performance appraisal. Challenges do also arise around patient workflow: admission, scheduling, and resource allocation. To model solutions to these process and workflow challenges, simple statistics, stochastic [128], mathematical [129], artificial intelligence [130], lean [131], agile [132], six-sigma [131] and total quality management [133] based models have been variously proposed and used. Sometimes, inadequate data may warrant simulation to fill in deterministic and non-deterministic data gaps [134,135]. This obviously comes with the need for adequate computing and storage capabilities.

The optimum framework for modelling and simulating a particular use-case depends on the availability, structure and size of data [126]. Other considerations will be if the system should be automated or not, if they are sophisticated, deterministic or not. The choice of model and/or simulation technique can ultimately be influenced by available computing power and storage space. How user-friendly such a system is, will be a major consideration as well. Opportunities for application of one or more of these modelling, simulation and prediction techniques to address some of the lingering healthcare challenges is huge.

6   HPC-Enabled Modelling and Simulation for Socio-Economical and Physical Sciences

Many types of decisions in society are supported by modelling and simulation. Some examples are political decisions based on predictive simulations of future climate changes, evacuation planning based on faster-than-real-time simulation of tsunamis, and financial market decisions based on mathematical models emulating current market conditions. In all of these situations, large amounts of data such as global geographical information, measurements of the current physical or financial state, and historical data are used both in the model building and model calibration processes.

We can roughly divide the applications within the large and diverse area, that we here call socio-economical and physical sciences, into two groups. Classical HPC applications, where we build a large-scale complex model and simulate this in order to produce data as a basis for decisions, and Big data applications, where the starting point is a data set, that is processed and analyzed to learn the behaviour of a system, to find relevant features, and to make predictions or decisions.

In classical HPC applications, the need for HPC arises from the fact that we have a large-scale model or a computationally heavy software implementation, that needs to make use of large-scale computational resources, and potentially also large-scale storage resources in order to deliver timely results.

Some particularly challenging problem features are high-dimensionality (e.g., in finance or quantum physics) where the computational costs grow exponentially with the dimension, multi-scale physics (e.g., in climate and tsunami simulations) where scales that differ in orders of magnitude need to be resolved to capture the relevant physical processes, and computations under uncertainty, where the impact of uncertain measurements, parameters and models is quantified through multiple evaluations or extended models leading to an increased computational cost (e.g., in safety critical decision problems).

Highly advanced algorithms and implementations for many different application areas have been developed over decades. A huge challenge is that these legacy codes are not optimized for modern computer architectures and cannot efficiently exploit massively parallel systems [136]. HPC knowledge and innovation is needed to merge the software and hardware state-of-the-art into highly efficient application simulation tools. An opportunity that is brought by the increase in available computer power is instead that the limits of what can be simulated are expanding outwards. The recent increase in research on uncertainty quantification [137] is one example of how this has changed the computational research landscape.

Big data processing as opposed to classical HPC simulation is a relatively young field. The amount of data that is being harvested is following an exponential trend, while hardware development, often in relation to cloud environments, and software development with a specific focus on machine learning and AI is struggling to keep up. The opportunities for using data in new ways are endless, but as is suggested in [138], data and algorithms together can provide the *whats*, while the innovation and imagination of human interpreters is still needed to answer the *whys*. Areas where we see a rapidly growing need for HPC solutions is the internet of things [139], where the expected vast amounts of data provides new challenges for the extraction of knowledge, as well as in the social media context [140], where all kinds of real world events or personal preferences provide footprints that can be tracked and exploited.

In the following paragraphs of this section, we highlight some of the work and contributions of the participants in this Action within the diverse subfields in the wider physical and socio-economical application area. Some of the topics are also represented as individual chapters later in this volume.

Classical HPC Applications. In this sub-field, the interplay of the algorithms with the parallel implementation is crucial, and we provide two examples, both with industrial design applications.

Wing design is one of the essential procedures of aircraft manufactures and it is a compromise between many competing factors and constraints. Efficient numerical optimization methods are important to speed-up the design procedure, especially for design parameters of $\mathcal{O}(10\text{--}100)$. In wing shape optimization, necessary derivatives can easily be calculated by applying finite-difference methods. However, finite difference methods are in general significantly more expensive, requiring at least one additional flow solution per parameter. By using the method of modular analysis and unified derivatives (MAUD), we can unify all methods for computing total derivatives using a single equation with associated distributed-memory, sparse data-passing schemes. Moreover, the wing design requires a set of benchmark cases for the shape optimization to find solutions of many candidate shapes by applying computational fluid dynamics (CFD) analysis with turbulence models. High-fidelity CFD simulations must be carried out in parallel to reduce the total run-time using HPC resources [141].

An application problem that is also discussed later in an individual chapter is electromagnetic scattering, with applications to, e.g., aircraft antenna design. These problems have millions or billions of unknown variables, and the code needs to run on a cluster due to the memory requirements. However, few of the existing (legacy) implementations are parallelised for multicore-based computational nodes. We show results from a pilot implementation using a task-parallel programming model [142], and discuss how to develop this further into a complete distributed implementation.

HPC in Computational Intelligence. As a thriving application platform, HPC excels in supporting execution and it's speedup through parallellisation when running Computational Intelligence (CI) algorithms. The likes of CI algorithms supported by this action includes development of some of most efficient optimization algorithms for continuous optimization as defined with benchmark functions competition framework from Congress on Evolutionary Computation (CEC) 2017 [143,144]. Specifically useful, in [144] a Differential Evolution (DE) algorithm is enhanced with a new mechanism, the distance based parameter adaptation in the context of Success-History based DE (SHADE), the winner strategy of several previous CEC competitions. An important contribution of an expert system for underwater glider path planning using DE was published in [145], where the application of SHADE strategy enabled significant advances in improved path planning over mesoscale ocean current structures. Another CI technique in learning pipeline is Stability Selection (SS), yet another computationally demanding technique like DE, and SS was improved through a discrete optimization algorithm [146]. In [147], a recent whole pipeline survey overview for black-box discrete optimization benchmarking (BB-DOB) is provided, defining taxonomy, evaluation, and ranking for BB-DOB algorithms. Also, in the case of EU project RIVR (Upgrading National Research Structures in Slovenia) supported by European Regional Development Fund (ERDF), an important side-effect of cHiPSet COST action was leveraging it's experts' inclusiveness to gain capacity recognition at a national ministry for co-financing HPC equipment[1]. In the view of future possibilities for modelling and simulation in CI context, gain from HPC is clearly seen in improving upon techniques with DE like in

---

[1] https://www.rtvslo.si/znanost-in-tehnologija/v-mariboru-vzpostavljajo-superracunalniski-center/475543.

energy applications [148], constrained trajectory planning [149], artificial life of full ecosystems [150] including HPC-enabled evolutionary computer vision in 2D [151,152] and 3D [151], many other well recognized real-world optimization challenges [153], or even insight to deep inner dynamics of DE over full benchmarks, requiring large HPC capacities [154].

IoT, Smart Cities, and Big Data Applications. Monitoring the real-world environment is a big challenge given the number of variables that can be sensed nowadays in IoT environments, as for example GPS-position, temperature, humidity, presence, people location, ultraviolet radiation, air quality, hazardous gases, pressure, proximity, acceleration. IoT assumes that multiple sensors can be used to monitor the real-world and this information can be stored and processed, jointly with information from soft-sensor (RSS, web, etc.) [155], to for example assist elderly people in the street [156], develop intelligent interfaces [157] or detect anomalies in industrial environments [158]. In any case, the developed global system needs to fuse heterogeneous data for obtaining a complete view of actual situation and inferring future dangerous situations. These two tasks need Cloud capabilities and HPC.

One of the critical aspects of management within the "smart city" concept is Intelligent Transport Systems, and in particular road traffic control. Off-line traffic simulation is perfect for designing road systems and planning traffic light timings, but does not allow to tackle unexpected or rare situation in real time. Short-term traffic forecasting [159], especially using data-driven (i.e. *learning*) methods, provides a complementary approach. With the availability of smart sensing technologies, like automatic vehicle counting from standard surveillance cameras, it is possible to devise decentralised solutions that measure the current situation of traffic flow on each road, perform local communication between nodes, and forecast the conditions for the immediate future using machine learning algorithms [160]. These may be augmented with evaluations of unexpectedness and per-node traffic jam prediction. Concentration of these data at a decision-making location may also allow travel time estimation, exploitation of network locality information, as well as comparison with the estimates provided by a traffic management system, which can be evaluated for effectiveness on the medium term and possibly tuned accordingly.

Further topics that are discussed in later chapters of this volume look at such diverse questions as how to use data from mobile cellular networks for applications such as urban sensing and event detection, and how sentiment analysis can be applied to forecast the value of cryptocurrencies.

Small Data Applications. The growing big data processing field is well known, but in parallel, there is also a growing interest in a specific type of small data applications. With the increasing instability of the financial and political systems, and of the global climate, there is an increased occurrence of extreme events. Within the big data sets, there are small data sets, that sample the extreme events. To understand their behaviour has applications, e.g., in financial risk management, in insurance, and in prediction of catastrophic climate events. In a later chapter, methods for extreme value estimation are surveyed.

7   Summary and Conclusion

HPC and M&S form two previously largely disjoint and disconnected research communities. The COST Action IC1406 *High-Performance Modelling and Simulation for Big Data Applications* brings these two communities together to tackle the challenges of big data applications from diverse application domains. Experts from both communities jointly study these applications and application scenarios and cooperatively develop solutions that benefit from the cross-pollination of expertise. Different perspectives on the same topic lead to creative solutions and ultimately to the common goal of HPC-enabled M&S.

The purpose of this paper is to set the scene for individual applications bringing together HPC and M&S. We have argued why high-performance modelling matters for big data applications. Following this line of reasoning we looked at the subject matter from the four angles of the four working groups into which the COST Action is organised. Throughout the previous two sections we have presented a myriad of application opportunities and technological challenges for HPC-enabled modelling and simulation in life, socio-economical and physical sciences. These are complemented by comprehensive surveys of the current state of the art with respect to HPC technology and tools, both from the perspective of programming models as well as from middleware solutions.

Bringing together specialists from all these communities is the central contribution of the COST Action. Having set the scene in this paper, the other papers of this volume exemplify the achievements of the COST Action. Each addresses a specific application or application scenario from the life, socio-economical or physical sciences and explores how the application of state-of-the-art HPC tools and technologies may lead to superior solutions in the near future.

Acknowledgments. This work was supported by the ICT COST Action IC1406 *High-Performance Modelling and Simulation for Big Data Applications*. We would like to thank all members of the COST Action for their direct or indirect contributions to this work and the success of the COST Action in general.

We particularly thank Christoph Kessler, Linköping University, Sweden; Salvatore Vitabile, University of Palermo, Italy; Marco Beccuti, University of Torino, Italy; Lalit Garg, University of Malta, Malta; Jing Gong, KTH Royal Institute of Technology, Stockholm, Sweden; Aleš Zamuda, University of Maribor, Slovenia; José Manuel Molina Lopez, Universidad Carlos III de Madrid, Spain; Amr Abdullatif, Alberto Cabri, Francesco Masulli, and Stefano Rovetta, University of Genova and Vega Research Laboratories, Genova, Italy, for their contributions to this chapter.

References

1. Bracciali, A., et al.: PWHATSHAP: efficient haplotyping for future generation sequencing. BMC Bioinform. **17**, 342 (2016)
2. Misale, C., Ferrero, G., Torquati, M., Aldinucci, M.: Sequence alignment tools: one parallel pattern to rule them all? BioMed. Res. Int. **2014**, 12 p. (2014). Article ID 539410. https://doi.org/10.1155/2014/539410
3. Aldinucci, M., Ruggieri, S., Torquati, M.: Porting decision tree algorithms to multicore using FastFlow. In: Balcázar, J.L., Bonchi, F., Gionis, A., Sebag, M. (eds.) ECML PKDD 2010. LNCS (LNAI), vol. 6321, pp. 7–23. Springer, Heidelberg (2010). https://doi.org/10.1007/978-3-642-15880-3_7
4. Buono, D., Danelutto, M., Lametti, S., Torquati, M.: Parallel patterns for general purpose many-core. In: 21st Euromicro International Conference on Parallel, Distributed, and Network-Based Processing, pp. 131–139 (2013)
5. Aldinucci, M., et al.: Parallel stochastic systems biology in the cloud. Brief. Bioinform. **15**, 798–813 (2014)
6. Aldinucci, M., Drocco, M., Misale, C., Tremblay, G.: Languages for big data analysis. In: Sakr, S., Zomaya, A. (eds.) Encyclopedia of Big Data Technologies, pp. 1–12. Springer, Cham (2018). https://doi.org/10.1007/978-3-319-63962-8_142-1
7. Tordini, F., Aldinucci, M., Viviani, P., Merelli, I., Liò, P.: Scientific workflows on clouds with heterogeneous and preemptible instances. In: Proceedings of the International Conference on Parallel Computing, ParCo 2017, 12–15 September 2017, Bologna, Italy. Advances in Parallel Computing. IOS Press (2018)
8. Akhter, N., Othman, M.: Energy aware resource allocation of cloud data center: review and open issues. Cluster Comput. **19**, 1163–1182 (2016)
9. Mastelic, T., Oleksiak, A., Claussen, H., Brandic, I., Pierson, J.M., Vasilakos, A.V.: Cloud computing: survey on energy efficiency. ACM Comput. Surv. **47**, 33 (2015)
10. Niewiadomska-Szynkiewicz, E., Sikora, A., Arabas, P., Kamola, M., Mincer, M., Kołodziej, J.: Dynamic power management in energy-aware computer networks and data intensive systems. Future Gener. Comput. Syst. **37**, 284–296 (2014)
11. Antal, M., et al.: MoSiCS: modeling, simulation and optimization of complex systems - a case study on energy efficient datacenters. Simul. Model. Pract. Theory (2018). https://doi.org/10.1016/j.simpat.2018.12.004
12. Karpowicz, M.: Energy-efficient CPU frequency control for the Linux system. Concurrency Comput.: Pract. Exp. **28**, 420–437 (2016)
13. Karpowicz, M.P., Arabas, P., Niewiadomska-Szynkiewicz, E.: Energy-aware multilevel control system for a network of Linux software routers: design and implementation. IEEE Syst. J. **12**, 571–582 (2018)
14. Cotes-Ruiz, I., Prado, R., Garcia-Galan, S.: Dynamic voltage frequency scaling simulator for real workflows energy-aware management in green cloud computing. PLoS ONE **12**, e0169803 (2017)
15. Healy, P.D., Lynn, T., Barrett, E., Morrison, J.P.: Single system image: a survey. J. Parallel Distrib. Comput. **90–91**, 35–51 (2016)
16. Oussous, A., Benjelloun, F., Lahcen, A.A., Belfkih, S.: Big data technologies: a survey. J. King Saud Univ. - Comput. Inf. Sci. **30**, 431–448 (2018)
17. Berman, F., Fox, G., Hey, A.: Grid Computing: Making the Global Infrastructure a Reality. Wiley, Hoboken (2003)
18. Sehgal, N., Bhatt, P.C.P.: Cloud Computing. Concepts and Practices. Springer, Heidelberg (2018). https://doi.org/10.1007/978-3-319-77839-6

19. MOSIX. www.mosix.org
20. OpenSSI. www.openssi.org/cgi-bin/view?page=openssi.html
21. Kerrighed. www.kerrighed.org
22. UNICORE. www.unicore.eu
23. Globus Toolkit. toolkit.globus.org
24. Cannataro, M.: Handbook of Research on Computational Grid Technologies for Life Sciences, Biomedicine, and Healthcare. IGI Global, Hershey (2009)
25. Walters, R.J., Crouch, S., Bennett, P.: Building computational grids using ubiquitous web technologies. In: Camarinha-Matos, L.M., Xu, L., Afsarmanesh, H. (eds.) PRO-VE 2012. IAICT, vol. 380, pp. 254–261. Springer, Heidelberg (2012). https://doi.org/10.1007/978-3-642-32775-9_26
26. Hwu, W.H. (ed.): GPU Computing Gems, Emerald edn. Morgan Kaufman, Waltham (2011)
27. Singh, A., Bhat, J., Raju, R., D'Souza, R.: Survey on various load balancing techniques in cloud computing. Adv. Comput. **7**, 28–34 (2017)
28. Zhang, J., Yu, F.R., Wang, S., Huang, T., Liu, Z., Liu, Y.: Load balancing in data center networks: a survey. IEEE Commun. Surv. Tutor. **20**, 2324–2352 (2018)
29. Staples, G.: Torque resource manager. In: Proceedings of the 2006 ACM/IEEE Conference on Supercomputing. ACM, New York (2006)
30. Slurm Workload Manager. slurm.schedmd.com
31. Mohamed, E., Hong, Z.: Hadoop-MapReduce job scheduling algorithms survey. In: 2016 7th International Conference on Cloud Computing and Big Data (CCBD), pp. 237–242 (2016)
32. White, T.: Hadoop: The Definitive Guide. O'Reilly Media, Newton (2015)
33. Apache Spark. spark.apache.org
34. Apache Storm. storm.apache.org
35. Apache Flink. flink.apache.org
36. RapidMiner Studio. rapidminer.com
37. Orange. orange.biolab.si
38. Frank, E., Hall, M.A., Witten, I.H.: Data Mining: Practical Machine Learning Tools and Techniques. Morgan Kaufmann, Burlington (2016)
39. Milne, I., et al.: Tablet-next generation sequence assembly visualization. Bioinformatics **26**, 401–403 (2010)
40. Carver, T., Böhme, U., Otto, T., Parkhill, J., Berriman, M.: BamView: viewing mapped read alignment data in the context of the reference sequence. Bioinformatics **26**, 676–677 (2010)
41. Rutherford, K., et al.: Artemis: sequence visualization and annotation. Bioinformatics **16**, 944–949 (2000)
42. Desale, D.: Top tools for social network analysis and visualisation (2018). www.kdnuggets.com/2015/06/top-30-social-network-analysis-visualization-tools.html/3
43. Sikora, A., Niewiadomska-Szynkiewicz, E.: A federated approach to parallel and distributed simulation of complex systems. Int. J. Appl. Math. Comput. Sci. **17**, 99–106 (2007)
44. Inostrosa-Psijas, A., Gil-Costa, V., Marin, M., Wainer, G.: Semi-asynchronous approximate parallel DEVS simulation of web search engines. Concurrency and Computation: Pract. Exp. **30**, e4149 (2018)
45. Miller, J., Cotterell, M., Buckley, S.: Supporting a modeling continuum in scalation: from predictive analytics to simulation modeling. In: Proceedings of Winter Simulation Conference: Simulation: Making Decisions in a Complex World, pp. 1191–1202. IEEE Press (2013)

46. Niewiadomska-Szynkiewicz, E., Sikora, A.: A software tool for federated simulation of wireless sensor networks and mobile ad hoc networks. In: Jónasson, K. (ed.) PARA 2010. LNCS, vol. 7133, pp. 303–313. Springer, Heidelberg (2012). https://doi.org/10.1007/978-3-642-28151-8_30
47. Song, X., Wu, Y., Ma, Y., Ciu, Y., Gong, G.: Military simulation big data: background, state of the art, and challenges. Math. Probl. Eng. **2015**, 1–20 (2015). https://doi.org/10.1155/2015/298356
48. Fidjeland, A.K., Roesch, E.B., Shanahan, M.P., Luk, W.: NeMo: a platform for neural modelling of spiking neurons using GPUS. In: 2009 20th IEEE International Conference on Application-specific Systems, Architectures and Processors, pp. 137–144 (2009)
49. Szynkiewicz, P.: A novel GPU-enabled simulator for large scale spiking neural networks. J. Telecommun. Inf. Technol. **2**, 34–42 (2016)
50. Martínez-del-Amor, M.A., Macías-Ramos, L.F., Valencia-Cabrera, L., Riscos-Núñez, A., Pérez-Jiménez, M.J.: Accelerated simulation of P systems on the GPU: a survey. In: Pan, L., Păun, G., Pérez-Jiménez, M.J., Song, T. (eds.) BIC-TA 2014. CCIS, vol. 472, pp. 308–312. Springer, Heidelberg (2014). https://doi.org/10.1007/978-3-662-45049-9_50
51. Beyer, J., Hadwiger, M., Pfister, H.: A survey of GPU-based large-scale volume visualization. In: Proceedings of the Eurographics Conference on Visualization (Eurovis 2014), pp. 1–19 (2014)
52. Maeda, R., et al.: Jade: a heterogeneous multiprocessor system simulation platform using recorded and statistical application models. In: Proceedings of HiPEAC Workshop on Advanced Interconnect Solutions and Technologies for Emerging Computing Systems, pp. 1–6 (2016)
53. Casanova, H., Giersch, A., Legrand, A., Quinson, M., Suter, F.: Versatile, scalable, and accurate simulation of distributed applications and platforms. J. Parallel Distrib. Comput. **74**, 2899–2917 (2014)
54. Calheiros, R., Ranjan, R., Beloglazov, A., Rose, C.D., Buyya, R.: CloudSim: a toolkit for modeling and simulation of cloud computing environments and evaluation of resource provisioning algorithms. Softw. Pract. Exp. **41**, 23–50 (2011)
55. Multi2Sim Workload Manager. www.multi2sim.org
56. Nasir, M.A.U., Morales, G.D.F., García-Soriano, D., Kourtellis, N., Serafini, M.: The power of both choices: practical load balancing for distributed stream processing engines. CoRR abs/1504.00788 (2015)
57. Zaharia, M., Chowdhury, M., Franklin, M.J., Shenker, S., Stoica, I.: Spark: cluster computing with working sets. In: Proceedings of the 2nd USENIX Conference on Hot Topics in Cloud Computing, HotCloud 2010, p. 10. USENIX Association, Berkeley (2010)
58. Dean, J., Ghemawat, S.: MapReduce: simplified data processing on large clusters. CACM **51**, 107–113 (2008)
59. Apache Software Foundation: Hadoop. http://hadoop.apache.org/. Accessed 2018
60. Intel Corp.: Threading Building Blocks. Accessed 2018
61. Park, I., Voss, M.J., Kim, S.W., Eigenmann, R.: Parallel programming environment for OpenMP. Sci. Program. **9**, 143–161 (2001)
62. Pacheco, P.S.: Parallel Programming with MPI. Morgan Kaufmann Publishers Inc., San Francisco (1996)
63. Khronos Compute Working Group: OpenACC Directives for Accelerators. http://www.openacc-standard.org. Accessed 2018

64. Aldinucci, M., Danelutto, M., Meneghin, M., Torquati, M., Kilpatrick, P.: Efficient streaming applications on multi-core with FastFlow: the biosequence alignment test-bed. In: Advances in Parallel Computing, vol. 19. Elsevier, Amsterdam (2010)
65. Aldinucci, M., Danelutto, M., Kilpatrick, P., Torquati, M.: FastFlow: high-level and efficient streaming on multi-core. In: Pllana, S., Xhafa, F. (eds.) Programming Multi-core and Many-core Computing Systems. Parallel and Distributed Computing. Wiley, New York (2017)
66. Enmyren, J., Kessler, C.W.: SkePU: a multi-backend skeleton programming library for multi-GPU systems. In: Proceedings of the Fourth International Workshop on High-level Parallel Programming and Applications, HLPP 2010, pp. 5–14. ACM, New York (2010)
67. Grelck, C., Scholz, S.: SAC: a functional array language for efficient multithreaded execution. Int. J. Parallel Program. **34**, 383–427 (2006)
68. Grelck, C., Scholz, S., Shafarenko, A.: Asynchronous stream processing with S-net. Int. J. Parallel Program. **38**, 38–67 (2010)
69. Lee, E.A., Parks, T.M.: Dataflow process networks. Proc. IEEE **83**, 773–801 (1995)
70. Misale, C., Drocco, M., Aldinucci, M., Tremblay, G.: A comparison of big data frameworks on a layered dataflow model. Parallel Process. Lett. **27**, 1740003 (2017)
71. Aldinucci, M., Danelutto, M., Anardu, L., Torquati, M., Kilpatrick, P.: Parallel patterns + macro data flow for multi-core programming. In: Proceedings of International Euromicro PDP 2012: Parallel Distributed and Network-Based Processing, pp. 27–36. IEEE, Garching (2012)
72. Dean, J., Ghemawat, S.: MapReduce: simplified data processing on large clusters. In: Proceedings of 6th USENIX Symposium on Operating Systems Design & Implementation, pp. 137–150 (2004)
73. Cole, M.: Algorithmic Skeletons: Structured Management of Parallel Computations. Research Monographs in Parallel and Distributed Computing. Pitman, London (1989)
74. Chu, C.T., et al.: Map-reduce for machine learning on multicore. In: Proceedings of the 19th International Conference on Neural Information Processing Systems, pp. 281–288 (2006)
75. Zaharia, M., et al.: Resilient distributed datasets: a fault-tolerant abstraction for in-memory cluster computing. In: Proceedings of the 9th USENIX Conference on Networked Systems Design and Implementation (2012)
76. Carbone, P., Fóra, G., Ewen, S., Haridi, S., Tzoumas, K.: Lightweight asynchronous snapshots for distributed dataflows. CoRR abs/1506.08603 (2015)
77. Toshniwal, A., et al.: Storm@twitter. In: Proceedings of the ACM SIGMOD International Conference on Management of Data, pp. 147–156 (2014)
78. Akidau, T., et al.: The dataflow model: a practical approach to balancing correctness, latency, and cost in massive-scale, unbounded, out-of-order data processing. Proc. VLDB Endowment **8**, 1792–1803 (2015)
79. Kitchenham, B., Brereton, O.P., Budgen, D., Turner, M., Bailey, J., Linkman, S.: Systematic literature reviews in software engineering - a systematic literature review. Inf. Softw. Technol. **51**, 7–15 (2009)
80. Calzone, L., Fages, F., Soliman, S.: BIOCHAM: an environment for modeling biological systems and formalizing experimental knowledge. Bioinformatics **22**, 1805–1807 (2006)
81. Zechner, C., Seelig, G., Rullan, M., Khammash, M.: Molecular circuits for dynamic noise filtering. Proc. Natl. Acad. Sci. **113**, 4729–4734 (2016)

82. Fages, F., Soliman, S.: On robustness computation and optimization in BIOCHAM-4. In: Proceedings of Computational Methods in Systems Biology - 16th International Conference, CMSB 2018, Brno, Czech Republic, 12–14 September 2018, pp. 292–299 (2018)
83. Nasti, L., Gori, R., Milazzo, P.: Formalizing a notion of concentration robustness for biochemical networks. In: Mazzara, M., Ober, I., Salaün, G. (eds.) STAF 2018: Software Technologies: Applications and Foundations. LNCS, vol. 11176, pp. 81–97. Springer, Cham (2018). https://doi.org/10.1007/978-3-030-04771-9_8
84. Proceedings of the 12th International Joint Conference on Biomedical Engineering Systems and Technologies. In: BIOINFORMATICS 2019 (2019, in Press)
85. Sansom, C., Castiglione, F., Lio, P.: Metabolic disorders: how can systems modelling help? Lancet Diabetes Endocrinol. **4**, 306 (2016)
86. Bartocci, E., Liò, P.: Computational modeling, formal analysis, and tools for systems biology. PLOS Comput. Biol. **12**, 1–22 (2016)
87. Capobianco, E., Liò, P.: Comorbidity networks: beyond disease correlations. J. Complex Netw. **3**, 319–332 (2015)
88. Capobianco, E., Liò, P.: Comorbidity: a multidimensional approach. Trends Mol. Med. **19**, 515–521 (2013)
89. Bartocci, E., Liò, P., Merelli, E., Paoletti, N.: Multiple verification in complex biological systems: the bone remodelling case study. In: Priami, C., Petre, I., de Vink, E. (eds.) Transactions on Computational Systems Biology XIV. LNCS, vol. 7625, pp. 53–76. Springer, Heidelberg (2012). https://doi.org/10.1007/978-3-642-35524-0_3
90. Liò, P., Paoletti, N., Moni, M., Atwell, K., Merelli, E., Viceconti, M.: Modelling osteomyelitis. BMC Bioinform. **13**(Suppl. 14), S12 (2012)
91. Paoletti, N., Liò, P., Merelli, E., Viceconti, M.: Multilevel computational modeling and quantitative analysis of bone remodeling. IEEE/ACM Trans. Comput. Biol. Bioinform. **9**, 1366–78 (2012)
92. Liò, P., Merelli, E., Paoletti, N., Viceconti, M.: A combined process algebraic and stochastic approach to bone remodeling. Electron. Notes Theor. Comput. Sci. **277**, 41–52 (2011). The Second International Workshop on Interactions Between Computer Science and Biology
93. Luisi, P.L., Ferri, F., Stano, P.: Approaches to semi-synthetic minimal cells: a review. Naturwissenschaften **93**, 1–13 (2006)
94. Kuruma, Y., Stano, P., Ueda, T., Luisi, P.L.: A synthetic biology approach to the construction of membrane proteins in semi-synthetic minimal cells. Biochimica et Biophysica Acta (BBA)-Biomembranes **1788**, 567–574 (2009)
95. Lorenzo, C., Ospri, L.L., Marangoni, R.: On fine stochastic simulations of liposome-encapsulated pure systems. Commun. Comput. Inf. Sci. **587**, 146–158 (2016)
96. Lazzerini-Ospri, L., Stano, P., Luisi, P., Marangoni, R.: Characterization of the emergent properties of a synthetic quasi-cellular system. BMC Bioinform. **13**, S9 (2012)
97. Fanti, A., Gammuto, L., Mavelli, F., Stano, P., Marangoni, R.: Do protocells preferentially retain macromolecular solutes upon division/fragmentation? A study based on the extrusion of POPC giant vesicles. Integr. Biol. **10**, 6–17 (2017)
98. Calviello, L., Stano, P., Mavelli, F., Luisi, P.L., Marangoni, R.: Quasi-cellular systems: stochastic simulation analysis at nanoscale range. BMC Bioinform. **14**, S7 (2013)
99. The 1000 Genomes Project Consortium: A global reference for human genetic variation. Nature **526**, 68–74 (2015)

100. The Computational Pan-Genomics Consortium: Computational pan-genomics: status, promises and challenges. Brief. Bioinform. **19**, 118–135 (2018)
101. Huang, L., Popic, V., Batzoglou, S.: Short read alignment with populations of genomes. Bioinformatics **29**, 361–370 (2013)
102. Bille, P., Landau, G.M., Raman, R., Sadakane, K., Satti, S.R., Weimann, O.: Random access to grammar-compressed strings. In: 22nd Annual ACM-SIAM Symposium on Discrete Algorithms (SODA), pp. 373–389 (2011)
103. Navarro, G.: Indexing highly repetitive collections. In: 23rd International Workshop on Combinatorial Algorithms (IWOCA), pp. 274–279 (2012)
104. Gagie, T., Gawrychowski, P., Puglisi, S.J.: Faster approximate pattern matching in compressed repetitive texts. In: 22nd International Symposium on Algorithms and Computation (ISAAC), pp. 653–662 (2011)
105. Iliopoulos, C.S., Kundu, R., Pissis, S.P.: Efficient pattern matching in elastic-degenerate texts. In: Drewes, F., Martín-Vide, C., Truthe, B. (eds.) LATA 2017. LNCS, vol. 10168, pp. 131–142. Springer, Cham (2017). https://doi.org/10.1007/978-3-319-53733-7_9
106. Danecek, P., et al.: The variant call format and VCFtools. Bioinformatics **27**, 2156–2158 (2011)
107. Holub, J., Smyth, W.F., Wang, S.: Fast pattern-matching on indeterminate strings. J. Discret. Algorithms **6**, 37–50 (2008)
108. Grossi, R., et al.: On-line pattern matching on a set of similar texts. In: CPM. LIPIcs (2017)
109. Bernardini, G., Pisanti, N., Pissis, S.P., Rosone, G.: Pattern matching on elastic-degenerate text with errors. In: Fici, G., Sciortino, M., Venturini, R. (eds.) SPIRE 2017. LNCS, vol. 10508, pp. 74–90. Springer, Cham (2017). https://doi.org/10.1007/978-3-319-67428-5_7
110. Pissis, S.P., Retha, A.: Dictionary matching in elastic-degenerate texts with applications in searching VCF files on-line. In: 17th International Symposium on Experimental Algorithms (SEA), pp. 16:1–16:14 (2018)
111. Aoyama, K., Nakashima, Y., Inenaga, S., Bannai, H., Takeda, M.: Faster online elastic degenerate string matching. In: 29th Annual Symposium on Combinatorial Pattern Matching, (CPM). LIPIcs, pp. 9:1–9:10 (2018)
112. Alzamel, M., et al.: Degenerate string comparison and applications. In: 18th International Workshop on Algorithms in Bioinformatics (WABI). LIPIcs, pp. 21:1–21:14 (2018)
113. Patterson, M., et al.: WhatsHap: weighted haplotype assembly for future-generation sequencing reads. J. Comput. Biol. **22**, 498–509 (2015). PMID: 25658651
114. Aldinucci, M., Bracciali, A., Marschall, T., Patterson, M., Pisanti, N., Torquati, M.: High-performance haplotype assembly. In: di Serio, C., Liò, P., Nonis, A., Tagliaferri, R. (eds.) CIBB 2014. LNCS, vol. 8623, pp. 245–258. Springer, Cham (2015). https://doi.org/10.1007/978-3-319-24462-4_21
115. Vitabile, S., Conti, V., Lanza, B., Cusumano, D., Sorbello, F.: Metabolic networks robustness: theory, simulations and results. J. Interconnection Netw. **12**, 221–240 (2012)
116. Vitabile, S., Conti, V., Lanza, B., Cusumano, D., Sorbello, F.: Topological information, flux balance analysis, and extreme pathways extraction for metabolic networks behaviour investigation. IOSPress, no. 234, pp. 66–73 (2011)
117. Vitello, G., Alongi, A., Conti, V., Vitabile, S.: A bio-inspired cognitive agent for autonomous urban vehicles routing optimization. IEEE Trans. Cogn. Dev. Syst. **9**, 5–15 (2017)

118. Conti, V., Ruffo, S., Vitabile, S., Barolli, L.: BIAM: a new bio-inspired analysis methodology for digital ecosystems based on a scale-free architecture. Soft Comput. **23**(4), 1133–1150 (2019)

119. Beccuti, M., et al.: GPU accelerated analysis of treg-teff cross regulation in relapsing-remitting multiple sclerosis. In: Mencagli, G., et al. (eds.) Euro-Par 2018. LNCS, vol. 11339, pp. 626–637. Springer, Cham (2019). https://doi.org/10.1007/978-3-030-10549-5_49

120. Totis, N., et al.: Overcoming the lack of kinetic information in biochemical reactions networks. ACM SIGMETRICS Perform. Eval. Rev. **44**, 91–102 (2017)

121. Bardozzo, F., Lió, P., Tagliaferri, R.: A study on multi-omic oscillations in Escherichia coli metabolic networks. BMC Bioinform. **19**, 194 (2018)

122. Suravajhala, P., Kogelman, L.J.A., Kadarmideen, H.N.: Multi-omic data integration and analysis using systems genomics approaches: methods and applications in animal production, health and welfare. Genet. Sel. Evol. **48**, 38 (2016)

123. Serra, A., Galdi, P., Tagliaferri, R.: Machine learning for bioinformatics and neuroimaging. Wiley Interdisc. Rev. Data Min. Knowl. Discov. **8**, e1248 (2018)

124. McClean, S., Gillespie, J., Garg, L., Barton, M., Scotney, B., Kullerton, K.: Using phase-type models to cost stroke patient care across health, social and community services. Eur. J. Oper. Res. **236**, 190–199 (2014)

125. WHO: World Health Statistics 2018: Monitoring the SDGs. Technical report (2018)

126. Garg, L., McClean, S., Barton, M.: Can management science methods do more to improve healthcare? (2014)

127. Jahangirian, M., et al.: A rapid review method for extremely large corpora of literature: applications to the domains of modelling, simulation, and management. Int. J. Inf. Manag. **31**, 234–243 (2011)

128. Garg, L., Barton, M., Meenan, B.J., Fullerton, K.: Intelligent patient management and resource planning for complex, heterogeneous, and stochastic healthcare systems. IEEE Trans. Syst. Man Cybern. - Part A Syst. Hum. **42**, 1332–1345 (2012)

129. Garnett, G., Cousens, S., Hallett, T., Steketee, R., Walker, N.: Mathematical models in the evaluation of health programmes. Lancet **378**, 515–525 (2011)

130. Shanmugam, S., Garg, L.: Model employee appraisal system with artificial intelligence capabilities. J. Cases Inf. Technol. **17**, 30–40 (2015)

131. Aleem, S.: Translating 10 lessons from lean six sigma project in paper-based training site to electronic health record-based primary care practice: challenges and opportunities. Qual. Manag. Health Care **22**, 224 (2013)

132. Kannan, V., Fish, J.C., Willett, D.L.: Agile model driven development of electronic health record-based specialty population registries (2016)

133. Heidari Gorji, A., Farooquie, J.: A comparative study of total quality management of health care system in India and Iran. BMC Res. Notes **4**, 566 (2011)

134. Garg, L., Dauwels, J., Earnest, A., Leong, K.P.: Tensor-based methods for handling missing data in quality-of-life questionnaires. IEEE J. Biomed. Heal Inform. **18**, 1571–1580 (2014)

135. McClean, S., Barton, M., Garg, L., Fullerton, K.: A modeling framework that combines Markov models and discrete-event simulation for stroke patient care. ACM Trans. Model. Comput. Simul. **21**, 25 (2011)

136. Herlihy, M., Luchangco, V.: Distributed computing and the multicore revolution. SIGACT News **39**, 62–72 (2008)

137. Smith, R.C.: Uncertainty Quantification: Theory, Implementation, and Applications, vol. 12. SIAM (2013)

138. John Walker, S.: Big Data: A Revolution that will Transform How We Live, Work, and Think. Houghton Mifflin Harcourt, Boston (2014)
139. Al-Fuqaha, A., Guizani, M., Mohammadi, M., Aledhari, M., Ayyash, M.: Internet of Things: a survey on enabling technologies, protocols, and applications. IEEE Commun. Surv. Tutor. **17**, 2347–2376 (2015)
140. Kennedy, H.: Post, Mine, Repeat: Social Media Data Mining Becomes Ordinary. Springer, London (2016). https://doi.org/10.1057/978-1-137-35398-6
141. Zhang, M., Melin, T., Gong, J., Barth, M., Axner, L.: Mixed fidelity aerodynamic and aero-structural optimization for wings. In: 2018 International Conference on High Performance Computing and Simulation, pp. 476–483 (2018). QC 20180808
142. Zafari, A., et al.: Task parallel implementation of a solver for electromagnetic scattering problems (2018). https://arxiv.org/abs/1801.03589
143. Viktorin, A., Senkerik, R., Pluhacek, M., Kadavy, T., Zamuda, A.: Distance based parameter adaptation for differential evolution. In: 2017 IEEE Symposium Series on Computational Intelligence (SSCI), pp. 1–7. IEEE (2017)
144. Viktorin, A., Senkerik, R., Pluhacek, M., Kadavy, T., Zamuda, A.: Distance based parameter adaptation for success-history based differential evolution. Swarm Evol. Comput. (2018)
145. Zamuda, A., Sosa, J.D.H.: Success history applied to expert system for underwater glider path planning using differential evolution. Expert Syst. Appl. **119**, 155–170 (2019)
146. Zamuda, A., Zarges, C., Stiglic, G., Hrovat, G.: Stability selection using a genetic algorithm and logistic linear regression on healthcare records. In: Proceedings of the Genetic and Evolutionary Computation Conference Companion (GECCO 2017), pp. 143–144 (2017)
147. Zamuda, A., Nicolau, M., Zarges, C.: A black-box discrete optimization benchmarking (BB-DOB) pipeline survey: taxonomy, evaluation, and ranking. In: Proceedings of the Genetic and Evolutionary Computation Conference Companion (GECCO 2018), pp. 1777–1782 (2018)
148. Glotić, A., Zamuda, A.: Short-term combined economic and emission hydrothermal optimization by surrogate differential evolution. Appl. Energy **141**, 42–56 (2015)
149. Zamuda, A., Sosa, J.D.H., Adler, L.: Constrained differential evolution optimization for underwater glider path planning in sub-mesoscale eddy sampling. Appl. Soft Comput. **42**, 93–118 (2016)
150. Zamuda, A., Brest, J.: Environmental framework to visualize emergent artificial forest ecosystems. Inf. Sci. **220**, 522–540 (2013)
151. Zamuda, A., Brest, J.: Vectorized procedural models for animated trees reconstruction using differential evolution. Inf. Sci. **278**, 1–21 (2014)
152. Zamuda, A., Mlakar, U.: Differential evolution control parameters study for self-adaptive triangular brushstrokes. Informatica - Int. J. Comput. Inform. **39**, 105–113 (2015)
153. Zamuda, A., Brest, J.: On tenfold execution time in real world optimization problems with differential evolution in perspective of algorithm design. In: 2018 25th International Conference on Systems, Signals and Image Processing (IWSSIP), pp. 1–5. IEEE (2018)
154. Zamuda, A., Brest, J.: Self-adaptive control parameters' randomization frequency and propagations in differential evolution. Swarm Evol. Comput. **25**, 72–99 (2015)
155. Blázquez Gil, G., Berlanga, A., Molina, J.M.: InContexto: multisensor architecture to obtain people context from smartphones. Int. J. Distrib. Sens. Netw. **8** (2012)

156. Cristina-Bicharra, A., Vivacqua, C., Sanchez-Pi, N., Martí, L., Molina, J.M.: Crowd-based ambient assisted living to monitor elderly health in outdoor settings. IEEE Softw. **34**, 53–57 (2017)
157. Griol, D., Molina, J.M., Sanchis, A.: Integration of context-aware conversational interfaces to develop practical applications for mobile devices. J. Ambient Intell. Smart Environ. (JAISE) **9**, 561–577 (2017)
158. Marti, L., Sanchez-Pi, N., Molina, J.M., Bicharra, A.C.: Anomaly detection based on sensor data in petroleum industry applications. Sensors **15**, 2774–2797 (2015)
159. Vlahogianni, E.I., Karlaftis, M.G., Golias, J.C.: Short-term traffic forecasting: where we are and where we're going. Transp. Res. Part C: Emerg. Technol. **43**, 3–19 (2014)
160. Abdullatif, A., Masulli, F., Rovetta, S.: Tracking time evolving data streams for short-term traffic forecasting. Data Sci. Eng. **2**, 210–223 (2017)

Parallelization of Hierarchical Matrix Algorithms for Electromagnetic Scattering Problems

Elisabeth Larsson[1]([✉])(iD), Afshin Zafari[1], Marco Righero[2](iD),
M. Alessandro Francavilla[3], Giorgio Giordanengo[2], Francesca Vipiana[4](iD),
Giuseppe Vecchi[4], Christoph Kessler[5](iD), Corinne Ancourt[6](iD),
and Clemens Grelck[7](iD)

[1] Scientific Computing, Department of Information Technology,
Uppsala University, Uppsala, Sweden
elisabeth.larsson@it.uu.se, afshin.zafari@gmail.com
[2] Antenna and EMC Lab (LACE), LINKS Foundation, Turin, Italy
{marco.righero,giorgio.giordanengo}@linksfoundation.com
[3] ASML Netherlands BV, Veldhoven, Netherlands
alessandro.francavilla@asml.com
[4] Department of Electronics and Telecommunications,
Politecnico di Torino, Turin, Italy
{francesca.vipiana,giuseppe.vecchi}@polito.it
[5] Department of Computer and Information Science, Linköping University,
Linköping, Sweden
christoph.kessler@liu.se
[6] MINES ParisTech, PSL University, CRI, Paris, France
corinne.ancourt@mines-paristech.fr
[7] Informatics Institute, University of Amsterdam, Amsterdam, Netherlands
c.grelck@uva.nl

Abstract. Numerical solution methods for electromagnetic scattering problems lead to large systems of equations with millions or even billions of unknown variables. The coefficient matrices are dense, leading to large computational costs and storage requirements if direct methods are used. A commonly used technique is to instead form a hierarchical representation for the parts of the matrix that corresponds to far-field interactions. The overall computational cost and storage requirements can then be reduced to $\mathcal{O}(N \log N)$. This still corresponds to a large-scale simulation that requires parallel implementation. The hierarchical algorithms are rather complex, both regarding data dependencies and communication patterns, making parallelization non-trivial. In this chapter, we describe two classes of algorithms in some detail, we provide a survey of existing solutions, we show results for a proof-of-concept implementation, and we provide various perspectives on different aspects of the problem.

The list of authors is organized into three subgroups, Larsson and Zafari (coordination and proof-of-concept implementation), Righero, Francavilla, Giordanengo, Vipiana, and Vecchi (definition of and expertise relating to the application), Kessler, Ancourt, and Grelck (perspectives and parallel expertise).

J. Kołodziej and H. González-Vélez (Eds.): cHiPSet, LNCS 11400, pp. 36–68, 2019.
https://doi.org/10.1007/978-3-030-16272-6_2

Keywords: Electromagnetic scattering · Hierarchical matrix ·
Task parallel · Fast multipole method ·
Nested equivalent source approximation

1   Introduction

In this chapter, we consider how efficient solution algorithms for electromagnetic scattering problems can be implemented for current multicore-based and heterogeneous cluster architectures. Simulation of electromagnetic fields [42] is an important industrial problem with several application areas. One of the most well known is antenna design for aircraft, but electromagnetic behavior is important, e.g., also for other types of vehicles, for satellites, and for medical equipment. A common way to reduce the cost of the numerical simulation is to assume time-harmonic solutions, and to reformulate the Maxwell equations describing the electromagnetic waves in terms of surface currents [49]. That is, the resulting numerical problem is time-independent and is solved on the surface of the body being studied, see Fig. 1 for an example of a realistic aircraft surface model.

Fig. 1. Surface currents on an aircraft model from a boundary element simulation with around 2 million unknowns.

The size N of the discretized problem, which for a boundary element discretization takes the form of a system of equations with a dense coefficient matrix, can still be very large, on the order of millions of unknowns going up to billions, and this size increases with the wave frequency. If an iterative solution method is applied to the full (dense) matrix, the cost for each matrix-vector multiplication is $\mathcal{O}(N^2)$, and direct storage of the matrix also requires memory resources of $\mathcal{O}(N^2)$. Different (approximate) factorizations of the matrices, that can reduce the costs to $\mathcal{O}(N \log N)$ or even $\mathcal{O}(N)$, have been proposed in the literature such as the MultiLevel Fast Multipole Algorithm (MLFMA), see, e.g., [43,51]; FFT-based factorization, see, e.g., [50,57]; factorizations based on the Adaptive Cross Approximation (ACA), see, e.g., [67]; or based on H2 matrices as the Nested Equivalent Source Approximation (NESA) [37–39].

All these approximations can be seen as decomposing the original dense matrix into a sparse matrix accounting for near field interactions, and a hierarchical matrix structure with low storage requirements accounting for far field interactions.

A large investment in terms of research and development has been made in constructing and implementing these rather complex algorithms efficiently. A large part of this effort was made before the advent of multicore architectures. Then, the focus was much more on minimizing the amount of computations, optimizing for a powerful server, potentially with a few processors (cores). Now, clusters are built from regular computers with large numbers of cores, and sometimes the additional complexity of accelerators. Memory bandwidth is often the limiting factor in this case. The question for companies as well as researchers with advanced application codes is how to make these codes run on their own or their customers' clusters, with the least effort in terms of changes to the code, and with the maximum output in terms of utilization of the cluster and computational efficiency.

Some of the properties of the hierarchical matrix algorithms that make parallel implementation challenging are first the general form of the algorithm, with interleaved stages of interactions in the vertical direction between parents and children in a tree structure, and horizontally between the different branches at each level of the tree. The stages typically have different levels of parallelism and work loads, and there is a bottleneck when the algorithm reaches the coarsest level of the tree structure, and the amount of parallelism is the smallest. That is, the algorithm itself is generally heterogeneous. Furthermore, the tree can be unbalanced in different ways due to the geometry of the underlying structure, and the groups at the finest level can contain different number of unknowns depending on how the scattering surface cuts through space. An overview of the challenges inherent in the implementation of the fast multipole method (FMM), which is one of the algorithms in this class, on modern computer architectures can be found in [13].

In the following sections, we first provide a high-level description of two types of hierarchical algorithms for electromagnetic scattering. Then in Sect. 3 we provide a survey of literature and software in this area. Section 4 discusses two task-parallel implementations of a simplified algorithm for shared memory. Then in Sect. 5, different perspectives regarding the question of how to eventually port the software to clusters and heterogeneous architecture are given.

2   Two Classes of Algorithms and Their Properties

In this section, we will go deeper into the MLFMA and NESA algorithm classes, and describe their properties from the parallelization perspective. For the mathematical details of the algorithms, see [43] for MLFMA and [37–39] for NESA.

2.1   Interaction Matrices

Solving a system of equations for the unknown surface currents given measured field values can be seen as an inverse problem. When using an iterative method, we transform the inverse problem to repeated solutions of the forward problem, which is easier to address.

The forward problem consists of computing an electromagnetic field given a distribution of sources/charges. We will use two examples to make it more concrete. A well known model problem is to compute the electrostatic potential,

$$\phi(\boldsymbol{x}) = \sum_{j=1}^{N} K(\boldsymbol{x}, \boldsymbol{x}_j) q_j, \tag{1}$$

generated by the point charges q_j located at the points $\boldsymbol{x}_j$. The kernel $K(\cdot, \cdot)$, which is logarithmic in two dimensions and proportional to the inverse distance in three dimensions, represents the interaction between the field points and the charges.

The corresponding scattering problem that is of real interest in industry and for research has a similar structure and consists of computing the electric and/or magnetic fields generated by surface currents on for example a metallic object such as an aircraft. We write this in simplified form as

$$E(\boldsymbol{r}) = \int_{\partial\Omega} \left(G(\boldsymbol{r}, \boldsymbol{r}') \boldsymbol{j}(\boldsymbol{r}') + \frac{1}{k^2} \nabla \left(G(\boldsymbol{r}, \boldsymbol{r}') \nabla \cdot \boldsymbol{j}(\boldsymbol{r}') \right) \right) d\boldsymbol{r}', \tag{2}$$

where $\boldsymbol{r}$ is a point in space, $\partial\Omega$ is the surface of the object, and $G(\cdot, \cdot)$ is a Green's function.

To render the problems tractable for computer simulation, they are discretized. In the first case, we already have discrete charges. In the second case, a boundary integral formulation of the problem is used, where we represent the fields and surface currents by a set of basis functions v_j and corresponding coefficients, which we denote by E_j and q_j, $j = 1, \ldots, N$. Henceforth, we will refer to q_j as sources, and to individual basis functions as locations. The fields are evaluated in the same discrete locations as where the sources are located. This allows us to express the forward problem as a matrix–vector multiplication

$$E = Zq, \tag{3}$$

where E is the vector of the field variables, Z is an $N \times N$ interaction matrix where element z_{ij} describes the contribution from a unit source at location j to the field at location i, and q is the vector of source values.

2.2   The Hierarchical Algorithm

The basis for the fast algorithms is that interactions between locations near to each other are stronger then distant interactions. In the algorithms, near-field interactions are computed directly, while far-field interactions are approximated in such a way that the required storage and the amount of computations is decreased while still respecting a given error tolerance.

The computational domain is hierarchically divided into groups (boxes), which can be represented as an oct-tree (quad-tree in two dimensions) with levels $\ell = L_0, \ldots, \ell_{\max}$. Since the charges are located only on the surface of the body, many of the groups, especially on the finer levels, are empty of charges, and are pruned from the tree. When we construct the hierarchical algorithm, we consider interactions between groups. We let E_i denote the field variables in group i at level $\ell_{\max}$, and we let E_i^j be the contribution from group j at level $\ell_{\max}$ to E_i, such that

$$E_i = \sum_j E_i^j. \tag{4}$$

Using the direct matrix–vector multiplication, we have that

$$E_i^j = Z_{i,j} Q_j, \tag{5}$$

where $Z_{i,j}$ is a matrix block, and Q_j is the vector of charges in group j at level $\ell_{\max}$. In the hierarchical fast matrix–vector multiplication algorithm, only the near-field interactions are computed directly. These are here defined as interactions between groups that are neighbours at the finest level. The far-field interactions are instead approximated. At each level of the tree structure, starting from level L_0, the far-field groups are identified as those that are not neighbours to the target group. As much of the far-field interaction as possible is treated at each level, to minimize the total number of groups to interact with. In Fig. 2, we show the layout of the near and far-field for computing the field at one location (the black box) in a two-dimensional geometry.

Fig. 2. Illustration of a two-dimensional domain that is hierarchically divided into three levels of boxes. Charges are located on the wavy curve. For the black target box, the near-field consists of the six dark gray neighbouring boxes. The far-field at each level consists of the four large, five medium, and five small light gray boxes that are not neighbours of the target box.

The far-field approximation for one interaction has the following general form

$$E_i^j = Z_{i,j} Q_j \approx R_i \underbrace{\mathcal{P}_{\ell_{\max}-1}^{\ell_{\max}} \cdots \mathcal{P}_{\bar{\ell}}^{\bar{\ell}+1}}_{\text{descending}} T_{i,j}^{\ell} \underbrace{\mathcal{P}_{\bar{\ell}+1}^{\bar{\ell}} \cdots \mathcal{P}_{\ell_{\max}}^{\ell_{\max}-1}}_{\text{ascending}} S_j Q_j, \tag{6}$$

and can be described in terms of the five steps described in Algorithm 1.

Radiation:

The sources Q_j are converted into an intermediate representation $X_j^{\ell_{\max}} = S_j Q_j$.

Source transfer:

The intermediate representation is propagated up through the parent groups $X_j^{\ell-1} = \mathcal{P}_\ell^{\ell-1} X_j^\ell$ until level $\bar{l}$, where the far-field interaction takes place.

Translation:

The far-field interaction between groups i and j is computed at level $\bar{\ell}$. The result is an intermediate field representation $Y_i^{\bar{\ell}} = T_{i,j}^{\bar{\ell}} X_j^{\bar{\ell}}$.

Field transfer:

The intermediate field representation is propagated down through the child groups $Y_i^{\ell+1} = \mathcal{P}_\ell^{\ell+1} Y_i^\ell$ until the finest level is reached.

Reception:

The intermediate field representation is evaluated at the actual field locations, $E_i^j = R_i Y_i^{\ell_{\max}}$.

Algorithm 1. The algorithm for computing one interaction term.

If we change the view, and instead see the algorithm from the perspective of one particular group at level ℓ that takes part in several interactions, the work related to that group can be expressed as Algorithm 2.

Upward Phase:

if $\ell = \ell_{\max}$ then

| Compute $X_j^{\ell_{\max}} = S_j Q_j$ for local sources.

else

| Receive source contributions from all child groups.

end

if $\ell > L_0$ then

| Send accumulated source contribution to parent.

end

Translation Phase:

| Compute $Y_i^\ell = T_{i,j}^\ell X_j^\ell$ according to interaction list.

Downward Phase:

if $\ell > L_0$ then

| Receive field contribution from parent.

end

if $\ell < \ell_{\max}$ then

| Send field contribution to all child groups.

else

| Compute $E_j = R_j Y_j^{\ell_{\max}}$ for local target points.

end

Algorithm 2. The algorithm seen from the view of one particular group.

For the parallel implementation, there are several relevant aspects to keep in mind. For the upward and downward phases, communication is performed vertically in the tree, between parent and child groups. The translation operations on the other hand need horizontal communication. Due to the hierarchical structure, each group has an interaction list of limited size. The three phases of the algorithm can be overlapped, since different groups complete the phases at different times. Even more important is that the near-field interactions for disjunct groups are independent and can be interspersed with the far-field computations.

The memory savings that the fast algorithms provide stem from the fact that the far-field part of the interaction matrix is replaced with the operators in (6). These are the same for groups that have the same position relative to each other. That is, only a limited number of operators are needed at each level.

2.3 Specific Properties of the NESA Algorithm

In the NESA algorithm, all of the far-field operations consist in expressing sources and field in terms of equivalent charges. The actual sources in a group at level ℓ_{max} can through a low rank approximation be represented by a set of equivalent sources that generate a matching field at some control points located at an exterior test surface. In the same way, the equivalent sources in a child group can be represented by another set of equivalent sources at the parent group. This is schematically shown for a two-dimensional problem in Fig. 3. The number of equivalent charges Q is the same in each group, which is why we can save significantly in the far-field computation. The translation and field transfers are managed similarly. We will not go into all details here, instead we refer to [37].

Fig. 3. A parent group and one of its children are illustrated. The points on the solid circles are where the equivalent sources are located, and the points on the dashed circle are where the fields are matched.

To understand the computational properties of the NESA algorithm, we characterize each operation in terms of how much memory it needs to load counted in double precision numbers, and how many floating point operations (flop) are performed. We also provide the computational intensity, in flop/double. The results

Table 1. Characterization of the matrix–vector products in the NESA algorithm. The number of sources in group j is denoted by n_j.

Operator	Data size	Compute size	Intensity
Near field			
$Z_{i,j}$	$n_i \times n_j$	$2n_i n_j$	2
Far field			
S_j	$Q \times n_j$	$2n_j Q$	2
$\mathcal{P}_\ell^{\ell-1}$	$Q \times Q$	$2Q^2$	2
$\mathcal{T}_{i,j}^\ell$	$Q \times Q$	$2Q^2$	2
$\mathcal{P}_\ell^{\ell+1}$	$Q \times Q$	$2Q^2$	2
R_i	$n_i \times Q$	$2n_i Q$	2

are listed in Table 1. All of the operations in the NESA algorithm are dense matrix–vector products, with the same computational intensity of 2 flop/double. For modern multicore architectures, a computational intensity of 30–40 is needed in order to balance bandwidth capacity and floating point performance, see for example the trade-offs for the Tintin and Rackham systems at UPPMAX, Uppsala University, calculated in [64]. This means that we need to exploit data locality (work on data that is cached locally) in order to overcome bandwidth limitations and scale to the full number of available cores.

2.4 Specific Properties of the MLFMA Algorithm

In the MLFMA algorithm, the intermediate representation of sources and fields is given in terms of plane wave directions $\hat{\kappa} = (\theta, \phi)$, where θ is the polar angle, and ϕ is the azimuthal angle in a spherical coordinate system. When computing far-field interactions, the Green's function can be represented using an integral over the directions, which numerically is done through a quadrature method. The accuracy of the approximation depends on the number of directions that are used. A difference compared with the NESA method is that the number of directions that are needed scale with the box size.

Table 2. An example of the number of directions N_ℓ needed at each level in the MLFMA algorithm, starting from the finest level $\ell = \ell_{\max}$.

$\ell_{\max} - \ell$	0	1	2	3	4	5	6	7	8	9
L_ℓ	5	7	10	15	23	38	66	120	224	428
N_ℓ	72	128	242	512	1152	3042	8978	29282	101250	368082

To compute the number of directions needed for a box at level ℓ, we first compute the parameter L_ℓ from the wave number of the electromagnetic wave,

Fig. 4. A unit sphere discretized for $L_\ell = 23$ with 24 points in θ (latitudes) and 48 points in ϕ (longitudes).

the diagonal d_ℓ of the box, and the desired error tolerance τ [43, Sect. 5.3]. Then the box is discretized with $L_\ell + 1$ points in the θ-direction and $2L_\ell + 2$ points in the ϕ-direction giving a total number of $N_\ell = 2L_\ell^2 + 4L_\ell + 2$. Using a realistic tolerance $\tau = 1e - 4$ and an appropriate box size for the finest level leads to the sequence of sizes given in Table 2. Figure 4 shows the discretized sphere for $L_\ell = 23$. The wide range of sizes for the representations at different levels does pose a challenge for parallel implementations.

The interpolation step between parent and child or vice versa can be realized in different ways. Here, we consider the Lagrange interpolation method described in [43]. Then the value at one point at the new level is computed using the m nearest neighbours in each coordinate direction. The operations of one interpolation step are shown schematically in Fig. 5.

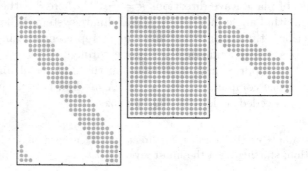

Fig. 5. To interpolate the data (middle) from a child $L = 10$ to a parent $L = 15$, a sparse interpolation matrix (left, right) is applied to each of the data dimensions. The matrix sizes are here 32×22, 22×17, and 17×16. The data matrix is extended with $m/2$ columns to each side to manage the periodicity at the poles.

Similarly as for the NESA algorithm in the previous subsection, we characterize the work performed during the algorithm and evaluate its computational

Table 3. Characterization of the steps in the MLFMA algorithm. The number of sources in group j is denoted by n_j.

Operator	Data size	Compute size	Intensity
Near field			
$Z_{i,j}$	$n_i \times n_j$	$2n_i n_j$	2
Far field			
S_j	$N_\ell \times n_j$	$2n_j N_\ell$	2
$\mathcal{P}_\ell^{\ell-1}$	$(2L_\ell \times L_\ell)$	$2m\left(2L_\ell L_{\ell-1} + 2L_{\ell-1}^2\right)$	$2m\left(\frac{L_{\ell-1}}{L_\ell} + \left(\frac{L_{\ell-1}}{L_\ell}\right)^2\right)$
$\mathcal{T}_{i,j}^\ell$	$2\left(2L_\ell \times L_\ell\right)$	$\left(2L_\ell^2\right)$	0.5
$\mathcal{P}_\ell^{\ell+1}$	$(2L_\ell \times L_\ell)$	$2m\left(2L_\ell L_{\ell+1} + 2L_{\ell+1}^2\right)$	$2m\left(\frac{L_{\ell+1}}{L_\ell} + \left(\frac{L_{\ell+1}}{L_\ell}\right)^2\right)$
R_i	$n_i \times N_\ell$	$2n_i N_\ell$	2

intensity. The results are given in Table 3. The radiation and reception steps are matrix–vector products also in this case. The interpolation steps have a higher computational intensity. For $m = 6$ and the child to parent operation, we get 40–66 flop/data, while for the parent to child operations, we get 10–15 flop/data. The translation step is often a bottleneck in parallel implementation. It is an elementwise multiplication with an intensity less than one flop/data.

3   State of the Art

There is a rich literature on parallel implementation of hierarchical matrix algorithms. Many of the implementations are aimed at volume formulations (particles/charges are located in a volume), as opposed to surface formulations as for the scattering problem. The volume formulation is more likely to have a large number of particles in a group, and a more well-balanced tree structure.

The most common parallelization approach, targeting distributed memory systems, is to partition the tree data structure over the computational nodes, and use an MPI-based parallelization [34]. The resulting performance is typically a bit better for volume formulations then for boundary formulations, since the computational density is higher in the former case. A particular issue for the MLFMA formulation of electromagnetic scattering problems is that the work per element (group) in the tree data structure increases with the level, and additional partitioning strategies are needed for the coarser part of the structure [6,30,56].

The ongoing trend in cluster hardware is an increasing number of cores per computational node. When scaling to large numbers of cores, it is hard to fully exploit the computational resources using a pure MPI implementation, due to the rapid increase in the number of inter-node messages with the number of MPI processes for communication heavy algorithms [64]. As is pointed out in [35], a hybrid parallelization with MPI at the distributed level and threads within the computational nodes is more likely to perform well. That is, a need for efficient shared memory parallelizations of hierarchical algorithms to be used in combination with the distributed MPI level arises.

The emerging method of choice for implementing complex algorithms on multicore architectures is dependency-aware task-based parallel programming, which is available, e.g, through the StarPU [5], OmpSs [46], and SuperGlue [54] frameworks, but also in OpenMP, since version 4.0. Starting with [7], where StarPU is used for a task parallel implementation of an FMM algorithm, several authors have taken an interest in the problem. In [31], SuperGlue is used for a multicore CPU+GPU implementation of an adaptive FMM. The Quark [61] run-time system is used for developing an FMM solver in [40]. Since tasks were introduced in OpenMP, a recurring question is if the OpenMP implementations can reach the same performance as the specific run-times discussed above. An early OpenMP task FMM implementation is found in [2]. This was before the depend clause was introduced, allowing dependencies between sibling tasks. OpenMP, Cilk and other models are compared for FMM in [66], OpenMP and Klang/StarPU are compared in [1], and different OpenMP implementations and task parallel run-times are compared with a special focus on locking and synchronization in [4]. A common conclusion from these comparisons is that the commutative clause provided by most task parallel run-time systems is quite important for performance, and that this would be a useful upgrade of OpenMP tasks for the future.

An alternative track is to develop special purpose software components for the class of FMM-like algorithms, see, e.g., PetFMM [12] and Tapas [21].

An open source implementation of MLFMA is available through the Puma-EM software [47], parallelized with MPI. An example of a commercial MLFMA software is Efield [16] provided by ESI Group, parallelized for shared memory.

4   Proposed Solution and Proof of Concept

During the last decade task-parallel programming has emerged as the main programming paradigm to run scientific applications on modern multicore- and heterogeneous computer architectures. A recent and fairly complete overview of the current state of the art can be found in [52].

The key idea is that the programmer provides the sequential work-flow of an algorithm in terms of tasks. These are then submitted to a run-time system, which analyses the data dependencies of the tasks and schedules them onto available hardware resources to be executed in parallel. It can in some cases be possible to obtain higher performance by hand-tuning a code, but the cost in programming effort and the renewed cost if the system configuration changes are usually considered too high.

There are several arguments for using task parallel programming for the hierarchical matrix–vector products considered here.

- The work flow is already described in terms of *tasks* operating on data associated with the individual groups. Therefore, the overhead of converting the algorithm into a suitable form can be largely avoided.

- The data size varies between groups, the number of child groups and interactions across the tree structure. The amount of work varies with the level and the phase of the algorithm. All of this indicates that the asynchronous task execution provided by a run-time system is more likely to be efficient than a statically determined schedule.
- The dependencies between tasks are complex, problem dependent, and hard to analyze manually. With the run-time scheduling, dependencies are automatically managed, and tasks can run as soon as their dependencies have been met. Furthermore, the run-time guarantees correctness in the sense that if the sequential task flow of the application code is described correctly, the parallel execution guarantees to respect the order up to admissible interleavings.

As a proof of concept, we have implemented the NESA algorithm for the electrostatic potential problem using the SuperGlue [54] framework. A detailed description of the implementation details and the results can be found in [63]. A benefit of using the NESA algorithm is that the tasks are more similar both in size and type than for the MLFMA algorithm. The main arguments for choosing the SuperGlue framework are (i) that it has very low scheduling overhead, and can therefore handle small task sizes well, and (ii) that commutative data accesses are naturally included in the dependency management based on data-versioning. Commutative accesses relate to tasks that touch the same data, and that can therefore not run concurrently, but that can otherwise run in any order.

We have also implemented the NESA algorithm using OpenMP tasks, and provide some results and comments on how the two implementations compare.

In the following subsections, we provide a brief survey of task parallel programming frameworks, we discuss the SuperGlue and OpenMP implementations, and we provide some illustrative performance results.

4.1   A Task-Parallel Programming Overview

One of the key features of task parallel programming is that it makes it relatively easy for the programmer to produce a parallel application code that performs well. However, it is still important for the programmer to understand how to write a task parallel program and how various aspects of the algorithm are likely to impact performance.

The granularity of the tasks determines the number of tasks, which has a direct effect on the potential parallelism. As an application programmer, it is beneficial to be aware of how tasks interact with each other and with the data. That is, to understand the character of the data dependencies. There may be different ways of splitting the work that lead to different degrees of parallelism. In the NESA and MLFMA cases, a basic task size is given by the algorithm through the division of the domain into groups. The discussion to have is whether some groups need splitting (the coarse levels in MLFMA) or merging (the leaf groups).

The granularity of tasks also has an effect on how the tasks interact with the memory hierarchy. If the tasks are small enough, data may fit into the cache. If the run-time system is locality-aware such that tasks are scheduled at the cores where the data they need is cached, significant performance gains may be secured. As was discussed in Sects. 2.3 and 2.4, the computational intensity provided by the tasks of the NESA and MLFMA algorithms is not enough to scale well if all of the data is read from the main memory.

In [55] resource-aware task-scheduling is investigated. It is shown that the effect of, e.g, bandwidth contention between tasks can be reduced by co-scheduling a mix of diverse tasks. However, in the NESA case, all of the tasks have a similar computational intensity, so that approach is not applicable.

From the user perspective, it would be ideal if there were only one framework for task parallelism, or at least one common standard for task parallel programming implemented by different frameworks. Steps are being taken in this direction, see also the implementation in [62], but it will take some time until it is in place. Meanwhile, we provide an overview of some of the more relevant initiatives.

The StarPU framework [5,52] was initially developed to manage scheduling between the CPU and GPU resources in one computational node. It has over time been developed in different ways and has become one of the most widely adopted general purpose run-time systems. In StarPU, an important component is the management of data transfers and data prefetching. Advanced performance prediction based on performance measurements is used in the different scheduling algorithms. StarPU has very good performance for large scale problems with relatively large task sizes. When task sizes become too small, the overhead of the advanced scheduling is too large, and performance goes down.

Another important run-time system is OmpSs [15], which is the current representative of the StarSs family [46]. In OmpSs, the tasks are defined through compiler directives in the same way as in OpenMP. In fact, the development of the OpenMP standard in terms of tasks and task dependencies is driven by the development of OmpSs. In this way, the constructs and implementations are well tested before being adopted by the standard. The use of directives can be seen as less intrusive when transforming legacy code into task parallel code compared with the use of specific APIs for task submission.

LAPACK [3], which implements a large selection of linear algebra operations, is one of the most widely used libraries in scientific computing. With the advent of multicore architectures, a number of projects were started to provide multicore and GPU support. These have now converged into using the PaRSEC run-time system [8], which has excellent performance both for large and small task sizes. PaRSEC can be used for all types of algorithms, but it requires the task dependencies to be expressed in a specific data flow language. This allows to build a parametrized task graph that can be used efficiently by the run-time system, but it can be an obstacle for the application programmer.

The SuperGlue framework [54] was developed mainly for research purposes with a focus on performance. It is a general-purpose task parallel framework for multicore architectures. It is very lightweight, it uses an efficient representation of dependencies through data versions, and has very low overhead, such that comparatively small tasks can be used without loosing performance.

Tasks with dependencies were introduced in OpenMP 4.0. The dependencies are only between sibling tasks submitted in the same parallel region, and there is not yet support for commutative tasks, which are relevant for the NESA and MLFMA types of algorithms. The main reason for using OpenMP is that it is a standard and is likely to remain, making it a relatively secure investment in coding.

4.2   The SuperGlue Task Parallel Implementation

SuperGlue is implemented in C++ as a headers only library. In order to write a task-based version of the NESA algorithm for SuperGlue, we need to define a SuperGlue task class for the matrix–vector product that is the computational kernel used in all the tasks. In Program 1.1 we show a slightly simplified code that emphasizes the most relevant parts. The task class contains the data that is touched by the task, a constructor, and a run method. In the constructor, the types of data accesses are registered. In this case, it is a commutative (add) access to the output vector. The read accesses to the input data are not registered as that data is not modified during execution. The access information is used for tracking dependencies, and extra dependencies increase the overhead cost.

The constructor is called at task submission, while the run method is called at task execution time.

```
1 class SGTaskGemv : public Task<Options,3>{
2 private:
3   SGMatrix *A,*x,*y;
4 public:
5   SGTaskGemv(SGMatrix &A_, SGMatrix &x_, SGMatrix &
        y_)
6   {
7     A = &A_;
8     x = &x_;
9     y = &y_;
10    Handle<Options> &hy = y->get_handle();
11    register_access(ReadWriteAdd::add, hy);
12  }
13
14  void run(){
15    double *Mat= A->get_matrix()->get_data_memory();
16    double *X  = x->get_matrix()->get_data_memory();
17    double *Y  = y->get_matrix()->get_data_memory();
18    cblas_dgemv(Mat, X, Y);
19  }
20 };
```

Program 1.1. The MVP task class

In the application code all former calls to the matrix–vector product sub-routine should be replaced by the corresponding task submission. If we hide the task submission statement in a subroutine, the syntax of the application code does not need to change at all. The new subroutine that replaces the original matrix–vector product by the task submission is provided as Program 1.2.

```
1 void gemv(SGMatrix &A, SGMatrix &x, SGMatrix &y){
2     SGTaskGemv *t= new SGTaskGemv(A, x, y);
3     sgEngine->submit(t);
4 }
```

Program 1.2. The subroutine that submits an MVP task.

There are also other small changes such as starting up the SuperGlue run-time, and the SGMatrix data type, which equips the 'ordinary' matrix type with the data handle that is used when registering accesses. A longer description of the implementation can be found in [63], and the full implementation is available at GitHub[1].

4.3 The OpenMP Task-Parallel Implementation

An implementation with a similar functionality as the task-parallel implementation described above can—with some care—be created with OpenMP as well. A simple *task* construct was introduced in OpenMP 3.0, and a *depend* clause was added in OpenMP 4.0, to allow dependencies between sibling tasks, i.e, tasks created within the same parallel region. This means that if we create several parallel regions for different parts of the algorithm, there will effectively be barriers in between, and the tasks from different regions cannot mix.

```
1 #pragma omp parallel
2 {
3   #pragma omp single
4   {
5     // Submit tasks for near-field multiplication
6     FMM::mv_near_field(OT, C, Q);
7     // Submit tasks for far-field multiplication
8     FMM::mv_far_field(OT, C, Q);
9   }
10 }
11 #pragma omp taskwait
12 #pragma omp barrier
```

Program 1.3. The structure of the OpenMP implementation. There is one global parallel region (lines 1–10), and within this region only one thread can submit tasks (lines 3–9).

---

[1] https://github.com/afshin-zafari/FMM/.

The proper way to do it is to create one parallel region that covers the whole computation, and then make sure that only one thread generates tasks such that the sequential order is not compromised. An excerpt from the OpenMP main program that illustrates this is shown in Program 1.3. The tasks are implicitly submitted from the near-field and far-field subroutines, whenever the cblas_dgemv subroutine is invoked.

The tasks are defined using the task pragma with the depend clause, see Program 1.4. Only the (necessary) inout dependence for the output data vector is included. Adding the (nonessential) read dependencies on the matrix and input data vector was shown in the experiments to degrade performance.

```
1 #pragma omp task depend(inout:Y[0:N])
2 cblas_dgemv(Mat, X, Y);
```

Program 1.4. The OpenMP task pragma that defines a gemv task.

As can be seen, the implementation is not so difficult, but there are several ways to make mistakes that lead to suboptimal performance. The programmer needs to understand how the task generation, the task scheduling, and the parallel regions interact.

4.4 Performance Results

In this section we summarize the experimental results from [63] and relate these to the arguments we gave for using a task-based parallel implementation. The ease of implementation was discussed in the previous two subsections. The next two arguments concerned the benefits of asynchronous task execution, dynamic and automatic scheduling, and mixing of computational phases.

Execution traces for the SuperGlue implementation, when running on one shared memory node of the Tintin cluster at the Uppsala Multidisciplinary Center for Advanced Computational Science (UPPMAX), are shown in Fig. 6. The simulation parameters P and Q are the average number of sources in one group at the finest level (the average of n_j), and the number of auxiliary sources in each group, respectively. The near-field trace (top) nicely illustrates how tasks of different sizes are scheduled asynchronously onto 16 worker threads with no visible idle time between the tasks. The far-field trace furthermore illustrates that the different computational phases can be interleaved to a large extent using a schedule that it would be difficult to construct statically. Finally the last trace shows that the far-field tasks can be embedded in the near-field computation. As will be discussed below, this is beneficial since the far-field tasks have a lower computational intensity, and in this case are also smaller. The idle time that can be seen in the beginning for thread 0 in the middle and bottom panels is the time for task submission.

Another question that was investigated using the proof of concept implementation was how the task size impacts scalability, and how small tasks can be used without loosing performance. The same problem with $N = 100\,000$ source points is solved in all experiments, but the method parameters P (the average number

Fig. 6. Execution traces for the near field computation (top), the far field computation (middle), and the combined execution (bottom) for $Q = 100$ and $P = 400$. Each task is shown as a triangle, and the color indicates which phase of the algorithm it belongs to. Near-field (dark gray), radiation (medium gray), source transfer (light gray), translation (black), field transfer (light gray), and reception (medium gray).

of source points at the finest level) and Q (the number of auxiliary points used for each group) are varied between the experiments.

We compute the speedup S_p using p cores as $S_p = T_1/T_p$. Each node of the Tintin cluster consists of two AMD Opteron 6220 (Bulldozer) processors. A peculiarity of the Bulldozer architecture is that each floating point unit (FPU) is shared between two cores. This means that the theoretical speedup when using $2p$ threads (cores) is only p, and the highest theoretical speedup on one node with 16 threads is 8.

Figure 7 shows the results for different task sizes. The near-field computation scales relatively well for all of the task sizes, but the performance improves with size P. For the far-field, there is no scalability when both P and Q are small. The situation improves when the sizes increase, but the scalability is significantly worse than for the near-field. For the combined computation, the results are better than the far-field results with the same sizes, and for the larger tasks even better than the near-field results. That is, the mixing of the two phases allows the limited scalability of the far-field computation to be hidden behind the better performance of the near-field computations. We can however conclude that $Q = 10$ and $P = 50$, which are reasonable numbers for the two-dimensional case results in tasks that are too small for scalability. Using $Q = 100$, which is suitable for the three-dimensional problem, is however enough for shared memory scalability. This is an indication that the proof of concept approach can be used for the real three-dimensional problem.

Fig. 7. Speedup for the near-field computation (left), the far-field computation (middle) for $P = 400$ (solid lines) and for $P = 50$ (dashed lines), and the combined computation (right).

In Table 4, we compare the execution times, the speedup, and the utilization for execution with small tasks and with larger tasks. The utilization is defined as the fraction of the total execution time that is spent in executing tasks. That

Table 4. The parallel execution time T_p, the speedup S_p, the speedup in relation to the theoretical speedup S_p^*, and the utilization U_p computed as the fraction of time spent executing tasks, for two problem settings.

p	T_p [ms]	S_p	S_p/S_p^*	U_p
$Q = 10, P = 50$				
1	244	1.0	1.00	0.90
4	111	2.2	1.10	0.55
8	137	1.8	0.44	0.29
16	156	1.6	0.20	0.21
$Q = 100, P = 300$				
1	1192	1	1.00	0.99
4	401	3.0	1.49	0.98
8	228	5.2	1.31	0.98
16	163	7.3	0.92	0.96

is, the lack of utilization reveals overhead, idle time and load imbalance. For the problem with larger tasks, both utilization and speed are close to optimal. For the problem with small tasks, the utilization goes down to 21% for 16 threads. Then one might expect that the execution time $T_{16} = T_1/16/0.21$, leading to a speedup $S_{16} = 3.4$, but this is not at all the case. Figure 8 shows the slowdown of individual task execution as a function of the number of threads. A factor of 2 is expected for 16 threads due to the Bulldozer architecture. This is also the case for the larger tasks. For the smaller tasks, the far-field computations exhibit a slowdown of 4, which limits the potential scalability to maximum 4 at 16 threads. The computational intensity does not change with the task size, but a potential explanation can be found when looking at the scheduling in the run-time system. For large enough tasks, the run-time system has time to use the knowledge of which data is needed by a task to place it in the work queue of the thread where that data is cached, thereby ensuring data locality. However, for too small task sizes, task execution becomes faster than task submission, and the opportunity to find the next task 'in time' is lost. Then the threads try to steal work from each other. This results in contention on the work queues as well as a loss of data locality.

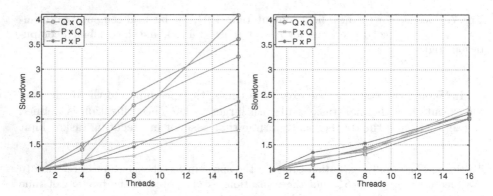

Fig. 8. Increase in individual task execution times for the complete execution for $P = 50$, $Q = 10$ (left) and for $P = 300$, $Q = 100$ (right).

The final question we ask in this section is whether OpenMP is efficient enough to use for this problem. We already mentioned the fact that OpenMP currently does not support commutative tasks. The performance of the OpenMP run-time implementations has increased over time, and will most likely continue to do so.

The experiments were carried out both on a node of the Tintin cluster, described in the previous section, and on a local shared memory system with 4 sockets of Intel Xeon E5-4650 Sandy Bridge processors, yielding a total of 64 cores. On Tintin, the codes were compiled with gcc version 4.9.1 and OpenMP 4.0, while on Sandy Bridge the compiler was gcc 6.3.0 combined with OpenMP 4.5.

We compare the execution times using SuperGlue (SG) and using OpenMP (OMP) for the full execution and for two different task sizes. The results, given in Tables 5 and 6, show that OpenMP is slower for small task sizes, and especially when small sizes are combined with large numbers of threads. However, for the larger problem sizes, the differences are small 5–10%, and the results vary between the two hardware systems. We do not see the effect of the missing commutative clause. As long as tasks are large enough. These results indicate that OpenMP can be used for this type of problem.

Table 5. Execution times in ms for the SuperGlue (SG) and OpenMP (OMP) implementations executed on a Tintin node.

p	$P = 50, Q = 10$			$P = 300, Q = 100$		
	SG	OMP	OMP/SG	SG	OMP	OMP/SG
1	244	285	1.17	1192	1186	1.00
4	111	134	1.21	363	345	0.95
8	137	110	0.80	210	186	0.89
16	156	254	1.63	145	139	0.96

Table 6. Execution times in ms for the SuperGlue (SG) and OpenMP (OMP) implementations executed on the Sandy Bridge system.

p	$P = 50, Q = 10$			$P = 300, Q = 100$		
	SG	OMP	OMP/SG	SG	OMP	OMP/SG
1	438	476	1.09	2318	2556	1.10
4	166	260	1.57	811	913	1.13
8	100	197	1.97	422	469	1.11
16	107	170	1.59	244	253	1.04
32	135	237	1.76	154	157	1.02
64	141	535	3.79	127	133	1.05

5 Perspectives and Future Directions

Our proof-of-concept implementation demonstrates that a task parallel implementation provides the expected benefits. As long as the task granularity is not too small relative to the overhead of the run-time system the proposed solution performs well. Thus, we can recommend this general direction of parallelization, but there are many further aspects to consider; we discuss some of them in the following subsections.

5.1   Recommendations for a Task Parallel 3-D Implementation

When performing large scale three-dimensional simulations, it becomes necessary to use distributed computer systems, and hence distributed parallel programming (or a partitioned global address space (PGAS) model). In [64] it was
shown that a hierarchical task-parallel programming model was beneficial for the
distributed implementation. Larger tasks are communicated between computational nodes, and then split into subtasks that are executed in parallel within
each node.

For the upward and downward phases it seems natural to let a larger task represent operations within a subtree. For the communication-intensive translation
phase, it is less clear what the best type of task is. Perhaps translations between
subtrees can be performed as one larger task, but this reduces the opportunities
to interleave the translation stage with the other stages.

The partitioning of the global tree structure into subtrees would be performed at a level where the number of groups is at least equal to the number
of computational nodes. Then the question is how to share the work and the
data for the levels above the splitting point. For the NESA algorithm, this is not
such a big problem as the amount of work at these lower levels is small. However, for the MLFMA algorithm, the work increases significantly for the lower
levels, as can be seen in Table 2. In this case, the work for these levels needs to
be divided between the computational nodes, while the data could potentially
be shared by all. A drawback of such an approach could be that this kind of
splitting becomes more intrusive from the programming perspective, than just
making each subroutine call into one task.

As we saw in the proof-of-concept implementation, small task sizes can also
become a problem, but from the programming perspective we do not want to
explicitly merge work into larger tasks. In a preliminary implementation, which
is not yet finished, we performed experiments with batching of small tasks. When
tasks are submitted to the run-time system, they are saved in a buffer until there
is enough work to actually start a batched task, which then executes all of them
at once.

The question of which run-time system or programming model to use is
a difficult one. Especially for a company, it is important to know what kind
of long-term support of a programming model can be expected, and whether
permissions and licenses for using it remain stable. This would be an argument
for using OpenMP for the shared memory part. For distributed task-parallel
programming, however, there is no similarly established standard as of yet. The
choice is then to either develop a custom run-time which is unlikely to be as
good as the already existing ones, or to trust an existing one, which may at
some point no longer be supported.

5.2   Automatically Mapping Workloads to Accelerators

Applications that perform regular computations on a large number of data are
often good candidates for efficient execution on accelerators such as GPUs. However, mapping some parts of the applications onto a GPU is not easy, especially

when the application is written in C++. Indeed, in C++ references to array elements or certain values such as loop bounds can be hidden in function calls. Automatic tools that detect data dependencies statically and generate parallel code and GPU kernels need this information explicitly. Otherwise, dynamic analysis and code instrumentation are required.

Initially, the mapping consists in detecting loops that meet the criteria of the accelerator. These criteria express the adequacy between the loop nest patterns and the target accelerator hierarchy: external parallel loops will be mapped directly to streaming cores and sequential internal loops in threads. The loop nest sizes must be large enough to compensate for communication time and less than the number of possible accelerator threads. Finally, an estimation of the kernel memory footprint is required to fit the overall memory of the GPU.

If we take into account only the pieces of application that naturally respect these constraints, we miss many pieces of code that can benefit from optimization. Gouin presents a methodology to increase the number of application pieces that can benefit from accelerator optimization and describes all necessary mapping stages [24, 25].

The actual programming of GPU kernels, preferably specified within the same source file as the calling CPU code, and of the necessary device memory management and data transfers to/from GPU device memory can be made easier for the programmer by adopting a high-level parallel programming model supporting GPU execution. For example, *OpenACC* allows to write kernels by annotating sequential loop-based code in a style similar to OpenMP parallel loop annotations. The OpenMP task model supports code generation for GPU execution of tasks since *OpenMP 4.0/4.5* with the introduction of the `target` directive for offloading computations to accelerator devices. *SYCL* (https://www.khronos.org/sycl) is a high-level programming layer atop OpenCL that provides a single-source abstraction for OpenCL based accelerator programming. For improved programmability, task-based runtime systems for heterogeneous programming such as StarPU can also be coupled with higher-level programming abstraction layers such as *SkePU* [14], which, from high-level constructs such as skeleton function calls, automatically generate the API calls for the management of tasks, data buffers and their dependencies by the runtime system.

5.3   Optimizing the Task Sizes

In the application the basic task size is given by the algorithm through the division of the domain into groups. As the tiling transformation makes it possible to optimize task granularity at the loop level, adjusting task and group sizes can:

- improve data locality
- improve cache reuse and
- reduce communication overhead.

The new decomposition must be performed in order to balance computations and communications. Considering the OpenMP implementation and a large number of small tasks, merging could also reduce the global thread creation over-heads and thread scheduling run-time.

Task and group sizes are multi-dimensional spaces and the optimal decomposition parameters depend on the target architecture constraints (memory size, number of cores). Finding these optimal parameters is complex since they are dynamic variables. Autotuner techniques combining profiling information might be used to develop heuristics and to limit the maximum task sizes at each level of the application.

5.4   Limiting Recursive Task Creation on CPU

Task-based computations over recursively defined sparse hierarchical domains such as quadtrees/octrees could, if applicable for the underlying computational problem, choose to stop the recursive subdivision at a certain depth limit and, for example, switch to computations over dense representations below this limit or sequentialize the independent subcomputations instead of creating a smaller task for each of them. For example, OpenMP 4.x provides the `if` clause to the `task` construct for conditional task creation. Such cut-off depth/condition, as well as the degree of task unrolling in general, can be used as a tuning parameter to balance the trade-off between computational work to perform, degree of data parallelism in tasks, and tasking and synchronization overhead. For example, Thoman *et al.* [53] describe a combined compiler and runtime approach for adaptive granularity control in recursive CPU task-parallel programs.

5.5   Techniques for Task and Data Granularity Adaptation on GPU

The task granularity in dynamically scheduled task-based computations on a heterogeneous system can have a major impact on overall performance. Each task executing on an accelerator typically contains just one kernel call, or possibly several kernel calls that execute in sequence on the same accelerator unit. For the application considered in this chapter, tasks/kernels of size 50×50 turn out to be too fine-grained for GPU execution in practice, as most of the GPU's computation capacity remains unused and the task management overhead (which is for StarPU in the order of several dozen microseconds) becomes large in relation to the task's work.

A number of task-based programming environments allow to control task granularity already at task creation, in particular for CPU-based tasks by introducing conditions for recursive task creation, as described in Sect. 5.4.

Moreover, a number of static and dynamic techniques exist for adapting task granularity in a GPU execution context. In the remainder of this section we review a number of such granularity adaptation techniques specifically for GPU task execution, which could be leveraged in future extensions of this work.

– Overpartitioning of a data-parallel computation into more than one task/kernel call leads to finer granularity, which can enable automated hybrid CPU-GPU computing but also incurs increased runtime overhead for the management of the additional tasks.

- Kernel fusion is an optimization for accelerator computations that tries to merge fine-grained tasks/kernel calls into fewer, coarser-grained ones.
- Persistent kernels on GPU are applicable to scenarios with many subsequent kernel calls of one or few statically known types, and can significantly reduce the accumulated kernel latencies for small GPU tasks.
- Operand transfer fusion is a granularity coarsening optimization for the communication of kernel operand data between main memory and accelerator memory.

Overpartitioning. Task-based computations can be generated from higher-level parallel programming models. As an example, we could consider the skeleton programming framework *SkePU* (www.ida.liu.se/labs/pelab/skepu) for GPU-based systems [17,18]. SkePU provides for each supported skeleton (map, reduce, stencil etc.) multiple back-ends (target-specific implementations), e.g. for single-threaded CPU execution, multithreaded CPU execution using OpenMP, and GPU execution in CUDA or OpenCL. Moreover, SkePU also provides a back-end that generates tasks for the StarPU runtime system [14]. From a single skeleton call, a user-defined number of asynchronously executed tasks can be generated, by partitioning the work and thus converting some of the skeleton call's data parallelism into task parallelism. Such "overpartitioning" automatically exploits hybrid CPU-GPU computing via StarPU's dynamic heterogeneous task scheduler [32] at the expense of increased runtime overhead for the management of the additional tasks.

Kernel Fusion. Kernel fusion is an agglomeration optimization for accelerator computations that merges multiple kernels resp. kernel calls into a single one. The purpose of this coarsening of the granularity of accelerator usage is to either improve data locality, or to reduce kernel startup overhead, or to improve the overall throughput by combining memory-bound with arithmetics-bound kernels. Kernel fusion is a special case of the classical *loop fusion* transformation, namely, for the case of parallel loops executing on an accelerator with many parallel hardware threads, such as a GPU.

Kernel fusion can be done in two different ways: *parallel fusion* (by co-scheduling of independent kernels) or *serial fusion* (by serialization of possibly dependent kernels), see also Fig. 9 for illustration.

Serial fusion is particularly effective if it can internalize inter-kernel flow of bulk operand data (i.e., intermediate (sub-)vectors or -matrices) between producer and consumer kernels, and moves the time points of production and consumption of each such data element much closer to each other. Hence, these data elements can now be stored and reused in registers or fast on-chip memory, which reduces the amount of slow off-chip memory accesses and thus increases the arithmetic intensity of the code.

In contrast, parallel fusion does not change the arithmetic intensity of the code, but eliminates kernel startup time overhead, improves thread occupancy and thus utilization of the accelerator especially for kernels with relatively small operands. Moreover, it can lead to overall improved throughput by co-scheduling

Fig. 9. Left: Serial kernel fusion by sequencing code from (calls to) different kernels in the same parallel loop, preserving per-element data flow dependencies between kernels in the fused code.—Right: Parallel kernel fusion by co-scheduling two previously independent kernel executions within the same "superkernel". Adapted from [59].

memory-bound with arithmetics-bound kernels [60]. For GPUs, parallel fusion can be done at the granularity of individual threads or of thread blocks, the latter of which should give better performance [60].

A number of static kernel fusion techniques especially for compilers targeting GPUs have been presented in the literature, e.g. by Wang et al. [59], Wahib and Maruyama [58] and Filipovic et al. [20]. Filipovic and Benkner [19] evaluate the effectiveness of parallel kernel fusion on GPU, Xeon Phi and CPU. Wen et al. [60] apply parallel kernel fusion in a just-in-time compiler that tries to pair memory-bound with arithmetics-bound kernels. Qiao et al. [48] study serial kernel fusion for image processing DSLs.

Persistent Kernel. For scenarios with many small tasks that all execute the same (or just a few different) statically known code, using a *persistent kernel* [29] is another technique to reduce the GPU kernel start-up overhead time (which is, for current CUDA GPUs, in the order of several microseconds, thus significant for small tasks). In contrast to starting a new kernel execution for each GPU task that is supplied with all its input data at its start and that delivers all output data on exit, a persistent kernel is started just once in the beginning and continuously runs on the GPU until it is eventually terminated by the CPU. When idle, the persistent kernel performs busy waiting on its input data buffers until it finds new data to work on, i.e. after it was written (transferred) there by the CPU. It then performs the corresponding operation and writes the data to the corresponding output buffer. The CPU can finally terminate the kernel by writing a special "poison pill" value into an input field that the GPU kernel polls regularly during busy waiting. For example, Maghazeh et al. [41] describe how the persistent-kernel technique was used in a packet processing application in telecommunications.

Operand Transfer Fusion. Heterogeneous systems that expose a (physically) distributed memory architecture to the low-level programmer require the explicit memory allocation and transfer of not yet uploaded kernel operand data from main memory to accelerator memory before kernel execution and the transfer of the kernel's output operands back to main memory (or possibly to other accelerator memories) if needed there for subsequent computations. Accelerator APIs provide functions for memory allocation and transfer of operands, such as cudaMalloc and cudaMemcpy, respectively.

The data transfer time for a bulk operand (e.g., a (sub-)vector or -matrix) of N elements can generally be modeled by a linear cost function $t_{comm} = \alpha + \beta N$, which is characterized by the transfer startup time α and the word transfer time β. On PCIe 3.0-attached GPUs the startup time α can be in an order of about $10\mu s$, with $\alpha/\beta \approx 10^4$ floats [36]. For tasks with small operands, the transfer startup time is thus a none-negligible overhead. Likewise, there is a significant overhead for device memory allocation where required.

A key observation is that multiple operands that can be stored adjacently in both main memory and accelerator memory can be transferred in a single, larger message, thus saving transfer startups compared to separate transfers for each operand. Likewise, device memory can be allocated for such operands by a single call to cudaMalloc.

Li and Kessler [36] present a dynamic optimization based on lazy allocation. They replace the standard API functions for lazy execution operand memory allocation and operand transfer by lazy-execution variants that defer their effect until kernel call execution time. At the kernel call, the operands and their (non-) availability in accelerator memory (hence the need for allocation and transfer) are definitely known, even in cases where static analysis could not resolve this information, e.g. due to variable aliasing or statically unknown task mapping. Then, operands to be transferred together will be allocated *consecutively* in memory if possible. This greedy optimization applies to one kernel call at a time.

5.6   High-Level Macro-dataflow Coordination

A common characteristic of the task-parallel programming frameworks discussed so far is that they, despite all abstractions from concrete hardware, do require a considerable expertise in parallel programming to get things right and even more such expertise to get things efficient. One reason is that they intertwine two different aspects of program execution: algorithmic behaviour, i.e., what is to be computed, and organization of task-parallel execution, i.e., how a computation is performed on multiple execution units, including the necessary problem decomposition, communication and synchronization requirements.

The aim of coordination programming is precisely to separate application-centric code from organization-centric code. The term goes back to the seminal work of Gelernter and Carriero [22], but has seen many variations since. For example, S-Net [27] is a declarative coordination language whose design thoroughly avoids the intertwining of computational and organizational aspects.

S-NET achieves a near complete separation of the concern of writing sequential application building blocks (i.e., *application engineering*) from the concern of composing these building blocks to form a parallel application (i.e., *concurrency engineering*).

S-NET defines the coordination behaviour of networks of asynchronous, stateless components and their orderly interconnection via typed streams. We deliberately restrict S-NET to coordination aspects and leave the specification of the concrete operational behaviour of basic components, named *boxes*, to conventional programming languages.

An S-NET box is connected to the outside world by two typed streams, a single input stream and a single output stream. The operational behaviour of a box is characterized by a stream transformer function that maps a single data item from the input stream to a (possibly empty) stream of data items on the output stream. S-NET effectively promotes functions implemented in a standard programming language into asynchronously executed stream-processing components.

In order to facilitate dynamic reconfiguration of networks, a box has no internal state, and any access to external state (e.g. file system, environment variables, etc.) is confined to using the streaming network. This allows us to cheaply migrate boxes between computing resources and even having individual boxes process multiple data items concurrently. Boxes execute fully asynchronously: as soon as data is available on the input stream, a box may start computing and producing data on the output stream. Boxes usually represent non-trivial units of computation instead of basic operations as in the original data-flow approach. Hence, S-NET effectively implements a macro data flow model.

It is a distinguishing feature of S-NET that it neither introduces streams as explicit objects nor that it defines network connectivity through explicit wiring. Instead, it uses algebraic formulae to describe streaming networks. The restriction of boxes to a single input and a single output stream (SISO) is essential for this. S-NET provides five network combinators: serial and parallel composition, serial and parallel replication as well as feedback. Any combinator preserves the SISO property: any network, regardless of its complexity, again is a SISO entity.

To summarize, S-NET is an abstract notation to express concurrency in application programs in an abstract and intuitive way. It avoids the typical annoyances of machine-level concurrent programming. Instead, S-NET borrows the idea of streaming networks of asynchronous, stateless components, which segregates applications into their natural building blocks and exposes the data flow between them. We have developed a highly tuned run-time system customized to the specific needs of S-NET [23]. In addition we have developed Distributed S-NET for cluster architectures [26].

S-NET is not at all confined to classical streaming applications as we have demonstrated through a number of numerical application case studies [28,44,45]. We have not yet implemented any of the methods for electromagnetic scattering problems described earlier in this paper, and, unfortunately, for the time being we lack the resources to do so. However, the closest matching algorithm we do have implemented with S-Net is Tiled Cholesky Factorization, another hierarchical matrix algorithm [10]. Here, S-Net compared very favourably against yet another established task-parallel approach: Intel's Concurrent Collections (CnC) [9,11,33]. In fact, S-Net outperformed CnC both with respect to code size and ease of programming as well as performance and scalability [65].

An interesting question for future work is whether or not—or better to what extent—we may be able to re-produce these positive results for the not dissimilar algorithms discussed in this paper.

6   Summary and Conclusions

In this chapter, we have discussed the properties of hierarchical matrix algorithms arising in electromagnetic scattering problems, and how to parallelize these problems on multicore, heterogeneous, and distributed hardware architectures.

Two different classes of algorithms were discussed in more detail, MLFMA and NESA algorithms. The main difference between these from a parallelization perspective is that in the former, the work performed for groups at different levels varies significantly, while in the latter, the work size per group is uniform. Because of this, a fine-grained parallelization of MLFMA needs to be more intrusive, since the work in coarse level groups needs to be split over threads/processes.

Both the data structures and the interaction patterns in the hierarchical matrix algorithms are irregular, which is why we suggest to use a parallel programming model that supports asynchronous execution. A pilot implementation using a task parallel programming model for shared memory architectures showed promising results regarding the potential to mix the computational phases during the execution and regarding the resulting utilization of the hardware. A challenging aspect was the relatively small work sizes for individual groups. We discuss different approaches to managing task granularity that could be implemented in future projects.

When working with industrial, or academic, legacy codes, several potentially conflicting interests influence the choices. To change which algorithm is used is typically a major investment, since it is unlikely that this part is well separated from the rest of the code. If the software was started from scratch today, perhaps other algorithmic choices would be made in light of the current prevailing hardware architectures. To achieve the best possible performance probably requires some refactoring of the code, while minimizing the changes to the existing code is relevant both from a cost perspective and a maintainability perspective. Finally, when using high-level programming models which build on some particular implementation of a run-time system, external dependencies are introduced that complicate the administration of the software, and introduce a risk of future incompatibility or discontinuation.

In this chapter we have tried to shed light on some of these choices, to support further work in the area.

References

1. Agullo, E., Aumage, O., Bramas, B., Coulaud, O., Pitoiset, S.: Bridging the gap between OpenMP and task-based runtime systems for the fast multipole method. IEEE Trans. Parallel Distrib. Syst. **28**(10), 2794–2807 (2017). https://doi.org/10.1109/TPDS.2017.2697857

2. Agullo, E., Bramas, B., Coulaud, O., Darve, E., Messner, M., Takahashi, T.: Task-based FMM for multicore architectures. SIAM J. Sci. Comput. **36**(1), C66–C93 (2014). https://doi.org/10.1137/130915662

3. Anderson, E., et al.: LAPACK Users' Guide, 3rd edn. Society for Industrial and Applied Mathematics, Philadelphia (1999)

4. Atkinson, P., McIntosh-Smith, S.: On the performance of parallel tasking runtimes for an irregular fast multipole method application. In: de Supinski, B.R., Olivier, S.L., Terboven, C., Chapman, B.M., Müller, M.S. (eds.) IWOMP 2017. LNCS, vol. 10468, pp. 92–106. Springer, Cham (2017). https://doi.org/10.1007/978-3-319-65578-9_7

5. Augonnet, C., Thibault, S., Namyst, R., Wacrenier, P.: StarPU: a unified platform for task scheduling on heterogeneous multicore architectures. Concurr. Comput.: Pract. Exper. **23**(2), 187–198 (2011). https://doi.org/10.1002/cpe.1631

6. Benson, A.R., Poulson, J., Tran, K., Engquist, B., Ying, L.: A parallel directional fast multipole method. SIAM J. Sci. Comput. **36**(4), C335–C352 (2014). https://doi.org/10.1137/130945569

7. Bordage, C.: Parallelization on heterogeneous multicore and multi-GPU systems of the fast multipole method for the Helmholtz equation using a runtime system. In: Omatu, S., Nguyen, T. (eds.) Proceedings of the Sixth International Conference on Advanced Engineering Computing and Applications in Sciences, pp. 90–95. International Academy, Research, and Industry Association (IARIA), Curran Associates Inc., Red Hook (2012)

8. Bosilca, G., Bouteiller, A., Danalis, A., Faverge, M., Hérault, T., Dongarra, J.J.: PaRSEC: exploiting heterogeneity to enhance scalability. Comput. Sci. Eng. **15**(6), 36–45 (2013)

9. Budimlić, Z., Chandramowlishwaran, A., Knobe, K., Lowney, G., Sarkar, V., Treggiari, L.: Multicore implementations of the Concurrent Collections programming model. In: 14th Workshop on Compilers for Parallel Computing, Zürich, Switzerland (2009)

10. Buttari, A., Langou, J., Kurzak, J., Dongarra, J.: A class of parallel tiled linear algebra algorithms for multicore architectures. Parallel Comput. **35**(1), 38–53 (2009)

11. Chandramowlishwaran, A., Knobe, K., Vuduc, R.: Performance evaluation of Concurrent Collections on high-performance multicore computing systems. In: 24th IEEE International Parallel and Distributed Processing Symposium (IPDPS 2010), Atlanta, USA, pp. 1–12. IEEE, April 2010

12. Cruz, F.A., Knepley, M.G., Barba, L.A.: PetFMM–a dynamically load-balancing parallel fast multipole library. Int. J. Numer. Methods Eng. **85**(4), 403–428 (2011). https://doi.org/10.1002/nme.2972

13. Darve, E., Cecka, C., Takahashi, T.: The fast multipole method on parallel clusters, multicore processors, and graphics processing units. Comptes Rendus Mécanique **339**(2), 185–193 (2011). https://doi.org/10.1016/j.crme.2010.12.005

14. Dastgeer, U., Kessler, C., Thibault, S.: Flexible runtime support for efficient skeleton programming on hybrid systems. In: Proceedings of the ParCo-2011 International Conference on Parallel Computing, Ghent, Belgium, September 2011. Advances in Parallel Computing, vol. 22, pp. 159–166. IOS press (2012). https://doi.org/10.3233/978-1-61499-041-3-159

15. Duran, A., et al.: OmpSs: a proposal for programming heterogeneous multi-core architectures. Parallel Proces. Lett. **21**(02), 173–193 (2011)

16. Efield®. http://www.efieldsolutions.com/

17. Enmyren, J., Kessler, C.: SkePU: a multi-backend skeleton programming library for multi-GPU systems. In: Proceedings of the 4th Internatioanl Workshop on High-Level Parallel Programming and Applications (HLPP-2010). ACM, September 2010. https://doi.org/10.1145/1863482.1863487

18. Ernstsson, A., Li, L., Kessler, C.: SkePU 2: flexible and type-safe skeleton programming for heterogeneous parallel systems. Int. J. Parallel Program. **46**(1) (2018). https://doi.org/10.1007/s10766-017-0490-5

19. Filipovic, J., Benkner, S.: OpenCL kernel fusion for GPU, Xeon Phi and CPU. In: Proceedings of the 27th International Symposium on Computer Architecture and High-Performance Computing (SBAC-PAD 2015), pp. 98–105. IEEE (2015). https://doi.org/10.1109/SAC-PAD.2015.29

20. Filipovic, J., Madzin, M., Fousek, J., Matyska, L.: Optimizing CUDA code by kernel fusion: application on BLAS. J. Supercomput. **71**, 3934–3957 (2015). https://doi.org/10.1007/s11227-015-1483-z

21. Fukuda, K., Matsuda, M., Maruyama, N., Yokota, R., Taura, K., Matsuoka, S.: Tapas: an implicitly parallel programming framework for hierarchical n-body algorithms. In: 2016 IEEE 22nd International Conference on Parallel and Distributed Systems (ICPADS), pp. 1100–1109, December 2016. https://doi.org/10.1109/ICPADS.2016.0145

22. Gelernter, D., Carriero, N.: Coordination languages and their significance. Commun. ACM **35**(2), 97–107 (1992)

23. Gijsbers, B., Grelck, C.: An efficient scalable runtime system for macro data flow processing using S-Net. Int. J. Parallel Program. **42**(6), 988–1011 (2014). https://doi.org/10.1007/s10766-013-0271-8

24. Gouin, F.: Methodology for image processing algorithms mapping on massively parallel architectures. Technical report, MINES ParisTech (2018)

25. Gouin, F., Ancourt, C., Guettier, C.: An up to date mapping methodology for GPUs. In: 20th Workshop on Compilers for Parallel Computing (CPC 2018), Dublin, Ireland, April 2018. https://hal-mines-paristech.archives-ouvertes.fr/hal-01759238

26. Grelck, C., Julku, J., Penczek, F.: Distributed S-Net: cluster and grid computing without the hassle. In: 12th IEEE/ACM International Conference on Cluster, Cloud and Grid Computing (CCGrid 2012), Ottawa, Canada. IEEE Computer Society (2012). https://doi.org/10.1109/CCGrid.2012.140

27. Grelck, C., Scholz, S., Shafarenko, A.: Asynchronous stream processing with S-Net. Int. J. Parallel Program. **38**(1), 38–67 (2010). https://doi.org/10.1007/s10766-009-0121-x

28. Grelck, C., Scholz, S.B., Shafarenko, A.: Coordinating data parallel SAC programs with S-Net. In: Proceedings of the 21st IEEE International Parallel and Distributed Processing Symposium (IPDPS 2007), Long Beach, California, USA. IEEE Computer Society Press, Los Alamitos (2007). https://doi.org/10.1109/IPDPS.2007.370408

29. Gupta, K., Stuart, J.A., Owens, J.D.: A study of persistent threads style GPU programming for GPGPU workloads. In: Innovative Parallel Computing - Foundations and Applications of GPU, Manycore, and Heterogeneous Systems (INPAR 2012), pp. 1–14. IEEE, May 2012. https://doi.org/10.1109/InPar.2012.6339596
30. Gürel, L., Ergül, O.: Hierarchical parallelization of the multilevel fast multipole algorithm (MLFMA). Proc. IEEE **101**(2), 332–341 (2013). https://doi.org/10.1109/JPROC.2012.2222331
31. Holm, M., Engblom, S., Goude, A., Holmgren, S.: Dynamic autotuning of adaptive fast multipole methods on hybrid multicore CPU and GPU systems. SIAM J. Sci. Comput. **36**(4) (2014). https://doi.org/10.1137/130943595
32. Kessler, C., et al.: Programmability and performance portability aspects of heterogeneous multi-/manycore systems. In: Proceedings of the DATE-2012 Conference on Design, Automation and Test in Europe, pp. 1403–1408. IEEE, March 2012. https://doi.org/10.1109/DATE.2012.6176582
33. Knobe, K.: Ease of use with Concurrent Collections (CnC). In: USENIX Workshop on Hot Topics in Parallelism (HotPar 2009), Berkeley USA (2009)
34. Kurzak, J., Pettitt, B.M.: Massively parallel implementation of a fast multipole method for distributed memory machines. J. Parallel Distrib. Comput. **65**(7), 870–881 (2005). https://doi.org/10.1016/j.jpdc.2005.02.001
35. Lashuk, I., et al.: A massively parallel adaptive fast multipole method on heterogeneous architectures. Commun. ACM **55**(5), 101–109 (2012). https://doi.org/10.1145/2160718.2160740
36. Li, L., Kessler, C.: Lazy allocation and transfer fusion optimization for GPU-based heterogeneous systems. In: Proceedings of the Euromicro PDP-2018 International Conference on Parallel, Distributed, and Network-Based Processing, pp. 311–315. IEEE, March 2018. https://doi.org/10.1109/PDP2018.2018.00054
37. Li, M., Francavilla, M., Vipiana, F., Vecchi, G., Chen, R.: Nested equivalent source approximation for the modeling of multiscale structures. IEEE Trans. Antennas Propag. **62**(7), 3664–3678 (2014)
38. Li, M., Francavilla, M., Vipiana, F., Vecchi, G., Fan, Z., Chen, R.: A doubly hierarchical MoM for high-fidelity modeling of multiscale structures. IEEE Trans. Electromagn. Compat. **56**(5), 1103–1111 (2014)
39. Li, M., Francavilla, M.A., Chen, R., Vecchi, G.: Wideband fast kernel-independent modeling of large multiscale structures via nested equivalent source approximation. IEEE Trans. Antennas Propag. **63**(5), 2122–2134 (2015). https://doi.org/10.1109/TAP.2015.2402297
40. Ltaief, H., Yokota, R.: Data-driven execution of fast multipole methods. Concurr. Comput.: Pract. Exp. **26**(11), 1935–1946 (2014). https://doi.org/10.1002/cpe.3132
41. Maghazeh, A., Bordoloi, U.D., Dastgeer, U., Andrei, A., Eles, P., Peng, Z.: Latency-aware packet processing on CPU-GPU heterogeneous systems. In: Proceedings of the Design Automation Conference (DAC), pp. 41:1–41:6. ACM (2017). https://doi.org/10.1145/3061639.3062269
42. Mautz, J.R., Harrington, R.F.: Electromagnetic scattering from homogeneous material body of revolution. Arch. Electron. Übertragungstech **33**, 71–80 (1979)
43. Nilsson, M.: Fast numerical techniques for electromagnetic problems in frequency domain. Ph.D. thesis, Division of Scientific Computing, Department of Information Technology, Uppsala University (2003)
44. Penczek, F., Cheng, W., Grelck, C., Kirner, R., Scheuermann, B., Shafarenko, A.: A data-flow based coordination approach to concurrent software engineering. In: 2nd Workshop on Data-Flow Execution Models for Extreme Scale Computing (DFM 2012), Minneapolis, USA. IEEE (2012). https://doi.org/10.1109/DFM.2012.14

45. Penczek, F., et al.: Parallel signal processing with S-Net. Procedia Comput. Sci. **1**(1), 2079–2088 (2010). https://doi.org/10.1016/j.procs.2010.04.233. http://www. sciencedirect.com/science/article/B9865-506HM1Y-88/2/87fcf1cee7899f0eeaadc90 bd0d56cd3, iCCS 2010

46. Pérez, J.M., Badia, R.M., Labarta, J.: A dependency-aware task-based program-ming environment for multi-core architectures. In: Proceedings of the 2008 IEEE International Conference on Cluster Computing, Tsukuba, Japan, 29 September–1 October 2008, pp. 142–151 (2008). https://doi.org/10.1109/CLUSTR.2008. 4663765

47. Puma-EM. https://sourceforge.net/projects/puma-em/

48. Qiao, B., Reiche, O., Hannig, F., Teich, J.: Automatic kernel fusion for image processing DSLs. In: Proceedings of the 21th International Workshop on Software and Compilers for Embedded Systems (SCOPES 2018). ACM, May 2018. https:// doi.org/10.1145/3207719.3207723

49. Rao, S., Wilton, D., Glisson, A.: Electromagnetic scattering by surfaces of arbitrary shape. IEEE Trans. Antennas Propag. **30**(3), 409–418 (1982)

50. Seo, S.M., Lee, J.F.: A fast IE-FFT algorithm for solving PEC scattering problems. IEEE Trans. Magn. **41**(5), 1476–1479 (2005)

51. Song, J., Lu, C.C., Chew, W.C.: Multilevel fast multipole algorithm for electromag-netic scattering by large complex objects. IEEE Trans. Antennas Propag. **45**(10), 1488–1493 (1997)

52. Thibault, S.: On Runtime Systems for Task-based Programming on Heterogeneous Platforms. Habilitation à diriger des recherches, L'Université Bordeaux (2018)

53. Thoman, P., Jordan, H., Fahringer, T.: Adaptive granularity control in task parallel programs using multiversioning. In: Wolf, F., Mohr, B., an Mey, D. (eds.) Euro-Par 2013. LNCS, vol. 8097, pp. 164–177. Springer, Heidelberg (2013). https://doi.org/ 10.1007/978-3-642-40047-6_19

54. Tillenius, M.: SuperGlue: a shared memory framework using data versioning for dependency-aware task-based parallelization. SIAM J. Sci. Comput. **37**(6) (2015). https://doi.org/10.1137/140989716

55. Tillenius, M., Larsson, E., Badia, R.M., Martorell, X.: Resource-aware task schedul-ing. ACM Trans. Embedded Comput. Syst. **14**(1), 5:1–5:25 (2015). https://doi.org/ 10.1145/2638554

56. Velamparambil, S., Chew, W.C.: Analysis and performance of a distributed mem-ory multilevel fast multipole algorithm. IEEE Trans. Antennas Propag. **53**(8), 2719–2727 (2005). https://doi.org/10.1109/TAP.2005.851859

57. Vipiana, F., Francavilla, M., Vecchi, G.: EFIE modeling of high-definition multi-scale structures. IEEE Trans. Antennas Propag. **58**(7), 2362–2374 (2010)

58. Wahib, M., Maruyama, N.: Scalable kernel fusion for memory-bound GPU applica-tions. In: Proceedings of the International Conference for High-Performance Com-puting, Networking, Storage and Analysis (SC 2014), pp. 191–202. IEEE (2014). https://doi.org/10.1109/SC.2014.21

59. Wang, G., Lin, Y., Yi, W.: Kernel fusion: an effective method for better power efficiency on multithreaded GPU. In: Proceedings of the IEEE/ACM International Conference on Green Computing and Communications and International Confer-ence on Cyber, Physical and Social Computing, pp. 344–350 (2010). https://doi. org/10.1109/GreenCom-CPSCom.2010.102

60. Wen, Y., O'Boyle, M.F., Fensch, C.: MaxPair: enhance OpenCL concurrent kernel execution by weighted maximum matching. In: Proceedings of the GPGPU-11. ACM (2018). https://doi.org/10.1145/3180270.3180272

61. YarKhan, A., Kurzak, J., Dongarra, J.: Quark users' guide: queueing and runtime for kernels. Technical report. ICL-UT-11-02 (2011)
62. Zafari, A.: TaskUniVerse: a task-based unified interface for versatile parallel execution. In: Wyrzykowski, R., Dongarra, J., Deelman, E., Karczewski, K. (eds.) PPAM 2017. LNCS, vol. 10777, pp. 169–184. Springer, Cham (2018). https://doi.org/10.1007/978-3-319-78024-5_16
63. Zafari, A., et al.: Task parallel implementation of a solver for electromagnetic scattering problems. CoRR abs/1801.03589 (2018). http://arxiv.org/abs/1801.03589
64. Zafari, A., Larsson, E., Tillenius, M.: DuctTeip: an efficient programming model for distributed task-based parallel computing (2019, submitted)
65. Zaichenkov, P., Gijsbers, B., Grelck, C., Tveretina, O., Shafarenko, A.: The cost and benefits of coordination programming: two case studies in Concurrent Collections (CnC) and S-Net. Parallel Process. Lett. **26**(3) (2016). https://doi.org/10.1142/S0129626416500110
66. Zhang, B.: Asynchronous task scheduling of the fast multipole method using various runtime systems. In: 2014 Fourth Workshop on Data-Flow Execution Models for Extreme Scale Computing, pp. 9–16 (2014). https://doi.org/10.1109/DFM.2014.14
67. Zhao, K., Vouvakis, M.N., Lee, J.F.: The adaptive cross approximation algorithm for accelerated method of moments computations of EMC problems. IEEE Trans. Electromagn. Compat. **47**(4), 763–773 (2005)

Tail Distribution and Extreme Quantile Estimation Using Non-parametric Approaches

Imen Rached[1]([✉])(iD) and Elisabeth Larsson[2](iD)

[1] Allianstic Research Laboratory, EFREI Paris, Ecole d'Ingénieurs Généraliste
Informatique et Technologies du Numérique,
30–32 Avenue de la République, 94800 Villejuif, France
imen.rached@efrei.fr
[2] Scientific Computing, Department of Information Technology, Uppsala University,
Box 337, 751 05 Uppsala, Sweden
elisabeth.larsson@it.uu.se

Abstract. Estimation of tail distributions and extreme quantiles is important in areas such as risk management in finance and insurance in relation to extreme or catastrophic events. The main difficulty from the statistical perspective is that the available data to base the estimates on is very sparse, which calls for tailored estimation methods. In this chapter, we provide a survey of currently used parametric and non-parametric methods, and provide some perspectives on how to move forward with non-parametric kernel-based estimation.

Keywords: Risk measures · Extreme value theory ·
Kernel estimation · Bandwidth selection

1 Introduction

This chapter presents a position survey on the overall objectives and specific challenges encompassing the state of the art in tail distribution and extreme quantile estimation of currently used parametric and non-parametric approaches and their application to Financial Risk Measurement. What is envisioned, is an enhanced non-parametric estimation method based on the Extreme Value Theory approach. The compounding perspectives of current challenges are addressed, like the threshold level of excess data to be chosen for extreme values and the bandwidth selection from a bias reduction perspective. The application of the kernel estimation approach and the use of Expected Shortfall as a coherent risk measure instead of the Value at Risk are presented. The extension to multivariate data is addressed and its challenges identified.

Overview of the Following Sections. In the following sections, Financial risk measures are presented in Sect. 2. Section 3, covers Extreme Value Theory, Sect. 4,

© The Author(s) 2019
J. Kołodziej and H. González-Vélez (Eds.): cHiPSet, LNCS 11400, pp. 69–87, 2019.
https://doi.org/10.1007/978-3-030-16272-6_3

Parametric estimation and Semi-parametric estimation methods, Sect. 5, Non-Parametric estimation methods and Sect. 6, the perspectives identified by the addressed challenges when estimating the presented financial risk measures.

2   Financial Risk Measures

The Long Term Capital Management collapse and the 1998 Russian debt crisis, the Latin American and Asian currency crises and more recently, the U.S. mortgage credit market turmoil, followed by the bankruptcy of Lehman Brothers and the world's biggest-ever trading loss at Société Générale are some examples of financial disasters during the last twenty years. In response to the serious financial crises, like the recent global financial crisis (2007–2008), regulators have become more concerned about the protection of financial institutions against catastrophic market risks. We recall that market risk is the risk that the value of an investment will decrease due to movements in market factors. The difficulty of modelling these rare but extreme events has been greatly reduced by recent advances in Extreme Value Theory (EVT). Value at Risk (VaR) and the related concept of Expected Shortfall (ES) have been the primary tools for measuring risk exposure in the financial services industry for over two decades. Additional literature can be found in [39] for Quantitative Risk Management and in [42] or in [25] for the application of EVT in insurance, finance and other fields.

2.1   Value at Risk

Consider the loss X of a portfolio over a given time period δ, then VaR is a risk statistic that measures the risk of holding the portfolio for the time period δ. Assume that X has a cumulative distribution function (cdf), F_X, then we define VaR at level $\alpha \in (0,1)$ as

$$\text{VaR}_\alpha^\delta(X) = \inf\{x \in \mathbb{R} : P(X > x) \leq 1 - \alpha\} = \inf\{x \in \mathbb{R}, F_X(x) \geq \alpha\} = F_X^\leftarrow(\alpha), \quad (1)$$

$F_X^\leftarrow$ is the generalized inverse of the cdf F_X. Typical values of α are 0.95 and 0.99, while δ usually is 1 day or 10 days. Value-at-Risk (VaR) has become a standard measure for risk management and is also recommended in the Basel II accord. For an overview on VaR in a more economic setting we refer to [37] and [23]. Despite its widespread use, VaR has received criticism for failing to distinguish between light and heavy losses beyond the VaR. Additionally, the traditional VaR method has been criticized for violating the requirement of sub-additivity [4]. Artzner et al. analysed risk measures and stated a set of properties/axioms that should be desirable for any risk measure. The four axioms they stated are:

- Monotonicity: Higher losses mean higher risk.
- Translation Equivariance: Increasing (or decreasing) the loss increases (decreases) the risk by the same amount.
- Subadditivity: Diversification decreases risk.
- Positive Homogeneity: Doubling the portfolio size doubles the risk.

Any risk measure which satisfies these axioms is said to be coherent. A related concept to VaR, which accounts for the tail mass is the conditional tail expectation (CVaR), or Expected Shortfall (ES). ES is the average loss conditional on the VaR being exceeded and gives risk managers additional valuable information about the tail risk of the distribution. Due to its usefulness as a risk measure, in 2013 the Basel Committee on Bank Supervision has even proposed replacing VaR with ES to measure market risk exposure.

2.2 Conditional Value at Risk or Expected Shortfall

$$\text{CVaR}_\alpha(X) := E[X|X \geq \text{VaR}_\alpha(X)] \tag{2}$$

Acerbi and Tasche proved in [1] that CVaR satisfies the above axioms and is therefore a coherent risk measure.

Conditional Value-at-Risk can be derived from VaR in the case of a continuous random variable and another possibility to calculate CVaR is to use Acerbi's Integral Formula:

$$\text{CVaR}_\alpha(X) = \frac{1}{1-\alpha} \int_\alpha^1 \text{VaR}_\beta(X)d\beta \tag{3}$$

Estimating ES from the empirical distribution is generally more difficult than estimating VaR due to the scarcity of observations in the tail. As in most risk applications, we do not need to focus on the entire distribution. Extreme value theory is then a practical and useful tool for modeling and quantifying risk. Value at Risk and Extreme value theory is covered well in most books on risk management and VaR in particular (also ES with much less extent), see for example [33,37,39], and [22]. Vice versa, VaR is treated in some Extreme value theory literature, such as [26] and [17].

3   Extreme Value Theory: Two Main Approaches

Extreme value theory (EVT) is the theory of modelling and measuring events which occur with very small probability: More precisely, having an $X_1, ..., X_n$ sample of n random variables independently and identically following a distribution function $F(\cdot)$, we want to estimate the real x_{p_n} defined by

$$x_{p_n} = \bar{F}^\leftarrow(p_n), \quad \text{with} \quad p_n < 1/n. \tag{4}$$

where p_n is a known sequence and $\bar{F}^\leftarrow(u) = \inf\{x \in \mathbb{R}, \bar{F}(x) \leq u\}$. $\bar{F}^\leftarrow$ is the generalized inverse of the survival function $\bar{F}(\cdot) = 1 - F(\cdot)$. Note that x_{p_n} is the order quantile $1 - p_n$ of the cumulative distribution function F.

A similar problem to the estimate of x_{p_n} is the estimate of "small probabilities" p_n or the estimation of the tail distribution. In other words, for a series of fixed (c_n) reals, we want to estimate the probability p_n defined by

$$p_n = P(X > c_n), \quad \text{with} \quad c_n > x_{n,n}. \tag{5}$$

The main result of Extreme Value Theory states that the tails of all distributions fall into one of three categories, regardless of the overall shape of the distribution. Two main approaches are used for implementing EVT in practice: Block maxima approach and Peaks Over Thresholds (POT).

3.1 Block Maxima Approach

The Fisher and Tippett [29] and Gnedenko [30] theorems are the fundamental results in EVT. The theorems state that the maximum of a sample of properly normalized independent and identically distributed random variables converges in distribution to one of the three possible distributions: the Weibull, Gumbel or the Fréchet.

Theorem 1 (Fisher, Tippett, Gnedenko).
Let $X_1, ..., X_n \sim^{i.i.d.} F$ and $X_{1,n} \leq ... \leq X_{n,n}$. If there exist two sequences a_n and b_n and a real γ such that

$$P\left(\frac{X_{n,n} - a_n}{b_n} \leq x\right) \longrightarrow H_\gamma(x), \tag{6}$$

when $n \longrightarrow +\infty$, then

$$H_\gamma(x) = \begin{cases} \exp\left(-(1 + \gamma x)^{-1/\gamma}\right) & \text{if } \gamma \neq 0, \quad 1 + \gamma x > 0. \\ \exp(-\exp(-x)) & \text{if } \gamma = 0, \quad x \in \mathbb{R}. \end{cases} \tag{7}$$

We say that F is in the domain of attraction of H_γ and denote this by $F \in \mathrm{DA}(H_\gamma)$. The distribution function $H_\gamma(\cdot)$ is called the Generalized Extreme Value distribution (GEV).

This law depends only on the parameter called the tail index. The density associated is shown in Fig. 1 for different values of γ. According to the sign of γ, we define three areas of attraction:

Fig. 1. The GEV distribution for $\gamma = -0.5$ (solid line), $\gamma = 0$ (dashed line), and $\gamma = 0.5$ (dash-dot line).

- If $\gamma > 0$, $F \in$ DA (Fréchet): This domain contains the laws for which the survival function decreases as a power function. Such tails are know as "fat tails" or "heavy tails". In this area of attraction, we find the laws of Pareto, Student, Cauchy, etc.
- If $\gamma = 0$, $F \in$ DA (Gumbel): This domain groups laws for which the survival function declines exponentially. This is the case of normal, gamma, log-normal, exponential, etc.
- if $\gamma < 0$, $F \in$ DA (Weibull): This domain corresponds to thin tails where the distribution has a finite endpoint. Examples in this class are the uniform and reverse Burr distributions.

The Weibull distribution clearly has a finite endpoint ($s_+(F) = \sup\{x, F(x) < 1\}$). This is usually the case of the distribution of mortality and insurance/re-insurance claims for example, see [20]. The Fréchet tail is thicker than the Gumbel's. Yet, it is well known that the distributions of the return series in most financial markets are heavy tailed (fat tails). The term "fat tails" can have several meanings, the most common being "extreme outcomes occur more frequently than predicted by the normal distribution".

The block Maxima approach is based on the utilization of maximum or minimum values of these observations within a certain sequence of constant length. For a sufficiently large number k of established blocks, the resulting peak values of these k blocks of equal length can be used for estimation. The procedure is rather wasteful of data and a relatively large sample is needed for accurate estimate.

3.2 Peaks Over Threshold (POT) Approach

The POT (Peaks-Over-Threshold) approach consists of using the generalized Pareto distribution (GPD) to approximate the distribution of excesses over a threshold. This approach has been suggested originally by hydrologists. This approach is generally preferred and forms the basis of our approach below. Both EVT approaches are equivalent by the Pickands-Balkema-de Haan theorem presented in [5, 40].

Theorem 2 (Pickands-Balkema-de Haan). *For a large class of underlying distribution functions F,*

$$F \in DA(H_\gamma) \quad \Longleftrightarrow \quad \sup_{x \in [0,\, s_+(F)[} |F_u(x) - G_{\gamma,\, \sigma(u)}(x)| \xrightarrow{u \to s_+(F)} 0, \quad (8)$$

where $s_+(F) = \sup\{x, F(x) < 1\}$ is the end point of the distribution, $F_u(x) = \mathbf{P}(X - u \le x | X > u)$ is the distribution of excess, and $G_{\gamma, \sigma}$ is the Generalized Pareto Distribution (GPD) defined as

$$G_{\gamma,\, \sigma}(x) = \begin{cases} 1 - (1 + \dfrac{\gamma}{\sigma}x)^{-1/\gamma} & \text{if } \gamma \neq 0, \ \sigma > 0, \\ 1 - \exp(-x/\sigma) & \text{if } \gamma = 0, \ \sigma > 0. \end{cases} \quad (9)$$

This means that the conditional excess distribution function F_u, for u large, is well approximated by a Generalized Pareto Distribution. Note that the tail index γ is the same for both the GPD and GEV distributions. The tail shape parameter σ and the tail index are the fundamental parameters governing the extreme behavior of the distribution, and the effectiveness of EVT in forecasting depends upon their reliable and accurate estimation. By incorporating information about the tail through our estimates of γ and σ, we can obtain VaR and ES estimates, even beyond the reach of the empirical distribution.

4   Parametric and Semi-parametric Estimation Methods

The problem of estimating the tail index γ has been widely studied in the literature. The most standard methods are of course the method of moments and maximum likelihood. Unfortunately, there is no explicit form for the parameters, but numerical methods provide good estimates. More generally, the two common approaches to estimate the tail index are:

- Semi-parametric models (e.g., the Hill estimator).
- Fully parametric models (e.g., the Generalized Pareto distribution or GPD).

4.1   Semi-parametric Estimation

The most known estimator for the tail index $\gamma > 0$ of fat tails distribution is without contest the Hill estimator [31]. The formal definition of fat tail distributions comes from regular variation. The cumulative distribution is in the Fréchet domain if and only if as $x \to \infty$, the tails are asymptotically Pareto-distributed:

$$F(x) \approx 1 - Ax^{-\tau}, \tag{10}$$

where $A > 0$ and $\tau = 1/\gamma$. Based on this approximation, the Hill estimator is written according to the statistics order $X_{1,n} \leq ... \leq X_{n,n}$ as follows:

$$H_{k_n,n} = 1/k_n \sum_{j=1}^{k_n} \ln X_{n-j+1,n} - \ln X_{n-k_n,n}. \tag{11}$$

where k_n is a sequence so that $1 \leq k_n \leq n$. Other estimators of this index have have been proposed by Beirlant et al. [6,7] using a regression exponential model to reduce the Hill estimator bias and by [28] that introduce a least squares estimator. The use of a kernel in the Hill estimator has been studied by Csörgő et al. [18]. An effective estimator of the extreme value index has been proposed by Falk and Marohn in [27]. A more detailed list of the different works on the estimation of the index of extreme values is found in [19]. Note that the Hill estimator is sensitive to the choice of threshold $u = X_{n-k_n,n}$ (or the number of excess k_n) and is only valid for fat-tailed data.

4.2 Parametric Estimation

The principle of POT is to approximate the survival function of the excess distribution by a GPD after estimating its parameters from the distribution of excess over a threshold u as explained in the following two steps:

- **First step—Tail distribution estimation**

  Let $X_1, ..., X_n$ follow a distribution F and let $Y_1, ..., Y_{N_n}, (Y_i = X_i - u_n)$ be the exceedances over a chosen threshold u_n. The distribution of excess F_{u_n} is given by:

$$F_{u_n}(y) = P(X - u_n \leq y \,|\, X > u_n) \tag{12}$$

  and then, the distribution F, of the extreme observations, is given by:

$$F(u_n + y) = F(u_n) + \bar{F}_{u_n}(y) \times \bar{F}(u_n) \tag{13}$$

  The distribution of excess F_{u_n} is approximated by $G_{\gamma, \sigma(u_n)}$ and the first step consists in estimating the parameters of this last distribution using the sample $(Y_1, ..., Y_{N_n})$. The parameter estimations can be done using MLE. Different methods have been proposed to estimate the parameters of the GPD. Other estimation methods are presented in [26]. The Probability Weighted Moments (PWM) method proposed by Hosking and Wallis [32] for $\gamma < 1/2$ was extended by Diebolt et al. [21] by a generalization of PWM estimators for $\gamma < 3/2$, as for many applications, e.g., in insurance, distributions are known to have a tail index larger than 1.

- **Second step—Quantile estimation**

  In order to estimate the extreme quantile x_p defined as

$$x_{p_n} : \bar{F}(x_{p_n}) = 1 - F(x_{p_n}) = p_n, \quad np_n \to 0. \tag{14}$$

  We estimate $F(u)$ by its empirical counterpart N_u/n and we approximate F_{u_n} by the approximate Generalized Pareto Distribution $GPD(\hat{\gamma}_n, \hat{\sigma}_n)$ in the Eq. (1). Then, for the threshold $u = X_{n-k,n}$, the extreme quantile is estimated by

$$\hat{x}_{p_n, k} = X_{n-k,n} + \hat{\sigma}_n \frac{\left(\frac{k}{np_n}\right)^{\hat{\gamma}_n} - 1}{\hat{\gamma}_n}. \tag{15}$$

The application of POT involves a number of challenges. The early stage of data analysis is very important in determining whether the data has the fat tail needed to apply the EVT results. Also, the parameter estimates of the limit GPD distributions depend on the number of extreme observations used. The choice of a threshold should be large enough to satisfy the conditions to permit its application (u tends towards infinity), while at the same time leaving sufficient observations for the estimation. A high threshold would generate few excesses, thereby inflating the variance of our parameter estimates. Lowering the threshold would necessitate using samples that are no longer considered as being in the tails which would entail an increase in the bias.

5   Non-parametric Estimation Methods

A main argument for using non-parametric estimation methods is that no specific assumptions on the distribution of the data is made *a priori*. That is, model specification bias can be avoided. This is relevant when there is limited information about the 'theoretical' data distribution, when the data can potentially contain a mix of variables with different underlying distributions, or when no suitable parametric model is available. In the context of extreme value distributions, the GPD and GEV distributions discussed in Sect. 3 are appropriate parametric models for the univariate case. However, for the multivariate case there is no general parametric form.

We restrict the discussion here to one particular form of non-parametric estimation, kernel density estimation [44]. Classical kernel estimation performs well when the data is symmetric, but has problems when there is significant skewness [9, 24, 41].

A common way to deal with skewness is transformation kernel estimation [45], which we will discuss with some details below. The idea is to transform the skew data set into another variable that has a more symmetric distribution, and allows for efficient classical kernel estimation.

Another issue for kernel density estimation is boundary bias. This arises because standard kernel estimates do not take knowledge of the domain of the data into account, and therefore the estimate does not reflect the actual behaviour close to the boundaries of the domain. We will also review a few bias correction techniques [34].

Even though kernel estimation is non-parametric with respect to the underlying distribution, there is a parameter that needs to be decided. This is the bandwidth (scale) of the kernel function, which determines the smoothness of the density estimate. We consider techniques intended for constant bandwidth [35], and also take a brief look at variable bandwidth kernel estimation [36]. In the latter case, the bandwidth and the location is allowed to vary such that bias can be reduced compared with using fixed parameters.

Kernel density estimation can be applied to any type of application and data, but some examples where it is used for extreme value distributions are given in [8, 9]. A non parametric method to estimate the VaR in extreme quantiles, based on transformed kernel estimation (TKE) of the cdf of losses was proposed in [3]. A kernel estimator of conditional ES is proposed in [13, 14, 43].

In the following subsections, we start by defining the classical kernel estimator, then we describe a selection of measures that are used for evaluating the quality of an estimate, and are needed, e.g, in the algorithms for bandwidth selection. Finally, we go into the different subareas of kernel estimation mentioned above in more detail.

5.1   Classical Kernel Estimation

Expressed in words, a classical kernel estimator approximates the probability density function associated with a data set through a sum of identical, symmetric kernel density functions that are centered at each data point. Then the sum is normalized to have total probability mass one.

We formalize this in the following way: Let $k(\cdot)$ be a bounded and symmetric probability distribution function (pdf), such as the normal distribution pdf or the Epanechnikov pdf, which we refer to as the kernel function.

Given a sample of n independent and identically distributed observations $X_1, \ldots, X_n$ of a random variable X with pdf $f_X(x)$, the classical kernel estimator is given by

$$\hat{f}_X(x) = \frac{1}{n} \sum_{i=1}^{n} k_b(x - X_i), \tag{16}$$

where $k_b(\cdot) = \frac{1}{b} k(\frac{\cdot}{b})$ and b is the bandwidth. Similarly, the classical kernel estimator for the cumulative distribution function (cdf) is given by

$$\hat{F}_X(x) = \frac{1}{n} \sum_{i=1}^{n} K_b(x - X_i), \tag{17}$$

where $K_b(x) = \int_{-\infty}^{x} k_b(t)dt$. That is, $K(\cdot)$ is the cdf corresponding to the pdf $k(\cdot)$.

5.2   Selected Measures to Evaluate Kernel Estimates

A measure that we would like to minimize for the kernel estimate is the mean integrated square error (MISE). This is expressed as

$$\text{MISE}(b) = \mathbb{E}\left[\int_{\Omega} \left(\hat{f}_X(x) - f_X(x) \right)^2 dx \right], \tag{18}$$

where Ω is the domain of support for $f_X(x)$, and the argument b is included to show that minimizing MISE is one criterion for bandwidth selection. However, MISE can only be computed when the true density $f_X(x)$ is known. MISE can be decomposed into two terms. The integrated square bias

$$\int_{\Omega} \left(\mathbb{E}\left[\hat{f}_X(x) \right] - f_X(x) \right)^2 dx, \tag{19}$$

and the integrated variance

$$\int_{\Omega} \text{Var}\left[\hat{f}_X(x) \right] dx. \tag{20}$$

To understand these expressions, we first need to understand that $\hat{f}_X$ is a random variable that changes with each sample realization. To illustrate what it means, we work through an example.

Example 1. Let X be uniformly distributed on $\Omega = [0, 1]$, and let $k(\cdot)$ be the Gaussian kernel. Then

$$f_X(x) = \begin{cases} 1, & 0 \leq x \leq 1 \\ 0, & \text{otherwise.} \end{cases} \tag{21}$$

For each kernel function centered at some data point y we have that

$$\mathbb{E}_X\left[k_b(x-y)\right] = \int_0^1 k_b(x-y) \cdot 1dy = K_b(x) - K_b(x-1). \tag{22}$$

If we apply that to the kernel estimator (16), we get the integrated square bias

$$\int_0^1 \left(K_b(x) - K_b(x-1) - 1\right)^2 dx. \tag{23}$$

By first using that $\text{Var}(X) = \mathbb{E}[X^2] - \mathbb{E}[X]^2$, we get the following expression for the integrated variance

$$\int_0^1 \left(\int_0^1 k_b(x-y)^2 \cdot 1dy - (K_b(x) - K_b(x-1))^2\right) dx. \tag{24}$$

The integrals are evaluated for the Gaussian kernel, and the results are shown in Fig. 2. The bias, which is largest at the boundaries, is minimized when the bandwidth is very large, but a large bandwidth also leads to a large variance. Hence, MISE is minimized by a bandwidth that provides a trade-off between bias and variance.

Fig. 2. The square bias (left) and the variance (middle) as a function of x for $b = 0.3, 0.4, 0.5, 0.6$. The curve for $b = 0.3$ is shown with a dashed line in both cases. MISE (right) is shown as a function of b (solid line) together with the integrated square bias (dashed line) and the integrated variance (dash-dot line).

To simplify the analysis, MISE is often replaced with the asymptotic MISE approximation (AMISE). This holds under certain conditions involving the sample size and the bandwidth. The bandwidth depends on the sample size, and we can write $b = b(n)$. We require $b(n) \downarrow 0$ as $n \longrightarrow \infty$, while $nb(n) \longrightarrow \infty$ as $n \longrightarrow \infty$. Furthermore, we need $f_X(x)$ to be twice continuously differentiable. We then have [44] the asymptotic approximation

$$\text{AMISE}(b) = \frac{1}{nb}R(k) + \frac{1}{4}m_2(k)^2 b^4 R(f''), \tag{25}$$

where $R(g) = \int g(x)^2 \, dx$ and $m_p(k) = \int x^p k(x) \, dx$. The bandwidth that minimizes AMISE can be analytically derived to be

$$b_{\text{opt}} = \left(\frac{R(k)}{m_2(k)^2 R(f'')} \frac{1}{n} \right)^{\frac{1}{5}}, \tag{26}$$

leading to

$$\text{AMISE}(b_{\text{opt}}) = \frac{5}{4} \left(\frac{m_2(k)^2 R(k)^4 R(f'')}{n^4} \right)^{\frac{1}{5}}. \tag{27}$$

The optimal bandwidth can then be calculate for different kernel functions. We have, e.g., for the Gaussian kernel [11]

$$b_{\text{opt}}^G = \left(\frac{1}{2\sqrt{\pi} R(f'')} \frac{1}{n} \right)^{\frac{1}{5}}. \tag{28}$$

The difficulty in using AMISE is that the norm of second derivative of the unknown density needs to be estimated. This will be further discussed under the subsection on bandwidth selectors.

We also mention the skewness γ_X of the data, which is a measure that can be used to see if the data is suitable for classical kernel estimation. We estimate it as

$$\hat{\gamma}_X = \frac{\frac{1}{n} \sum_{i=1}^{n} (X_i - \bar{X})^3}{\left(\frac{1}{n} \sum_{i=1}^{n} (X_i - \bar{X})^2 \right)^{\frac{3}{2}}}. \tag{29}$$

It was shown in [44], see also [41], that minimizing the square integrated error (ISE) for a specific sample is equivalent to minimizing the cross-validation function

$$\text{CV}(b) = \int_\Omega \left(\hat{f}_X(x) \right)^2 dx - \frac{2}{n} \sum_{i=1}^{n} \hat{f}_i(x_i), \tag{30}$$

where $\hat{f}_i(\cdot)$ is the kernel estimator obtained when leaving the observation x_i out. Other useful measures of the goodness of fit are also discussed in [41].

5.3   Bias-Corrected Kernel Estimation

As was illustrated in Example 1, boundaries where the density does not go to zero generate bias. This happens because the kernel functions cross the boundary, and some of the mass ends up outside the domain. We want from the kernel method that $\mathbb{E}[\hat{f}_X(x)] = f_X(x)$ in all of the support Ω of the density function, but this condition does not hold at boundaries, unless we also have that the density is zero there. An overview of the topic, and of simple boundary correction methods, is given in [34]. By employing a linear bias correction method, we can make the moments of order 0 and 1 satisfy the consistency requirements $m_0 = 1$ (total probability mass) and $m_1 = 0$, such that the expectation is consistent to order

b^2 at the boundary. A general linear correction method for a density supported on $\Omega = [x_0, \infty]$ that is shown to perform well in [34] has the form

$$\tilde{k}_b(y) = \frac{(a_2 - a_1 y)k_b(y)}{a_0 a_2 - a_1^2}, \qquad (31)$$

for a kernel function centered at the data location x. The coefficients $a_j = a_j(b, x)$ are computed as

$$a_j(b, x) = \int_{x_0}^{z} y^j k_b(x - y)dy, \qquad (32)$$

where z is the end point of the support of the kernel function. An example with modified Gaussian kernels close to a boundary is shown in Fig. 3. At the boundary, the amplitude of the kernels becomes higher to compensate for the mass loss, while away from the boundary they resume the normal shape and size. The kernel functions closest to the boundary become negative in a small region, but this does not affect the consistency of the estimate.

Fig. 3. Bias corrected kernel functions using the linear correction approach near a boundary (dashed line).

A more recent bias correction method is derived in [38], based on ideas from [15]. This type of correction is applied to the kernel estimator for the cdf, and can be seen as a Taylor expansion. It also improves the capturing of valleys and peaks in the distribution function, compared with the classical kernel estimator. It requires that the density is four times differentiable, that the kernel is symmetric, and at least for the theoretical derivations, that the kernel is compactly supported on $\Omega = [-1, 1]$. The overall bias of the estimator is $\mathcal{O}(b^4)$ as compared with $\mathcal{O}(b^2)$ for the linear correction method, while the variance is similar to what is achieved with the uncorrected estimator. This boundary correction approach is used for estimating extreme value distributions in [9].

$$\tilde{F}_X(x) = \frac{\hat{F}_X(x) + \lambda(\hat{F}_1(x) + \hat{F}_2(x))}{1 + 2\lambda}, \qquad (33)$$

where $\hat{F}_{1,2}(x) = \hat{F}_X(x \mp \ell b) \pm \ell b \hat{f}_X(x \mp \ell b)$, and

$$\ell(\lambda) = \sqrt{\frac{(1+2\lambda)m_2(k)}{2\lambda}}. \tag{34}$$

The parameter λ is kernel dependent, and should be chosen such that AMISE is minimized, but according to [15], the estimator is not that sensitive to the choice. An explicit expression for AMISE with this correction is derived in [38], and is also cited in [9], where the value $\lambda = 0.0799$ is also given as an (approximate) minimizer of the variance for the Epanechnikov kernel.

5.4 Transformation Kernel Estimation

The objective in transformation kernel estimation is to find a transformation of the random variable X, which for example has a right-skewed distribution into a symmetric random variable Y. Then classical kernel estimation can be successfully applied to Y.

The transformation function $T(\cdot)$ should be monotonic and increasing. For a right-skewed true density, it should also be concave. It also needs to have at least one continuous derivative. The transformation is applied to the original data to generate a transformed data sample

$$y_i = T(x_i), \quad i = 1, \ldots, n. \tag{35}$$

For the pdfs of the two random variables it holds that

$$f_X(x) = T'(x)f_Y(y), \tag{36}$$

and for the cdfs we have that $F_X(x) = F_Y(y)$. We apply the kernel density estimator to the transformed data, leading to the following estimator for the original density:

$$\hat{f}_X(x) = T'(x)\hat{f}_Y(y) = T'(x)\frac{1}{n}\sum_{i=1}^{n} k_b(T(x) - T(x_i)). \tag{37}$$

Several different transformation classes have been proposed for heavy tailed data. The shifted power transformation family was proposed in [45]

$$T(x) = \begin{cases} \mathrm{sign}(\lambda_2)(x + \lambda_1)^{\lambda_2}, & \lambda_2 \neq 0, \\ \ln(x + \lambda_1), & \lambda_2 = 0, \end{cases} \tag{38}$$

where $\lambda_1 > -\min(x_i)$ and $\lambda_2 \leq 1$. An algorithm for choosing the transformation parameters is given in [10]. First a restriction is made to parameters $\lambda_{1,2}$ that give close to zero skewness (29) for the transformed data. Then AMISE (27) of the classical kernel estimation for the density $f_Y(y)$ is minimized assuming an asymptotically optimal bandwidth. This is equivalent to minimizing $R(f_Y'')$. As we do not know the true density, an estimator is needed. The estimator suggested in [10] is

$$\hat{R}(f_Y'') = \frac{1}{n(n-1)} \sum_{i=1}^{n-1} \sum_{j=1+1}^{n} \frac{1}{c^5} k * k(y_i - y_j), \tag{39}$$

where the convolution $k * k(u) = \int k(u-s)k(s)ds$, and c is the bandwidth used in this estimate.

The Möbius-like mapping introduced in [16] takes data in $\Omega_X = [0, \infty)$ and maps it to $\Omega_Y = [-1, 1)$.

$$T(x) = \frac{x^\alpha - M^\alpha}{x^\alpha + M^\alpha}. \tag{40}$$

The scale M is determined by minimizing $R(\hat{f}_Y'')$. Given a scale M, α is determined such that no probability mass spills over at the right boundary. That is, the resulting density does not have mass at (or beyond) infinity.

A modified Champernowne distribution transformation is derived in [12], with transformation function

$$T(x) = \frac{\alpha(x+c)^{\alpha-1}((M+c)^\alpha) - c^\alpha}{((x+c)^\alpha + (M+c)^\alpha - 2c^\alpha)^2}, \tag{41}$$

where M can be chosen as the median of the data, and α and c are found by maximizing a log likelihood function, see [12].

So far, we have only considered the possibility of performing one transformation, but one can also transform the data iteratively, or perform two specific consecutive transformations. Doubly transformed kernel estimation is discussed, e.g., in [9]. The idea is to first transform the data to something close to uniform, and then to apply an inverse beta transformation. This makes the final distribution close to a beta distribution, and the optimal bandwidth can then easily be computed.

5.5 Bandwidth Selection

As briefly mentioned in Sects. 5.2 and 5.4, the choice of bandwidth b in kernel estimation has a significant impact on the quality of the estimator, but choosing the appropriate bandwidth requires the use of one estimator or another. The rule-of-thumb bandwidth estimator of Silverman [44],

$$b = \left(\frac{4}{3n}\right)^{\frac{1}{5}} \hat{\sigma}_X, \tag{42}$$

is often cited, but it assumes that the underlying density can be approximated by a normal density. This is hence not appropriate for heavy-tailed, right-skewed distributions.

Many bandwidth selection methods use a normal reference at some step in the process [11], but this introduces a parametric step in the non-parametric estimation. An interesting alternative, the Improved Sheather-Jones bandwidth selection algorithm, is also described in [11], where the normal reference is eliminated by formulating a non-linear equation for the optimal bandwidth.

We start from the point of how to estimate $R(f''_X) = \|f''_x\|^2$. There are at least two possible plug-in estimators, based on the equality

$$\|\widehat{f_X^{(j)}}\|^2 = (-1)^j \mathbb{E}[f^{(2j)}]. \tag{43}$$

The two types of estimators are

$$\|\widehat{f_X^{(j)}}\|^2 = \frac{1}{n^2} \sum_{k=1}^{n} \sum_{m=1}^{n} \int_{\mathbb{R}} k_b^{(j)}(x - x_k) k_b^{(j)}(x - x_m) dx \tag{44}$$

and

$$(-1)^j \widehat{\mathbb{E}[f^{(2j)}]} = \frac{(-1)^j}{n^2} \sum_{k=1}^{n} \sum_{m=1}^{n} k_b^{(2j)}(x_k - x_m). \tag{45}$$

By requiring the two estimators to have the same asymptotic mean square error, we get a condition on the bandwidth. A derivation for the Gaussian kernel is provided in [11], and we summarize these result here to illustrate the bandwidth selection algorithm. Requiring (44) and (45) to be asymptotically equivalent gives the following relation between the bandwidths for two consecutive derivatives:

$$\hat{b}_j^* = \left(\frac{1 + \frac{1}{2^{j+\frac{1}{2}}}}{3} \frac{(2j-1)!!}{N\sqrt{\frac{\pi}{2}} \|\widehat{f^{(j+1)}}\|^2} \right)^{\frac{1}{3+2j}} = \gamma_j(\hat{b}_{j+1}^*), \tag{46}$$

and, for the Gaussian kernel, (44) for $j + 1$ becomes

$$\|\widehat{f_X^{(j+1)}}\|^2 = \frac{(-1)^j}{n^2} \sum_{k=1}^{n} \sum_{m=1}^{n} k_{\sqrt{2}b_{j+1}^*}^{(2j)}(x_k - x_m). \tag{47}$$

The two relations (46) and (47) together define the function $\gamma_j(b)$. We also have Eq. (28) for the bandwidth of the Gaussian kernel. Combining this with (46) for $j = 1$ allows us to eliminate $\|\widehat{f''}\|^2$ to get

$$b^* = \left(\frac{6\sqrt{2} - 3}{7} \right)^{\frac{1}{5}} b_1^* \equiv \xi b_1^*. \tag{48}$$

Now we can apply (46) recursively to get a relation

$$b^* = \xi \gamma^{[\ell]}(b_{\ell+1}^*), \tag{49}$$

where $\gamma^{[\ell]}(b) = \gamma_1(\cdots \gamma_{\ell-1}(\gamma_\ell(b)) \cdots)$, for $\ell \geq 1$. Here, it would be possible to assume a normal distribution to estimate $\|\widehat{f^{\ell+2}}\|^2$ in order to compute $b_{\ell+1}^*$, and then all the other bandwidths. However, this does not work well if the true distribution is far from normal [11]. In the improved Sheather-Jones algorithm, we instead assume that $b^*_{\ell+1} = b$ for some large enough ℓ. The experiments in [11] indicate that $\ell = 5$ should be enough. We then get a non-linear equation to solve for b

$$b = \xi \gamma^{[\ell]}(b). \tag{50}$$

Using this relation, no assumptions on the true distribution are made, and this bandwidth selector is shown to perform well also for non-normal distributions.

6 More Challenges in Estimating the Risk Measures—Financial Time Series and Multivariate Case

A Dynamic Approach. Highlighting the underlying assumptions is relevant for understanding model uncertainty when estimating rare or extreme events. The VaR and ES are estimated given that the distribution of asset returns does not change over time. In the last two sections, when applying the POT approach to the returns in order to calculate these risk measures, their distribution was assumed to be stationary. A dynamic model which captures current risk is then more realistic. EVT can also be used based on a stochastic time series model. These dynamic models use an ARCH/GARCH type process along with the POT to model VaR and ES which depend on and change due to the fluctuations of the market. This approach, studied in [2], reflects two stylized facts exhibited by most financial return series, namely stochastic volatility and the fat-tailedness of conditional return distributions over short time horizons.

The Multivariate Case for EVT. When estimating the VaR of a multi-asset portfolio, under financial crises, correlations between assets often become more positive and stronger. Assuming that the variables are independent and identically distributed is a strong hypothesis. Portfolio losses are the result not only of the individual asset's performance but also, and very importantly, the result of the interaction between assets. Hence, from the accuracy point of view, ideally we would prefer the multivariate approach.

An extension of the univariate EVT models using a dependence structure leads to a parametric model and is then expected to be less efficient for scarce data. A non-parametric approach should be preferred to estimate portfolio tail risk. Transformation kernel density estimation is used in [8] for studying multivariate extreme value distributions in temperature measurement data. Future directions involve to apply this type of methodology to real and simulated portfolio data.

References

1. Acerbi, C., Tasche, D.: On the coherence of expected shortfall. J. Bank. Finance **26**(7), 1487–1503 (2002)
2. McNeil, A.J., Frey, R.: Estimation of tail-related risk measures for heteroscedastic financial time series: an extreme value approach. J. Empir. Finance **7**, 271–300 (2000)
3. Alemany, R., Bolancé, C., Guillén, M.: A nonparametric approach to calculating value-at-risk. Insur. Math. Econ. **52**(2), 255–262 (2013)
4. Artzner, P., Delbaen, F., Eber, J.M., Heath, D.: Coherent measures of risk. Math. Finance **9**(3), 203–228 (1999)
5. Balkema, A.A., de Haan, L.: Residual life time at great age. Ann. Probab. **2**(5), 792–804 (1974)
6. Beirlant, J., Dierckx, G., Goegebeur, Y., Matthys, G.: Tail index estimation and an exponential regression model. Extremes **2**(2), 177–200 (1999)
7. Beirlant, J., Dierckx, G., Guillou, A., Staăricaă, C.: On exponential representations of log-spacings of extreme order statistics. Extremes **5**(2), 157–180 (2002)
8. Beranger, B., Duong, T., Perkins-Kirkpatrick, S.E., Sisson, S.A.: Exploratory data analysis for moderate extreme values using non-parametric Kernel methods. arXiv:1602.08807 [stat.ME] (2016)
9. Bolancé, C., Bahraoui, Z., Alemany, R.: Estimating extreme value cumulative distribution functions using bias-corrected Kernel approaches. XREAP2015-01 (2015)
10. Bolancé, C., Guillén, M., Perch Nielsen, J.: Kernel density estimation of actuarial loss functions. Insur. Math. Econ. **32**(1), 19–36 (2003)
11. Botev, Z.I., Grotowski, J.F., Kroese, D.P.: Kernel density estimation via diffusion. Ann. Stat. **38**(5), 2916–2957 (2010)
12. Buch-larsen, T., Nielsen, J.P., Guillén, M., Bolancé, C.: Kernel density estimation for heavy-tailed distributions using the Champernowne transformation. Statistics **39**(6), 503–516 (2005)
13. Cai, Z., Wang, X.: Nonparametric estimation of conditional VaR and expected shortfall. J. Econ. **147**(1), 120–130 (2008)
14. Chen, S.: Non-parametric estimation of expected shortfall. J. Financ. Econ. **6**, 87–107 (2008)
15. Choi, E., Hall, P.: On bias reduction in local linear smoothing. Biometrika **85**(2), 333–345 (1998)
16. Clements, A., Hurn, S., Lindsay, K.: Mobius-like mappings and their use in Kernel density estimation. J. Am. Stat. Assoc. **98**(464), 993–1000 (2003)
17. Coles, S.: An Introduction to Statistical Modeling of Extreme Values. Springer Series in Statistics. Springer, London (2001). https://doi.org/10.1007/978-1-4471-3675-0
18. Csörgő, S., Deheuvels, P., Mason, D.: Kernel estimates of the tail index of a distribution. Ann. Stat. **13**(3), 1050–1077 (1985)
19. Csörgő, S., Viharos, L.: Estimating the tail index. In: Szyszkowicz, B. (ed.) Asymptotic Methods in Probability and Statistics, pp. 833–881. North-Holland, Amsterdam (1998)
20. Danielsson, J.: Financial Risk Forecasting. Wiley, Hoboken (2011)
21. Diebolt, J., Guillou, A., Rached, I.: Approximation of the distribution of excesses through a generalized probability-weighted moments method. J. Stat. Plan. Infer. **137**(3), 841–857 (2007)
22. Dowd, K.: Measuring Market Risk. Wiley, Hoboken (2005)

23. Duffie, D., Pan, J.: An overview of value at risk. J. Deriv. **4**(3), 7–49 (1997)
24. Eling, M.: Fitting insurance claims to skewed distributions: are the skew-normal and skew-student good models? Insur. Math. Econ. **51**(2), 239–248 (2012)
25. Embrechts, P. (ed.): Extremes and Integrated Risk Management. Risk Books, London (2000)
26. Embrechts, P., Klüppelberg, C., Mikosch, T.: Modelling Extremal Events: for Insurance and Finance. Springer, Heidelberg (1997). https://doi.org/10.1007/978-3-642-33483-2
27. Falk, M., Marohn, F.: Efficient estimation of the shape parameter in Pareto models with partially known scale. Stat. Decis. **15**, 229–239 (1997)
28. Feuerverger, A., Hall, P.: Estimating a tail exponent by modelling departure from a Pareto distribution. Ann. Stat. **27**(2), 760–781 (1999)
29. Fisher, R.A., Tippett, L.H.C.: Limiting forms of the frequency distribution of the largest or smallest member of a sample. Math. Proc. Camb. Philos. Soc. **24**(2), 180–190 (1928)
30. Gnedenko, B.: Sur la distribution limite du terme maximum d'une série aléatoire. Ann. Math. **44**(3), 423–453 (1943)
31. Hill, B.M.: A simple general approach to inference about the tail of a distribution. Ann. Stat. **3**, 1163–1174 (1975)
32. Hosking, J.R., Wallis, J.R.: Parameter and quantile estimation for the generalized Pareto distribution. Technometrics **29**(3), 339–349 (1987)
33. Hull, J.C.: Risk Management and Financial Institutions. Prentice Hall, Upper Saddle River (2006)
34. Jones, M.C.: Simple boundary correction for Kernel density estimation. Stat. Comput. **3**(3), 135–146 (1993)
35. Jones, M.C., Marron, J.S., Sheather, S.J.: A brief survey of bandwidth selection for density estimation. J. Am. Stat. Assoc. **91**(433), 401–407 (1996)
36. Jones, M.C., McKay, I.J., Hu, T.C.: Variable location and scale Kernel density estimation. Ann. Inst. Stat. Math. **46**(3), 521–535 (1994)
37. Jorion, P.: Value at Risk: The New Benchmark for Managing Financial Risk. McGraw-Hill, New York (2001)
38. Kim, C., Kim, S., Park, M., Lee, H.: A bias reducing technique in Kernel distribution function estimation. Comput. Stat. **21**(3–4), 589–601 (2006)
39. McNeil, A.J., Frey, R., Embrechts, P.: Quantitative Risk Management: Concepts, Techniques and Tools. Princeton Series in Finance. Princeton University Press, Princeton (2005)
40. Pickands, J.: Statistical inference using extreme order statistics. Ann. Stat. **3**(1), 119–131 (1975)
41. Pitt, D., Guillen, M., Bolancé, C.: Estimation of parametric and nonparametric models for univariate claim severity distributions - an approach using R. XREAP2011-06 (2011)
42. Reiss, R.D., Thomas, M.: Statistical Analysis of Extreme Values: with Applications to Insurance, Finance, Hydrology and Other Fields. Birkhäuser, Basel (2007)
43. Scaillet, O.: Nonparametric estimation of conditional expected shortfall. Insur. Risk Manag. J. **74**(1), 639–660 (2005)
44. Silverman, B.W.: Density Estimation for Statistics and Data Analysis, Monographs on Statistics and Applied Probability, vol. 26. Chapman & Hall/CRC, London (1986)
45. Wand, M.P., Marron, J.S., Ruppert, D.: Transformations in density estimation. J. Am. Stat. Assoc. **86**(414), 343–353 (1991)

Towards Efficient and Scalable Data-Intensive Content Delivery: State-of-the-Art, Issues and Challenges

Irene Kilanioti[1]([✉]), Alejandro Fernández-Montes[2], Damián Fernández-Cerero[2], Anthony Karageorgos[4], Christos Mettouris[1], Valentina Nejkovic[3], Nikolas Albanis[4], Rabih Bashroush[5], and George A. Papadopoulos[1]

[1] Department of Computer Science, University of Cyprus, Nicosia, Cyprus
irenekilanioti@gmail.com, {mettour,george}@cs.ucy.ac.cy
[2] Departamento de Lenguajes y Sistemas Informáticos, Universidad de Sevilla, Seville, Spain
{afdez,damiancerero}@us.es
[3] Faculty of Electronic Engineering, University of Nis, Niš, Serbia
valentina@elfak.ni.ac.rs
[4] TEI of Thessaly, Karditsa, Greece
karageorgos@computer.org, nikosbit@gmail.com
[5] University of East London, London, UK
r.bashroush@qub.ac.uk

Abstract. This chapter presents the authors' work for the Case Study entitled "Delivering Social Media with Scalability" within the framework of High-Performance Modelling and Simulation for Big Data Applications (cHiPSet) COST Action 1406. We identify some core research areas and give an outline of the publications we came up within the framework of the aforementioned action. The ease of user content generation within social media platforms, e.g. check-in information, multimedia data, etc., along with the proliferation of Global Positioning System (GPS)-enabled, always-connected capture devices lead to data streams of unprecedented amount and a radical change in information sharing. Social data streams raise a variety of practical challenges: derivation of real-time meaningful insights from effectively gathered social information, a paradigm shift for content distribution with the leverage of contextual data associated with user preferences, geographical characteristics and devices in general, etc. In this article we present the methodology we followed, the results of our work and the outline of a comprehensive survey, that depicts the state-of-the-art situation and organizes challenges concerning social media streams and the infrastructure of the data centers supporting the efficient access to data streams in terms of content distribution, data diffusion, data replication, energy efficiency and network infrastructure. The challenges of enabling better provisioning of social media data have been identified and they were based on the context of users accessing these resources. The existing literature has been systematized and the main research points and industrial efforts in the area were identified and analyzed. In our works, in the framework of the Action, we came up with

© The Author(s) 2019
J. Kołodziej and H. González-Vélez (Eds.): cHiPSet, LNCS 11400, pp. 88–137, 2019.
https://doi.org/10.1007/978-3-030-16272-6_4

potential solutions addressing the problems of the area and described how these fit in the general ecosystem.

1   Introduction

1.1   Social Data Streams Features

Herein some basic terminology for the topic of our Case Study entitled "Delivering Social Media with Scalability" within the framework of High-Performance Modelling and Simulation for Big Data Applications (cHiPSet) COST Action 1406 is introduced. The terminology appears in published works [111] and [108], as well.

Social networks, media and platforms enable communication, exchange, business and knowledge acquisition as well as social network users connection with each other with the purpose of sharing content. Social data is the information that social media users share, e.g. check-in information, multimedia data, tags, annotations, and likes, and may include metadata such as the user's location, native language, biographical data and shared links, whereas 'streams' denotes various approaches have been performed that we do not refer to static datasets, but rather to dynamic information generated and transmitted over the Online Social Network (OSN).

Formally, an OSN is depicted by a directed graph $G = (V, E)$, where V is the set of the vertices of the graph representing the nodes of the network and E are the edges between them, denoting various relationships among the edges of the graph [69]. The semantics of these edges vary, and their interpretation is expanded for various OSNs from personal acquaintance, to common interests, microblogging services or business contact. As far as the directionality of the edges of the social graph is concerned, it is associated with the concept of the OSN: for Facebook, an edge denotes mutual friendship between the endpoints of a link, for Twitter, if the edge between A and B points at B, A's posts (tweets) appear in B's main Twitter page, and so on. A social node centrality is indicative of the importance of a node within a social network. It is given in terms of a real-valued function on the vertices of a graph, where the values produced are expected to provide a ranking which identifies the most important nodes [40, 41].

In Rogers' classic work [150], the author defines *information diffusion* as the process in which an innovation is communicated through certain channels over time among the members of a social system. In this context, the innovation is defined as the first spread of information from an originator. A *social cascade* is a specific case of information diffusion and practically occurs within an OSN, when a piece of information is extensively retransmitted after its initial publication from a user. Cascades can be represented as rooted directed trees where the initiator of the cascade is the root of the tree [26] and the length of the cascade is the height of the resulting tree. Each vertex in the cascade tree can have the information of the user, and the identity of the item replicated in the cascade. Figure 1 depicts an example of the evolution of a social cascade in a directed

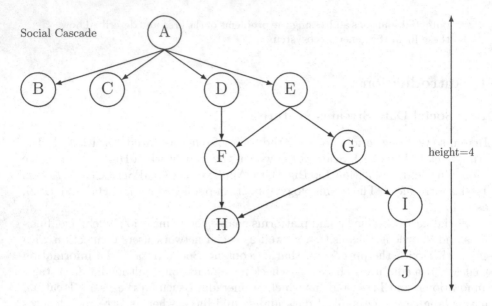

Fig. 1. The evolution of a social cascade in Twitter

graph. The cascade follows the arrows' direction. For example, in Twitter, B, C, D, E are followers of A, whereas the adopters of a new information piece could be the nodes, that after having been exposed in a video link, they retransmit it, contributing remarkably to Internet traffic [1].

1.2   Challenges for Distribution of Social Data Streams

In the survey [108] we wrote in the framework of (cHiPSet) COST Action 1406 we identified the challenges of enabling better provisioning of social media data based on the context of users accessing these resources. In our works [109–111], that we produced in the framework of the Action, we came up with potential solutions addressing the problems of the area and described how these fit in the general ecosystem.

Distributing social data streams largely depends on the exploitation of usage patterns found in OSNs, and can be improved either through the selective prefetching of content (**cost-effectiveness**) or through the strategic placement/selection of the employed infrastructure (**energy-efficiency**). The cost of scaling such content might be the number of replicas needed for a specific source or it may take into account the optimal use of memory and processing time of a social-aware built system. Optimization of energy efficiency for data centers that support social data interaction and analysis includes tasks such as data growth, data center federation and Content Delivery Network (CDN)-load-balancing at data center level. In our taxonomy (Fig. 2), pillars associated with cost-effectiveness include Context-aware Computing, Content/Information Diffusion Models and Content Distribution challenges, whereas Software for

Fig. 2. Taxonomy of challenges for distribution of social data streams.

Infrastructure Efficiency is associated with energy-efficiency. This taxonomy includes solutions or approaches to the 'Challenges for Distribution of Social Data Streams'. These solutions or approaches require enough effort, hence they can also be considered as a challenge for the research community.

Context-Aware Computing: Application of social contextual information, such as profiles, images, videos, biometrical, geolocation data and local data, in situations where conventional bandwidth-intensive content scaling is infeasible, could largely facilitate: the spreading of information, the identification of potential information sources, as well as a paradigm shift in the way users access and control their personal data. User-generated multimedia content is especially difficult due to its long tail nature, with each item probably not popular enough to be replicated in a global scale, but with the long-tail altogether getting sufficient accesses [20]. Social analysis tasks interweaved with context-aware computing could pave the ground for preactive caching mechanisms in the framework of a content delivery infrastructure of streaming providers.

Software for Infrastructure Efficiency: The industry has made several efforts to address challenges associated with optimization of energy efficiency for data centers that support social data interaction and analysis [42,129,163] such as data growth, isolation, real-time interactions, data center federation and CDN-load-balancing at data center level, but usually lacks from focusing on energy consumption of the employed infrastructures. The challenges in the area of energy-efficient data-centers include workload consolidation and shut-down techniques, Virtual Machines (VMs) consolidation and migration, data replication and placement, and energy-aware scheduling algorithms.

Content/Information Diffusion Models: Prevalence of OSNs has transformed the landscape of content exchange. Popularity of relatively data heavy multimedia user generated content (UGC) has also risen [6], resulting in data deluge across all media platforms [12,127,141]. Measurement studies, such as [48], attribute the recent increases in HTTP/HTTPS traffic to the extended use of OSNs [28,49,69]. Elaborate data manipulation presupposes coping with the size of social graphs with billions of nodes and edges [174]. Facebook, for example, reported that had 1.47 billion daily active users on average for June 2018 and 2.23 billion monthly active users as of June 30, 2018 [4]. Its custom built-in data warehouse and analytics infrastructure [11] has to apply ad-hoc queries and custom MapReduce jobs [55] in a continuous basis on over half a petabyte of new data every 24 h for the creation of meaningful aggregations and analysis. It is also acknowledged that a large proportion of bandwidth-intensive media is distributed via reposted OSN links, contributing significantly to Internet traffic [1], [46]. These challenges are closely associated with the Content/Information Diffusion Models used to represent the diffusion of information over OSNs and facilitate relevant algorithmic solutions (Fig. 2).

Content Distribution: The delivery infrastructure of video operators is made up of scattered geo-distributed servers, which with specific cache selection mechanisms direct users to the closest servers hosting the requested data. Transmission Control Protocol (TCP), however, is subject to delay jitter and throughput variations and clients are required to preload a playout buffer before starting the video playback [111]. Thus, the quality of experience (QoE) of media platform users is primarily determined by stalling effects on the application layer. For the YouTube case cache server selection is also highly Internet Service Provider (ISP)-specific, with geographical proximity not being the primary criterion and DNS level redirections for load-balancing purposes occurring quite frequently and substantially contributing to the initial startup delay of the playback. Several network-level and client-level approaches are focused on the detection of such interruptions, that negatively affect the user experience [94]. With the growing popularity of OSNs and the increased traffic due to outspread of information via the latter, the improvement of user experience through scaling bandwidth-demanding content largely depends on the exploitation of usage patterns and geolocation data associated with OSNs. These challenges are closely associated with the Architectures, Systems and Techniques within the 5G infrastructure.

Some key factors contributing to the problem of diffusion of bandwidth-intensive media content over OSNs are discussed below.

Large-Scale Datasets. In order to harness the power of social networks diffusion over CDN infrastructure, the key areas of interest that need to be explored include the large size of the graphs, and also the fact that diffusion of links is multiplied through dissemination over sites like YouTube, and amplified by the proliferation of smartphones and cheap broadband connections. The amount of information in OSNs is an obstacle, since elaborate manipulation of the data may be needed. An open problem is the efficient handling of graphs with billions of nodes and edges.

The desired scaling property refers to the fact that the throughput of the proposed approaches should remain unchanged with the increase in the data input size, such as the large datasets that social graphs comprise and the social cascades phenomena that amplify the situation. Cost of scaling such content can be expressed in different ways. For instance, it may be matched with the number of replicas needed for a specific source. Future experimentations may take into account the optimal use of memory and processing time of an OSN aware built system.

Internet of Things (IoT) is a global infrastructure that interconnects things based on interoperable information and communication technologies, and through identification, data capture, processing and communication capabilities enables advanced services [5]. Things are objects of the physical world (physical things, such as devices, vehicles, buildings, living or inanimate objects augmented with sensors) or the information world (virtual things), capable of being identified and integrated into communication networks. It is estimated that the number of Internet-connected devices has surpassed the human population in 2010 and that there will be about 50 million devices by 2020 [9]. Thus, the still ongoing significant IoT innovation is expected to generate massive amounts of data from diverse locations, that will need to be collected, indexed, stored, and analyzed.

OSN Evolution. Existent works examine valuable insights into the dynamic world by posing queries on an evolving sequence of social graphs (e.g. [146]). Time evolving graphs are increasingly used as a paradigm for the emerging area of OSNs [71]. However, the ability to scalably process queries concerning the information diffusion remains to a great extent unstudied. With the exception of sporadic works on specialized problems, such as that of inference of dynamic networks based on information diffusion data [149], at the time of writing the authors are not aware of relative studies on the information diffusion through OSNs under the prism of graphs dynamicity.

5G Approaches. The demand for high-speed data applications that has risen in recent decade lead to development of Fifth Generation Wireless (5G) communications. Development of efficient mechanisms for supporting mobile multimedia and data services is prerequisite for 5G networks. Real bottleneck of todays' mobile networks is the radio access network and the backhaul. Caching in the intermediate nodes, servers, gateways, routers, and mobile users' devices can reduce doubled transmission from content providers and core mobile networks.

Known caching techniques that can be used within 5G are: content distribution network, information-centric networks, content-centric networking, http web caching, evolved packet core caching, radio access network caching, device to device caching, proactive caching, predictive caching, cooperative caching [23]. Those techniques are using different algorithms and models. Analysis presented in [23] has shown that the deployment of those caching techniques in mobile network can reduce redundant traffic in backhaul, minimize the traffic load, increase the transfer rate in mobile network and reduce the latency. Correlation of several caching methods and procedures could result in improving network performance and obtaining better results.

On the other hand, well known bottleneck that 5G brings is the complex heterogeneity of the network. Particularly, network consists of different technologies that coexist, where some technologies could potentially disable the transmission of data of equipment that use other technologies. Thus, we need a solution that efficiently handles resources in space, frequency, and device dimensions. Semantic coordination could alternatively be used in such networks [135, 164].

The nodes in the system can communicate and share knowledge in terms of the spectrum utilization in the network. In [164], the authors proposed to model the spectrum usage coordination as an interactive process between a number of distributed communicating agents, where agents share their specific information and knowledge. The information includes the current spectrum usage state, spatial coordinates of the device, available communication protocols, usage policy, spectrum sensing capabilities of the device, spectrum needs, etc. An approach for such coordination is presented in [164] and it is based on semantic technologies and communication between heterogeneous agents with potentially different capabilities and a minimal common compliance. The core knowledge is represented by ontologies whose representation and usage is specified in a standardized way. The approach is used as dynamic spectrum coordination algorithms used for coordination among different wireless technologies in 5G networking [135, 164]. This semantic technologies based approach can be used for wide diapason of problems within 5G heterogeneous networks, such as network states predictions, network analysis, minimizing traffic load, content distribution coordination etc. This approach could be used in combination with caching techniques in order to improve content distribution in 5G, but further research should be done in this area.

Mobile CDNs and the Cloud. Mobile computing (MC) [13] has created enormous demand for online experience, that OSN-aware CDNs are required to satisfy. Almost-ubiquitous Wi-Fi coverage and rapid extension of mobile-broadband provide undisrupted connectivity for mobile devices, whereas devices that hop seamlessly from WiFi to cellular networks, and technologies such as 5G, will be optimised for uses that put a premium on continuous connectivity regardless of the user location [5]. Mobile-specific optimizations for applications along with drastically simplified and more intuitive use of devices (e.g. with multi-touch interactions instead of physical keyboards) contribute to mobile applications becoming the premium mode of accessing the Internet, at least in the US [6].

Cellular networks have become the main way citizens connect to the Internet worldwide, specially in developing countries. Thanks to the development of mobile devices and their networking capacities, as well as the arrival of fast and reliable networks such as 5G, a high quality connectivity is ensured everywhere and any time. The irruption of new paradigms, such as IoT, has increased the number of connected devices (sensors, actuators, etc.) which requires infrastructures that provide higher throughput networking, specially in use cases where high definition videos are involved and even new scenarios are yet to emerge.

Mobile Computing entails the processing and transmission of data over a medium, that does not constraint the human-medium interaction to a specific location or a fixed physical link. Figure 3 depicts a general overview of the MC paradigm in its current form. It is the present decade that signifies the proliferation of MC around the world, although handheld devices have been widely used for around two decades in the form of Personal Digital Assistants (PDAs) and early smartphones. Almost ubiquitous Wi-Fi coverage and rapid extension of mobile-broadband (around 78 active subscriptions per 100 inhabitants in Europe and America) provide undisrupted connectivity for mobile devices, whereas 97% of the world's population is reported to own a cellular subscription in 2015 [5]. Moreover, the MC paradigm is nowadays further combined with other predominant technology schemes leading to the paradigms of Mobile Cloud Computing [15], Mobile Edge Computing [8], Anticipatory Mobile Computing [138], etc.

Today's mobile devices include smartphones, wearables, carputers, tablet PCs, and e-readers. They are not considered as mere communication devices, as they are in their majority equipped with sensors that can monitor a user's location, activity and social context. Thus, they foster the collection of Big Data by allowing the recording and extension of the human senses [115].

Mobile social networking involves the interactions between users with similar interests or objectives through their mobile devices within virtual social networks [44]. Recommendation of interesting groups based on common geo-social patterns, display of geo-tagged multimedia content associated to nearby places, as well as automatic exchange of data among mobile devices by inferring trust from social relationships are among the possible mobile social applications benefiting from real-time location and place information.

1. *Industrial Applications*: Maintenance, service, optimization of distributed plant operations is achieved through several distributed control points, so that risk is reduced and the reliability of massive industrial systems is improved [139].
2. *Automotive Applications*: Automotive applications capture data from sensors embedded in the road that cooperate with car-based sensors. They aim at weather adaptive lighting in street lights, monitoring of parking spaces availability, promotion of hands-free driving, as well as accident avoidance through warning messages and diversions according to climate conditions and traffic congestion. Applications can promote massive vehicle data recording (stolen vehicle recovery, automatic crash notification, etc.) [7].
3. *Retail Applications*: Retail applications include, among many others, the monitoring of storage conditions along the supply chain, the automation of restocking process, as well as advising according to customer habits and preferences [139].

Fig. 3. Social data streams over mobile computing [108].

4. *Healthcare & Telemedicine Applications*: Physical condition monitoring for patients and the elderly, control of conditions inside freezers storing vaccines, medicines and organic elements, as well as more convenient access for people in remote locations with usage of telemedicine stations [98].

5. *Building Management Applications*: Video surveillance, monitoring of energy usage and building security, optimization of space in conference rooms and workdesks [7].

6. *Energy Applications*: Applications that utilize assets, optimize processes and reduce risks in the energy supply chain. Energy consumption monitoring and management [10,172], monitoring and optimization of performance in solar energy plants [167].

7. *Smart homes & Cities Applications*: Monitoring of vibrations and material conditions in buildings, bridges and historical monuments, urban noise monitoring, measuring of electromagnetic fields, monitoring of vehicles and pedestrian numbers to optimize driving and walking routes, waste management [81].

8. *Embedded Mobile Applications*: Applications for recommendation of interesting groups based on common geo-social patterns, infotainment, and automatic exchange of data among mobile devices by inferring trust from social relationships. Visual effects streaming workflow will give users on-demand, cloud-based access to visual effects tools, that can be accessed via web, given enough low-latency bandwidth to maintain a connection for streaming the User Interface from the cloud. Video Game streaming workflow will give players the option of streaming graphically-rich content that requires near-instant interaction between the game controller and the graphics on the TV screen [139].

9. *Technology Applications*: Hardware manufacture, among many others, is improved by applications measuring peformance and predicting maintenance needs of the hardware production chain [139].

Roadmap: Our chapter is organized as follows: Sect. 2 discusses existent surveys concerning modelling, simulation and performance evaluation in the examined bibliographical field. The association of context-aware computing with social networks is given in Sect. 3. Infrastructure efficiency of deployed data centers for the distribution of social content is analyzed in Sect. 4 in terms of software solutions, as well as data center scheduling frameworks. Section 5 presets a categorization of most predominant models for the depiction of the information diffusion process in a social network. Section 6 discusses various architectures, systems and techniques for efficient content distribution based on social data streams, along with diverse studies that corroborate them as well as the way 5G network infrastructure affects the social data streams. Section 7 concludes and finally gives the outline of future research directions.

2   Related Work

In a manner that resembles the utilization of social data streams Anjum et al. [21] review the deployment of peer-assisted content delivery solutions. They present challenges caused due to heterogeneity in user access patterns and the variety of contextual information, such as interests and incentives of Internet Service Providers, End-Users and Content Providers. Furthermore, Perera et al. [139] survey context awareness from an IoT perspective. They indicate that the technology in the IoT is expected to enable expansion of conventional content delivery systems to a broader network of connected devices. They systematize the collection, modeling, reasoning, and distribution of context in relation to sensor data in a work that resembles the social data harvesting in terms of volume, variety and velocity. The survey also addresses a broad range of methods, models, systems, applications, and middleware solutions related to context awareness in the realm of IoT, that could be potentially applicable to social data streams, too.

In [111] Kilanioti et al. study various experiments on a modified content delivery simulation framework and compare miscellaneous policies for dynamic content delivery based on analysis of social data streams. The incorporation of an OSN-aware dynamic mechanism becomes indispensable for content delivery services, since (i) significantly large proportion of Internet traffic results from bandwidth-intensive multimedia content, that is produced via online media services and transmitted over OSNs, and (ii) multimedia content providers, such as YouTube, often rely on ubiquitous content distribution infrastructures. The policies presented take patterns of user activity over OSNs and exploit geo-social properties of users participating in extensive retransmissions of items over OSNs. The authors proceed to incorporate diverse caching schemes of the underlying infrastructure, miscellaneous policies for the handling of OSN data and various approaches that take into account the most efficient timing for content placement. The simulation framework introduced in [107] serves in this study as the basis of further parameterized content delivery experimentation that exploits information transmission over OSNs and decreases replication costs by selectively copying items to locations where items are bound to be consumed.

Downloads of large size multimedia contents are explored through several studies together with techniques that try to reduce doubled content transmissions using intelligent caching strategies in mobile networking [14, 23, 101]. The main idea is redistribution of mobile multimedia traffic in order to eliminate duplicated downloads of popular contents. Intelligent caching strategies would enable access to popular contents from caches of nearby nodes of a mobile network operator. Those strategies allow content providers to reduce access delays to the requested content. Many caching algorithms for content distribution already exist [23]. Efficient caching strategy could enhance the energy efficiency of 5G networks, thus the cooperative caching architecture is presented in [101]. This strategy addressed the increasing demand for mobile multimedia and data services in energy efficiency in emerging 5G systems using content caching and distribution.

We are not aware of surveys in the bibliography suggesting an holistic approach for the utilization of social data streams towards facilitation of content distribution decisions and social analysis tasks other than [108]. The diverse parameters we review in this work (modelling, simulation, performance evaluation) take into account low-level decisions and high-level considerations, including energy efficiency of employed data centers, in-memory keeping solutions and various network approaches for time-critical applications. We review combined aspects such as optimal route selection, data redundancy, data localization and data center optimizations.

3 Social Networks and Context-Aware Computing

A social network is a network of social bindings between people. Computer-Supported Cooperative Work (CSCW) has contributed much in offering advanced collaborative systems for leveraging human connections and improving human interactions in workspace environments, but these systems mostly focus on business-driven interactions where connections among people tend to be formal and structured [43]. Recently however, social and computing disciplines focused specifically on the design of social-networking services, i.e. applications that support human social interactions and can be more informal.

The advancement of wireless networks, as well as mobile, context-aware and ubiquitous computing, enabled the improvement of social-networking services by enabling social encounters between proximate users with common interests in an anywhere and anytime fashion, as in Ubiquitous Computing systems [43]. Thus, there has been a shift of the application focus from virtual to physical social spaces using ubiquitous technologies [43]. This shift introduces a great number of possibilities, however it also introduces a number of challenges that are related to ubiquitous computing. While social-network systems for ubiquitous computing environments are an emerging trend in social computing, due to the fact that ubiquitous-computing environments are more dynamic and heterogeneous than Internet based environments, appropriate solutions and design guidelines are required to facilitate their ubiquitous aspect.

Ubiquitous Computing, first introduced in the nineties, refers to the shifting of the computing paradigm from the desktop Personal Computer (PC) to a more distributed and embedded form of computing [170]. Together with Pervasive Computing (for many these terms are synonymous), Ubiquitous Computing introduced the concept of "anywhere, anytime computing", allowing users to interact with computers embedded in every-day objects in an "anywhere and anytime" manner. Ubiquitous Computing specifies also that the interaction of users with such devices must be straightforward to the degree that the user would not be aware of such an interaction. Thus, in order for ubiquitous and pervasiveness to be achieved, computers must disappear from the front-end, be embedded to common objects that humans use daily and provide computational and informational services without expecting from users to explicitly and consciously interact with them.

Challenges in Ubiquitous Computing can be categorized to (Want and Pering [170]): (i) power management issues: refers to how mobile devices deal with processing power and storage space and the kind of wireless technology to use in every given situation, (ii) limitations in connecting devices: this issue has to do with how all these small devices will be connected and managed, (iii) user interface issues: since Ubiquitous Computing demands for many different small-scale devices of various types of interfaces and displays of various sizes, the challenge in user interfaces lies in developing user friendly and interactive interfaces to the level where users will be motivated in using them, (iv) issues related to Location Aware Computing. Henricksen et al. [88] add to the above list the challenge of managing heterogeneous devices of different hardware and software specifications, such as sensors and actuators, embedded devices in objects such as shoes, home and office appliances such as videos, mobile devices and traditional desktop computers, in order for these devices to interact seamlessly. Another challenge they mention has to do with maintaining network connections while devices move between networks of different nature and characteristics. In ubiquitous environments, people tend to use many devices simultaneously, therefore there is a need for these devices to communicate and exchange data. Another challenge Satyanarayanan [152] notes is tracking user intentions. This is important in Pervasive Computing in order for the system to understand what system actions could help the user and not hinder him/her.

An important challenge on context-awareness is to build context-aware systems that detect and manipulate the context in a human-like manner, i.e. making decisions proactively based on the context and provoke actions based on those decisions that assist the user through his/her task; the aforementioned should be done without any user participation or disturbance, except maybe in case of emergency. Another important issue is obtaining contextual information. Contextual information can be any information related to the user, the computing system, the environment of the user and any other relevant information regarding the interaction of the user and the system [63]. User's personal computing space can be used as the user's context (any information regarding the user taken from her personal profile, calendars, to-do lists etc.), various types of context can be sensed in real time like location, people and objects nearby, while contextual parameters could also include the current emotional and physiological state of the user. Contextual challenges also include the way context is represented (ontologies can be used or other context modeling techniques), the way this information is to be combined with the system information, as well as how frequently should context information be considered. Hinze and Buchanan [90] differentiate the static context from the fluent context. An example of static context is users profile information, while fluent context is dynamic, real-time context, e.g. time. The authors propose that a context model should be defined for each important entity, such as the user, the locations, etc. The authors mention as challenges the capturing of the context (whether it should be done automatically at particular times or manually by the user) and the process of storing the context (whether it should be stored on the client, on the server or both). On the process of accessing contextual information, Hinze and Buchanan propose that context-awareness can help in reducing the amount of data to be accessed in real time, by pre-retrieving any relevant pre-known data, e.g. the static context [90], to increase efficiency.

User modelling in another challenge in developing ubiquitous systems. User modeling in ubiquitous environments is challenging: a user often changes roles depending on the context and the current environment he acts into; the big challenge is how to capture these changes and how to react on them [90].

Perhaps one of the most important contextual parameters is location, as it plays an important role in context-aware systems and ubiquitous systems. An issue with location as a contextual parameter is the type of location sensing technology to be used, while privacy is another issue. The issue with privacy is whether user privacy should be sacrificed for location awareness and to what extent. A third issue is the semantic (and contextual) representation of the location in order to utilize more contextual parameters than just the location itself. For example, by semantically representing locations, one can attach to them various information resources such as a webpage, a user profile, various objects with semantic representation etc. Schilit et al. [154], proposed the movement from the simplified concept of location to more contextually rich notions of place where people and activities should also be considered. Possible problems towards this concept include the difficulty in managing large scale positioning data, privacy concerns regarding location-awareness and the challenge of how to associate information objects, such as a web page, with a real-world location. Privacy issues regarding location-awareness are related to human psychology: users often consider privacy issues when their location is to be known by a system, but at the same time they provide private information such as credit card numbers and addresses to online systems without hesitation. This happens because in the first case they simply do not see the benefit of providing their location to be used by a simple application (e.g. finding friends in the proximity), while at the latter case they clearly see the benefit of buying goods online. The authors also argue that the centralized nature of the most location tracking applications (having a central server on which all user personal data are stored) discourages users from providing any personalized information, because centralized data can be accessed by anyone, not only illegally (e.g. hackers) but also the government, corporations with interest in user data (e.g. advertisers) etc. A solution can be the use of a decentralized schema where any personal data is stored and calculated on the client side, i.e. the user's device. An example of such a technology is the well known Global Positioning System (GPS): the client device uses satellite links to calculate locally the user's current position.

Context-Awareness and Adaptation related challenges and issues include

1. **Modelling the context:** which method is more appropriate to use
2. **Observing the context:** automatically or manually
3. **Context sensing:** how are contextual parameters retrieved (sensors, user profiles etc.). In retrieving context data from various sources (e.g. sensors), how are inconsistencies between these data resolved

4. **Accuracy of contextual information** should be well known during the design of ubiquitous systems
5. **Storing the context:** on server (privacy issues), on client or on both
6. **Accessing the context**
7. **Using the context**
8. **How are the user and the environment connected and interact**
9. **How will the application modify its behaviour (be adapted) based on the context**
10. **Systems should be more context-aware than just the location.** A place is more than a location (also a Location related challenge)
11. **Devices should not operate based only on their own context, but based on the context of the whole system**
12. **Contextual information should be used to reduce the amount of input that is needed from users** (also a Human-Computer Interaction related challenge)
13. **How to capture changes in the user's role** deals with capturing the current context (i.e. the environment and the various circumstances) and user modelling (what possible role could a person play according to context)
14. **Context should be processed and various components should adapt to it without interfering with user's task** – no user explicit interaction should be necessary
15. **Adaptation in ubiquitous environments:** may need to adopt various devices separately and at the same time, while the user maintains a consistent view for the system/application

Context-aware computing has evolved over time from desktop applications, web applications, mobile computing, pervasive/ubiquitous computing to IoT over the last decade [139]. Context-aware computing became more popular with the introduction of the term 'ubiquitous computing' by Mark Weiser, while the term 'context-aware' was first used by Schilit and Theimer [155] in 1994. Context-aware computing has proven to be successful in understanding sensor data. Advances in sensor technology led to more powerful, cheaper and smaller sensors. The number of employed sensors is expected to grow over the next decade [161], generating ultimately big data [139, 140].

In settings where social communities become mobile, i.e. users not only interact, meet and communicate via social networks, but are mobile as well (move into the environment, interact with others, etc.), the concept of group awareness is met [53, 134, 176] where context related to the group is exploited to enable ubiquitous applications and services to function and serve people's concerns and needs in a pervasive manner. There is a need, thus, for formulating dynamic communities aiming to facilitate people in performing common tasks. It is often the case that such dynamic communities are resolved after the current goals have been achieved [134]. It is evident, thus, that the context within which such dynamic communities are created, act, achieve goals and are then resolved is important, and that, through this context, we can understand the groups' interests and, thus, personalize the applications and services offered [134].

A bibliography study [134] on mobile social network applications and platforms states that the context features that these applications and platforms use can be summarized as follows: Location, Interest, Time, Personal, Activity and Social Interaction. Here, context is "any information that can be used to characterize the situation of an entity" [62] and social context is "the information relevant to the characterization of a situation that influences the interactions of one user with one or more other users" [169]. Moreover, in [134] a context-aware Mobile Social Network model is proposed aiming to facilitate the creation of dynamic social networks based on a combination of multiple contexts, including location, users' profile, domain specific data and OSN data, along with services for fostering the interaction among users.

4   Infrastructure Efficiency

4.1   Software Solutions for Infrastructure Efficiency

Regarding infrastructure efficiency, various models have been proposed for the optimization of such infrastructures that support social networks data centers. These approaches have also been proposed by industry partners addressing various challenges [42,129,163]. Among these challenges, the following have been identified. (a) data volume increase, (b) confinement, (c) interactions made in real-time or near real time, (d) federation of data center infrastructures and (e) cdn-load-balancing between data centers, but usually not focused on cost effectiveness. One of the main data center costs is energy consumption of both the IT equipment as well as the supporting Mechanical and Electrical (M&E) infrastructure. A widely used indicator that measures the energy effectiveness of the M&E infrastructure overhead is Power Usage Effectiveness (PUE) [25], which is calculated as the *Total facility energy/Total IT energy* and has a theoretical minimum of 1.

Figure 2 shows the categories on which the research community and other stakeholders have developed solutions for the improvement of costs and efficiency:

- **Workload Consolidation and Shut-down Techniques,**
- **VM Consolidation and Migration,**
- **Data Replication and Placement, and**
- **Energy-aware Scheduling Algorithms.**

The main objective based on these solutions is to reduce the idleness of computing and storage nodes (throttle resources), while switching off unused machines without jeopardizing Service Level Agreements. Some representative examples from each category are shown in Table 1.

Regarding **Workload Consolidation and Shut-down Techniques,** heuristics for energy-aware consolidation of jobs and maximization of resource utilization are presented in [117]. These approaches estimate resource consumption in terms of CPU utilized by tasks and encourage resources to execute multiple tasks in parallel. The proposal from [102] is an algorithm that search for a minimum multi-objective function, taking into account energy-consumption and running time by combining resource allocation and heuristic rules and simulating Directed Acyclic Graph (DAG) based workloads.

One of the most popular approaches to increase efficiency is to switch off idle servers [75,78], which is usually tested in dedicated simulation tools [74]. Several models, including games theory models [72,73], are used to balance opposite requirements in data centers, such as performance and energy consumption. Even models utilized for economic environments, such as Data Envelopment Analysis, are employed to analyze the efficiency in various realistic large-scale data centers and propose corrections to improve data-center efficiency [76].

In addition, techniques for energy conservation like **Virtual Machine (VM) Migration and Consolidation** are widely studied and already employed. In [35], a resource manager solution focused on virtualized data centers, which enables lower energy consumption by applying VM migrations and allocations based on current CPU usage, is proposed. An extension of VM migration is presented in [34] where Service Level Agreement (SLA) restrictions are considered. Allocation and migration of VMs is also the target in [159] where a Bayesian Belief network algorithm is presented. Moreover, a day/night pattern is taken into account for an energy manager in [148], based on the aggregation of traffic during low usage periods and shutting down idle machines.

Solutions for improving energy proportionality through **Data Replication and Placement**, are also available. A power-proportional distributed file system approach that tries to store data on non-overlapping subsets of machines is presented in [18]. Such subsets of machines contain only one copy of each file and administrators can decide how many subsets will be turned on to serve incoming requests. On the other hand, a division of the cluster in non-overlapped zones is proposed in [162], enabling operators to shut down zones. In a similar way, in [105] the authors present a variation of the Hadoop File System (HDFS) that divides the cluster in *Hot Zones* that store recent data and *Cold Zones* where low [e.g. spatial or temporal] popularity files are stored. Then a power off policy is applied to the *Cold Zones*. A non-uniform replica placement on data popularity is also presented in [125].

Energy-Aware Scheduling Algorithms is the last family of solutions. A green scheduling algorithm based on neural networks is proposed by [68], focusing on the prediction of workload demand with the purpose of applying power-off policies to idle servers. Experiments presented simulate a medium sized data center that runs homogeneous workload that is intended to respond to end-user requests. Energy-aware scheduling policies combined with Dynamic Voltage and Frequency Scaling (DVFS) is presented in [100]. In [77], a multi-objective scheduling algorithm is proposed, based on genetic algorithms, which takes into account energy efficiency, performance and security constraints.

We have classified the related word under consideration in terms of their final objective, including: (a) modelling, (b) simulation, (c) performance. Such classification is shown in Table 2.

Table 1. Related work summary

Ref [68]	Title: Performance evaluation of a green scheduling algorithm for energy savings in cloud computing	Savings ~ 45%
	Category:	Workload consolidation and power off policies (power off policy based on a neural network predictor)
	Evaluation:	[8-512] nodes cluster simulation
	Workload:	End user homogeneous requests that follow a day/night pattern
Ref [117]	Title: Energy efficient utilization of resources in cloud computing systems	Savings [5-30]%
	Category:	Workload consolidation and power off policies (energy-aware task consolidation heuristic based on different cost functions)
	Evaluation:	Simulation of a not stated size cluster
	Workload:	Synthetic workload in terms of number of tasks, inter arrival time and resource usage
Ref [148]	Title: Saving energy in data center infrastructures	Savings [20-70]%
	Category:	Workload consolidation and shut-down techniques (safety margin power-off policy)
	Evaluation:	100 and 5000 nodes cluster simulation
	Workload:	Synthetic workload that follows a day/night pattern
Ref [35]	Title: Energy efficient resource management in virtualized cloud data centers	Savings ~ 80%
	Category:	VM consolidation and migration
	Evaluation:	100 nodes cluster simulation using CloudSim
	Workload:	Synthetic workload that simulates services that fulfill the capacity of the cluster
Ref [102]	Title: dynamic energy-aware scheduling for parallel task-based application in cloud computing	Savings [20-30]%
	Category:	Energy-aware scheduling algorithms (polynomial-time and multi-objective scheduling algorithm for DAG jobs)
	Evaluation:	Experimentation on a 64 nodes cluster
	Workload:	Synthetic directed acyclic graph-based workload

4.2   Data Center Scheduling Frameworks

Resource managers have direct impact on the efficiency of the infrastructure since they are responsible for the application of energy-aware scheduling models. The responsibility for actually deciding resource negotiation and tasks deployment have range from traditional approaches to fully managed solutions such as data centers which are used by many entities with multiple users and various kind of applications and requirements [30, 38].

Table 2. Classification of approaches according to their objective. The green color represents that the work focuses strongly on that objective, and the red color represents opposite.

Reference	Modelling	Simulation	Performance
[101]	●	●	●
[103]	●	●	●
[118]	●	●	●
[34]	●	●	●
[36]	●	●	●
[160]	●	●	●
[149]	●	●	●
[69]	●	●	●
[18]	●	●	●
[106]	●	●	●
[126]	●	●	●
[163]	●	●	●

The constraints imposed by diverse applications in terms of size, inter-arrival and duration, may lead to various resource efficiency, latency rates and security levels.

Current trends aim to utilize the same hardware resources to deploy various kind of applications and frameworks with diverse requirements, which increases the complexity since diverse data are to be processed.

We present the main categories of the scheduling resource-managing models following several approaches and we show their limitations summarized in Table 3.

Monolithic models, where a centralized manager is responsible for all scheduling and resource managing decisions came first. Such models [96] are a good choice when the workload is composed of a relative low number of Batch jobs, due to these schedulers being omniscient [55], since such kind of workload does not usually have strict latency requirements [60]. Monolithic resource managers perform near-optimal scheduling operations [58,85,175] as they are able to completely examine the data center. This detailed inspection allows the determination in terms of performance implications and impact on shared resources. [83,128,133,158,173]. Due to this detailed cluster inspection, monolithic centralized schedulers usually utilize resources at a higher level than other approaches [168]. Monolithic centralized schedulers also achieve high-quality decisions which result in shorter makespans, near-optimal load balancing and predictable performance and availability [59,156,177].

Table 3. Cluster scheduling approaches.

Frameworks	Strategy	Optimal environment	Near-optimal environments
Paragon [58]	Centralized	Low number of long-running and non-latency sensitive jobs	Mid and high number of jobs
Quasar [59]	Monolithic		Mixed workloads
Borg [168]			
YARN [166]	Centralized Two-level	Mid number of diverse long-running, non latency sensitive jobs	Latency-sensitive workloads
Mesos [89]			
Omega [156]	Centralized Shared-state	Mid number of heterogeneous workloads	High number of short and latency-sensitive jobs
Canary [142]	Distributed	High number of short, non resource-demanding, latency-sensitive jobs	Long, resource-demanding jobs
Tarcil [60]			Mixed workloads
Sparrow [137]			
Mercury [103]	Hybrid	Mixed workloads composed of 90% of short, latency-sensitive jobs and 10% of long-running,resource-demanding jobs	Homogeneous workloads Other workloads patterns Evolving patterns
Hawk [57]			
Eagle [56]			

With the arrival of new computation paradigms such as microservices, current trends tend to divide jobs into smaller parts which usually are more latency-sensitive. This new scenario with huge amounts of small jobs overcome the capacity of Monolithic models. Two new centralized resource managing models were proposed to overcome this limitation by dividing the responsibility of resource managing and scheduling:

– Two-level resource managers, such as Mesos [89], and YARN [166] employ a central resource manager which coordinates a set of independent schedulers. The parallel schedulers pessimistically block the data center in order to make a scheduling decision. Such manager offers resource schedulers, and as a response, the set of schedulers perform scheduling decisions for deciding which machines will execute a particular task. The down side of this model is that, opposed to Monolithic models, the schedulers are not omniscient. In this model, data-center state and tasks requirements are not always available to make optimal scheduling decisions.
– Shared-state resource managers, such as Omega [156], employ a centralized manager which orchestrates a set of parallel scheduling agents. In contrast to Two-level resource managers, each scheduling agent makes scheduling decisions based on a partially out-of-date copy of the whole data-center state.

Instead of blocking the data center to apply their decisions, they follow a transactional approach. If a transaction ends up in a conflict, the data-center state is requested and the scheduling restarts.

However, all the aforementioned proposals suffer from a performance bottlenecks when huge latency-sensitive workloads composed of millions of tasks are under consideration, as they employ centralized coordinators for resource managing or even for resource managing as well as scheduling [137].

Distributed schedulers such as Sparrow and Canary [67,137,142,143] are built to work optimally when the aforementioned scenarios are considered. Distributed models employ faster and simpler algorithms in order to analyze smaller areas of the data center, which leads to sub-optimal decisions with higher throughput and lower latency rates.

The frameworks and applications served by data centers are constantly evolving. Current trends show that in most cases heterogeneous workloads are being deployed in large-scale realistic clusters [50,145]. Such workloads are composed by two main kinds of jobs: (a) Jobs such as web servers and data-center frameworks, which represent 10% of jobs. These jobs consume, however, more than 80% of computing resources because they run for long periods; and (b) Jobs such as MapReduce tasks, which represent 90% of jobs. These jobs run for shorter periods and consume less than 20% of computing resources [19,144,147,175]. In such environment, sub-optimal scheduling operations may severely impact on the aforementioned large jobs. Hence, distributed models may achieve worse results in terms of performance compared to those achieved by centralized models.

Finally, hybrid models, such as Hawk and Mercury [56,57,103] were developed to work well under the aforementioned scenario. These models employ centralized and distributed approaches in order to overcome the limitations discussed. Hybrid models use a centralized scheduler for long-running jobs to provide high-quality scheduling and, on the other hand, they employ a distributed approach for those short jobs which need quick scheduling to achieve latency goals.

Beyond workload consolidating and resource throttling, other research has explored the impact IT hardware refresh and optimization could have on data centre energy consumption [31]. Additionally, it was shown that addressing energy efficiency at the design stage of software systems presents a significant opportunity to reduce infrastructure energy consumption [32].

5   Content Diffusion Models for Social Data Streams

This section outlines the most predominant models for the depiction of the content/information diffusion process in a social network described in [108]. Most of the existent algorithmic solutions for content distribution are built on them, thus the assumption that content circulation over social data streams is depicted by one of them is of crucial importance for the suggested solutions. The main algorithmic problems studied in the bibliography are related with the discovery of nodes that are most prone to diffuse content to the greatest extent, and the categorization of nodes according to their influence degree. The categorization of the models is depicted in Fig. 4. The models presented are the most recent in the bibliography and there are no prior recent models to the best of our knowledge. The first-level discrimination of models is based on whether they take the structure of the network into consideration (*network-aware*) or not (*holistic*). In other words the discrimination criterion is if they incorporate knowledge about underlying associations of the nodes (edges) or, to the contrary, follow an aggregate-level approach.

Information Diffusion Models Classification. Li et al. in [120] classify information diffusion issues as a "3W issue", that is with regard to "What", "Why" and "Where". They consider "What" to refer to the question "what latent information is there to be found in social networks?" and they provide as an example the findings, such as the way that an individual's shopping habits relate to his/her profession, that can be included in a large volume of consumer data. Furthermore, their proposal considers "Why", to refer to the question "why has the information propagated in this way?" This question refers to the factors that have affected the diffusion result, for example the factors that have produced a particular social cascade. Finally in their view "Where", refers to the question "where will the information be diffused to in the future?". This question refers to the future diffusion path that will be followed. For example if two influential users receive the same information from a common contact in a social network, but have a different perspective on the information, then it is important to estimate how they will respond and whether they will propagate the information through the network.

Based on the "3W issue" they classify information diffusion models as predictive and explanatory. Explanatory models aim to discover answers to important questions concerning the information diffusion process, such the determination of the main factors that affect information diffusion and the most influential nodes in the network. Predictive models, on the other hand, are used to predict the future information diffusion process in social networks based on certain factors, for example the quality of information diffused.

In a similar manner Luu et al. in [126] classify information diffusion models in non-network and network diffusion models. The former refers to user communities without any knowledge about the user relationship network and the latter is more applicable to the social networks where user relationships networks are given (e.g. Facebook, blog networks). For each model category Luu et al. describe representative models, notable model extensions, as well as model applications. The surveyed applications include Influence Maximization and Contamination Minimization. Model extensions are asynchronous models that incorporate time delay factors into the basic models.

An important class of information diffusion models are inspired from natural and biological systems. A typical example is provided by Dewi and Kim [61], who propose a bio-inspired model for information diffusion in complex networks using ant colony optimization. The model introduces selfishness in forwarder nodes and unacquainted nodes and employs ant colony optimization to find shortest path and manage the selfish nodes and disjoined nodes. The authors provide simulation results in two types of networks: lattice networks and scale free networks, and the results show that the ant-colony model has higher performance and higher reachability than a selected baseline epidemic model.

Influence Maximization. Influence maximization is an important issue in social network analysis domain which concerns finding the most influential nodes in a social network. Determining the influential nodes is made with respect to information diffusion models and is based on the observation that most of the existing models only contain trust relationships. In this respect Hosseini-Pozveh et al. in [93] classify influence maximization models in two classes: cascade-based and threshold-based. They evaluate all models in comparison with selected benchmark models through two real data sets, the Epinions and Bitcoin OTC. Based on the evaluation results a main conclusion is drawn: when a distrusted user performs an action or adopts an opinion, the target users may tend not to do it.

The efficiency of influence maximization algorithms is subject to active research since the problem is known to be NP-hard. In this respect Kempe et al. proposed a greedy algorithm (referred to as SimpleGreedy) that guarantees 63% influence spread of its optimal solution [106]. Along this line Ko et al. in [113] propose an improved algorithm, termed Hybrid-IM, which by combines PBIM (Path Based Influence Maximization) and CB-IM (Community Based Influence Maximization). Ko et al. further provide evaluation results from extensive experiments with four real-world datasets. They show that Hybrid-IM achieves great improvement (up to 43 times) in performance over state-of-the-art methods and finds the seed set that provides the influence spread very close to that of the state-of-the-art methods.

5.1   Holistic View Models

Rogers' theory [150] is quantified by the Bass model [33]. The Bass model is based on the notion that "the probability of adopting by those who have not yet adopted is a linear function of those who had previously adopted" (F.Bass). It predicts the number of adopters $n(t) \in N$ of an innovation at time t (in the information diffusion scenario the number of retransmitters of an information piece):

$$n(t) = pM + (q - p)N(t) - q/M \left(N(t) \right)^2 \tag{1}$$

where N(t) is the cumulative number of adopters by time t, M is the potential market (the ultimate number of adopters), $p \in [0, 1]$ is the coefficient of innovation (the external influences, expressing the individuals influenced by the mass media), and q is the coefficient of imitation (internal influence, expressing the individuals influenced by the early adopters). This approach, however, largely ignores the underlying network structure.

Models under the same concept of holistic view of the social behaviour make use of differential equations, and include, among others, the "multi-step flow model" by Katz and Lazarsfeld [104], the Daley-Kendall rumours model [54], and also, more recent ones, such as, the Van den Bulte and Joshi model of influentials and imitators [47].

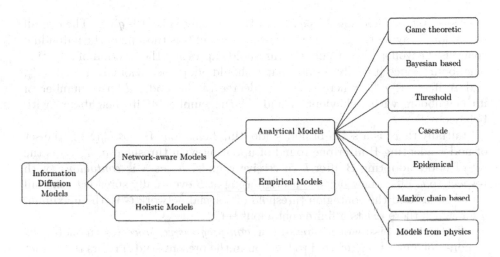

Fig. 4. Content/information diffusion models

5.2   Network-Aware Models

These include completely novel models, but also variations of the afore-mentioned (holistic) models, such as the Nekovee variation [136] of the Daley-Kendall model, and are separated in following categories, based on whether they are mathematically formulated (*Analytical models*) and then applied or are the outcome of empirical methods, such as regression, regression trees etc. (*Empirical models*).

Analytical Models. The first mathematical models based on nodes' thresholds for the depiction of information diffusion were developed by Schelling [157] and Granovetter [86]. A categorization of the most predominant models is presented.

Game-Theoretic Models. In [112], Kleinberg proposes a simple networked coordination games model. The author assumes that there are two behaviours a node $v \in V$ in the graph $G = (V, E)$ can follow, A and B. The model is based on the notion that for each individual the benefits of adopting a new behaviour increase as more of its neighbours adopt the new behaviour. At discrete time steps each node updates its choice of A or B according to the behaviour of its neighbours. The objective of the nodes is to switch each time to the behaviour that reaps the maximum benefit for them. For the nodes v and w there is a motivation for behaviour matching, expressed in the following way, where parameter q is a real number $0 < q < 1$:

– if v and w both choose behaviour A, they both receive a q payoff
– if v and w both choose behaviour B, they both receive a $1 - q$ payoff
– if v and w choose different behaviours, they both receive a 0 payoff

v's payoff for choosing A is qd_v^A and for choosing B is $(1 - q)d_v^B$. The overall payoff for v playing the game with its neighbours in G is the sum of the individual (pairwise) payoffs; q is actually the threshold expressing the fraction of adopting neighbours, since it easily results that v should adopt behaviour B if $d_v^B > qd_v$, and A if $d_v^B < qd_v$, where d_v is the degree of the node, d_v^A the number of its neighbours with behaviour A and d_v^B the number of its neighbours with behaviour B.

Initially there is a set S of nodes adopting behaviour B and $h_q(S)$ is the set of nodes adopting B after one round of updating with threshold q. $h_q^k(S)$ is the set of nodes adopting B after k successive rounds. A set S is *contagious* (with respect to h_q) if "a new behaviour originating at S eventually spreads to the full set of nodes"and the contagion threshold of a social network G is "the maximum q for which there exists a finite contagious set".

The technical issue of *progressive* or *non-progressive processes* (monotonous or non-monotonous as referred to later on in the present study) refers to the fact that when a node v following till then the behaviour A updates to behaviour B in time step t, it will be following B in all subsequent time steps. Although, intuitively, we would expect progressive processes to give finite contagious sets more easily (because of lack of early adopters setbacks that would hinder the cascade), Kleinberg points out that both the progressive and non-progressive models have the same contagion thresholds [131], which in both cases is at most $1/2$ ("a behaviour can't spread very far if it requires a strict majority of your friends to adopt it") [131].

More game-theoretic models can be found in the work of Arthur [22], who proposes a simple cascade model of sequential decisions with positive externalities, manifested by a term that adds to the payoff of a decision. Namely in the scenario of two competing products, the latter become more valuable as they are used by more users (for a social media site or a smartphone, for example, it will aquire better third-party applications and support as its users grow). Also game-theoretic models are introduced by Banerjee [29] and Bikhchandani et al. [39], that are based on influence not due to positive externalities, but because of information conveyed from earlier decisions. The proposed game-theoretic models, however, have the drawback of not taking heterogeneity into consideration, in the notion that all nodes have the same threshold, and all their neighbours contribute the same in making a node change its behaviour.

Bayes-Based Models. Combining nodes' private information and their observations of earlier adoptions, in [69], Kleinberg and Easley present a Bayes based model to formulate information cascades, answering questions such as "What is the probability this is the best restaurant given the reviews I have read and the crowds I see there?".

$$Pr\left[A|B\right] = \frac{Pr\left[A\right]Pr\left[B|A\right]}{Pr\left[B\right]} \qquad (2)$$

Three factors are taken into consideration:

- The states of the world;
- Payoffs; and
- Signals.

The first factor expresses whether an option is good or bad (if a new restaurant is a good or a bad choice). Supposing that the two options of the world are K (the option is a good idea) and B (the option is a bad idea), the world is placed in K with probability p and in B with probability $1 - p$ ($Pr\left[K\right] = p$, $Pr\left[B\right] = 1 - Pr\left[K\right] = 1 - p$). Payoffs for a node v are defined as follows:

- If v rejects the option, the payoff is 0.
- If v adopts a good idea, it receives a positive $v_g > 0$ payoff.
- If v adopts a bad idea, it receives a negative $v_b > 0$ payoff.
- If v adopts without any prior knowledge, the payoff is 0.

The signals refer to private information each individual gets about the benefit or not of a decision: a high signal (H) suggests that adoption is a good idea, whereas a low signal (L) suggests that it is a bad idea. If accepting is indeed a good idea, then $Pr\left[H|K\right] = q > \frac{1}{2}$ and $Pr\left[H|K\right] = 1 - q < \frac{1}{2}$. In the restaurant example the private information could be a review that an individual reads about the first restaurant, with a high signal corresponding to a review comparing it favorably to restaurant B. If choosing the first restaurant is indeed good, there should be a higher number of such reviews, so $Pr\left[H|K\right] = q > \frac{1}{2}$. Kleinberg and Easley [69] consider how individual decisions are made using (Eq. 2) when they get a sequence of independently generated signals consisting of a number of high signals and a number of low signals, thus making interesting observations about situations where individuals can observe others' earlier decision, but do not have access to their knowledge.

The basic propagation models on which most generalizations for information diffusion are based are the Linear Threshold Model (LTM) [86,157,171] and the Independent Cascade Model (ICM) [82] with many proposed extensions (LTM: [106,171], ICM: [82,87,106]) and also a proposed unification [106].

Linear Threshold Model. Based on the assumption that some node can be either active (adopts a new idea/transmits a piece of information) or inactive and taking into account the monotonicity assumption, namely that nodes can turn from inactive to active with the pass of time but not the opposite, we can say that the LTM is based on the following notion: Each node v has a predefined activation threshold $\theta_v \in [0,1]$, which expresses how difficult it is for the node to be influenced when its neighbors are active ("the weighted fraction of the

neighbors of node that must become active in order for node to become active"),
and is influenced by each one of its neighbors w according to a weight b_{vw},
so that $\sum_{w \in \Gamma(v)} b_{vw} \leq 1$. The thresholds can be produced randomly with a
uniform distribution, but some approaches investigate a uniform threshold for
all the nodes of the network, e.g. [37]. The process takes place in discrete steps
and the nodes that satisfy the constraint $\sum_{w \in \Gamma(v)} b_{vw} > \theta_v$ are gradually added
as active to the initial set of nodes. It's worth mentioning that LTM can result
as a modification of the networked coordinations game referred in the previous
paragraph with the differentiation of payoffs for different pairs of nodes.

LTM expresses the idea that the influence of the neighbours of a node is
additive, but when the rule of influence can not be expressed by a simple weighed
sum, for example a node becomes active when one of its acquaintances and two
of its co-workers do so, the arbitrary function g_v substitutes the weighed sum.
In the *General Threshold Model* for time steps $t = 1, 2, 3...$ a node v becomes
active if the set of active neighbours at t satisfy $g_v(X) > \theta_v$.

Independent Cascade Model. Under the ICM model [82], there is also a set
of initially active nodes, the process takes place in discrete steps, but when
node v becomes active, it has only one chance of activating each of its inactive
neighbors w until the end of the process with a probability p_{vw} independent of
the activations history and with an arbitrary order.

Exact evaluation of activation probabilities is exponential to the number of
edges of the graph. Improving the performance of the works in [86] and [160],
there are works studying the calculation of these probabilities such as [84] (based
on a General Threshold Model with the assumption that each parent's influence
is fixed), or [64] (based on the ICM). In the latter, sampling from the twitter
dataset is conducted in an efficient Markov-Chain Monte Carlo fashion using
the Metropolis-Hastings algorithm [51] and the problem is tackled with two
differentiations, one of which considering the past paths of data known (retweets
for the twitter dataset) and one considering only the past path endpoints known
(hashtags and urls) and joint probabilities are taken into consideration, reflecting
also model uncertainty.

Epidemical Models. In the case of epidemical models a single activated
("infected") node causes the change of state of a neighbour susceptible node,
whereas in the afore-mentioned threshold and game-theoretic models a node has
to interact with multiple neighbour nodes to evolve (complex contagion).

Epidemical models were introduced on the assumption that information
would propagate like diseases. They constitute another category with an almost
straightforward pairing with the ICM. The ICM captures the notion of contagion
more directly, and also allows us to incorporate the idea that a node's receptive-
ness to influence does not depend on the past history of interactions with its
neighbors.

Epidemical models variations include the simple branching processes model,
where a node infects a number of nodes and the contagion proceeds in subsequent
waves with a probability π. This model is characterized by the basic reproductive

number of the disease $R_0 = k\pi$, where k is the number of new people somebody meets, which expresses the anticipated number of new cases of the disease that a single node will cause.

Extensions of the epidemical models are the SIR, SIS, and SIRS models: S stands for susceptible nodes, nodes that have not been infected yet and have no immunity to the contagion. I stands for infected nodes, nodes contagious to their susceptible neighbours, and R stands for recovered nodes, with the recovery considered as permanent in SIR and temporary in the case of SIRS [114]. The sequence of the letters in the acronyms of the models explains the flow of the epidemic. In SIR model nodes pass from the state of being susceptible to the state of being infected and then recover. In SIS model nodes are immediately susceptible once they have recovered (like in the case of common cold, recovery does not imply immunity that lasts for long). In the SIRS model recovered nodes free of infection may rejoin the susceptible nodes.

Markov Chain Models. Markov chains [65] are used to describe transitions from one state of a system to another in a finite set of possible states. Their memoryless nature (*Markov property*) has to do with the fact that the next state each time is independent of the preceding states. More formally: With a set of states $\{\xi_1, \xi_2, .., \xi_r\}$ the process moves successively from one state to another in so-called *steps*, and specifically from state ξ_i to state ξ_j with a probability p_{ij} (*transition probability*) independent of the previous states of the chains, or remains in the same state with a probability p_{ii}. A particular state is picked from Ξ as the initial state. Markov chains are usually depicted with a directed graph, where the edges' labels denote the transition probabilities.

Markov models are widely used for analysing the web navigation of users. PageRank [45] is based on a Markov model and is used for ranking of information in the World Wide Web. By assigning weights that denote the relative importance of an hyperlinked document in a set of documents, the likelihood that a person will reach a specific page through random clicks is, essentially, represented.

In [160], Song et al. use a Continuous-Time Markov Chain Model (CTMC), namely a Markov model that describes the transition among states after some time of stay in a particular state. This time is exponentially distributed and does not affect the transition probability to the next state. The information diffusion model is introduced on a network $G(V, w, \tau)$. G contains a set V of n nodes and E edges between nodes representing the information diffusion paths. w denotes the set of the edges' weights ("amount of information to flow from one node to another") and τ the set of the time delay on the information diffusion paths. Thus, the representation of the graph matches the CTMC in the notion that each node represents a state, each weight a transition probability and the delay is represented as the time-to-stay in each state.

Voter Model. The basic voter model introduced by Clifford and Sudbury [52] and Holley and Liggett [91], is defined in an undirected network and allows the spread of two opinions. In discrete time steps, a node adopts the opinion of a randomly chosen neighbour. For a node $v \in V$ in graph $G = (V, E)$, $\Gamma(v)$ is the set of neighbors of v in G and initially the nodes are arbitrarily endowed with a 0/1 state. At time step t each node adopts the opinion of one uniformly picked neighbour. With an initial assignment $f_0 : V \to \{0, 1\}$ inductively we define

$$f_{t+1}(v) = \begin{cases} 1, with\ probability\ a \\ 0, with\ probability\ b \end{cases} \tag{3}$$

where $a = \frac{|\{u \in \Gamma(v) : f_t(u) = 1\}|}{|\Gamma(v)|}$ and $b = \frac{|\{u \in \Gamma(v) : f_t(u) = 0\}|}{|\Gamma(v)|}$.

Even-Dar and Shapira [70] argue that it is one of the most natural probabilistic models to capture the information diffusion in a social network. It is suitable for depicting the spread of a technological product, as it is proved that under this model consensus is reached with probability 1. Even-Dar and Shapira refer to the (almost) consensus of products such as Google as a search engine, YouTube as a video-sharing website etc.

Models from Physics. Models from physics include the Ising model [97] serving for the description of magnetic systems, and bootstrap percolation [16] serving for the description of magnetic systems, neuronal activity, glassy dynamics, etc.

The Ising model [97] was first proposed in statistical physics and encompasses the notion of a ground state (in physics the state with the minimum energy), and that of the "self-optimizing" nature of the network.

Similarly to the basic voter model, there can be two competing "opinions", in favour of or against a subject, let's say depicted by a "+1" and a "−1", which in physics express the correspondence of an atom forming a network to a spin variable (can be considered as the basic unit of magnetization) state $\sigma_i = \pm 1$. The total energy of the system under this model (Hamiltonian) is defined as:

$$H = H(\sigma) = -\sum_{<i,j>} E\sigma_i\sigma_j - \sum_i J\sigma_i \tag{4}$$

for each configuration $\sigma = (\sigma_1, ..., \sigma_N)$, with the parameter J associated with an "external magnetic field" and E with the "nearest-neighbours interaction", N the number of the atoms. The ground state is the lowest energy configuration s_g (in physics the zero temperature configuration), so that $s_g \in argmin_s H(s)$. In a social network can be seen as the state with the most likely opinion, minimizing conflicts among its members (atoms).

In the standard bootstrap percolation process [16] a node is initially either active with a given probability f or inactive. It becomes active if k ($k = 2, 3, ...$) of its nearest neighbors are active. In that notion it resembles the k-core problem of random graphs [124], where k-core is the maximal subgraph within which all vertices have at least k neighbors, but whereas bootstrap percolation starts from a subset of seed vertices according to the above-mentioned activation rule, the k-core of the network can be found by a subsequent pruning of vertices which have less than k neighbors.

Empirical Models. Before the advent of machine-readable traces, the potential of networks in the transmission of information and messages was stated already by Milgram in his renowned experiment [130] or Christakis [79], who suggested in a study of 12000 participants that risks, such as the risk of becoming obese or benefits, such as stopping of smoking, are propagated through social ties. However, it is large scale and time-resolved machine-readable traces that, through the step-by-step track of interactions in OSNs (although not compulsorily easily accessible/collectible), have driven to the formulation of a plethora of empirical models.

Some generic observations concerning the empirical models are the following. Many of them lack insight of information content, unlike works, such as that of Huberman et al. [24], who formulate a model taking into consideration solely the features of an information item (a news item in Twitter). Sometimes the discovered patterns in empirical models are at odds with the predictions based on theoretical (analytical) models. For example, in unison with the epidemical model, Leskovec et al. in [119] claim that cascades (depicting the blogosphere information diffusion) are mostly tree-like. More specifically, they notice that the number of edges in the cascade increases almost linearly with the number of nodes, suggesting that the average degree in the cascade remains constant as the cascade grows (a trees property). Moreover, Leskovec et al. claim that these trees are balanced, as they notice that the cascade diameter increases logarithmically with the size of the cascade. In contradiction to the above, the trees derived from the chain-letter diffusion model of Liben Nowell and Kleinberg in [121] are inconsistent with the epidemic model, as they are very narrow and deep, with the majority of their nodes having one child and a median distance from their root to the their leaves being of hundreds steps.

Precisely, in [121] the spread of a chain-letter is represented by a tree. Copies of the chain-letter represent paths through the tree, the root represents the originator and the leaves represent the recipients of a message (w is a child of v if w appends its name in the copy of the letter directly below v). In order to produce trees with the characteristics mentioned in the previous paragraph, the probabilistic model suggested (i) incorporates asynchrony: after receiving a message, each recipient waits for a time t before acting on it, and if it receives more copies of the item in this time interval, it acts upon only one of them, and (ii) encompasses a back-rate β, as a node can either forward the message to its neighbours with probability $1 - \beta$ or group-reply to his corecipients with a probability β.

In [27], Bakshy et al. attempt to model the information diffusion in Twitter with the use of regression trees. Twitter is convenient for information diffusion modeling, since it is explicitly diffusion-oriented: users subscribe to the content of other users. The retweet feature, moreover, helps in the acknowledgement (though does not guarantee it) of reposts. Seeders are users posting original (not retweeted) content and reposting instead of the conventional retweeting (RT @username) is taken into account. Influence is measured in terms of the size of the whole diffusion tree created, and not just the plain number of explicit retweets. The three different cases studied ascribe the influence to the first one having posted a link, the most recent one or follow a hybrid approach.

As far as the seed users are concerned, the predictors used include: the number of followers, number of friends, number of tweets and date of joining, and regarding the past influence of seed users: the average, minimum and maximum total influence and average, minimum and maximum local influence (local refers to the average number of reposts by a user's immediate friends over a period of one month and total to the average total cascade size over that period).

Bakshy et al. [27] come to the conclusion that although large cascades have in their majority previously successful individuals with many followers as initiators, individuals with these characteristics are not necessarily bound to start a large cascade. Thus, because of the fact that estimations cannot be made at an individual level, marketers should rely on the average performance. By studying the return on investment, on the whole, with a cost function of the number of followers per individual i: $c_i = ac_f + f_i c_f$, where a is acquisition cost c_f cost per follower and f_i is the number of followers, they conclude that relatively ordinary users of average influence and connectivity are most cost-efficient.

Content-related features are, also, according to Bakshy et al. not expected to discriminate initiators of large cascades from non-successful ones, due to the large number of non-successes. In order to take content into account, the regression analysis is repeated encompassing the following features: rated interestingness, perceived interestingness to an average person, rated positive feeling, willingness to share via email, IM, Twitter, Facebook or Digg, some indicator variables for type of URL, and some indicator variables for category of content.

Moreover, Lerman et al. [118] claim that exploiting the proximity of users in the social graph can serve as an adding-value factor for the prediction of information diffusion. They discriminate proximity as coming from conservative or non-conservative processes (denoting that the amount of spread information in the network remains or not constant, respectively). For the case the underlying network is not fully known [132], Najar et al. focus on predicting the final activation state of the network when an initial activation is given. They find the correspondence between the initial and final states of the network without considering the intermediate states. Their work is based on the analogy between predictive and generative approaches for discrimination or regression problems (predictive models depicting a better performance, when the real data distribution can't be captured).

In [174], Yang and Leskovec use a time series model for modeling the global influence of a node through the whole network. For each node u, an influence function $I_u(l)$ is the number of mentions of an information l time units after the node u adopted the information (at t_u), and with $V(t)$ being the number of nodes that mention the information at time t, it applies:

$$V(t+1) = \sum_{u \in \in A(t)} I_u(t - t_u) \tag{5}$$

where A(t) are the nodes that got activated before t, $t_u \leq t$. For the modeling of the influence functions a non-parametric formulation followed allows greater accuracy and deviation, as no assumptions are made.

A study of the social news aggregator Digg [66] crawling data from the site, story, user and social network perspective, suggests the presence of previously unconsidered factors for the steering of information spread in OSNs. Doerr et al. suggest, that, beyond the bare OSN topology two factors matter: the temporal alignment between user activities (i.e. whether users are visiting the site in the same narrow time window) and a hidden logical layer of interaction patterns occurring in their majority outside the social graph.

In the direction of studying the information diffusion as social graphs evolve, Ren et al. [146] study the evolution steps for shortest paths between two nodes, (so that they can ascribe them to a disjoint path, a short-circuiting bridge or a new friend between them), and furthermore, metrics such as closeness centrality, and global metrics, like the graph diameter, across snapshots of gradually evolving graphs. To this end, they adopt an efficient algorithm and an efficient storage scheme.

Firstly, they cluster (in an incremental procedure not requiring all snapshots to be present in memory) successive graphs exploiting their many resemblances (daily snapshots). As $G_\cup$ and $G_\cap$ essentially "bound" the graphs in the cluster, with $G_\cap$ being the intersection (the largest common subgraph) of all snapshots in cluster C, and $G_\cup$ the union (the smallest common supergraph) of all snapshots in C, grouping of snapshots into clusters can be based in the idea of the graph edit similarity between these two graphs ($G_\cup$, $G_\cap$). The graph edit similarity to capture the similarity requirement of a cluster is defined as:

$$ges(G_a, G_b) = \frac{2 \mid E(G_a \cap G_b) \mid}{\mid E(G_a) \mid + \mid E(G_b) \mid} \tag{6}$$

Secondly, they exploit the idea that, denoting the shortest-path between the vertices v and u, by $\tilde{P}_*(u, v)$ in a graph G_*, where $* = 1, 2, ..., n, \cap, \cup$, the solution can easily be found by the intersection or union (two graphs) of graphs in the cluster, or be "fixed" using these two graphs, and they propose a "finding-verifying-fixing framework".

As far as the storage schemes variations are concerned, for a cluster of snapshots $C = G_1, ..., G_k$ the deltas $\Delta(G_i, G_\cap), \forall 1 \leq i \leq k$ consist a small fraction of the snapshot, and their size depends on the threshold value used for clusters' similarity. The penalty of decompression overheads needed is surpassed by savings in I/O. Variations of the storage schemes include the following:

$$SM1(C) = \{G_\cap, \Delta(G_\cup, G_\cap), \Delta(G_i, G_\cap) | 1 \leq i \leq k\} \tag{7}$$

$$SM2(C) = \{G_\cap, \Delta(G_\cup, G_\cap), \Delta(G_1, G_\cap), \mathcal{D}(G_i, G_{i-1}) | 2 \leq i \leq k\} \tag{8}$$

$$SM\_FVF(C) = \{\mathcal{D}(G_\cap, G_{p\cap}), \Delta(G_\cup, G_\cap), \Delta(G_1, G_\cap), \mathcal{D}(G_i, G_{i-1}) | 2 \leq i \leq k\} \tag{9}$$

In (7) the authors consider only the edge sets of $\Delta(G_i, G_\cap)$ and $G_\cap$ to execute their algorithms on a snapshot G_i and the snapshots, G_i's, of the cluster need not be explicitly stored. For further compression of data of an evolving graph sequence similarity of successive snapshots is exploited: In (8) $\mathcal{D}(G_i, G_{i-1}) =$

(E_i^+, E_i^-), where $E_i^+ = E(G_i) - E(G_{i-1})$ and $E_i^- = E(G_{i-1}) - E(G_i)$ are the changes made to snapshot G_{i-1} to obtain the next snapshot Gi. Authors observe that the size of the set of edge changes $D(Gi, Gi-1)$ is on average just $1/10$ the size of $\Delta(G_i, G_\cap)$. Hence, representing an EGS in terms of the D's is much more space efficient than in term of the Δ's. Further compression can be achieved by exploiting inter-cluster redundancy (9).

6   Distribution of Social Data Streams

6.1   Content Distribution for Social Data Streams

This subsection provides a description of architectures, systems and techniques [108] for the distribution of social data content.

Architectures. In [99], Jacobson et al. introduce Content Centric Networking (CCN), noting that network use has evolved to be dominated by content distribution and retrieval. CCN has no notion of host at its lowest level - a packet "address" names content, not location, while simultaneously preserving the design decisions that make TCP/IP simple, robust and scalable. Content is treated as a primitive, and with new approaches, Jacobson et al. simultaneously achieve scalability and performance.

To share resources within the context of a social network with the use of the cloud business model, Chard et al. in [49] propose the SocialCloud architecture. Users register in cloud services (computational capacity, photo storage etc.), and their friends can consume and provide these services through a Facebook application. The allocation of resources (trading or reciprocal use between friends) is conducted by an underlying market infrastructure, whereas the Social Cloud application passes a SLA to the service. The advertisement of the service, so that it can be included in the market is done with XML based metadata stored in Globus Monitoring and Discovery System (MDS).

An interesting approach [116] applicable to the realm of content delivery is based on an architecture which combines global learning and local caches with small population. It is shown that age-based thresholds can timely exploit time-varying popularities to improve caching performance. Moreover, the caching efficiency is maximized by a combination of global learning and clustering of access locations, accompanied by score mechanisms to help with practical issues at local caches. Practical considerations include, though, the size of the content that circulates over OSN and the long-tail effect, since the goal of the authors is first to learn a good estimate at the global point and then feed it back to the local caches in the form of content scores, thus, making the approach possibly prohibitive for OSN-aware content delivery.

Systems. In Buzztraq [151], Sastry et al. build a prototype system that takes advantage of the knowledge of the users' friends' location and number, to generate hints for the placement of replicas closer to future accesses. Comparing their strategy with location based placement, which instead uses the geographical location of recent users, they find substantial decrease of cost, when requests as part of cascades are more than random accesses of content. Furthermore, their system reacts faster when there is a new region shift, since it starts counting friends of previous users in a new region, even before a request comes from that region. The key concept of Buzztraq is to place replicas of items already posted by a user closer to the locations of friends, anticipating future requests. The intuition is that social cascades are rapidly spread through populations as social epidemics. The experimental results indicated that social cascade prediction can lower the cost of user access compared to simple location-based placement. Buzztrack is a simple system that only provides hints as to where to place objects. Other more complex constraints that the present work covers, such as server bandwidth and storage, are not taken into account. Moreover, social cascade is indirectly analyzed because there has to be a third-party page where users connect to view the videos and have access to their social profile.

In the direction of distributing long-tailed content while lowering bandwidth costs and improving QoS, although without considering storage constraints, Traverso et al. in [165] exploit the time differences between sites and the access patterns that users follow. Rather than naively pushing UGC immediately, which may not be consumed and contribute unnecessarily to a traffic spike in the upload link, the system can follow a pull-based approach, where the first friend of a user in a Point of Presence (PoP) asks for the content. Moreover, rather than pushing content as soon as a user uploads, content can be pushed at the local time that is off-peak for the uplink and be downloaded in a subsequent time bin, also off-peak for the downlink. The larger the difference is between the content production bin and the bin in which the content is likely to be read, the better is the performance of the system.

In [153], Scellato et al. study how Twitter can be used to examine social cascades of UGC from YouTube and discover popular objects for replication. They improve the temporary caching policy by placing content after accounting for the distance between users. For the model CDN system constructed and tested, Scellato et al. used the Limelight network properties with 19 clusters of servers worldwide. To test the system, two different video weights were used: geosocial, in which node locality values are calculated from all the users that have posted a message about the item (even without being involved in a cascade), and geocascade, in which node locality values are calculated from the users participating in the item's social cascade. It was shown that the model improved performance against a no weight policy, with geocascade weight performing better.

Techniques. The introduction of concrete, unified metrics for the characterization of the extent of the social dissemination (local or global cascades phenomena) is an open issue. A systematic incorporation of this quantified knowledge into the existent underlying content delivery infrastructure would be salutary for proactive steps towards the improvement of user experience.

Furthermore, novel techniques aim to incorporate the information extracted from OSNs in the way that users share content and in how the content ultimately reaches the users. Some of these works use the information directly from OSNs, whereas others use such information indirectly. The research goals vary: the decision for copying content, improvement of policy for temporary caching, etc.

Zhou et al. [178] leverage the connection between content exchange and geographic locality (using a Facebook dataset they identify significant geographic locality not only concerning the connections in the social graph, but also the exchange of content) and the observation that an important fraction of content is "created at the edge" (*is user-generated*), with a web based scheme for caching using the access patterns of friends. Content exchange is kept within the same Internet Service Provider (ISP) with a drop-in component, that can be deployed by existing web browsers and is independent of the type of content exchanged. Browsing users online are protected with k-anonymity, where k is the number of users connected to the same proxy and are able to view the content.

In [92], Hoque and Gupta propose a technique with a logical addressing scheme for putting together in the disk blocks containing data from friends. The large scale of OSNs and the predominant tail effect do not allow use of techniques such as those used in multimedia file systems or web servers, where items are globally popular, and, techniques keeping related blocks together tracking the access pattern of blocks, respectively. To this purpose, in [92] the social graph is divided into communities. The organization of blocks in the disk is conducted with a greedy heuristic that finds a layout for the users within the communities and organizes the different communities on the disk by considering inter-community tie strength. The system is implemented on top of the Neo4j graph database as a layout manager.

Instead of optimizing the performance of UGC services exploiting spatial and temporal locality in access patterns, Huguenin et al., in [95], show on a large (more than 650,000 videos) YouTube dataset that content locality (induced by the related videos feature) and geographic locality are in fact correlated. More specifically, they show how the geographic view distribution of a video can be inferred to a large extent from that of its related videos, proposing a UGC storage system that proactively places videos close to the expected requests. Such an approach could be extended with the leverage of information from OSNs.

Kilanioti et al. in [109–111] propose miscellaneous policies for dynamic OSN-aware content delivery over a content delivery simulation framework. The authors propose policies that take patterns of user activity over OSNs and exploit geo-social properties of users participating in social cascades, proceed to incorporate various caching schemes of the underlying infrastructure, different policies for the handling of OSN data and various approaches that take into account the efficient timing of prefetching. Given an efficient placement of surrogate servers with maximum performance and minimum infrastructure cost, they apply contextual features of the user as heuristics to find the best content diffusion placement, either in a global or in a local scale, i.e., which content will be copied in the surrogate servers and to what extent, not overlooking memory, time and computational cost. Moreover they study temporal aspects of diffusion, related to the most efficient timing of the content placement. The simulation framework they introduce can serve as the basis of further parameterized content delivery experimentation that exploits information transmission over OSNs and decreases replication costs by selectively copying items to locations where items are likely to be consumed.

In terms of performance, Kilanioti et al. note a significant improvement over the respective improvement (39.43% only for the plain Social Prefetcher approach [107], up to 42.32% for selected caching mechanisms, compared to 30% in [165]) performing better than existent pull-based methods employed by most CDNs, even though these methods additionally overlook storage issues of the distributed infrastructure.

Last but not least, of more concurrent cascades happening it would be interesting to know which of them will evolve as global and which of them will evolve as local, possibly making some associations with their content or context features. It is challenging to discover contextual associations among the topics, which are by nature implicit in the user-generated content exchanged over OSNs and spread via social cascades. In other words it would be useful to derive semantic relations. This way the identification of a popular topic can be conducted in a higher, more abstract level with the augmentation of a semantic annotation. While the topic of a single information disseminated through an OSN can be explicitly identified, it is not trivial to identify reliable and effective models for the adoption of topics as time evolves [80,123] characterized with some useful emergent semantics. Therefore efficient semantic annotation can be seen as a solution for the challenge of characterization of the extent of the social dissemination.

6.2   Content Distribution in 5G Environments and Technologies

Content became the main information item exchanged between different actors in the Internet. Video and multimedia content counts for 80–90% of the total global traffic. Rich multimedia content lead to rapid mobile traffic growth that current mobile radio network, mobile backhaul, the capacity of the wireless link and mobile core network cannot support. 5G could overcome these bottlenecks introducing high increasing ratio of mobility communications and strong orientation towards content-related services and applications for content delivery over wireless technology, high throughput, low data delivery latency, and high scalability enabling huge number of devices [17].

Environment. 5G represents the 5th generation network of mobile systems which opens new possibilities, increase radio link capacity and brings plenty of new trends such as [17,122]: heterogeneous networks (HetNets); new use cases based on connections and communications between device to device, massive Machine-Type Communications, and Internet of Things (IoT); evolution of radio access technologies; cloudification throughout SDN and network function virtualization (NFV) paradigms; flexible spectrum management; cell densification; etc.

NFV and SDN capabilities in 5G systems are expected to enable network programmability. Content delivery could be affected by 5G cloudification through different SDN/NFV paradigms [122]. Programmable network control and the virtualization of all the RAN elements into virtual appliances by flexible NFV management are included within 5G networks. This enable content focused resources allocation. Agile design of new network functions and their control are possible. Network providers could extend network with new function that includes custom designed information, such as services that can offer to the online media service providers. The collaboration between the network provider and the online media service provider by means of the edge cache could be enabled by media delivery solutions designed for 5G. The control of the network will be kept by the network provider. The network provider would give only the relevant information for the online media service provider, while the online media service provider will keep the control of the delivery process and decide whether the cache shall be used, what and how information or resources are cached [3].

Technologies. New technologies such as LTE-A, LTE-U, WiFi and ZigBee, SDN and NFV rapidly change networks and services and lead to changes to content delivery. For example, mobile video will generate more than 69% of mobile data traffic by 2019 [2]. It is expected to witness an increase to 75% by 2021, which is much greater from 46% in 2016 on the share of smart devices and connections, while the amount of traffic offloaded from 4G was 63% at the end of 2016, and it will be 66% percent by 2021 [2].It is also expected to witness higher offload rates when the 5G network arrives. The main challenges in a wireless or mobile environment that have impact on content delivery services are reflected to the limited spectrum and bandwidth in wireless, heterogeneous networks, wireless link characteristics that are dependent on location and time, radio congestion, handoff issues, etc.

5G Use Cases. Future 5G developments is dependent on service providers, technology enablers and customers. All these actors are directly involved in decisions which use cases to pursue first, as well what technology is needed for the use cases. The 5G standards development process is also dependent on decisions which use cases first to deploy. All these ongoing developments will directly affect content delivery mechanisms, models and systems architectures. The main 5G use cases currently are reflected to [3]:

1. Gigabit broadband to home, related to deliver streams rated from 100 Mbit/sec to 1 Gbit/sec, which are needed to deliver television with higher resolution than 4K, virtual and augmented reality. Specific applications require special network configuration, for example in order to minimize latency in virtual reality applications.
2. Next generation mobile user experience.
3. Future corporate networks, addressed to better service providing, which require operators to dynamically manage network and to use software defined networking and network function virtualization.

4. Digital industrial ecosystems include agriculture, smart cities and healthcare applications, which imply network configurations that every industry participant can benefit from.
5. Infrastructure as a service approach is for service providers that lack the resources to invest in nationwide 5G coverage.

5G Solutions and Approaches. The demand for high-speed data applications has been on the rise in the recent decade, which led to the development of 5G. Development of efficient mechanisms for supporting mobile multimedia and data services is prerequisite for 5G networks. The real bottleneck of todays' mobile networks is access radio network and the backhaul. Caching in the intermediate nodes, servers, gateways, routers, and mobile users' devices can reduce doubled transmission from content providers and core mobile networks.

Known caching techniques that can be used within 5G are: content distribution network, information-centric networks, content-centric networking, http web caching, evolved packet core caching, radio access network caching, device to device caching, proactive caching, predictive caching, cooperative caching [23]. Those techniques are using different algorithms and models. Analysis presented in [23] showed that the deployment of those caching techniques in mobile network can reduce redundant traffic in backhaul, minimize the traffic load, increase the transfer rate in mobile network and reduce the latency. Correlation of several caching methods and procedures could result in improving network performance and obtaining better results.

5G brings complex heterogeneity of the network with different technologies that coexist, where some technologies could totally disable transmission of data of equipment that use other technologies. Solutions that efficiently handles resources in space, frequency, and device dimensions are needed. One possible efficient solution is semantic coordination in such networks is given in [135, 164].

The nodes in the system can communicate and share knowledge of their perspective of the spectrum utilization in the network. In [164] authors proposed to model the spectrum usage coordination as an interactive process between a number of distributed communicating agents, where agents share their specific information and knowledge. The information includes the current spectrum usage state, spatial coordinates of the device, available communication protocols, usage policy, spectrum sensing capabilities of the device, spectrum needs, etc. Approach for such coordination presented in [164] is based on semantic technologies, and harmonize communication between heterogeneous agents with potentially different capabilities with a minimal common compliance. The core knowledge is represented by ontologies whose representation and usage is specified in a standardized way. This semantic technologies-based approach can be used for a wide spectrum of problems within 5G heterogeneous networks, such as network states predictions, network analysis, minimizing traffic load, content distribution coordination etc. This approach could be used in combination with caching techniques in order to improve content distribution in 5G, but further research should be carried out in this area.

7   Conclusions

This article describes the results of the collaborative work performed as part of High-Performance Modelling and Simulation for Big Data Applications (cHiPSet) COST Action 1406. The presented case study focused on multimedia big data from entertainment and social media, medical images, consumer images, voice and video, that drives research and development of related technologies and applications and is steadily becoming a valuable source of information and insights [109–111], [108]. In fact, this work describes the general landscape and how our approach fits in the general ecosystem. Multimedia content providers such as YouTube strive to efficiently deliver multimedia big data to a large amount of users over the Internet, with currently more than 300 h of video content being uploaded to the site every minute. Traditionally, these content providers often rely on social data content distribution infrastructures. However, some measurement studies depict that a significantly large proportion of HTTP traffic results from bandwidth-intensive multimedia content circulating through OSNs. Consequently the user activity extracted from OSNs can be exploited to reduce the bandwidth usage. By incorporating patterns of information transmission over OSNs into a simulated content distribution infrastructure, the performance of content distribution mechanisms can be remarkably improved.

CDN services are increasingly being used to enable the delivery of bandwidth-demanding large media data to end-users of multimedia content providers and extend the capabilities of the Internet by deploying massively distributed infrastructures to accelerate content delivery. Next generation CDNs are being leveraged in an array of ways to overcome the challenges of providing a seamless customer experience across multiple devices with varying connectivity and corresponding to the call for enterprise application delivery. They have to go beyond efficient resource discovery and retrieval tasks of the established CDNs and support refined mechanisms for data placement, replication and distribution for a large variety of resource types and media formats. OSNs on the other hand create a potentially transformational change in user navigation and from this angle the rapid proliferation of OSNs sites is expected to reshape the architecture and design of CDNs. The challenges and opportunities highlighted in the interdisciplinary field of OSN-aware content delivery are bound to foster some interesting future developments, including innovative cache replacement strategies as a product of the systematic research of temporal, structural and geographical properties of social cascades.

Particularly today that HTTP traffic ascribed to media circulating over OSNs has grown, an OSN-awareness mechanism over content distribution schemes has become essential. This mechanism aims to exploit patterns of social interactions of the users to reduce the load on the origin server, the traffic on the Internet, and ultimately improve the user experience. By addressing the issue of which content will be copied in the surrogate servers of a CDN, it ensures a near-optimal content diffusion placement. At the same time, it moderates the impact on bandwidth that the Big Data transmitted via OSNs has, offering scalable solutions to existing CDNs or OSNs providers. Furthermore, it paves the way for experimentation with variations on caching schemes, timing parameters of content delivery and context of the OSN and the media platform.

A future target is to potentially leverage the CDN services of cloud service providers in order to lower costs while increasing simplicity. CDNs, often operated as Software as a Service (SaaS) in cloud providers (Amazon Cloud-Front, Microsoft Azure CDN, etc.) aim at addressing the problem of smooth and transparent content delivery. A CDN actually drives cloud adoption through enhanced performance, scalability and cost reduction. With the limitation for both CDNs and cloud services being the geographic distance between a user asking for content and the server where the content resides, cloud acceleration and CDN networks are both complementary to achieving a goal of delivering data in the fastest possible way. Cloud mainly handles. Utilization of OSN-aware CDNs in cloud computing, where content is constantly changing and, thus, not easily cached, is likely to have profound effects on large data download.

References

1. Alexa. http://alexa.com/topsites. Accessed 20 Dec 2018
2. Cisco visual networking index: global mobile data traffic forecast update, 2016–2021 white paper
3. Ericsson research blog. 5G media delivery. https://www.ericsson.com/research-blog/5g-media-delivery/. Accessed 20 Dec 2018
4. Facebook Newsroom. http://newsroom.fb.com/Key-Facts. Accessed 20 Dec 2018
5. International Telecommunication Union. ICT facts and figures in 2017. https://www.itu.int/en/ITU-D/Statistics/Documents/facts/ICTFactsFigures2017.pdf. Accessed 20 Dec 2018
6. Internet Society. Global Internet Report 2017. Mobile Evolution and Development of the Internet. https://future.internetsociety.org/wp-content/uploads/2017/09/2017-Internet-Society-Global-Internet-Report-Paths-to-Our-Digital-Future.pdf. Accessed 20 Dec 2018
7. Management of Networks with Constrained Devices: Use Cases. IETF Internet Draft. https://goo.gl/cT5pXr. Accessed 15 Mar 2016
8. Mobile-edge computing - introductory technical white paper. https://goo.gl/ybrCnq. Accessed 15 Mar 2016
9. The Internet of Things: how the next evolution of the Internet is changing everything. CISCO, San Jose, CA, USA, White Paper (2011). http://goo.gl/ugKAoN. Accessed 15 Mar 2016
10. The Smart Grid: An Introduction. US Department of Energy. http://goo.gl/jTNgf. Accessed 15 Mar 2016
11. Under the Hood: Scheduling MapReduce jobs more efficiently with Corona, Facebook engineering. goo.gl/XJRNN. Accessed 20 Dec 2018
12. YouTube Statistics. https://www.youtube.com/yt/press/statistics.html. Accessed 20 Dec 2018
13. cHiPSet - Research Work Results. Grant Period 1 (2017). http://chipset-cost.eu/wp-content/uploads/2017/05/report-1.pdf#page=13. Accessed 20 Dec 2018
14. Abedini, N., Shakkottai, S.: Content caching and scheduling in wireless networks with elastic and inelastic traffic. IEEE/ACM Trans. Netw. **22**(3), 864–874 (2014)

15. Abolfazli, S., Sanaei, Z., Ahmed, E., Gani, A., Buyya, R.: Cloud-based augmentation for mobile devices: motivation, taxonomies, and open challenges. IEEE Commun. Surv. Tutor. **16**(1), 337–368 (2014). https://doi.org/10.1109/SURV. 2013.070813.00285
16. Aizenman, M., Lebowitz, J.L.: Metastability effects in bootstrap percolation. J. Phys. A: Math. Gen. **21**(19), 3801 (1999)
17. Akpakwu, G.A., Silva, B.J., Hancke, G.P., Abu-Mahfouz, A.M.: A survey on 5G networks for the internet of things: communication technologies and challenges. IEEE Access **6**, 3619–3647 (2018)
18. Amur, H., Cipar, J., Gupta, V., Ganger, G.R., Kozuch, M.A., Schwan, K.: Robust and flexible power-proportional storage. In: Proceedings of the 1st ACM Symposium on Cloud Computing, pp. 217–228. ACM (2010)
19. Ananthanarayanan, G., et al.: PACMan: coordinated memory caching for parallel jobs. In: Proceedings of the 9th USENIX Conference on Networked Systems Design and Implementation, p. 20. USENIX Association (2012)
20. Anderson, C.: The Long Tail: Why the Future of Business is Selling Less of More. Hyperion, Santa Clara (2008). Revised and Updated Edition
21. Anjum, N., Karamshuk, D., Shikh-Bahaei, M., Sastry, N.: Survey on peer-assisted content delivery networks. Comput. Netw. **116**, 79–95 (2017)
22. Arthur, W.B.: Competing technologies, increasing returns, and lock-in by historical events. Econ. J. **99**(394), 116–131 (1989)
23. Assila, B., Kobbane, A., El Koutbi, M.: A survey on caching in 5G mobile network (2017)
24. Asur, R.B.S., Bandari, R., Huberman, B.: The pulse of news in social media: forecasting popularity. In: Association for the Advancement of Artificial Intelligence, 1202 (2012)
25. Avelar, V., Azevedo, D., French, A., Power, E.N.: PUE: a comprehensive examination of the metric. White Paper 49 (2012)
26. Bakshy, E., Hofman, J.M., Mason, W.A., Watts, D.J.: Everyone's an influencer: quantifying influence on Twitter. In: Proceedings of the Fourth ACM International Conference on Web Search and Data Mining, pp. 65–74. ACM (2011)
27. Bakshy, E., Hofman, J.M., Mason, W.A., Watts, D.J.: Everyone's an influencer: quantifying influence on Twitter. In: Proceedings of the Forth International Conference on Web Search and Web Data Mining, WSDM 2011, Hong Kong, China, 9–12 February 2011, pp. 65–74 (2011). http://doi.acm.org/10.1145/1935826.1935845
28. Bakshy, E., Rosenn, I., Marlow, C., Adamic, L.A.: The role of social networks in information diffusion. In: Proceedings of the 21st World Wide Web Conference 2012, WWW 2012, Lyon, France, 16–20 April 2012, pp. 519–528 (2012). http://doi.acm.org/10.1145/2187836.2187907
29. Banerjee, A.V.: A simple model of herd behavior. Q. J. Econ. **107**(3), 797–817 (1992)
30. Barroso, L.A., Clidaras, J., Hölzle, U.: The datacenter as a computer: an introduction to the design of warehouse-scale machines. Synth. Lect. Comput. Arch. **8**(3), 1–154 (2013)
31. Bashroush, R.: A comprehensive reasoning framework for hardware refresh in data centers. IEEE Trans. Sustain. Comput. **3**(4), 209–220 (2018)
32. Bashroush, R., Woods, E.: Architectural principles for energy-aware internet-scale applications. IEEE Softw. **34**(3), 14–17 (2017)
33. Bass, F.M.: A new product growth for model consumer durables. Manag. Sci. **15**(5), 215–227 (1969)

34. Beloglazov, A., Abawajy, J., Buyya, R.: Energy-aware resource allocation heuristics for efficient management of data centers for cloud computing. Futur. Gener. Comput. Syst. **28**(5), 755–768 (2012)
35. Beloglazov, A., Buyya, R.: Energy efficient resource management in virtualized cloud data centers. In: Proceedings of the 2010 10th IEEE/ACM International Conference on Cluster, Cloud and Grid Computing, pp. 826–831. IEEE Computer Society (2010)
36. Beloglazov, A., Buyya, R.: Optimal online deterministic algorithms and adaptive heuristics for energy and performance efficient dynamic consolidation of virtual machines in cloud data centers. Concurr. Comput.: Pract. Exp. **24**(13), 1397–1420 (2012)
37. Berger, E.: Dynamic monopolies of constant size. J. Comb. Theory Ser. B **83**(2), 191–200 (2001)
38. Bhattacharya, A.A., Culler, D., Friedman, E., Ghodsi, A., Shenker, S., Stoica, I.: Hierarchical scheduling for diverse datacenter workloads. In: Proceedings of the 4th Annual Symposium on Cloud Computing, p. 4. ACM (2013)
39. Bikhchandani, S., Hirshleifer, D., Welch, I.: A theory of fads, fashion, custom, and cultural change as informational cascades. J. Polit. Econ. **100**, 992–1026 (1992)
40. Bonacich, P.: Power and centrality: a family of measures. Am. J. Sociol. **92**, 1170–1182 (1987)
41. Borgatti, S.P.: Centrality and network flow. Soc. Netw. **27**(1), 55–71 (2005) http://www.sciencedirect.com/science/article/pii/S0378873304000693
42. Borthakur, D., et al.: Apache Hadoop goes realtime at Facebook. In: Proceedings of the 2011 ACM SIGMOD International Conference on Management of Data, pp. 1071–1080. ACM (2011)
43. Bottazzi, D., Montanari, R., Toninelli, A.: Context-aware middleware for anytime, anywhere social networks. IEEE Intell. Syst. **22**(5), 23–32 (2007)
44. Boyd, D., Ellison, N.B.: Social network sites: definition, history, and scholarship. J. Comput.-Mediat. Commun. **13**(1), 210–230 (2007). https://doi.org/10.1111/j.1083-6101.2007.00393.x
45. Brin, S., Page, L.: The anatomy of a large-scale hypertextual web search engine. Comput. Netw. ISDN Syst. **30**(1), 107–117 (1998)
46. Brodersen, A., Scellato, S., Wattenhofer, M.: YouTube around the world: geographic popularity of videos. In: Proceedings of the 21st International Conference on World Wide Web, pp. 241–250. ACM (2012)
47. Van den Bulte, C., Joshi, Y.V.: New product diffusion with influentials and imitators. Mark. Sci. **26**(3), 400–421 (2007)
48. Cha, M., Kwak, H., Rodriguez, P., Ahn, Y., Moon, S.B.: I tube, you tube, everybody tubes: analyzing the world's largest user generated content video system. In: Proceedings of the 7th ACM SIGCOMM Conference on Internet Measurement 2007, San Diego, California, USA, 24–26 October 2007, pp. 1–14 (2007). https://doi.org/10.1145/1298306.1298309
49. Chard, K., Caton, S., Rana, O., Bubendorfer, K.: Social cloud: cloud computing in social networks. In: IEEE International Conference on Cloud Computing, CLOUD 2010, Miami, FL, USA, 5–10 July 2010, pp. 99–106 (2010). https://doi.org/10.1109/CLOUD.2010.28
50. Chen, Y., Alspaugh, S., Katz, R.: Interactive analytical processing in big data systems: a cross-industry study of mapreduce workloads. Proc. VLDB Endow. **5**(12), 1802–1813 (2012)
51. Chib, S., Greenberg, E.: Understanding the metropolis-hastings algorithm. Am. Stat. **49**(4), 327–335 (1995)

52. Clifford, P., Sudbury, A.: A model for spatial conflict. Biometrika **60**(3), 581–588 (1973)
53. Coutand, O., et al.: Context-aware group management in mobile environments. In: IST Mobile Summit (2005)
54. Daley, D., Kendall, D.G.: Stochastic rumours. IMA J. Appl. Math. **1**(1), 42–55 (1965)
55. Dean, J., Ghemawat, S.: MapReduce: simplified data processing on large clusters. Commun. ACM **51**(1), 107–113 (2008)
56. Delgado, P., Didona, D., Dinu, F., Zwaenepoel, W.: Job-aware scheduling in eagle: divide and stick to your probes. In: Proceedings of the Seventh ACM Symposium on Cloud Computing. No. EPFL-CONF-221125 (2016)
57. Delgado, P., Dinu, F., Kermarrec, A.M., Zwaenepoel, W.: Hawk: hybrid datacenter scheduling. In: USENIX Annual Technical Conference, pp. 499–510 (2015)
58. Delimitrou, C., Kozyrakis, C.: Paragon: QoS-aware scheduling for heterogeneous datacenters. ACM SIGPLAN Not. **48**, 77–88 (2013)
59. Delimitrou, C., Kozyrakis, C.: Quasar: resource-efficient and QoS-aware cluster management. ACM SIGPLAN Not. **49**, 127–144 (2014)
60. Delimitrou, C., Sanchez, D., Kozyrakis, C.: Tarcil: reconciling scheduling speed and quality in large shared clusters. In: Proceedings of the Sixth ACM Symposium on Cloud Computing, pp. 97–110. ACM (2015)
61. Dewi, R.R., Kim, T.-H.: A new approach to modeling of bio-inspired information diffusion with ant colony optimization in complex networks. In: Zelinka, I., Suganthan, P.N., Chen, G., Snasel, V., Abraham, A., Rössler, O. (eds.) Nostradamus 2014: Prediction, Modeling and Analysis of Complex Systems. AISC, vol. 289, pp. 131–140. Springer, Cham (2014). https://doi.org/10.1007/978-3-319-07401-6_13
62. Dey, A.K.: Understanding and using context. Pers. Ubiquit. Comput. **5**(1), 4–7 (2001)
63. Dey, A.K., Abowd, G.D., Salber, D.: A conceptual framework and a toolkit for supporting the rapid prototyping of context-aware applications. Hum.-Comput. Interact. **16**(2), 97–166 (2001)
64. Dickens, L., Molloy, I., Lobo, J., Cheng, P.C., Russo, A.: Learning stochastic models of information flow. In: 2012 IEEE 28th International Conference on Data Engineering (ICDE), pp. 570–581. IEEE (2012)
65. Dodge, Y., Cox, D., Commenges, D., Davison, A., Solomon, P., Wilson, S.: The Oxford Dictionary of Statistical Terms. Oxford University Press, Oxford (2006)
66. Doerr, C., Blenn, N., Tang, S., Van Mieghem, P.: Are friends overrated? A study for the social news aggregator digg.com. Comput. Commun. **35**(7), 796–809 (2012)
67. Dogar, F.R., Karagiannis, T., Ballani, H., Rowstron, A.: Decentralized task-aware scheduling for data center networks. In: ACM SIGCOMM Computer Communication Review, vol. 44, pp. 431–442. ACM (2014)
68. Duy, T.V.T., Sato, Y., Inoguchi, Y.: Performance evaluation of a green scheduling algorithm for energy savings in cloud computing. In: 2010 IEEE International Symposium on Parallel & Distributed Processing, Workshops and PhD Forum (IPDPSW), pp. 1–8. IEEE (2010)
69. Easley, D.A., Kleinberg, J.M.: Networks, Crowds, and Markets - Reasoning About a Highly Connected World. Cambridge University Press (2010). http://www.cambridge.org/gb/knowledge/isbn/item2705443/?site_locale=en_GB
70. Even-Dar, E., Shapira, A.: A note on maximizing the spread of influence in social networks. Inf. Process. Lett. **111**(4), 184–187 (2011). https://doi.org/10.1016/j.ipl.2010.11.015

71. Fard, A., Abdolrashidi, A., Ramaswamy, L., Miller, J.A.: Towards efficient query processing on massive time-evolving graphs. In: 8th International Conference on Collaborative Computing: Networking, Applications and Worksharing, CollaborateCom 2012, Pittsburgh, PA, USA, 14–17 October 2012, pp. 567–574 (2012). http://dx.doi.org/10.4108/icst.collaboratecom.2012.250532
72. Fernández-Cerero, D., Jakóbik, A., Fernández-Montes, A., Kołodziej, J.: Stackelberg game-based models in energy-aware cloud scheduling. In: Nolle, L. (ed.) Proceedings of 32nd European Conference on Modelling and Simulation ECMS 2018 (ECMS, Wilhelmshaven, Germany, May 2018), ECMS 2018, pp. 460–467. European Council for Modelling and Simulation, Dudweiler (2018)
73. Fernández-Cerero, D., Jakóbik, A., Fernández-Montes, A., Kolodziej, J.: Gamescore: game-based energy-aware cloud scheduler and simulator for computational clouds. Simul. Model. Pract. Theory (2018). http://www.sciencedirect.com/science/article/pii/S1569190X18301229
74. Fernández-Cerero, D., Fernández-Montes, A., Jakóbik, A., Kolodziej, J., Toro, M.: Score: simulator for cloud optimization of resources and energy consumption. Simul. Model. Pract. Theory **82**, 160–173 (2018). http://www.sciencedirect.com/science/article/pii/S1569190X18300030
75. Fernández-Cerero, D., Fernández-Montes, A., Ortega, J.A.: Energy policies for data-center monolithic schedulers. Expert. Syst. Appl. **110**, 170–181 (2018). http://www.sciencedirect.com/science/article/pii/S0957417418303531
76. Fernández-Cerero, D., Fernández-Montes, A., Velasco, F.: Productive efficiency of energy-aware data centers. Energies **11**(8), 2053 (2018). http://www.mdpi.com/1996-1073/11/8/2053
77. Fernández-Cerero, D., Jakóbik, A., Grzonka, D., Kolodziej, J., Fernández-Montes, A.: Security supportive energy-aware scheduling and energy policies for cloud environments. J. Parallel Distrib. Comput. **119**, 191–202 (2018). http://www.sciencedirect.com/science/article/pii/S0743731518302843
78. Fernández-Montes, A., Fernández-Cerero, D., González-Abril, L., Álvarez García, J.A., Ortega, J.A.: Energy wasting at internet data centers due to fear. Pattern Recognit. Lett. **67**, 59–65 (2015). http://www.sciencedirect.com/science/article/pii/S0167865515001907. Cognitive Systems for Knowledge Discovery
79. Fowler, J., Christakis, N.: Connected: The Surprising Power of Our Social Networks and How they Shape Our Lives. HarperCollins Publishers, New York City (2009)
80. García-Silva, A., Kang, J.H., Lerman, K., Corcho, O.: Characterising emergent semantics in Twitter lists. In: Proceedings of the 9th International Conference on the Semantic Web: Research and Applications (ESWC), Heraklion, Greece (2012)
81. Gea, T., Paradells, J., Lamarca, M., Roldan, D.: Smart cities as an application of Internet of Things: experiences and lessons learnt in Barcelona. In: 2013 Seventh International Conference on Innovative Mobile and Internet Services in Ubiquitous Computing (IMIS), pp. 552–557. IEEE (2013)
82. Goldenberg, J., Libai, B., Muller, E.: Talk of the network: a complex systems look at the underlying process of word-of-mouth. Mark. Lett. **12**(3), 211–223 (2001)
83. Govindan, S., Liu, J., Kansal, A., Sivasubramaniam, A.: Cuanta: quantifying effects of shared on-chip resource interference for consolidated virtual machines. In: Proceedings of the 2nd ACM Symposium on Cloud Computing, p. 22. ACM (2011)
84. Goyal, A., Bonchi, F., Lakshmanan, L.V.: Learning influence probabilities in social networks. In: Proceedings of the third ACM International Conference on Web Search and Data Mining, pp. 241–250. ACM (2010)

85. Grandl, R., Ananthanarayanan, G., Kandula, S., Rao, S., Akella, A.: Multi-resource packing for cluster schedulers. ACM SIGCOMM Comput. Commun. Rev. **44**(4), 455–466 (2015)
86. Granovetter, M.: Threshold models of collective behavior. Am. J. Sociol. **83**, 1420–1443 (1978)
87. Gruhl, D., Guha, R., Liben-Nowell, D., Tomkins, A.: Information diffusion through Blogspace. In: Proceedings of the 13th International Conference on World Wide Web, pp. 491–501. ACM (2004)
88. Henricksen, K., Indulska, J., Rakotonirainy, A.: Infrastructure for pervasive computing: challenges. In: GI Jahrestagung (1), pp. 214–222 (2001)
89. Hindman, B., et al.: Mesos: a platform for fine-grained resource sharing in the data center. NSDI **11**, 22 (2011)
90. Hinze, A., Buchanan, G.: Context-awareness in mobile tourist information systems: challenges for user interaction. In: International Workshop on Context in Mobile HCI at the Seventh International Conference on Human Computer Interaction with Mobile Devices and Services (2005)
91. Holley, R.A., Liggett, T.M.: Ergodic theorems for weakly interacting infinite systems and the voter model. Ann. Probab. **3**, 643–663 (1975)
92. Hoque, I., Gupta, I.: Disk layout techniques for online social network data. IEEE Internet Comput. **16**(3), 24–36 (2012)
93. Hosseini-Pozveh, M., Zamanifar, K., Naghsh-Nilchi, A.R.: Assessing information diffusion models for influence maximization in signed social networks. Expert Syst. Appl. **119**, 476–490 (2019)
94. Hoßfeld, T., Schatz, R., Biersack, E., Plissonneau, L.: Internet video delivery in YouTube: from traffic measurements to quality of experience. In: Biersack, E., Callegari, C., Matijasevic, M. (eds.) Data Traffic Monitoring and Analysis. LNCS, vol. 7754, pp. 264–301. Springer, Heidelberg (2013). https://doi.org/10.1007/978-3-642-36784-7_11
95. Huguenin, K., Kermarrec, A.M., Kloudas, K., Taïani, F.: Content and geographical locality in user-generated content sharing systems. In: Proceedings of the 22nd international workshop on Network and Operating System Support for Digital Audio and Video, pp. 77–82. ACM (2012)
96. Isard, M., Prabhakaran, V., Currey, J., Wieder, U., Talwar, K., Goldberg, A.: Quincy: fair scheduling for distributed computing clusters. In: Proceedings of the ACM SIGOPS 22nd Symposium on Operating Systems Principles, pp. 261–276. ACM (2009)
97. Ising, E.: Beitrag zur Theorie des Ferromagnetismus. Zeitschrift für Physik A Hadrons and Nuclei **31**(1), 253–258 (1925)
98. Istepanian, R., Hu, S., Philip, N., Sungoor, A.: The potential of Internet of m-health Things m-IoT for non-invasive glucose level sensing. In: 2011 Annual International Conference of the IEEE Engineering in Medicine and Biology Society, EMBC, pp. 5264–5266. IEEE (2011)
99. Jacobson, V., Smetters, D.K., Thornton, J.D., Plass, M.F., Briggs, N., Braynard, R.: Networking named content. Commun. ACM **55**(1), 117–124 (2012). https://doi.org/10.1145/2063176.2063204
100. Jakóbik, A., Grzonka, D., Kołodziej, J.: Security supportive energy aware scheduling and scaling for cloud environments (2017)
101. Jiang, L., Feng, G., Qin, S.: Content distribution for 5G systems based on distributed cloud service network architecture (2015)

102. Juarez, F., Ejarque, J., Badia, R.M.: Dynamic energy-aware scheduling for parallel task-based application in cloud computing. Futur. Gener. Comput. Syst. **78**, 257–271 (2016)
103. Karanasos, K., et al.: Mercury: hybrid centralized and distributed scheduling in large shared clusters. In: USENIX Annual Technical Conference, pp. 485–497 (2015)
104. Katz, E., Lazarsfeld, P.F.: Personal Influence, the Part Played by People in the Flow of Mass Communications. Transaction Publishers, Piscataway (1966)
105. Kaushik, R.T., Bhandarkar, M.: GreenHDFS: towards an energy-conserving, storage-efficient, hybrid Hadoop compute cluster. In: Proceedings of the USENIX Annual Technical Conference, p. 109 (2010)
106. Kempe, D., Kleinberg, J.M., Tardos, É.: Maximizing the spread of influence through a social network. In: Proceedings of the Ninth ACM SIGKDD International Conference on Knowledge Discovery and Data Mining, pp. 137–146. ACM (2003)
107. Kilanioti, I.: Improving multimedia content delivery via augmentation with social information. The social prefetcher approach. IEEE Trans. Multimed. **17**(9), 1460–1470 (2015). https://doi.org/10.1109/TMM.2015.2459658
108. Kilanioti, I., et al.: A survey on cost-effective context-aware distribution of social data streams over energy-efficient data centres. Simul. Model. Pract. Theory (2018). http://www.sciencedirect.com/science/article/pii/S1569190X18301709
109. Kilanioti, I., Papadopoulos, G.A.: Delivering social multimedia content with scalability. In: Pop, F., Kołodziej, J., Di Martino, B. (eds.) Resource Management for Big Data Platforms. CCN, pp. 383–399. Springer, Cham (2016). https://doi.org/10.1007/978-3-319-44881-7_18
110. Kilanioti, I., Papadopoulos, G.A.: Predicting video virality on Twitter. In: Pop, F., Kołodziej, J., Di Martino, B. (eds.) Resource Management for Big Data Platforms. CCN, pp. 419–439. Springer, Cham (2016). https://doi.org/10.1007/978-3-319-44881-7_20
111. Kilanioti, I., Papadopoulos, G.A.: Content delivery simulations supported by social network-awareness. Simul. Model. Pract. Theory **71**, 114–133 (2017)
112. Kleinberg, J.M.: Cascading behavior in networks: algorithmic and economic issues. In: Nisan, N., Roughgarden, T., Tardos, E., Vazirani, V. (eds.) Algorithmic Game Theory, pp. 613–632. Cambridge University Press (2007)
113. Ko, Y.Y., Cho, K.J., Kim, S.W.: Efficient and effective influence maximization in social networks: a hybrid-approach. Inf. Sci. **465**, 144–161 (2018)
114. Kuperman, M., Abramson, G.: Small world effect in an epidemiological model. Phys. Rev. Lett. **86**(13), 2909–2912 (2001)
115. Lane, N.D., Miluzzo, E., Lu, H., Peebles, D., Choudhury, T., Campbell, A.T.: A survey of mobile phone sensing. J. Supercomput. **48**(9), 140–150 (2010). https://doi.org/10.1109/MCOM.2010.5560598
116. Leconte, M., Paschos, G., Gkatzikis, L., Draief, M., Vassilaras, S., Chouvardas, S.: Placing dynamic content in caches with small population. In: IEEE INFOCOM 2016 - The 35th Annual IEEE International Conference on Computer Communications, pp. 1–9, April 2016
117. Lee, Y.C., Zomaya, A.Y.: Energy efficient utilization of resources in cloud computing systems. J. Supercomput. **60**(2), 268–280 (2012)
118. Lerman, K., Intagorn, S., Kang, J.H., Ghosh, R.: Using proximity to predict activity in social networks. In: Proceedings of the 21st International Conference on World Wide Web, pp. 555–556. ACM (2012)

119. Leskovec, J., McGlohon, M., Faloutsos, C., Glance, N., Hurst, M.: Patterns of cascading behavior in large blog graphs. In: Proceedings of SIAM International Conference on Data Mining (SDM) 2007. SIAM (2007)

120. Li, M., Wang, X., Gao, K., Zhang, S.: A survey on information diffusion in online social networks: models and methods. Information 8(4), 118 (2017)

121. Liben-Nowell, D., Kleinberg, J.: Tracing information flow on a global scale using Internet chain-letter data. Proc. Natl. Acad. Sci. 105(12), 4633–4638 (2008)

122. Liberal, F., Kourtis, A., Fajardo, J.O., Koumaras, H.: Multimedia content delivery in SDN and NFV-based towards 5G networks. IEEE COMSOC MMTC E-Lett. 10(4), 6–10 (2015)

123. Lin, C.X., Mei, Q., Jiang, Y., Han, J., Qi, S.: Inferring the diffusion and evolution of topics in social communities. Mind 3(d4), d5 (2011)

124. Łuczak, T.: Size and connectivity of the K-core of a random graph. Discrete Math. 91(1), 61–68 (1991)

125. Luo, X., Wang, Y., Zhang, Z., Wang, H.: Superset: a non-uniform replica placement strategy towards high-performance and cost-effective distributed storage service. In: 2013 International Conference on Advanced Cloud and Big Data (CBD), pp. 139–146. IEEE (2013)

126. Luu, M.D., Hoang, T.A., Lim, E.P.: A survey of information diffusion models and relevant problems (2011)

127. Maier, G., Feldmann, A., Paxson, V., Allman, M.: On dominant characteristics of residential broadband internet traffic. In: Proceedings of the 9th ACM SIGCOMM Internet Measurement Conference IMC, pp. 90–102. ACM (2009)

128. Mars, J., Tang, L.: Whare-map: heterogeneity in homogeneous warehouse-scale computers. In: ACM SIGARCH Computer Architecture News, vol. 41, pp. 619–630. ACM (2013)

129. Menon, A.: Big data@ Facebook. In: Proceedings of the 2012 Workshop on Management of Big Data Systems, pp. 31–32. ACM (2012)

130. Milgram, S.: The small world problem. Psychol. Today 2(1), 60–67 (1967)

131. Morris, S.: Contagion. Rev. Econ. Stud. 67(1), 57–78 (2000)

132. Najar, A., Denoyer, L., Gallinari, P.: Predicting information diffusion on social networks with partial knowledge. In: Proceedings of the 21st International Conference on World Wide Web, pp. 1197–1204. ACM (2012)

133. Nathuji, R., Kansal, A., Ghaffarkhah, A.: Q-clouds: managing performance interference effects for QoS-aware clouds. In: Proceedings of the 5th European Conference on Computer Systems, pp. 237–250. ACM (2010)

134. Navarro, N.D.A.B., Da Costa, C.A., Barbosa, J.L.V., Righi, R.D.R.: A context-aware spontaneous mobile social network. In: Ubiquitous Intelligence and Computing and 2015 IEEE 12th International Conference on Autonomic and Trusted Computing and 2015 IEEE 15th International Conference on Scalable Computing and Communications and Its Associated Workshops (UIC-ATC-ScalCom), pp. 85–92. IEEE (2015)

135. Nejković, V., Jelenković, F., Tošić, M., Milošević, N., Nikolić, Z.: CoordSS: an ontology framework for heterogeneous networks experimentation. Telfor J. 8(2), 70–75 (2016)

136. Nekovee, M., Moreno, Y., Bianconi, G., Marsili, M.: Theory of rumour spreading in complex social networks. Phys. A: Stat. Mech. its Appl. 374(1), 457–470 (2007)

137. Ousterhout, K., Wendell, P., Zaharia, M., Stoica, I.: Sparrow: distributed, low latency scheduling. In: Proceedings of the Twenty-Fourth ACM Symposium on Operating Systems Principles, pp. 69–84. ACM (2013)

138. Pejovic, V., Musolesi, M.: Anticipatory mobile computing: a survey of the state of the art and research challenges. ACM Comput. Surv. **47**(3), 47 (2015). https://doi.org/10.1145/2693843

139. Perera, C., Zaslavsky, A., Christen, P., Georgakopoulos, D.: Context aware computing for the internet of things: a survey. IEEE Commun. Surv. Tutor. **16**(1), 414–454 (2014)

140. Perera, C., Zaslavsky, A., Christen, P., Georgakopoulos, D.: Sensing as a service model for smart cities supported by internet of things. Trans. Emerg. Telecommun. Technol. **25**(1), 81–93 (2014)

141. Plissonneau, L., Vu-Brugier, G.: Mobile data traffic analysis: how do you prefer watching videos? In: Proceedings of the 22nd International Teletraffic Congress (ITC), pp. 1–8. IEEE (2010)

142. Qu, H., Mashayekhi, O., Terei, D., Levis, P.: Canary: a scheduling architecture for high performance cloud computing. arXiv preprint arXiv:1602.01412 (2016)

143. Rasley, J., Karanasos, K., Kandula, S., Fonseca, R., Vojnovic, M., Rao, S.: Efficient queue management for cluster scheduling. In: Proceedings of the Eleventh European Conference on Computer Systems, p. 36. ACM (2016)

144. Reiss, C., Tumanov, A., Ganger, G.R., Katz, R.H., Kozuch, M.A.: Heterogeneity and dynamicity of clouds at scale: Google trace analysis. In: Proceedings of the Third ACM Symposium on Cloud Computing, p. 7. ACM (2012)

145. Reiss, C., Wilkes, J., Hellerstein, J.L.: Google cluster-usage traces: format + schema. Technical report, Google Inc., Mountain View, CA, USA, November 2011. http://code.google.com/p/googleclusterdata/wiki/TraceVersion2. Accessed 20 Mar 2012

146. Ren, C., Lo, E., Kao, B., Zhu, X., Cheng, R.: On querying historial evolving graph sequences. Proc. VLDB Endow. **4**(11), 726–737 (2011)

147. Ren, K., Kwon, Y., Balazinska, M., Howe, B.: Hadoop's adolescence: an analysis of hadoop usage in scientific workloads. Proc. VLDB Endow. **6**(10), 853–864 (2013)

148. Ricciardi, S., Careglio, D., Sole-Pareta, J., Fiore, U., Palmieri, F., et al.: Saving energy in data center infrastructures. In: 2011 First International Conference on Data Compression, Communications and Processing (CCP), pp. 265–270. IEEE (2011)

149. Rodriguez, M.G., Leskovec, J., Schölkopf, B.: Structure and dynamics of information pathways in online media. In: Proceedings of ACM International Conference on Web Search and Data Mining (WSDM), Rome, Italy (2013)

150. Rogers, E.M.: Diffusion of Innovations. Simon and Schuster, New York (1995)

151. Sastry, N., Yoneki, E., Crowcroft, J.: Buzztraq: predicting geographical access patterns of social cascades using social networks. In: Proceedings of the Second ACM EuroSys Workshop on Social Network Systems, SNS 2009, Nuremberg, Germany, 31 March 2009, pp. 39–45 (2009). http://doi.acm.org/10.1145/1578002.1578009

152. Satyanarayanan, M.: Pervasive computing: vision and challenges. IEEE Pers. Commun. **8**(4), 10–17 (2001)

153. Scellato, S., Mascolo, C., Musolesi, M., Crowcroft, J.: Track globally, deliver locally: improving content delivery networks by tracking geographic social cascades. In: Proceedings of the 20th International Conference on World Wide Web, WWW 2011, Hyderabad, India, 28 March–1 April 2011, pp. 457–466 (2011). http://doi.acm.org/10.1145/1963405.1963471

154. Schilit, B.N., et al.: Challenge: ubiquitous location-aware computing and the place lab initiative. In: Proceedings of the 1st ACM International Workshop on Wireless Mobile Applications and Services on WLAN Hotspots, pp. 29–35. ACM (2003)

155. Schilit, B.N., Theimer, M.M.: Disseminating active map information to mobile hosts. IEEE Netw. **8**(5), 22–32 (1994)
156. Schwarzkopf, M., Konwinski, A., Abd-El-Malek, M., Wilkes, J.: Omega: flexible, scalable schedulers for large compute clusters. In: Proceedings of the 8th ACM European Conference on Computer Systems, pp. 351–364. ACM (2013)
157. Sendling, T.C.: Micromotives and Macrobehavior. Norton, New York (1978)
158. Shue, D., Freedman, M.J., Shaikh, A.: Performance isolation and fairness for multi-tenant cloud storage. OSDI **12**, 349–362 (2012)
159. Sohrabi, S., Tang, A., Moser, I., Aleti, A.: Adaptive virtual machine migration mechanism for energy efficiency. In: Proceedings of the 5th International Workshop on Green and Sustainable Software, pp. 8–14. ACM (2016)
160. Song, X., Chi, Y., Hino, K., Tseng, B.L.: Information flow modeling based on diffusion rate for prediction and ranking. In: Proceedings of the 16th International Conference on World Wide Web, pp. 191–200. ACM (2007)
161. Sundmaeker, H., Guillemin, P., Friess, P., Woelfflé, S.: Vision and challenges for realising the internet of things. Clust. Eur. Res. Proj. Internet Things Eur. Commision **3**(3), 34–36 (2010)
162. Thereska, E., Donnelly, A., Narayanan, D.: Sierra: practical power-proportionality for data center storage. In: Proceedings of the Sixth Conference on Computer systems, pp. 169–182. ACM (2011)
163. Torres, R., Finamore, A., Kim, J.R., Mellia, M., Munafo, M.M., Rao, S.: Dissecting video server selection strategies in the YouTube CDN. In: 2011 31st International Conference on Distributed Computing Systems (ICDCS), pp. 248–257. IEEE (2011)
164. Tosic, M., et al.: Semantic coordination protocol for LTE and Wi-Fi coexistence. In: 2016 European Conference on Networks and Communications (EuCNC), pp. 69–73. IEEE (2016)
165. Traverso, S., Huguenin, K., Trestian, I., Erramilli, V., Laoutaris, N., Papagiannaki, K.: TailGate: handling long-tail content with a little help from friends. In: Proceedings of the 21st World Wide Web Conference 2012, WWW 2012, Lyon, France, 16–20 April 2012, pp. 151–160 (2012). http://doi.acm.org/10.1145/2187836.2187858
166. Vavilapalli, V.K., et al.: Apache Hadoop YARN: yet another resource negotiator. In: Proceedings of the 4th Annual Symposium on Cloud Computing, p. 5. ACM (2013)
167. Vergara, E.J., Nadjm-Tehrani, S.: EnergyBox: a trace-driven tool for data transmission energy consumption studies. In: Energy Efficiency in Large Scale Distributed Systems - COST IC0804 European Conference, EE-LSDS 2013, Vienna, Austria, 22–24 April 2013, Revised Selected Papers, pp. 19–34 (2013). http://dx.doi.org/10.1007/978-3-642-40517-4_2
168. Verma, A., Pedrosa, L., Korupolu, M., Oppenheimer, D., Tune, E., Wilkes, J.: Large-scale cluster management at Google with Borg. In: Proceedings of the Tenth European Conference on Computer Systems, p. 18. ACM (2015)
169. Wang, Z., Zhou, X., Yu, Z., Wang, H., Ni, H.: Quantitative evaluation of group user experience in smart spaces. Cybern. Syst.: Int. J. **41**(2), 105–122 (2010)
170. Want, R., Pering, T.: System challenges for ubiquitous & pervasive computing. In: Proceedings of the 27th International Conference on Software Engineering, pp. 9–14. ACM (2005)
171. Watts, D.J.: A simple model of global cascades on random networks. Proc. Natl. Acad. Sci. **99**(9), 5766–5771 (2002)

172. Yan, Y., Qian, Y., Sharif, H., Tipper, D.: A survey on smart grid communication infrastructures: motivations, requirements and challenges. IEEE Commun. Surv. Tutor. **15**(1), 5–20 (2013)

173. Yang, H., Breslow, A., Mars, J., Tang, L.: Bubble-flux: precise online QoS management for increased utilization in warehouse scale computers. In: ACM SIGARCH Computer Architecture News, vol. 41, pp. 607–618. ACM (2013)

174. Yang, J., Leskovec, J.: Modeling information diffusion in implicit networks. In: Proceedings of the 10th IEEE International Conference on Data Mining (ICDM), pp. 599–608. IEEE (2010)

175. Zaharia, M., Borthakur, D., Sen Sarma, J., Elmeleegy, K., Shenker, S., Stoica, I.: Delay scheduling: a simple technique for achieving locality and fairness in cluster scheduling. In: Proceedings of the 5th European Conference on Computer Systems, pp. 265–278. ACM (2010)

176. Zhang, D., Yu, Z., Guo, B., Wang, Z.: Exploiting personal and community context in mobile social networks. In: Chin, A., Zhang, D. (eds.) Mobile Social Networking. CSS, pp. 109–138. Springer, New York (2014). https://doi.org/10.1007/978-1-4614-8579-7_6

177. Zhang, X., Tune, E., Hagmann, R., Jnagal, R., Gokhale, V., Wilkes, J.: CPI 2: CPU performance isolation for shared compute clusters. In: Proceedings of the 8th ACM European Conference on Computer Systems, pp. 379–391. ACM (2013)

178. Zhou, F., Zhang, L., Franco, E., Mislove, A., Revis, R., Sundaram, R.: WebCloud: recruiting social network users to assist in content distribution. In: Proceedings of the 11th IEEE International Symposium on Network Computing and Applications, Cambridge, MA, USA (2012)

Big Data in 5G Distributed Applications

Valentina Nejkovic[1(✉)], Ari Visa[2], Milorad Tosic[1], Nenad Petrovic[1],
Mikko Valkama[2], Mike Koivisto[2], Jukka Talvitie[2], Svetozar Rancic[3],
Daniel Grzonka[4], Jacek Tchorzewski[4], Pierre Kuonen[5],
and Francisco Gortazar[6]

[1] Faculty of Electronic Engineering, University of Nis, Nis, Serbia
valentina@elfak.ni.ac.rs
[2] Faculty of Computing and Electrical Engineering,
Tampere University of Technology, Tampere, Finland
[3] Faculty of Science and Mathematics, University of Nis, Nis, Serbia
[4] Cracow University of Technology, Cracow, Poland
[5] University of Applied Sciences of Western Switzerland, Fribourg, Switzerland
[6] Rey Juan Carlos University, Madrid, Spain

Abstract. Fifth generation mobile networks (5G) will rather supplement than
replace current 4G networks by dramatically improving their bandwidth,
capacity and reliability. This way, much more demanding use cases that simply
are not achievable with today's networks will become reality - from home
entertainment, to product manufacturing and healthcare. However, many of
them rely on Internet of Things (IoT) devices equipped with low-cost transmitters and sensors that generate enormous amount of data about their environment. Therefore, due to large scale of 5G systems, combined with their
inherent complexity and heterogeneity, Big Data and analysis techniques are
considered as one of the main enablers of future mobile networks. In this work,
we recognize 5G use cases from various application domains and list the basic
requirements for their development and realization.

Keywords: 5G · Big Data · Use cases

1 Introduction

The vision of 5G is becoming clearer as we move closer to the end of this decade. The
5G will feature increased network speed, and machines, cars, city infrastructure beside
people will be connected. It is expected that 5G networks will have always-on capabilities and to be energy efficient, which require new protocols and access technologies.
The 5G network represents highly complex and heterogeneous network that integrates
massive amount of sensor nodes and diversity of devices such as macro and small cells
with different radio access technologies such as GSM, WCDMA, LTE, and Wi-Fi that
coexist with one another. Such network vision is expected to lead to traffic volume of
tens of exabytes per month that further demands networks capacity 1000 times higher
than now [1, 2]. Such traffic volume is not supported with nowadays cellular networks.
Thus, practical deployment of 5G networking systems, in addition to traditional
technology drivers, needs some new critical issues to be resolved on different areas

J. Kołodziej and H. González-Vélez (Eds.): cHiPSet, LNCS 11400, pp. 138–162, 2019.
https://doi.org/10.1007/978-3-030-16272-6_5

such as: (1) coordination mechanism [3], (2) power consumption [4], (3) networking behavior prediction [5], (4) positioning and location-awareness [6] etc. Some operators already start their deployments and the standards process forward.

5G will be built upon the existing 4G LTE networks with features available as part of the LTE - Advanced standard. Some features will include carrier aggregation that enable using of existing spectrum efficiently with network capacity increase and higher throughput rates. Self-organizing networks will play key role as well as technologies such as coordinated multipoint that will enable operators to simultaneously transmit and process signals from multiple sites. Software-defined networks (SDN) and network functions virtualization (NFV) will be very important for operators in order to scale their networks quickly in migration from 4G to 5G [7]. SDN will play key role for carving virtual sub-networks, which can be used for huge bandwidth applications, which for example include video with requirement in speed of 10 Gb/s as well as lower bandwidth applications, which for example connect different user equipment that are less demanding on the network.

The 5G architecture and deployment will depend upon how the network is used. For example, applications such as streaming video, video conferencing and virtual reality require high speed with growth in the video traffic. In order to achieve this requirement, the network needs a lot of small cell coverage and higher bandwidth spectrum. Further, 5G will be the network for Internet of Things (IoT) with support for a lot of devices [8]. Such IoT network should be efficient in low-bandwidth transmissions with enhanced coverage. Because of the high scale of 5G systems combined with their inherent complexity and heterogeneity, Big Data techniques and analysis will be one of the main enablers of the new 5G critical issues.

Big Data refers to large data sets whose size is growing at enormous speed making it difficult to handle and manage them using the traditional techniques and software tools. It is a step forward from traditional data analysis, considering the following aspects (so-called five "five Vs") [9]: quantity of data (volume), different types of semi-structured and unstructured data (variety), the rate with which data is changing or how often it is created (velocity), the importance of results extracted from data (value), data quality, including trust, credibility and integrity (veracity). Taking into account the prediction that the number of connected devices will increase 10–100 by the time when 5G will be commercially used [10], it can be concluded that Big Data techniques will play an important role, as all the considered usage scenarios are based on extracting knowledge from the enormous amount of heterogeneous data generated by connected devices in order to support the decisioning and other mechanisms in future 5G networks.

In this chapter, we identify use cases and scenarios that could benefit from new capabilities provided by 5G network in synergy with Big Data technologies, list basic requirements for their application development, and consider some future challenges addressing positioning challenges and semantic-based solutions. The researcher community and service providers (business stakeholders) could benefit from this chapter. From one side, it provides an insight of recent trends in 5G research and development, while, from the other side, it discusses how the research outcomes could be used for development of future services to satisfy customer demands.

Section 2 of this chapter gives list 5G use cases requirements, while Sect. 3 gives identified 5g use case with short description of each. Section 4 gives future challenges targeting positioning systems, semantic based approaches, 5G security etc. Section 5 concludes the chapter.

2   5G Use Cases Requirements

The introduction of big data techniques in 5G distributed applications poses a challenge, as these techniques usually require huge computational resources. In general, there is a need for high performance computing infrastructure. This infrastructure would typically be available as a private or public cloud or grid. Cloud or grid resources will allow for consuming, storing and processing huge amounts of data. This data shall be prepared for consumption from the edge network. Depending on the nature of the data needed by end-users, we can envision two kinds of data processing methods: online and offline. Offline methods are easier to handle as the processing can be performed in the cloud or grid. This are supposed to be processes that are not critical. Online processing is used when a response is needed in a given amount of time, and therefore both the time required to give a response and the latency would have high impact on the set of use cases that will be available for 5G.

For online processing, in those cases where common off-the-shelf hardware is available at the edge, general Big Data solutions can be run on top of this commodity hardware, assuming that the constrained resources available are enough.

In general, we identify following requirements needed for 5G use cases:

- Network requirements: Network with 5G capabilities; faster and higher-capacity networks, which can deliver video and other content-rich services; massive connectivity of devices based on different technologies, etc.
- Application requirements: Consistent process mining over Big Data triple store; Network capability measurement module; Reasoning module; Learning and Prediction module (for example, Neural Network); Optimization module; Corresponding domain and application Ontologies; etc.
- Storage requirements: Big Data triple store; Possibility to handles large amounts (a petabyte or more) of data; Distributed redundant data storage; Massively parallel processing; Provides Semantic Big Data processing capabilities; Centrally managed and orchestrated.

Even though the 5G networks are primarily designed for enhanced communication purposes, high-accuracy positioning has been considered as one of the key features in 5G. Moreover, the standardization organization third generation partnership project (3GPP) has already published several technical reports and specifications regarding positioning in future 5G networks [11–14]. However, since the 5G specifications are still under development, detailed descriptions of different positioning approaches and related positioning protocols are yet unavailable. Despite this, in order to facilitate development of various future 5G-enabled use cases, 3GPP has introduced the first set of performance requirements considering different types of position-reliant use cases presented in [13]. For each use case, a specific positioning accuracy, including both horizontal and vertical directions, has been given according to the type of the area of interest and its 5G service characteristics. For certain use cases, when applicable, also accuracy requirements for velocity estimation and device bearing estimation are provided.

Similar to common 5G guidelines, besides focusing only on maximizing the positioning accuracy, also other important positioning service aspects have been considered in the existing reports given in [13]. One of the key performance indicators is positioning availability, which defines in which percent of the time the positioning method provides estimates with the specified accuracy level. Another important positioning performance indicator is latency, which indicates the elapsed time between triggering the positioning process and finally obtaining the position estimates. Moreover, the latency of the first position estimate at the initialization stage of the positioning process, referred to as the time-to-first-fix, has been separately specified typically with reduced performance requirements compared to the latency in general.

In addition to the above-described 5G positioning requirements, there are various other aspects, which have not yet been appropriately addressed in the reports and specifications, but should be considered according to the needs of users, operators and 3rd parties. Such aspects include, for example, energy consumption, security and privacy, estimation reliability and related confidence levels, and possible regulatory requirements (e.g., positioning during emergency calls) [12–14].

Mobile-network-based positioning approaches can be divided into two fundamental categories, which are network centric positioning and user-centric positioning. In network-centric positioning, the position estimates are obtained at the network side based on the signals transmitted by the user device. In this approach, all heavy computational load is located at the network side, which reduces the power consumption of the user device, and thus, increases the valuable battery life of the device. Moreover, when the positioning is done at the network side, all positioning related information, such as network BS locations, are already available for the positioning algorithms without introducing additional overhead from signaling the information over the radio interface. The fact that the position information is fundamentally located at the network side is especially useful for achieving the future targets of the 5G networks, as it facilitates numerous 5G-enabled mission-critical use cases where the latency and reliability of the position estimates are in a crucial role. In the user-centric positioning approach, where the user device performs the positioning based on the signals transmitted by the network nodes, the position information is not directly available at the network side. This approach increases user security and privacy, but on the other hand, it requires additional signaling overhead in order to utilize the device positions jointly as part of new 5G-enabled infrastructures such as traffic control and ITS, for instance.

3   5G Use Cases

In this section, we analyze how the current advances in 5G and related concepts can be leveraged in order to provide novel use cases that were not possible before or improve the existing services and solutions.

3.1 5G Coordination Mechanisms

The 5G network indicates the need for coexistence of multiple wireless technologies in the same environment [3, 15, 16]. The problem that raises in such environments is mutual interference among multiple wireless networks, which is consequence of an overlapping in usage of the same set of resources. Typically, such case happens when same radio frequencies are used for multiple communication channels that are based on different radio technologies [3, 15]. Coordination protocols defined by the technology standards traditionally address the problem when networks use same technology. New coordination concepts are needed in the case of co-existing networks based on heterogeneous technologies [16, 17].

We identify the following possible scenario. In a Home Network setting, a typical home can have several rooms each equipped with WiFi enabled HDTV set and a number of streaming audio appliances. At the same time and in the same building, a sensor network is used for home automation including presence detection, temperature and lighting regulation, doorbell indication and security and safety monitoring. Most homes also have at least one microwave oven and a number of Bluetooth Low Energy gadgets. During the typical evening, all of these devices are active and have to be actively coordinated in order to provide satisfactory level of service.

3.2 Power Consumption

A number of recently finished as well as currently on-going 5G related EU projects confirm a diversity of usage and applications of power consumption, efficiency and reliability in WSNs. These projects delivered a number of algorithms and protocols for reducing energy consumption that show the importance of the power consumption. Further, the design of the 5G wireless networks has to consider energy efficiency as very important pillar in order to optimize economic, operational, and environmental concerns [1, 18]. In presence of enormous high traffic volume, data-driven techniques such as intelligent distribution of frequently accessed content over the network nodes and content caching can result in relevant energy consumption reductions and prolong the lifetime of nodes that are low on battery energy.

3.3 Networking Behavior Prediction

Big Data Analytics solutions can predict how the needs in resources use change among places and throughout the time within a complex large-scale system. A 5G network that adopt such solution would have ability to learn from the previous situations and states and intelligently adopt to new demands [5, 19]. Particularly, using appropriate learning techniques the system will enable devices to learn from past observations in their surroundings.

For example, we identify the following use case scenario: (a) In a Smart City, traffic lights and pedestrian crossings (i.e. various presence detectors) are IEEE 802.15.4 technology equipped while community WiFi network is mounted on a number of light posts lining the same street. During rush hours, there is a high demand for WiFi traffic due to a large number of people using personal devices potentially impacting traffic management system; (b) Mobile users consume images, videos and music, which increase in volume over time. In such a case, network congestion is a consequence of the high dynamics in demands that exceeds the system potential for adaptability.

3.4 Positioning and Location-Awareness in Future 5G Networks

The world is changing rapidly. New services are needed and many of those new services require location-awareness. Autonomous vehicles, transportation, traffic control need this kind of service. If we consider the problem from the point of view of the smart city we notice that there are many new user groups, such as pedestrians, cleaning and maintenance services, management and administration. There are several approaches to help with positioning. One started with Long Range Positioning systems like Decca and LORAN and continued with Global Positioning System (GPS) that is a positioning system based on Medium Earth Orbit satellites. GPS is a part of Global Navigation Satellite System (GNSS) [20]. GNSS also includes, for example European Galileo and Russian GLONASS. However, satellites are not solving the positioning problem totally. In many regions positioning needs help from mobile communication networks that is called assisted GPS (A-GPS). The high latitudes in North and in South and cities with skyscrapers are for examples problematic regions

In contrast to the earlier and existing mobile generations, where positioning has been only an add-on feature, future 5G radio networks will allow for highly accurate positioning not only for personal navigation purposes but also for unforeseen location-aware services and applications like robotics, intelligent transportation systems (ITSs), and drones, just to name few. While seeking to meet the demanding communication requirements of 5G, e.g., in terms of capacity and data-rates, 5G networks will exploit large bandwidths and massive antenna arrays, which together with even denser base station (BS) deployments create also a convenient environment for 5G-based radio positioning. Hence, it is widely expected that future 5G networks should enable and even improve indoor and outdoor positioning techniques embedded to a radio access network (RAN) [11] as well as the ones that utilizes RAN-external measurements from GNSS or sensors.

3.5 Ultra/High Definition Live Video Streaming in Wireless Networks

In recent years, video streaming, both on-demand and live has become an important part of our everyday lives – from social networks, content delivery platforms to industrial, robotic and experimentation systems. Due to rise of processor power and camera sensor resolution of consumer devices, such as smartphones, the image quality criteria perceived by consumers has dramatically increased. High Definition video is becoming a must for all the use cases where video streaming is involved. Not only that, but also new video formats are emerging, such as stereoscopic 3D, 360-degree video and Ultra High Definition Video which contain even more data that has to be transmitted. Therefore, Internet service providers, mobile carriers and content providers are encountering many issues, as transmission of such content requires significantly larger bandwidth. Additionally, the issues become even more challenging due to device mobility, which can affect the Quality of Service and Quality of Experience, especially when it comes to live video broadcast in varying network conditions [21]. Here, we identify a potential use case of novel networking paradigms – SDN and VNF, in combination with Big Data technologies. Large amount of network equipment and status data is analyzed. The results of data analysis are semantically annotated and stored into RDF triple store, so semantic reasoning can be performed in order to draw new conclusions which could lead to re-deployment of virtual networking assets, generation of SDN rules, parameter tuning or other optimizations with objective to satisfy user-defined QoS parameters and maintain the quality of high definition live video streaming in varying network conditions, where devices are moving intensively (such as mobile robotic and experimentation systems).

In several publications so far, this topic has been discussed, problems identified and several solutions proposed. However, in most cases, these solutions suffer from low quality, large end-to-end latency in live streaming and frequent freezes in the video playout due to sudden drops of the available bandwidth [22]. In [22], it was shown network-based prioritization introduced by an OpenFlow, SDN-enabled controller can reduce video freezes caused by network congestion. Therefore, the utilization of SDN technologies in this case seems promising. In [23], results confirm that it is now possible to realize a short-range THz wireless communication system for commercial applications where Ultra HD video streaming is needed. However, it is not suitable for use cases like experimentation and mobile robot where long-range wireless communication is of utmost importance.

We can conclude that there are still many open questions in case of ultra/high definition live video streaming using wireless networks, which makes it suitable for future research and application of next generation networking in synergy with Big Data and semantic technologies.

3.6 Multi-party Trust Based on Blockchain for Process Monitoring

IoT and smart objects are key-enabler technologies for monitoring of complex business processes [24], especially in logistics domain and industrial production systems [25]. However, most of these processes involve multiple parties. In absence of central authority, the trust between these parties becomes an important issue [25, 26]. Despite the fact that artifact-driven monitoring enables to effectively keep track of the execution of processes where multiple organizations are involved, it does not fully solve the problem of trust among them. As the devices involved in monitoring process might belong to different organizations, there is still a possibility that one of the parties can misconfigure its devices in order to achieve some own goal in an illegal way, with possibility to disrupt the process execution itself, affecting the final outcome.

Blockchain technology is recognized as a solution for issues related to trust in multi-party process monitoring systems [25–27]. Blockchain provides a shared immutable ledger, which guarantees that the information can be accessed and validated by all the participants of a process both during its execution and after it is completed, which builds the trust among them.

This use case represents a potential area where we can make use of synergy of various novel technologies and paradigms, such as IoT, Big Data and next generation networking together with blockchain.

3.7 Trusted Friend Computing

With the advent of 5G networks, an increasing number of devices will be connected permanently and at high speed to the Internet and to each other. While many applications will benefit from this new connectivity by being able to interact more quickly with data providers, such as the cloud or other resources, there is also a growing need for privacy-conscious data sharing. This is particularly the case in the context of Big Data, which also includes the issue of moving large amounts of private data. One possible approach to this problem is to move calculations close to the data and provide access to both data and local computing resources.

The Trusted Friend Computing (TFC) concept aims to enable a community of users to securely share their IT resources without a central organization collecting and storing information. It is a distributed, resource-centered paradigm where data, computing power, software or the network can be shared reliably and resiliently. This paradigm defines an original IT architecture built around the notion of a community of users (called friends) of a given software application. Instead of using the traditional approach where the IT architecture is middleware-centric to share resources, the TFC approach focuses on the software application used by the community. One of the important advantages of this approach is to avoid heavy executable codes transfers since all friends already possess the calculation modules useful for the community. Inspired by the social network model and using a concept similar to virtual private networks (VPNs), the idea is to allow friends to invite other users of the software to join the community to share their resources. The community is therefore built by individual cooptation and is, by nature, distributed, decentralized and elastic.

To achieve this objective, several major technical challenges must be addressed. We can, among other things, mention:

- Clearly define a security model for sharing IT resources in the context of TFC applications;
- The definition of community management and accounting needs;
- The development of a platform to enable and facilitate the implementation of applications that comply with the TFC model.

Finally, a user community focused on using a specific application must be identified and the application must be enhanced with TFC features. One of these communities is that of physicians involved in the diagnosis of genetic diseases and using the GensearchNGS tool [28]. This Java software analyzes next-generation sequencing data (NGS) to detect changes in DNA sequences for the diagnosis of genetic diseases [29, 30]. In order to be able to easily integrate into any Java software, including GensearchNGS, TFC capabilities the POP-Java tool [31, 32] was used. This tool has been improved to support the different functionalities required for TFC-compatible applications [33].

TFC's security model is based on the notion of a "confidence link" as presented in [34]. A confidence link is a two-way channel that allows two friends to communicate safely at any time. The confidence link also authenticates users with a security certificate, ensuring the identification of communicating partners. Each member of a network can extend the network by creating additional confidence links with other friends, thus adding new members to the network. All friends as well as all confidence links form a connected graph where the nodes are friends and the arcs are the confidence links. We call such a graph a "community of trusted friends" or more simply a "community". None of the friends in the community have a global view of the infrastructure. Each friend only knows his direct friends, i.e. the users with whom he has established a confidence link.

Applications can publish resources on a network of friends or search and access the resources of other network members. When publishing a resource, specific access rights can be given to limit access to the resource, for example by differentiating between direct and indirect friends in a network.

The model also includes the ability to record the use of each member's resources, which allows the use of resources to be billed based on their utilization rate, thereby encouraging members to share their resources.

Today, and certainly even more so tomorrow, the use of mobile networks for professional applications will be a reality. These applications are less and less confined to work desktops but are now used outside the enterprise environment for efficiency and ease of use. A concept such as TFC can truly benefit from a high-performance mobile communications network such as 5G networks to provide professional communities with secure access, anytime, anywhere, to vast computing and data resources.

3.8   Virtual and Augmented Reality Applications

Virtual (VR) and augmented reality (AR) applications are not exceptions when it comes to potential use cases where utilization of 5G networks could be highly beneficial. The arrival of next-generation of mobile network will unlock the full potential of VR and AR technology, which is still limited by current network characteristics. The complex graphically-rich scenes and sophisticated input mechanisms that are used to create the VR and AR experiences require a large amount of data that has to be processed [35]. Lag, stutter, and stalls are unacceptable for user experience and comfort [36]. This is not a huge problem for local applications, but is quite challenging when done remotely, if the user is on the move and not using the fixed network connection [35]. In this case, the quality of VR and AR experience is heavily dependent on three network components: high capacity, low latency and uniform experience. This way, many novel services and applications that involve the usage of augmented and virtual reality would see lights of the day, such as immersive movies, video games, live shows, concerts, sport events, immersive education platforms, immersive social interactions, immersive professional project collaboration and many others [35–37]. To sum up, these services would affect the way that people play, learn and communicate [36].

4 Current Solutions and Future Challenges

4.1 5G Positioning

Possible Error Sources State of the Art

When considering the 5G positioning aspect, ultra-dense BS deployments, increased transmission bandwidths, and large antenna arrays enable efficient utilization of both ranging-based (e.g., time-of-arrival (ToA) and time-difference-of-arrival (TDoA)), and angle-based (e.g., direction-of-arrival (DoA)) positioning measurements. However, in order to exploit these types of measurements for positioning, specific prior knowledge about the network and user device is often assumed available. In case of temporal measurements, the clocks of the user device and network nodes are often assumed to be synchronized. More specifically, with ToA measurements, all clocks in the network, including the user device and the BSs, are typically assumed to be synchronized among each other, whereas with TDoA measurements, only the BS clocks are assumed to be synchronized. Nonetheless, clock synchronization errors can result in large inaccuracies in ranging measurements, and thus, has to be carefully considered in a practical positioning system implementation. Besides the aforementioned clock errors, the ranging measurements as well as angle-based measurements can be deteriorated by the errors related to BSs' locations. In addition to the inaccurate BSs' location information, uncertainties in the orientation of the BS antennas and/or the user device antennas may cause significant error to the positioning results when utilizing angle-based measurements like DoA measurements for positioning.

Whereas the BS position and antenna orientation error can be typically considered time-invariant, the clock errors are often time-variant with certain time-drifting behavior. However, it is appropriate to assume that the time-variant behavior of the BS clocks can be sufficiently small, and thus, there can be only a possible constant clock offset between the BS clocks. Nonetheless, any unknown (or uncertain) system parameter, such as clock offset, BS positions and antenna orientation, can be estimated using classical simultaneous localization and mapping (SLAM) approaches, where the user device position and the unknown system parameters are estimated simultaneously while the user device is moving within the network coverage area.

Since the 5G specifications are still under development and 5G networks are only beginning to emerge to the market, the state-of-the-art 5G positioning studies rely on high computational load computer simulations using realistic radio wave propagation models with extensive 3D ray tracing algorithms. In [38], a network-centric positioning approach was studied by considering asynchronous clocks in the user device and in the network BSs. It was shown that regardless of the clock errors, sub-meter positioning accuracy was achieved by using the ToA and DoA measurements. Moreover, while the user device was moving in the network, the network BSs were synchronized similar to the well-known SLAM principle. This type of approach was later used in [39] for investigating location-aware communications, including applications for proactive radio resource management and location-based geometric beamforming.

A user-centric positioning approach based on signals from a single BS was studied in [40]. In this case, by utilizing only a single BS for the positioning, requirements for the clock synchronization can be considerably alleviated. Based on the ToA and angle-of-arrival (AoA) measurements, the user device position was estimated with sub-meter accuracy and the antenna orientation of the user device with sub-degree accuracy. Moreover, the developed estimation algorithm was also designed to exploit reflected (or scattered) radio wave components, and therefore, it was able to provide position estimates also for the reflection locations. This type of utilization of non-line-of-sight radio paths introduces various new communications aspects from advanced beam-forming techniques to environment-aware interference management. The user-centric positioning approach was also studied in [41] for a high-speed train scenario utilizing 5G-specified downlink synchronization signal blocks for positioning purposes. Again, despite of the challenging BS geometry of the train scenario, sub-meter positioning accuracy was achieved by jointly using the ToA and AoA measurements.

The network-centric positioning with uncertain BS antenna orientations was studied in [42], where the positioning was based on type of signals used in conventional beam training procedures. By using beam-wise received signal power measurements the user device position and the unknown BS antenna orientations were jointly estimated achieving a sub-meter positioning error and a sub-degree antenna orientation error.

Semantic Analysis of Network Topology and Sensor Data for High-Precision Localization in 5G Networks Challenges

High-accuracy positioning has been considered as one of the key features of future generation network and still an open question in many areas, such as robotics, drone-based experimentation and exploration, autonomous vehicles and intelligent transportation systems.

This task becomes quite challenging in these cases, especially when it comes to indoor localization [43] and outdoor localization of fast-moving aerial devices [44] in varying network conditions (drones).

Mobile-network-based positioning can be divided in two categories: user-centric and network-centric. There are various positioning methods which perform with different values of accuracy, latency and time-to-fix in certain conditions.

It is identified that current research in 5G localization is going towards cooperation [45, 46]. Therefore, the semantic coordination of both user and network operator devices could be used for determining the precise location, taking into account two factors:

1. Network topology: how the devices are arranged in space within the network, such as distance, frequency band at which the device is operating etc. The information about network topology can be semantically annotated leveraging some domain-specific language as a representation.
2. Service utilization and sensor data: a large amount of service utilization and sensor data is collected from both the customer and network operator devices (such as monitoring and status). It can be analyzed leveraging various data analysis technique. Furthermore, the data can be semantically annotated according to the results obtained as output of data analysis techniques.

For this purpose, we define domain-specific ontologies and rules which are used to perform semantic reasoning about the precise location leveraging the semantic annotations about both the network topology and service utilization/sensor data, taking into account the user-defined performance metrics and QoS parameters, such as accuracy, latency and time-to-fix (Fig. 1).

Fig. 1. Semantic analysis of network topology and sensor data for high-precision localization in 5G networks.

4.2 Infrastructure Design of Semantic Driven Big Data in 5G Networking

Semantic Driven Big Data State of the Art
Problems of 5G coordination, power consumption and network behavior prediction feature smart adoption of high-volume data processing results by the system that we propose to address using semantics. In particular, core of the proposed infrastructure is a server, centralized or distributed, that collects relevant knowledge in the given environment and uses the knowledge to make necessary informative decisions, for example about network coordination, network sensors power consumption etc. The server collects networking data and interprets data semantically. For the knowledge representation, the server uses ontology framework approach. The first version of the framework has been previously successfully applied in the case of coordination of technologies that operate in the same unlicensed frequency band [17, 47]. The

coordination and spectrum sensing is modelled as an interactive process, where system nodes communicate and share knowledge about relevant spectrum conditions. Semantic channels are established within the system for the interaction between participating communication devices. The ontology framework could be extended for different cases such as solution presented in [48] that could give further directions for management of semantic Big Data for intelligence.

System that incorporates sensors and 5G user equipment acquire large collection of data. Collecting, storing, analyzing and retrieving data from industrial sensors or other machinery connected to the Internet of Things has become of increasing importance, as a growing number of organizations is looking to take advantage of available data.

One possible semantic framework approach has been successfully proven in many cases. In [17], the case of semantic LTE-U coordination is presented. The coordination and spectrum sensing is modelled as an interactive process, where system nodes communicate and share knowledge about relevant spectrum conditions. Ontologies are used for knowledge representation as bases for automatic reasoning about optimal channel allocations and for coordination. Moreover, in [49] the semantic technology was used for the implementation of network intelligence on top of the FIESTA-IoT platform by using reasoning for the network state estimation in order to perform the spectrum coordination. On the other side, in [50, 51], a semantic-driven approach for unmanned vehicle mission coordination in robotic experimentation testbeds is presented. In this case, the ontologies are used to represent the knowledge about device capabilities, constraints, domain expert knowledge and both the design-time (mission code) and run-time (sensor data) aspects that are taken into account during the generation of the coordinated device missions. Furthermore, in the paper [52] is presented the novel semantic-based approach and algorithm for automatic code generation with huge potential with its extension to 5G applications.

Semantic Driven 5G System Architecture Challenges
The challenge is to exploit semantic technologies at the backend as a flexible foundation for advanced frontend data processing tasks. Possible system architecture consists of five modules given in Fig. 2 and described in more details in the following.

(1) Data Acquisition Module (DAM): Redis is an in-memory database with option of persistence on disk, so it represents a tradeoff where very high write and read speed is achieved at the price of the limitation of data sets that can't be larger than memory [53–55]. We assume data sources at the order of million data series with about million measurements annually for few tens of years with several bytes of a data item size. Hence, size of the total data load could be estimated at the order of a petabyte (PB). The row data has low information density, and as such it is very susceptible for compression. Hence, it can be expected that a 100 times compression rate can be achieved easily (e.g. simple run-length encoding). Big Data technologies can be used for ultra-large scale data sets processing. Distributed storage and processing frameworks are used for that, such as the open source Apache Hadoop Framework [56]. Apache Hadoop enables distributed data processing across clusters of computers. Popular MapReduce distributed data-processing model, Hadoop Distributed File System (HDFS), and distributed table store HBase [57] are Hadoop components.

(2) The Pre-Processing Module (PPM) identifies instability intervals that are semantically annotated, stored, and retrieved later on during search by end user. Anomaly detection is an important problem that has been under extensive research in diverse application domains. We distinguish two basic types of approaches with respect to domain specification as well as online or offline processing. These approaches are not mutually exclusive but, in opposite, they can be used together to achieve a synergy effect. Results obtained in such a way can be used for instant reaction but also for longer term planning activities. They can provide users a valuable information, which can be used proactively, further improve system

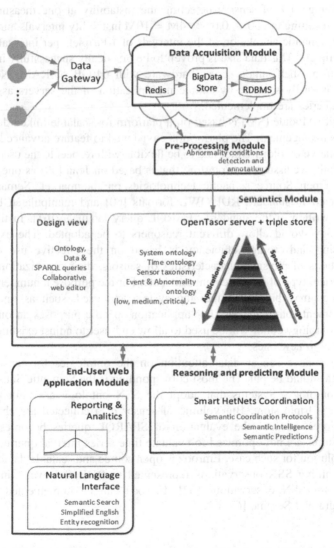

Fig. 2. System architecture for Semantic Driven Big Data in 5G networking.

efficiency and give competitive advantages. In most cases a refining of input data is needed as a first step. Anomaly detection in time series data obtained by sensors [58] is a very demanding task but really important in the same time.

A simple low-complexity algorithm for instability intervals detection is envisioned. The process complexity shall be encapsulated into a separate instability parameters construction module that would extract the parameters from data series in an independent batch-processing manner. Semantic description of the instability interval may be more or less complex depending on the end user application requirements. However, it contains pointer to the corresponding row data record that are stored separately such that semantic search may retrieve row data also. We estimate no more than 250 potential instability intervals within one series annually with average 1% of sensors detecting the instability at one measurement time instant, resulting in $250 \times 0.01 \times 4M = 10M$ instability intervals annually. If we assume semantic annotation of the intervals of 10 triplets per interval, it totals to 100M triplets. This data size is proven to be practically successfully implemented on a off-the-shelf single server hardware with 64 GB of RAM. Note that the system is easily scalable by simple multiplication of the servers assuming federated queries are implemented.

(3) Semantics Module (SM) is based on a platform for scalable linked data semantic datasets management. The platform is envisioned to feature advanced Web based collaborative ontology editor and to be flexible with respect to the used triplestore. By default, we assume a triplestore that is based on Jena [59] as one of the most proven Open Source semantic technologies on the market. Semantic data is represented in standard RDF/OWL formats [60] and manipulated by semantic queries written in the standard SPARQL query language [61]. In this way, the technology would allow different reasoners to be adopted. The expected data processing and storage efficiency is based on the effective use of semantic descriptions of physical characteristics of sensors, their organization and placement, price, type of measurement units, etc. For the purpose a number of standard ontologies may be loaded into the system and used, such as time ontology, measurements ontology, etc. For application specific purposes an online collaborative ontology editor will be used to allow end-user to adjust existing ontologies and develop new ones.

When we have sensor data, attention on the ontologies for sensor data and metadata should be put. The most corresponding is the Semantic Sensor Network (SSN) ontology. Systems that adopt the SSN ontology are built on an RDF database - triple store. Big volume of sensor data collected are challenging to triple stores, because the evaluation of SPARQL queries becomes expensive. Triple stores are not optimized to evaluate time series interval queries. Emrooz is good solution for such case. Emrooz is open source and scalable database capable of consuming SSN observations represented in RDF and evaluating SPARQL queries for SSN observations [62]. Emrooz can be implemented on Apache Cassandra and Sesame [62, 63].

(4) End-User Web Application Module (WAM) is envisioned to be implemented as an advanced Ajax front-end that communicates with back-end using RESTful service API and SPARQL queries. It should consist of the following sub-modules:

   (a) NLP Sub-Module: user enters search query in simplified English, such that low cognitive load for end user is required while in the same time certain domain language specifics are exploited in order to lower complexity of the language use and processing. The input is then processed and converted to SPARQL query for semantic search over the semantically annotated data. Data preprocessing algorithms can then be used to retrieve intervals of unstable states, with recorded date and time of the start and end of the data sequence. Every time series is semantically annotated also: name of the physical property, type of the measurement unit, name of the subsystem (and/or machine and/or location ...), attached sensor, etc. Semantic descriptions of data are automatically generated during preprocessing and are later used for making autocomplete recommendations to the user, to help him easily search the time series descriptions. Then, key segments are identified related to the given search query, where each of the segments can describe date, time, abnormality in measured physical unit (on some sensor with some features), and all/some unstable data overlapping with an extracted instability interval [64]. In this way, we are able to make more effective and user friendly queries.

   (b) Reporting & Analytics Sub-Module: Results of the data analysis are visually presented by means of visually appealing charts, graphs, tables, etc. Semantic filtering is applied for powerful faceted search and browsing through the search results. Also, data analysts are able to reconfigure online data presentation into simple web applications that could be instantly used by the other team members.

Semantic similarity between the input query and annotations of the instability intervals is used as the indicator of coincidence between data sets and the search query. Multilingual support can be provided by existing features defined in the standard RDF/XML language support. As a consequence of the NLP module that is based on representing concepts by the supporting ontologies, multilingualism is supported naturally. Though, some additional effort would be required depending on the type and number of additional languages.

Additional features: Different characterizations and taxonomies of the instability intervals are possible including for example classification of the abnormal events as low, middle, high or critical. We can also specify the intensity of the abnormality as a percentage of the deviation of maximal measured value in the instability interval from the target value. For example, we may define abnormality as "deviation between 7% and 20%". Estimation of conditional probability of overlapping of two or more instability intervals will be based on simple analytics algorithms such as counting ("x of y" or "x/y", 6 of 9 or 7/10, in searching results indicate overlapping of the instability intervals). Advanced user-friendly simplified English based search for causality chains for identification of the root cause is possible. Similarly, a set of intervals rooted by a specified interval can be determined as well.

(5) Reasoning and Predicting Module (RPM) is envisioned to be implemented as an advanced neural network. Neural networks can be adopted for learning component of the RPM. Neural networks have been proven effective in interference detection and classification within wireless networks [65, 66] as well as in time-series prediction tasks [67] that are crucial for coordination.

4.3　5G Security Challenges

Security solutions for 5G can be divided into five groups: Software Defined Network (SDN), Network Function Virtualization (NFV), Mobile Cloud (MC), communication channels and privacy policies [68]. Primary focuses with target technologies described in [68] are: security of centralized control points (SDN, NFV); flow rules verification in SDN switches (SDN); control access to SDN and core network elements (SDN, NFV, MC); isolation for VNFs and virtual slices (NFV); security of control channels (SDN and channels themselves); user identity verification for roaming and clouds services (privacy policies); security of users identity and location (privacy policies); encryption and anti-malware technologies (privacy policies); security of data, storage systems and web services in clouds (MC); service-based access control security for clouds (MC).

Each of this target and security technologies are deeply investigated in [68].

Security of 5G will be a big challenge because it will connect branches of critical infrastructures. However, to make 5G a safe technology, security solutions will consider not only this integrated critical infrastructure but also society as a whole, [68]. The basic challenges mentioned in [68] and [69] are:

- High network traffic - a huge number of IoT devices.
- Security of radio communications.
- Cryptographic integrity of user data plane.
- Roaming Security - updating security parameters between operators of networks.
- Denial of Service and Distributed Denial of Service attacks on infrastructure and end devices.
- Coordination of distributed control systems (like Non-Access Stratum layers of 3GPP protocols).
- Eavesdropping. This attack may lead to intercepting messages by an attacked receiver and is very hard to detect.
- Jamming. This attack may lead to disrupting a communication between legitimate users or block access to radio resources. Very often is realized via an infected receiver.
- Man in The Middle attack. Attacker takes control over communication between legitimate users.
- Basic requirements like authentication, authorization, availability or data confidentiality. Some of the current technologies fulfilling these requirements may be not effective enough in 5G context.

4.4   5G Simulations

A very popular method of finding problems, predicting behavior and developing improvements in system is analyzing the simulation of this system. In 5G cellular communication new simulation systems have to be developed because of a huge number of new services, applications requirements, and performance indicators, [70]. There are three basic types of simulations: link-level, system-level, and network-level. Authors in [70] describe the following challenges connected to all of these three types of simulation:

- Variety of application, technologies, environments and performance indicators.
- Complexity of simulation and simulators. It is caused by growing memory demands and time of simulation which is a result of huge MIMO and complexity of channels.
- Integration of all these three types of simulations. Integration of link-level and system-level simulation may be useful in the evaluation of nonlinear operations (like NOMA) in complex environments. Integration of system-level and network-level simulation is useful in the evaluation of the end to-end performance of all network.

Other challenges, like reusability, scalability, flexibility, multiple levels of abstraction or parallel processing are deeply investigated in [70].

4.5   Radio-Access Research and Propagation Issues

One of the expectations for 5G is to ensure prospective radio-access technologies which will be integrated and will allow creating a long-term networked society [71]. Seven main challenges in this field mentioned in [71] are multi-hop communication, device-to-device communication, cooperative devices, ultra-reliable communication, massive machine-type communication, inter-vehicular/vehicular-to-road communication, and ultra-dense deployments.

The principals of propagation of centimeter waves are very similar to millimeter waves but have different characteristic [72]. The most important differences in those characteristics are free space path loss, diffraction, reflection and scattering, material penetration. These problems can be solved by deploying a Multi Input Single Output System described in [72]. OFDM can be used as a base for developing a new system of encoding digital data on multiple carrier frequencies [72]. OFDM will allow to avoid multipath effect, gain spectral efficiency, and simplify equalization (in comparison with Single-Carrier Systems) [72].

4.6   Millimeter Waves and 5G Standardization

Millimeter waves have a bigger spectrum in cellular frequency bands then centimeters waves [71]. This provides new radio-design opportunities and challenges, like [71]:

- Very high capacity and data rates.
- "Short wavelengths necessitating large array antenna solutions to maintain useful link budgets".
- Antenna sizes will be smaller (design challenges).

Standardization of 5G is a still on-going process. However, some decisions have been already made. The World Radio Communication Conference promoted bands lower than 6 GHz or between 24–84 GHz in 2015 [71]. A Third Generation Partnership Project (3GPP) completed first 5G specification in 2018. Below 6 GHz bandwidth requirements regarding cellular network did not change because of similarity of propagation conditions in new and existing bands [71]. More technical information about higher bands and accepted by 3GPP standards can be found in [71] and [73].

4.7   5G Modulation Schemes

Extreme data rates, a huge number of IoT devices, high-speed high resolution streaming videos - this are only examples what 5G will be used for. The main challenge is to support very fast entry to the network, even for transferring trivial data, [74]. To achieve this goal proper modulation scheme have to be chosen.

Orthogonal Frequency Division Multiplexing is a classic modulation scheme based on dividing available bandwidth into several parallel sub-channels. Each of these sub-channels (called also sub-carriers) can transmit independent data. Multiplexing in time and frequency is possible. However, authors in [74] proposed three modulations schemes, with better Peak to Average Power Ratio and better spectrum efficiency. These modulations schemes are, [74]:

- Filter Bank Multi-carrier (FBMC) - each sub-carrier is filtered independently. Cycle prefix is not used. Offset-QAM is used for orthogonality.
- Generalized Frequency Division Multiplexing (GFDM) adaptable multiple carrier transmission methods. Each sub-carrier is filtered independently. There is no orthogonality. Available spectrum is spread into segments.
- Filtered Orthogonal Frequency Division Multiplexing (F-OFDM) - an extension of classic OFDM. Bandwidth is divided into sub-bands depending on the application. Each sub-band provide proper service. The spectrum is accommodating a range of services which optimize its usage.

Comparison of all these modulation schemes, results and conclusions can be found in [63].

4.8   Machine Learning in Software Defined Networks

The 5G technology entails a significant increase in the amount of processed data. The continuous collection and analysis of such data leads to a Big Data problems that are caused by the volume, variety and velocity properties [75].

However, a key aspect of the operation of each network is its management and control. Recently, most of a network functions (e.g. routing, switching, firewalling, conversion of protocols etc.) were realized by dedicated hardware. The complexity of a network infrastructure increases a number of challenges in organizing, managing and optimizing network operations. The popular idea for solving these problems is Software Defined Networking (SDN) paradigm. SDN allows to migrate many of network functions from the devices to the software-defined networking controllers. The SDN controller manages flow control, analyses network traffic and routes packets according to forwarding policies. Consequently, SDN controller serves as a sort of operating system for the network.

Taking into account aforementioned challenges and problem of processing large data sets, there is a need for developing efficient and much more complex management methods. Such management methods require making decisions in the real time. There are a lot of known data processing methods. However, many of them cannot be directly applied for effective processing and management of large data sets in modern environments, such as 5G networks. Modern solutions require complex decision making techniques that analyze historical, temporal and frequency network data [76].

One of the possible solutions could be the application of Machine Learning (ML) methods, which are successfully used in the processing of Big Data [77–80]. The capabilities of SDN (e.g. centralized control, global view of the network, software-based network analysis, and dynamic forwarding policies) may fit well to the application of Machine Learning techniques [81]. These possibilities are included in the FCAPS (Fault, Configuration, Accounting, Performance, Security) management ISO standard [82]. In each of the following areas of application one can find intelligent methods [78]:

In the fault management area, ML methods allow not only detection, but also solving the causes of failures in networks. Automation dealing with failures will allow for minimization of downtime and human intervention and, as a result, minimization of losses.

Machine Learning can play important role also in configuration management. Networks such as 5G are characterized by frequent topological changes. This requires modifications in the configuration, which can be prone to errors and difficult to optimize. Considering the multiplicity of configuration parameters, analyses of ML can help to automate this process, e.g. by dynamic resources allocation or services configuration. Appropriate methods can also allow verification of the used configuration and its possible withdrawal and rollback.

Accounting management is tightly connected with monitoring of network resources and pricing plans. ML methods can help identify fraud and dishonest activities of network users. It is also possible to analyze the use of resources and create new service packages. Smart solutions can also significantly improve the QoS level.

An important area of management is performance management. Guaranteeing adequate level of performance is a key factor for efficient network. The use of ML methods can result in traffic load prediction, and, in result, proactive and adaptive network performance management.

Security Management has become crucial issue in networks. Modern security approaches consist of tools for identifying threats and vulnerabilities. The use of ML methods can help in detection of anomalies finding and abuses verification in the network. However, this approach has a high risk of blocking the correct network traffic (high false positive rate). Identifying the nature of the cyber-attack is crucial to choosing appropriate remedies allowed returning to the proper functioning of the network.

The aforementioned opportunities show a wide field for applying ML methods in Software Defined Networking paradigm. Machine Learning can play the major role in autonomous network management for 5G networks. Some of the available solutions, such as IBM's MAPE-K or CogNet, are successfully supported by Machine Learning methods [76, 78].

5 Conclusion

Use case opportunities will increase enormously with 5G networks deployment. Not only that the existing applications and solutions will be enhanced, but many novel use cases and scenarios will become feasible. The potential for further 5G use cases in future services and applications is huge in industries and national priorities including domains from entertainment and telecommunication services, to healthcare, smart cities, remote industrial machine operation, virtual sports attendance and many others.

However, the future scenarios will place much more diverse requirements on the system that need to be explored and analyzed. It is identified that the main enablers of future 5G networks are Internet of Things (IoT), Big Data technologies, together with novel networking paradigms – Software-Defined Networking (SDN) and Network Functions Virtualization (NFV). New architectures will rely on large number of connected smart devices generating enormous amount of data each moment. The generated data needs to be analyzed in order to make the right decision as soon as possible, almost in real time. On the other side, the increased flexibility of network infrastructure management and fine-grained control is also required, which is enabled by NFV and SDN. Furthermore, there is a need for evolution of the current architectures by adding the additional network intelligence layer that would enable more complex scenarios, such as device coordination. The possible approaches for embedding the network intelligence are either using the semantic technology or machine learning techniques.

The future may seem far ahead but the phase for defining the requirements is now. Any new technology or system that we design for 5G needs to be deployed and evaluated, and it is expected to last at least until the end of the next decade.

References

1. Buzzi, S., et al.: A survey of energy-efficient techniques for 5G networks and challenges ahead. IEEE J. Sel. Areas Commun. **34**(4), 697–709 (2016)
2. The 1000x data challenge, Qualcomm, Technical report. http://www.qualcomm.com/1000x. Accessed 29 Jan 2019
3. Yang, L., Zhang, W.: Introduction. In: Yang, L., Zhang, W. (eds.) Interference Coordination for 5G Cellular Networks. SpringerBriefs in Electrical and Computer Engineering, pp. 1–11. Springer, Cham (2015). https://doi.org/10.1007/978-3-319-24723-6_1
4. Salem, F.E., et al.: A energy consumption optimization in 5G networks using multilevel beamforming and large scale antenna systems. In: Proceedings of 2016 IEEE Wireless Communications and Networking Conference, pp. 1–6 (2016). https://doi.org/10.1109/wcnc.2016.7564904
5. López, B., et al.: An approach to data analysis in 5G networks. Entropy **19**(74), 1–23 (2017). https://doi.org/10.3390/e19020074
6. Ejaz, W., et al.: Internet of Things (IoT) in 5G wireless communications. IEEE Access **4**, 10310–10314 (2016). https://doi.org/10.1109/ACCESS.2016.2646120
7. Pérez, M., et al.: Self-organizing capabilities in 5G networks: NFV & SDN coordination in a complex use case. In: Proceedings of EuCNC 2018, pp. 1–5 (2018)
8. Khan, M., et al.: Location awareness in 5G networks using RSS measurements for public safety applications. IEEE Access **5**, 21753–21762 (2017)

9. Mohammed, A.F., Humbe, V.T., Chowhan, S.S.: A review of big data environment and its related technologies. In: Proceedings of 2016 International Conference on Information Communication and Embedded Systems (ICICES), pp. 1–5 (2016)
10. Hu, F.: Opportunities in 5G Networks: A Research and Development Perspective. CRC Press, Boca Raton (2016)
11. 3GPP, TS 38.455 (V15.1.0): NG-RAN; NR Positioning Protocol A (NRPPa) (2018)
12. 3GPP, TR 38.913 (v14.3.0): Study on scenarios and requirements for next generation access technologies (2017)
13. 3GPP, TR 22.872 (v16.1.0): Study on positioning use cases; Stage 1 (2018)
14. 3GPP, TR 38.305 (v15.1.0). Stage 2 functional specification of User Equipment (UE) positioning in NG-RAN (2018)
15. Soret, B., et al.: Interference coordination for 5G new radio. IEEE Wirel. Commun. 25(3), 131–137 (2018)
16. Milosevic, N., Dimitrijevic, B., Drajic, D., Nikolic, Z., Tosic, M.: LTE and WiFi co-existence in 5 GHz unlicensed band. Facta Universitatis, Electron. Energ. 30(3), 363–373 (2017)
17. Tosic, M., et al.: Semantic coordination protocol for LTE and Wi-Fi coexistence. In: Proceedings of European Conference on Networks and Communications, EUCNC 2016, Athens, Greece, pp. 27–30 (2016)
18. Rizvi, S., et al.: An investigation of energy efficiency in 5G wireless networks. In: Proceedings of 2017 International Conference on Circuits, System and Simulation (ICCSS), pp. 142–145 (2017)
19. Abdalla, S., Ariffin, S.: The enhanced user history-based prediction in 5G. In: Proceedings of the Fourth International Conference on Advances in Computing, Communication and Information Technology - CCIT, pp. 1–5 (2016)
20. What is GNSS? https://www.gsa.europa.eu/european-gnss/what-gnss. Accessed 29 Jan 2019
21. Kacianka, S., Hellwagner, H.: Adaptive video streaming for UAV networks. In: Proceedings of the 7th ACM International Workshop on Mobile Video - MoVid 2015, pp. 25–30 (2015)
22. Petrangeli, S., et al.: Live streaming of 4K ultra-high definition video over the Internet. In: Proceedings of the 7th International Conference on Multimedia Systems Article No. 27, pp. 1–4 (2016). https://doi.org/10.1145/2910017.2910627
23. Nallappan, K., et al.: Live streaming of uncompressed 4K video using Terahertz wireless links. In: Proceedings of 2018 IEEE International Conference on Communications (ICC), pp. 1–7 (2018). https://doi.org/10.1109/icc.2018.8422216
24. Meroni, G., Di Ciccio, C., Mendling, J.: Artifact-driven process monitoring: dynamically binding real-world objects to running processes. In: Proceedings of the Forum and Doctoral Consortium Papers Presented at the 29th International Conference on Advanced Information Systems Engineering, CAiSE 2017, Essen, Germany, pp. 1–9 (2017)
25. Meroni, G., Plebani, P.: Combining artifact-driven monitoring with blockchain: analysis and solutions. In: Matulevičius, R., Dijkman, R. (eds.) CAiSE 2018. LNBIP, vol. 316, pp. 103–114. Springer, Cham (2018). https://doi.org/10.1007/978-3-319-92898-2_8
26. Baresi, L., et al.: mArtifact: an artifact-driven process monitoring platform. In: Proceedings of BPM Demo Track Co-Located with 15th International Conference on Business Process Modeling, BPM 2017, Barcelona, Spain, pp. 1–5 (2017)
27. Weber, I., Xu, X., Riveret, R., Governatori, G., Ponomarev, A., Mendling, J.: Untrusted business process monitoring and execution using blockchain. In: La Rosa, M., Loos, P., Pastor, O. (eds.) BPM 2016. LNCS, vol. 9850, pp. 329–347. Springer, Cham (2016). https://doi.org/10.1007/978-3-319-45348-4_19
28. Wolf, B., et al.: DNAseq workflow in a diagnostic context, and an example of a user friendly implementation. J. Biomed. Biotechnol. 2015(3), 1–11 (2015)

29. Wolf, B., et al.: Safe variant annotation sharing across laboratories. In: Variant Detection 2017, Spain (2017)
30. Böck, J., et al.: Single CpG hypermethylation, allele methylation errors, and decreased expression of multiple tumor suppressor genes in normal body cells of mutation-negative early-onset and high-risk breast cancer patients. Int. J. Cancer **143**, 1416–1425 (2018)
31. POP-Java: Parallel Programming with Java. https://icosys.ch/pop-java. Accessed 29 Jan 2019
32. Wolf, B., Kuonen, P., Dandekar, T.: POP-Java: Parallélisme et distribution orienté objet. In: Proceedings of the Conférence d'informatique en Parallélisme, Architecture et Système, Compas2014, Neuchâtel, Switzerland, pp. 1–13 (2014)
33. Wolf, B., Loïc, M., Kuonen, P.: FriendComputing: organic application centric distributed computing. In: Proceedings of the Second International Workshop on Sustainable Ultrascale Computing Systems, NESUS 2015, Krakow, Poland, pp. 117–119 (2015)
34. Kuonen, P., Clement, V., Bapst, F.: Securing the grid using virtualization: the ViSaG model. In: Proceedings of the Fifth International Conference on Cloud Computing, GRIDs, and Virtualization, Cloud Computing 2014, Venice, Italy, pp. 49–54 (2014)
35. Enabling Mobile Augmented and Virtual Reality with 5G Networks. AT&T (2018). https://about.att.com/content/dam/snrdocs/Foundry%20ARVR%20Public%20Whitepaper.pdf. Accessed 29 Jan 2019
36. VR and AR pushing connectivity limits. Qualcomm Technologies, Inc. (2018). https://www.qualcomm.com/media/documents/files/vr-and-ar-pushing-connectivity-limits.pdf. Accessed 29 Jan 2019
37. Augmented and Virtual Reality: the First Wave of 5G Killer Apps. Qualcomm Technologies, Inc. (2017). https://www.qualcomm.com/media/documents/files/augmented-and-virtual-reality-the-first-wave-of-5g-killer-apps.pdf. Accessed 29 Jan 2019
38. Koivisto, M., et al.: Joint device positioning and clock synchronization in 5G ultra-dense networks. IEEE Trans. Wirel. Commun. **16**(5), 2866–2881 (2017)
39. Koivisto, M., Hakkarainen, A., Costa, M., Kela, P., Leppänen, K., Valkama, M.: High-efficiency device positioning and location-aware communications in dense 5G networks. IEEE Commun. Mag. **55**(8), 188–195 (2017)
40. Talvitie, J., Valkama, M., Destino, G., Wymeersch, H.: Novel algorithms for high-accuracy joint position and orientation estimation in 5G mmWave systems. In: Proceedings of IEEE Globecom Workshops, pp. 1–7 (2017)
41. Talvitie, J., Levanen, T., Koivisto, M., Pajukoski K., Renfors, M., Valkama, M.: Positioning of high-speed trains using 5G new radio synchronization signals. In: Proceedings of IEEE Wireless Communications and Networking Conference, WCNC 2018, pp. 1–6 (2018)
42. Rastorgueva-Foi, E., Costa, M., Koivisto, M., Talvitie, J., Leppänen, K., Valkama M.: Beam-based device positioning in mmWave 5G systems under orientation uncertainties. In: Proceedings of Asilomar Conference on Signals, Systems, and Computers (2018)
43. Witrisal, et al.: High-accuracy positioning for indoor applications: RFID, UWB, 5G, and beyond. In: Proceedings of 2016 IEEE International Conference on RFID, pp. 1–7 (2016)
44. Nam, S.Y., Joshi, G.P.: Unmanned aerial vehicle localization using distributed sensors. Int. J. Distrib. Sens. Netw. **13**(9), 1–8 (2017)
45. Zhang, P., Lu, J., Wang, Y., Wang, Q.: Cooperative localization in 5G networks: a survey. ICT Express **3**(1), 27–32 (2017)
46. Dammann, A., Raulefs, R., Zhang, S.: On prospects of positioning in 5G. In: Proceedings of 2015 IEEE International Conference on Communication Workshop (ICCW), pp. 1–7 (2015)
47. Tosic, M., Nikolic, Z., Nejkovic, Dimitrijevic, B., Milosevic, N.: Spectrum sensing coordination for FIRE LTE testbeds, Invited Paper. In: Proceedings of 2nd International Conference on Electrical, Electronic and Computing Engineering, IcETRAN 2015 (2015)

48. Boury-Brisset, A.C.: Managing semantic big data for intelligence. Proc. STIDS **2013**, 41–47 (2013)
49. Nikolic, Z., Tosic, M., Milosevic, N., Nejkovic, V., Jelenkovic, F.: Spectrum coordination for intelligent wireless Internet of Things networks. In: Proceedings of 2017 25th Telecommunication Forum (TELFOR), Belgrade, Serbia, pp. 1–7 (2017). https://doi.org/ 10.1109/telfor.2017.8249326
50. Nejkovic, V., Petrovic, N., Milosevic, N., Tosic, M.: The SCOR ontologies framework for robotics testbed. In: 2018 26th Telecommunication Forum (TELFOR), Belgrade, Serbia, pp. 1–4 (2018). https://doi.org/10.1109/telfor.2018.8611841
51. Petrovic, N., Nejkovic, V., Milosevic, N., Tosic, M.: A semantic framework for design-time RIoT device mission coordination. In: Proceedings of 2018 26th Telecommunication Forum (TELFOR), Belgrade, Serbia, pp. 1–4 (2018). https://doi.org/10.1109/telfor.2018.8611845
52. Jelenkovic, F., Tosic, M., Nejkovic, V.: Semantic driven code generation for networking testbed experimentation. Enterp. Inf. Syst. 1–17 (2018). https://doi.org/10.1080/17517575. 2018.1509135
53. Redis. http://redis.io/topics/faq. Accessed 29 Jan 2019
54. Cois, C.A., Palko, T.: High-volume data collection and real time analytics using Redis. In: Proceedings of STRATA 2013. O'Reilly (2013)
55. Nakamura, S.: LINE Storage: Storing billions of rows in Sharded-Redis and HBase per Month. http://tech.naver.jp/blog/?p=1420
56. Apache Hadoop. http://hadoop.apache.org/. Accessed 29 Jan 2019
57. Apache HBase. http://hbase.apache.org/. Accessed 29 Jan 2019
58. Yao, Y., et al.: Online anomaly detection for sensor systems: a simple and efficient approach. Perform. Eval. **67**(11), 1059–1075 (2010)
59. Apache Jena. http://jena.apache.org/. Accessed 29 Jan 2019
60. OWL Web Ontology Language Overview. http://www.w3.org/TR/owl-features/. Accessed 29 Jan 2019
61. Prud'Hommeaux, E., Seaborne, A.: SPARQL query language for RDF. W3C recommendation, 15 (2008)
62. Stocker, M., Shurpali, N., Taylor, K., Burba, G., Rönkkö, M., Kolehmainen M.: Emrooz: a scalable database for SSN observations. In: Proceedings of First Joint International Workshop on Semantic Sensor Networks and Terra Cognita, SSN-TC/OrdRing@ISWC, pp. 1–12 (2015)
63. Broekstra, J., Kampman, A., van Harmelen, F.: Sesame: a generic architecture for storing and querying RDF and RDF schema. In: Horrocks, I., Hendler, J. (eds.) ISWC 2002. LNCS, vol. 2342, pp. 54–68. Springer, Heidelberg (2002). https://doi.org/10.1007/3-540-48005-6_7
64. Todorovic, B., Rancic, S., Markovic, I., Mulalic, E., Ilic, V.: Named entity recognition and classification using context hidden Markov model. In: 2008, 9th Symposium on IEEE Proceedings of Neural Network Applications in Electrical Engineering (NEUREL), pp. 1–4 (2008)
65. Hermans, F., et al.: A lightweight approach to online detection and classification of interference in 802.15. 4-based sensor networks. ACM SIGBED Rev. **9**(3), 11–20 (2012)
66. Iyer, V., Hermans, F., Voigt, T.: Detecting and avoiding multiple sources of interference in the 2.4 GHz spectrum. In: Abdelzaher, T., Pereira, N., Tovar, E. (eds.) EWSN 2015. LNCS, vol. 8965, pp. 35–51. Springer, Cham (2015). https://doi.org/10.1007/978-3-319-15582-1_3
67. Schmidhuber, J.: Deep learning in neural networks: an overview. Neural Netw. **61**, 85–117 (2015)
68. Ahmad, I., et al.: 5G security: analysis of threats and solutions. In: Proceedings of 2017 IEEE Conference 4 on Standards for Communications and Networking (CSCN), pp. 193–199 (2017)

69. Fang, D., Qian, Y., Hu, R.Q.: Security for 5G mobile wireless networks. IEEE Access **6**, 4850–4874 (2018)
70. Cho, S., et al.: System level simulation for 5G cellular communication systems. In: Proceedings of 2017 Ninth International Conference on Ubiquitous and Future Networks (ICUFN), pp. 296–299 (2017)
71. Mattisson, S.: Overview of 5G requirements and future wireless networks. In: Proceedings of ESSCIRC 2017 - 43rd IEEE European Solid State Circuits Conference, pp. 1–6 (2017)
72. Nichita, M.V., et al.: 5G propagation: current solutions and future proposals. In: Proceedings of 2016 12th IEEE International Symposium on Electronics and Telecommunications (ISETC), pp. 47–50 (2016)
73. Third Generation Partnership Project. http://www.3gpp.org/. Accessed 29 Jan 2019
74. Nagul, S.: A review on 5G modulation schemes and their comparisons for future wireless communications. In: Proceedings of 2018 Conference on Signal Processing and Communication Engineering Systems (SPACES), pp. 72–76 (2018)
75. Suthaharan, S.: Big data classification: problems and challenges in network intrusion prediction with machine learning. SIGMETRICS Perform. Eval. Rev. **41**, 70–73 (2014)
76. Casetti, C., et al.: Cognitive Network Management for 5G (white paper). In: 5GPPP Working Group on Network Management and QoS (2017). https://bscw.5g-ppp.eu/pub/bscw.cgi/d154625/NetworkManagement_WhitePaper_1.pdf. Accessed 29 Jan 2019
77. Al-Jarrah, O.Y., et al.: Efficient machine learning for big data: a review. Big Data Res. **2**, 87–93 (2015)
78. Ayoubi, S., et al.: Machine learning for cognitive network management. IEEE Commun. Mag. **56**(1), 158–165 (2018)
79. Imran, A., Zoha, A., Abu-Dayya, A.: Challenges in 5G: how to empower SON with big data for enabling 5G. IEEE Netw. **28**(6), 27–33 (2014)
80. Jakóbik, A.: Big data security. In: Pop, F., Kołodziej, J., Di Martino, B. (eds.) Resource Management for Big Data Platforms. CCN, pp. 241–261. Springer, Cham (2016). https://doi.org/10.1007/978-3-319-44881-7_12
81. Xie, J., et al.: A survey of machine learning techniques applied to software defined networking (SDN): research issues and challenges. IEEE Commun. Surv. Tutor. **1**, 1–39 (2018)
82. Abdallah, S., et al.: A network management framework for SDN. In: Proceedings of 2018 9th IFIP International Conference on New Technologies, Mobility and Security (NTMS), pp. 1–4 (2018)

Big Data Processing, Analysis and Applications in Mobile Cellular Networks

Sanja Brdar[1]([✉]), Olivera Novović[1], Nastasija Grujić[1],
Horacio González–Vélez[2], Ciprian-Octavian Truică[3], Siegfried Benkner[4],
Enes Bajrovic[4], and Apostolos Papadopoulos[5]

[1] BioSense Institute, University of Novi Sad, Novi Sad, Serbia
{sanja.brdar,novovic,n.grujic}@biosense.rs
[2] Cloud Competency Centre, National College of Ireland, Dublin 1, Ireland
horacio@ncirl.ie
[3] Computer Science and Engineering Department,
Faculty of Automatic Control and Computers, University Politehnica of Bucharest,
Bucharest, Romania
ciprian.truica@cs.pub.ro
[4] Faculty of Computer Science, University of Vienna, Vienna, Austria
{siegfried.benkner,enes.bajrovic}@univie.ac.at
[5] Department of Informatics, Aristotle University of Thessaloniki,
Thessaloniki, Greece
papadopo@csd.auth.gr

Abstract. When coupled with spatio-temporal context, location-based data collected in mobile cellular networks provide insights into patterns of human activity, interactions, and mobility. Whilst uncovered patterns have immense potential for improving services of telecom providers as well as for external applications related to social wellbeing, its inherent massive volume make such 'Big Data' sets complex to process. A significant number of studies involving such mobile phone data have been presented, but there still remain numerous open challenges to reach technology readiness. They include efficient access in privacy-preserving manner, high performance computing environments, scalable data analytics, innovative data fusion with other sources–all finally linked into the applications ready for operational mode. In this chapter, we provide a broad overview of the entire workflow from raw data access to the final applications and point out the critical challenges in each step that need to be addressed to unlock the value of data generated by mobile cellular networks.

Keywords: Data analysis · HPC · Big Data · Cellular networks

This article is based upon work from COST Action IC1406 High-Performance Modelling and Simulation for Big Data Applications (cHiPSet), supported by COST (European Cooperation in Science and Technology).

J. Kołodziej and H. González-Vélez (Eds.): cHiPSet, LNCS 11400, pp. 163–185, 2019.
https://doi.org/10.1007/978-3-030-16272-6_6

1 Mobile Cellular Networks - From Data to Applications

There is a tremendous growth of new applications that are based on the analysis of data generated within mobile cellular networks. Mobile phone service providers collect large amounts of data with potential value for improving their services as well as to enable social good applications [7]. As an example, every time a user makes via mobile phone interaction (SMS, call, internet), a *call detail record* (CDR) is created and stored by a mobile network operator. CDRs not only log the user activity for billing purposes and network management, but also provide opportunities for different applications such as urban sensing [5], transport planning [3,28], disaster management [38,46,64] socio-economic analysis [45,57] and monitoring epidemics of infectious diseases [10,11,36,62].

Several studies have reviewed applications to analyse CDRs, however most focus on specific aspects such as data analytics for internal use in telecom companies [26], graph analytics and applications [7], or public health [44]. This survey aims to cover the entire workflow from raw data to final application, with emphasis on the gaps to advance technology readiness. Figure 1 depicts our main concept which shall be used to summarise the state of the art work and identify open challenges.

Fig. 1. Mobile cellular networks - from location data to applications.

The rest of this paper is structured as follows. Section 2 provides some background on mobile cellular networks and the nature of the data sets available. It also sets the basis for different approaches to anonymization. Section 3 presents a discussion of data-intensive approaches and architectures to deal with the computationally-demanding nature of detecting patterns from telecom data. Then, Sect. 4 discusses approaches to analyze mobile operators data sets via graph analysis and machine learning. Section 5 enumerates some relevant external data sources that can complement mobile phone data, while Sect. 6

elaborates on diverse pertinent applications. Finally, Sect. 7 furnishes the summary and objectives for future research efforts.

2 Data Anonymization and Access

With the pervasive adoption of smartphones in modern societies, in addition to CDRs, there is now a growing interest in xDRs, Extended Data Records. They enclose information on visited web sites, used applications, executed transactions, etc. Coupled with cell-tower triangulation, applications can infer fine-grain phone locations [29], thus making data volumes even larger. Telecom data typically include spatial and temporal parameters to map device activity, connectivity, and mobility.

Telecom operators follow rigorous procedures for data anonymization to preserve privacy such that anonymized records cannot be linked to subscribers under any normal circumstances. Furthermore, before releasing any data to third parties, data sets are usually aggregated on temporal and/or spatial scales. For example, the numbers of calls as well as the duration of calls between any pair of antennas are aggregated hourly and movement trajectories are provided with reduced spatial resolution [1]. Differential privacy paradigm adds noise to original data up to the level not affecting the statistics significantly to preserve users' privacy. Another approach, suggested by the Open Algorithms (OPAL) initiative, proposes moving the algorithm to the data [35]. In their model, raw data are never exposed to outside parties, only vetted algorithms run on telecom companies' servers.

An example of preserving privacy of users by releasing only pre-aggregated data is Telecom Italia Big Data Challenge [4]. Opened data sets accumulated activity and connectivity across defined spatial cells of the city of Milan and in the Province of Trentino in 10 min resolution. Despite aggregation, data sets are still rich source of information, especially when fused with other data such as weather, news, social networks and electricity data from the city. To get some useful insight about the data we further describe and visualize activity and connectivity maps from Telecom Italia data sets and mobility from Telekom Srbija data set.

2.1 Activity

The activity data set consists of records with square id, time interval, sms-in activity, sms-out activity, call-in activity, call-out activity, internet traffic activity and country code, for each square of grid network. The data is aggregated in ten minutes time slots. We did further aggregation on daily level to gain overall insight into daily base activity. Figure 2 illustrates an aggregated activity of mobile phone users in the city of Milan. We observe that areas with highest activity refer to urban core of the city, whereas areas with lower activity levels refer to peripheral parts of the city. The same analysis is performed for the Province of Trentino and corresponding results are presented in Fig. 3. Although the inspected area of the Trentino Province exceeds significantly the urban area of the city of Trentno, the same pattern in distribution of mobile phone activity is present - high activity in urban area along lower activity in rural areas. From the visual inspection of Fig. 3 we observe that higher activity areas spatially refer to transit areas with main roads, which was expected.

Fig. 2. Aggregated activity over spatial area of the city of Milan.

2.2 Connectivity

Connectivity data provides directional interaction strength among the squares (cells) of the grid network. Records consist of *timestamp, square id1, square id2* and *strength* which represents the value (weight) of aggregated telecom traffic multiplied with a constant k to hide exact number of calls and sms recorded by single base station [4]. As in [43] we performed additional spatial aggregation, and analyzed connectivity patterns between different city zones of Milan through the lens of graph theory. For illustration purposes we created a single undirected, weighted graph for a typical working day from the data set. In Fig. 4 we present the obtained spatial graph of connectivity links. During the work week, the city center acts as a hub, the strongest links are gathered close to the city center, while on weekends and holidays the opposite pattern occurs [43].

The second type of connectivity data presents connectivity from the city of Milan to other Provinces in Italy. Additional aggregation is applied to extract

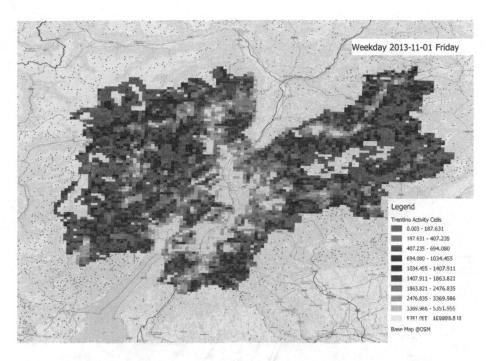

Fig. 3. Aggregated activity over spatial area of Trentino Province

Fig. 4. Connectivity across the city of Milan

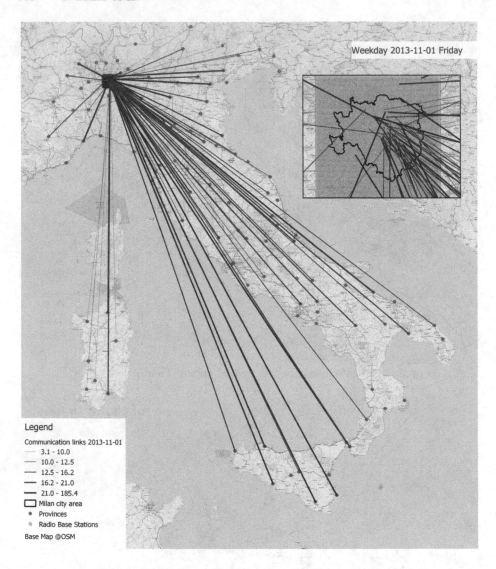

Fig. 5. Connectivity from the city of Milan to Provinces

daily base connectivity patterns. Figure 5 presents connectivity links from different areas of the city of Milan to Provinces in Italy. We may conclude that the distribution of connectivity links is regular to all Provinces, and that the majority of links start from central areas of the city of Milan.

2.3   Mobility

Mobile phone data can reveal the approximate location of a user and its mobility trace based on geographical location of the Radio Base Stations which registered

Fig. 6. Mobility across the city of Novi Sad, Serbia

the traffic. In [16] the authors proposed a novel computational framework that enables efficient and extensible discovery of mobility intelligence from large-scale spatial-temporal data such as CDR, GPS and Location Based Services data. In [25] the authors focus on usage of Call Detail Records (CDR) in the context of mobility, transport and transport infrastructure analysis. They analyzed CDR data associated with Radio Base Stations together with Open Street Map road network to estimate users mobility. CDR data can provide generalized view of users mobility, since data is collected only when the telecom traffic happens. To illustrate mobility data set we created Fig. 6 that presents a map with mobility traces across the city of Novi Sad on 3rd July 2017, for the time interval between 6am and 12pm extracted from raw CDR data through aggregation of visited locations' sequences of anonymous users. Data originate from Serbian national operator, Telekom Srbija, released under non-disclosure agreement. From mobility traces we can detect few locations in the city that acts as trajectory hubs.

3 Big Data Processing

The typical workflow applied for processing spatio-temporal data, such as mobile phone data used in this case study, contains numerous queries across locations and timestamps of interest, spatial/time aggregations and summarization.

Existing solutions are rarely focusing on the execution time, scalability, and throughput that are of high importance for the implementation and near real-time settings. In this section, we present briefly some important concepts and architectural issues related to processing Big Data.

3.1 Big Data Architectures

Over the last decade we have witnessed a tremendous progress and innovation in large-scale data processing systems and the associated data-driven computation. Among many others, these include MapReduce-based computational systems, data streaming technologies, and NoSQL database systems. A major challenge is to build systems that on the one hand could handle large volumes of batch data and on the other hand offer the required scalability, performance and low latency required for integration and real-time processing of massive, continuous data streams. In the following paragraphs, we discuss some of the architectural principles underlying Big Data systems that address this challenge, in particular the Lambda and the Kappa architectural alternatives.

Lambda Architecture. Big Data systems often face the challenge of how to integrate processing of "new" data that is being constantly ingested into a system with historical (batch) data. Newly arriving (real-time) data is usually processed using stream-based processing techniques, while historical data is periodically reprocessed using batch processing. The Lambda architecture [40] is a blueprint for a Big Data system that unifies stream processing of real-time data and batch processing of historical data.

The Lambda architecture pursues a generalized approach to developing Big Data systems with the goal of overcoming the complexities and limitations when trying to scale traditional data systems based on incrementally updated relational databases. In an incremental database system, the state of the database (i.e. its contents) is incrementally updated, usually when new data is processed. In contrast to incremental database systems, the Lambda architecture advocates a functional approach relying on immutable data, i.e., new data is added on top of the immutable historical data (batch data) already present in the system.

As opposed to traditional distributed database systems, e.g., where distribution of tables across multiple machines has to be explicitly dealt with by the developer, a key underlying principle of the Lambda architecture is to make the system aware of its distributed nature so that it can automatically manage distribution, replication and related issues. Another key aspect of the Lambda architecture is its reliance on immutable data as opposed to incrementally updated data in relational database systems. Reliance on immutable data is essential for achieving resilience with respect to human errors.

The Lambda architecture promises to tackle many important requirements of Big Data systems, including scalability, robustness and fault tolerance (including fault-tolerance with respect to human errors), support for low-latency reads and updates, extensibility, easier debugging and maintainability. At a high-level of abstraction, the Lambda architecture is comprised of three layers, the batch layer, the serving layer, and the speed layer.

The batch layer stores the raw data (also often referred to as batch data, historical data, or master data set), which is immutable. Whenever new data arrives, it is appended to the existing data in the batch layer. The batch layer is responsible for computing batch views taking into account all available data. The batch layer periodically recomputes the batch views from scratch so that also the new data that has been added to the system since the computation of the last batch views is processed.

The serving layer sits on top of the batch layer and provides read access to the batch views that have been computed by the batch layer. The serving layer usually constitutes a distributed database, which is populated with the computed batch views, and ensures that the batch views can be randomly accessed. The serving layer is constantly updated with new batch views once these become available. Since the serving layer only needs to support batch updates and random reads, but no random writes (updates), it is usually significantly less complex than a database that needs to support random reads and writes. While the serving layer enables fast read-only access to the pre-computed batch views, it must be clear that these views may not be completely up-to-date, since data that has been acquired since the latest batch views have been computed have not been considered.

The speed layer is provided on top of the serving layer in order to support real-time views on the data. The speed layer mitigates the high latency of the batch layer by processing the data on-the-fly, as it arrives in the system, using fast, incremental algorithms to compute real-time views of the data. As opposed to the batch layer, which periodically recomputes the batch views based on all historical data form scratch, the speed layer does not compute real-time views from scratch. To minimize latency, it only performs incremental updates of the real-time views taking into account just the newly arrived data. The real-time views provided by the speed layer are of temporary nature. Once the new data has arrived at the batch layer and has been included in the latest batch views, the corresponding real-time views can be discarded.

Figure 7 depicts the main architectural aspects of the Lambda architecture. Data streamed in from data sources (sensors, Web clients, etc.) is being fed in parallel both into the batch layer and the speed layer, which compute the corresponding batch views and real-time views, respectively.

The lambda architecture can be seen as a trade-off between two conflicting goals: speed and accuracy. While computation of real-time views is being done with very short latencies, computation of batch views is typically a very high-latency process. On the other hand, since the speed layer does not take into account all of the available data, real-time views are usually only approximations, while batch views provide accurate answers considering all data available in the master data store at a certain point in time. In order to get a view of all the available data (batch data and new data) queries have to be resolved such that

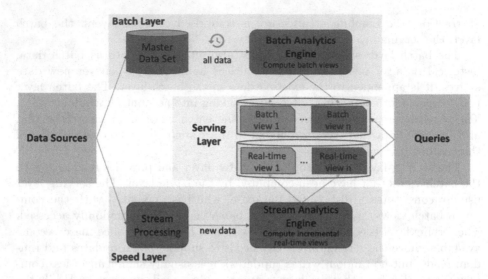

Fig. 7. The Lambda architecture.

they combine the corresponding batch-views and real-time views, which can either be done in the serving layer or by the client applications.

The Lambda architecture has been widely recognized as a viable approach to unifying batch and stream processing, by advocating real-time stream processing and batch re-processing on immutable data. There are, however, some potential drawbacks associated with the Lambda architecture. Although a major objective of the lambda architecture is to reduce the complexity as compared to traditional distributed database systems, this goal often cannot be fully realized. While the batch layer usually hides complexity from the developers, typically by relying on some high-level MapReduce framework (e.g., Hadoop), the speed layer may still exhibit significant complexities to the developers of Big Data solutions. In addition, having to develop and maintain two separate data processing components, the stream layer and the batch layer, adds to the overall complexity. Another potential issue with the Lambda architecture is that constantly recomputing the batch views from scratch might become prohibitively expensive in terms of resource usage and latency.

Kappa Architecture. A limitation of the Lambda architecture is that two different data processing systems, i.e., the stream layer and the batch layer, have to be maintained. These layers need to perform the same analytics, however realized with different technologies and tools. As a consequence, the system becomes more complex and debugging and maintenance become more difficult. This drawback is being addressed by the Kappa architecture [31].

The Kappa architecture constitutes a simplification of the Lambda architecture by uniformly treating real-time data and batch data as streams. Consequently, batch processing as done in the lambda architecture, is replaced by

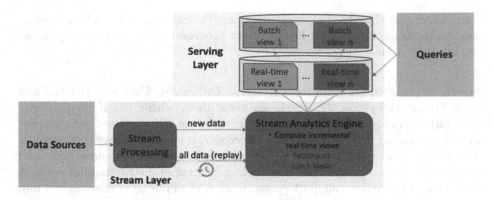

Fig. 8. The Kappa architecture

stream processing. The Kappa architecture assumes that (historical) batch data can also be viewed as a (bounded) stream, which is often the case. What is required, however, is that the stream processing component also supports efficient replay of historical data as a stream. Only if this is the case, batch views can be recomputed by the same stream analytics engine that is also responsible for processing real-time views. Besides the ability to replay historical data, the order of all data events must be strictly preserved in the system in order to ensure deterministic results.

Instead of a batch layer and a speed layer, the Kappa architecture relies on a single stream layer capable of handling the data volumes for computing both real-time views and batch views. Overall system complexity decreases with the Kappa architecture as illustrated in Fig. 8. However, it should be noted that the Kappa architecture is not a replacement of the Lambda architecture, since it will not be suitable for all use cases.

3.2 Big Data Frameworks

There is a plethora of Big Data frameworks and tools that have been developed in the past decade. As a result, both the Lambda architecture and Kappa architecture can be implemented using a variety of different technologies for the different system components. In the following, we briefly discuss a few frameworks that are most typically used to implement Big Data systems based on the Lambda or Kappa architecture.

Hadoop. The Apache Hadoop ecosystem is a collection of tools for developing scalable Big Data processing systems [63]. The Hadoop File System (HDFS) is a distributed file system for storing large volumes of data on distributed memory machines (clusters) transparently handling the details of data distribution, replication and fail-over. The Hadoop MapReduce engine utilizes HDFS to support transparent parallelism of large-scale batch processing that can be formulated according to the MapReduce programming model. Hadoop is often used to implement the batch layer in data processing systems that implement the Lambda Architecture.

Spark. Apache Spark introduces *Resilient Distributed Data sets* (RDDs) and *Data Frames* (DFs) [65,66]. Spark can work nicely within the Hadoop ecosystem, although this is not mandatory, since Spark is self-contained with respect to task scheduling and fault tolerance. Moreover, it supports a large collection of data sources, including HDFS. Spark supports iterative MapReduce tasks and improves performance by explicitly enabling caching of distributed data sets. A wide range of functions support categorization of application components into data transformations and actions. In addition, Spark provides stream processing functionality, a rich machine learning library, a powerful library for SQL processing on top of Data Frames and also a library specifically designed for graph processing (GraphX). Spark is often used for implementing the speed layer in a Lambda or the stream layer in a Kappa architecture.

Kafka. Apache Kafka [30,60] is a scalable message queuing and log aggregation platform for real-time data feeds. It provides a distributed message queue and a publish/subscribe messaging model for streams of data records, supporting distributed, fault-tolerant data storage. The framework is run as a so-called *Kafka cluster* on multiple servers that can scale over multiple data centers. Kafka supports efficient replay of data streams and thus it is often used to implement systems that resemble the Kappa architecture.

Samza. Apache Samza [42] is a scalable, distributed real-time stream processing platform that has been developed in conjunction with Apache Kafka and that is often used for implementing Big Data systems based on the Kappa architecture. Samza can be integrated easily with the YARN resource management framework.

Resource Management Frameworks. YARN is a resource negotiator included with Apache Hadoop. YARN decouples the programming paradigm of MapReduce from its resource management capabilities, and delegates many scheduling functions (e.g., task fault-tolerance) to per-application components. Apache Mesos is a fine-grained resource negotiation engine that supports sharing and management of a large cluster of machines between different computing frameworks, including Hadoop, MPI, Spark, Kafka, etc. The main difference between YARN and Mesos is the resource negotiation model. Whereas YARN implements a push-based resource negotiation approach, where clients specify their resource requirements and deployment preferences, Mesos uses a pull-based approach, where the negotiator offers resources to clients which they can accept or decline.

4 Data Analysis

Data Analysis is the scientific process of examining data sets in order to discover patterns and draw insights about the information they contain. In the case of data collected by mobile phone providers, typically in the form of CDRs, the analysis focuses in two main directions: (i) graph analysis and (ii) machine learning. Moreover, the data analysis must incorporate the spatial-temporal characteristics of such data.

4.1 Graph Analytics

Graph mining is a heavily active research direction with numerous applications [2,15] that uses novel approaches for mining and performing useful analysis on datasets represented by graph structures. Current research directions can be categorized into the following groups [52]: (i) Graph clustering used for grouping vertices into clusters; (ii) Graph Classification used for classifying separate, individual graphs into two or more categories; (iii) Subgraph mining used for producing a set of subgraphs occurring in at least some given threshold of the given input example graphs.

One of the core research directions in the area of graph clustering is the discovery of meaningful communities in a large network [20] from the perspective of spatial-temporal data that evolves over time. In the majority of real-life applications, graphs are extremely sparse usually following power-law degree distribution. However, the original graph may contain groups of vertices, called *communities*, where vertices in the same community are more well-connected than vertices across communities. In the case of CDR data, the graph corresponds to user interactions and communities correspond to groups of people with strong pair-wise activity within the group delimited by spacial-temporal boundaries. To enable efficient community detection in potentially massive amounts of data, the following problems must be tackled [58]: (*i*) the algorithmic techniques applied must scale well with respect to the size of the data, which means that the algorithmic complexity should stay below $\mathcal{O}(n^2)$ (where n is the number of graph nodes), and (*ii*) since these techniques are unsupervised, the algorithms used must be flexible enough to be able to infer the number of communities during the course of the algorithm. Moreover, the temporal dimension of the data must be taken into account when detecting communities to better understand the natural evolution of user interactions. Some algorithms that qualify for this task are LOUVAIN [8], Infomap [54], Walktrap [50], FastGreedy [14], etc.

The result of community detection analysis is a set of grouped vertices that have very strong inner connectivity. The results could be presented on the map, since telecom data is georeferenced. In Fig. 9 we present geographical map of Milan city with wide suburban area overlayed with the results of community detection analysis in 3D. Communities that have smaller overall area are presented with higher bars. From visual inspection of Fig. 9 we can notice that the dense urban area of the city has a larger number of small communities, while in the sparsely populated suburban area there are a few very large communities. High number of communities within small spatial area is reflecting dynamic nature of telecom traffic in urban areas, which is strongly related to people flow and its dynamic across the city.

Fig. 9. Communities over the city of Milan in 3D.

Collective classification and label propagation are two important research directions in the area of graph classification for vertex classification. Iterative classification is used for collective classification to capture the similarity among the points where each vertex represents one data point either labeled or unlabelled [55]. Label propagation is a converging iterative algorithm where vertices are assigned labels based on the majority vote on the labels of their neighbors [67]. In the case of CDR data, these algorithms can be used to draw insights about users and their neighborhoods by finding the correlations between the label of a user and (i) its observed attributes, (ii) the observed attributes (including observed labels) of other users in its neighborhood, (iii) the unobserved labels of users in its neighborhood. The spatial-temporal dimension of the data also plays an important role as the correlations will bring new insight into the propagation of labels and the way user neighborhood is built.

Subgraph mining deals with the identification of frequent graphs and subgraphs that can be used for classification tasks, graph clustering and building indices [51]. In the case of CDR data, subgraph mining can help to detect hidden patterns in active user communities delimited into spatial-temporal boundaries by contrasting the support of frequent graphs between various different graph classes or to classify user interaction by considering frequent patterns using the spatial-temporal dimensions as a cardinal feature.

4.2 Machine Learning

Spatial-temporal data analysis is an important and evolving domain of machine learning. The main direction when dealing with such data is forecasting and prediction in support of the decision-making process.

Classical machine learning techniques, from simple ones for sequential pattern mining (e.g., Apriori, Generalized Sequential Pattern, FreeSpan, PrefixSpan, SPADE) to more complex ones (e.g., Linear, Multilinear, Logistic, Poisson or Nonlinear Regression), can be used to capture the dependencies between spatial and temporal components and help with making accurate predictions into the future and extract new knowledge about the evolution of users and their interests.

With the increasing evolution and adoption of neural networks, new deep learning architectures are developed for the analysis of spatial-temporal data and used for making and quantifying the uncertainty associated with predictions [56]. These techniques can be employed in the process of making accurate predictions for spatial-temporal data when working in both big data and data scarce regimes managing to quantify the uncertainty associated with predictions in a real-time manner.

5 Data Fusion

Identified patterns from telecom data reach true value when combined with other sources. As illustrated in Fig. 10 processed and analyzed telecom data can be fused with diverse data sources in context of various applications. We summarized several fusion scenarios in Table 1. The list is not exhaustive, only highlights diversity of the combinations, and some of the examples might integrate mobile phone data with more than one external source. Satellite data, environmental data, IoT, Points-of-Interests (POI), National statistics and other sources can add to the value of mobile phone data. For example, satellite data can provide information on land cover types and changes and IoT can collect valuable ground truth measurements.

Bringing together heterogeneous datasets with mobile phone data and using them jointly is challenging due to typical mismatch in the resolutions of data, multimodal and dynamic nature of data. Some applications on mobile phone data demand external sources only for training and validation (e.g. learning model to predict socio-economic indicators based on features extracted from telecom data). Here special attention is needed to understand the bias and avoid spurious correlations. Other scenarios demand continuous information flow from external source and dynamic integration (e.g. air quality measurements fused with aggregated mobility from telecom data). The main challenge here is the timely processing of external data and proper alignment with mobile phone data.

Fusion scenarios reported in Table 1 illustrate heterogeneity of external data sources, all having an important role in unlocking the value of mobile phone data coming from telecom operators. The quality of final application depends on the

Table 1. Data fusion scenarios - mapping external data sources with telecom data.

External data source	Examples
Satellite data	NASAs Tropical Rainfall Measurement Mission (TRMM) satellite ⟷ anomalous patterns of mobility and calling frequency [38]
	Landsat-7 for deriving impact map of floods ⟷ aggregated activity by day and by antenna [46]
	SPOT-Vegetation satellite for calculating vegetation index ⟷ average number of calls between all market pairs [27]
Environmental data	The air quality estimated by regional model ⟷ staying at home and travel patterns [17]
	Availability of environmental freshwater measured as the total length of the rivers in each spatial unit ⟷ estimate of mobility obtained from CDRs [39]
	Logs of the climatic conditions: temperature, relative humidity, air pressure and wind speed from weather stations ⟷ inferring the social network for each subject [49]
POI	Events on famous POIs across city ⟷ users presences in the area [21]
	POIs from Google Earth for land use inference ⟷ aggregated number of calls managed by each of base transceiver station towers [48]
	Pokémon POIs ⟷ city-level aggregated distributions of number of connected devices and downloaded information from xDR records [24]
IoT	Inductive loop vehicle detectors ⟷ mobility, rush hours traffic [28]
Census, Surveys	Travel surveys ⟷ daily commuting from mobility traces patterns [3]
	Census on journey to work ⟷ activity and connectivity around laborshed area [5]
	Demographic and health surveys ⟷ connectivity and mobility across country [11]
	National statistics on socio-economic development ⟷ human mobility patterns [45]
	Household income and expenditure survey ⟷ top up credit amounts, mobility and social network features [57]
Infrastructure	The street network (highways and primary streets) from OpenStreetMap, metro network, bus routes ⟷ xDR data aggregated into origin-destination (OD) matrices [23]
	Customer sites of each power line per grid square and line measurement indicating the amount of flowing energy ⟷ aggregated people dynamics features from the mobile phone network activity [9]

Data Fusion

Fig. 10. Fusion of mobile phone data with other sources.

availability of external sources, efficiency of data processing and the quality of delivered information and its integration.

6 Applications

A plethora of research work has been published related to the usage of telecom data for a multitude of purposes. Telecom data contains rich user behaviour information, and it can reveal mobility patterns, activity related to specific locations, peak hours or unusual events. Extracting frequent trajectories, home and work location detection, origin destination matrices are further examples of knowledge that may be mined from rich telecom data. Telecom operators have a great interest to analyze collected data for optimizing their services. For example, time-dependent pricing schemes can maximize operators profit, as well as users grade of service. Dynamic data pricing frameworks combining both spatial and temporal traffic patterns [18] allow estimating optimal pricing rewards given the current network capacity.

Telecom data significantly enriched many different fields and boosted external social good applications. Studies in transportation, urban and energy planning, public health, economy and tourism have benefited most from this valuable new resource that surpasses all alternative sources in population coverage, spatial and temporal resolution.

Transportation planning applications need information on different modes of trips, purposes, and times of day. With telecom data transportation models can effectively utilize mobility footprints at large scale and resolution. This was validated by an MIT study [3] on the Boston metropolitan area where the authors demonstrated how CDR data can be used to represent distinct mobility patterns. In another example, origin destination matrices inferred from mobile phone data helped IBM to redesign the bus routes [6] in the largest city of Ivory Coast - Abidjan.

Mobility patterns derived from telecom data could be very valuable for public health applications, in particular epidemiology. Surveillance, prioritization and prevention are key efforts in epidemiology. Mobile phone data demonstrated utility for dengue [62], HIV [11,22], malaria [61], schistosomiasis [39], Ebola epidemic [47], and cholera outbreaks [19]. Another suitable public health application is concerned with air quality where recent studies embraced telecom data to better quantify individual and population level expose to air pollution. In [17] the authors highlighted the need to dynamically assess exposure to NO_2 that has high impact on peoples health. Their method incorporated individual travel patterns.

Urban studies highly explored the potential of mobile phone data and discovered that it can be used for urban planning [5], detecting social function of land use [48], in particular residential and office areas as well as leisure-commerce and rush hour patterns [53], and extracting relevant information about the structure of the cities [37]. Recent applications propose an analytical process able to discover, understand and characterize city events from CDR data [21] and a method to predict the population at a large spatio-temporal scale in a city [13]. All urban studies fit into the wider context of smart city applications and therefore more breakthroughs on the usage of mobile phone data are expected.

With the growing role of tourism there is increased interest to investigate utility of mobile phone data to understand tourists experiences, evaluate marketing strategies and estimate revenues generated by touristic events. Mobility and behaviour patterns have been recently used to derive trust and reputation models and scalable data analytics for the tourism industry [33,59]. The Andorra case study has proposed indicators in high spatial and temporal resolutions such as tourist flows per country of origin, flows of new tourists, revisiting patterns, profiling of tourist interests to uncover valuable patterns for tourism [34]. Special attention is given to large scale events that attract foreign people [12]. Arguably, tourists via their mobile devices have quickly become data sources for crowd-sourced aggregation with dynamic spatial and temporal resolutions [32].

Other high impact applications include social and economical development [45,57], disaster events management such as cyclones landfall [38] or earthquakes [64], and food security [27,68].

Although many studies demonstrated utility of mobile phone data in various applications, reaching the operational level is still not that close. If we recall the summary of workflow's steps provided in Fig. 1, all further described in the previous sections, we can realize that technologies used in each step need to match with specific application.

7   Summary and Vision

This chapter provided an overview of all steps in discovering knowledge from raw telecom data in the context of different applications. Knowledge about how people move across a city, where they are gathering, what are home, work and leisure locations along with corresponding time component are valuable for many applications. The biggest challenges in this process are privacy and regulation, real-time settings and data fusion with external sources.

Efforts directed toward providing access to telecom large-scale human behavioral data in a privacy-preserving manner [41] are necessary. Real-time settings raise critical issues concerning computational infrastructure, big data frameworks and analytics. There is a lack of research and benchmark studies that evaluate different computational architectures and big data frameworks. Only a few studies tackled issues of parallelization and distributed processing. In [16] authors proposed mobility intelligence framework based on Apache Spark for processing and analytics of large scale mobile phone data. Another example is the study [58] that provided computational pipeline for the community detection in mobile phone data, developed in Apache Hive and Spark technology, and benchmarked different architectures and settings. More of these studies are needed to choose the right architecture and processing frameworks. Graph analytics together with machine learning have become indispensable tools for telecom data analytics, but the streaming nature of data demands for change detection and online adaption. External data sources mentioned in the data fusion section are also advancing (e.g., new satellites launched, enhanced IoT ecosystems) and will help us to understand spatio-temporal context better.

Future research must address all critical aspects to reach technology readiness for operational environment. This will enable applications based on mobile phone data to have high impact on decision making in urban, transport, public health and other domains and will certainly open opportunities for new applications.

References

1. Acs, G., Castelluccia, C.: A case study: privacy preserving release of spatio-temporal density in Paris. In: 20th ACM SIGKDD International Conference on Knowledge Discovery and Data Mining-KDD 2014, pp. 1679–1688. ACM, New York (2014). https://doi.org/10.1145/2623330.2623361
2. Aggarwal, C.C., Wang, H.: Managing and Mining Graph Data. Springer, New York (2010). https://doi.org/10.1007/978-1-4419-6045-0
3. Alexander, L., Jiang, S., Murga, M., González, M.C.: Origin-destination trips by purpose and time of day inferred from mobile phone data. Transp. Res. Part C: Emerg. Technol. 58, 240–250 (2015). https://doi.org/10.1016/j.trc.2015.02.018
4. Barlacchi, G., et al.: A multi-source dataset of urban life in the city of milan and the province of trentino. Sci. Data 2, 150055 (2015)
5. Becker, R.A., et al.: A tale of one city: using cellular network data for urban planning. IEEE Pervasive Comput. 10(4), 18–26 (2011). https://doi.org/10.1109/MPRV.2011.44

6. Berlingerio, M., Calabrese, F., Di Lorenzo, G., Nair, R., Pinelli, F., Sbodio, M.L.: AllAboard: a system for exploring urban mobility and optimizing public transport using cellphone data. In: Blockeel, H., Kersting, K., Nijssen, S., Železný, F. (eds.) ECML PKDD 2013. LNCS (LNAI), vol. 8190, pp. 663–666. Springer, Heidelberg (2013). https://doi.org/10.1007/978-3-642-40994-3_50

7. Blondel, V.D., Decuyper, A., Krings, G.: A survey of results on mobile phone datasets analysis. EPJ Data Sci. **4**(1). https://doi.org/10.1140/epjds/s13688-015-0046-0

8. Blondel, V.D., Guillaume, J.L., Lambiotte, R., Lefebvre, E.: Fast unfolding of communities in large networks. J. Stat. Mech.: Theory Exp. **2008**(10), P10008 (2008). https://doi.org/10.1088/1742-5468/2008/10/P10008

9. Bogomolov, A., Lepri, B., Larcher, R., Antonelli, F., Pianesi, F., Pentland, A.: Energy consumption prediction using people dynamics derived from cellular network data. EPJ Data Sci. **5**(1), 13 (2016). https://doi.org/10.1140/epjds/s13688-016-0075-3

10. Bosetti, P., Poletti, P., Stella, M., Lepri, B., Merler, S., De Domenico, M.: Reducing measles risk in turkey through social integration of Syrian refugees. arXiv preprint arXiv:1901.04214 (2019)

11. Brdar, S., Gavrić, K., Ćulibrk, D., Crnojević, V.: Unveiling spatial epidemiology of HIV with mobile phone data. Sci. Rep. **6** (2016). https://doi.org/10.1038/srep19342

12. Callegari, C., Garroppo, R.G., Giordano, S.: Inferring social information on foreign people from mobile traffic data. In: 2017 IEEE International Conference on Communications (ICC), pp. 1–6. IEEE (2017)

13. Chen, J., et al.: Fine-grained prediction of urban population using mobile phone location data. Int. J. Geogr. Inf. Sci. **32**, 1770–1786 (2018)

14. Clauset, A., Newman, M.E., Moore, C.: Finding community structure in very large networks. Phys. Rev. E **70**(6), 066111 (2004)

15. Cook, D.J., Holder, L.B.: Mining Graph Data. Wiley, Hoboken (2006). https://doi.org/10.1002/0470073047

16. Dang, T.A., et al.: Mobility genome^{TM}-a framework for mobility intelligence from large-scale spatio-temporal data. In: 2017 IEEE International Conference on Data Science and Advanced Analytics (DSAA), pp. 449–458. IEEE (2017)

17. Dewulf, B., et al.: Dynamic assessment of exposure to air pollution using mobile phone data. Int. J. Health Geogr. **15**(1), 14 (2016)

18. Ding, J., Li, Y., Zhang, P., Jin, D.: Time dependent pricing for large-scale mobile networks of urban environment: feasibility and adaptability. IEEE Trans. Serv. Comput. (2017)

19. Finger, F., et al.: Mobile phone data highlights the role of mass gatherings in the spreading of cholera outbreaks. Proc. Natl. Acad. Sci. **113**(23), 6421–6426 (2016)

20. Fortunato, S.: Community detection in graphs. Phys. Rep. **483**(3), 75–174 (2010). https://doi.org/10.1016/j.physrep.2009.11.002

21. Furletti, B., Trasarti, R., Cintia, P., Gabrielli, L.: Discovering and understanding city events with big data: the case of rome. Information **8**(3), 74 (2017)

22. Gavric, K., Brdar, S., Culibrk, D., Crnojevic, V.: Linking the human mobility and connectivity patterns with spatial HIV distribution. NetMob D4D Challenge, pp. 1–6 (2013)

23. Graells-Garrido, E., Caro, D., Parra, D.: Inferring modes of transportation using mobile phone data. EPJ Data Sci. **7**(1), 49 (2018)

24. Graells-Garrido, E., Ferres, L., Caro, D., Bravo, L.: The effect of Pokémon go on the pulse of the city: a natural experiment. EPJ Data Sci. **6**(1), 23 (2017)

25. Gundlegård, D., Rydergren, C., Breyer, N., Rajna, B.: Travel demand estimation and network assignment based on cellular network data. Comput. Commun. **95**, 29–42 (2016)
26. He, Y., Yu, F.R., Zhao, N., Yin, H., Yao, H., Qiu, R.C.: Big data analytics in mobile cellular networks. IEEE Access **4**, 1985–1996 (2016)
27. Jacques, D.C., et al.: Social capital and transaction costs in millet markets. Heliyon **4**(1), e00505 (2018)
28. Järv, O., Ahas, R., Saluveer, E., Derudder, B., Witlox, F.: Mobile phones in a traffic flow: a geographical perspective to evening rush hour traffic analysis using call detail records. PloS ONE **7**(11), 1–12 (2012). https://doi.org/10.1371/journal.pone.0049171
29. Jiang, S., Fiore, G.A., Yang, Y., Ferreira Jr., J., Frazzoli, E., González, M.C.: A review of urban computing for mobile phone traces: current methods, challenges and opportunities. In: Proceedings of the 2nd ACM SIGKDD International Workshop on Urban Computing, p. 2. ACM (2013)
30. Kreps, J.: Kafka: a distributed messaging system for log processing. In: Proceedings of the 6th International Workshop on Networking Meets Databases (NetDB) (2011)
31. Kreps, J.: Questioning the Lambda Architecture, July 2014. https://www.oreilly.com/ideas/questioning-the-lambda-architecture. Accessed 15 Dec 2018
32. Leal, F., Malheiro, B., González-Vélez, H., Burguillo, J.C.: Trust-based modelling of multi-criteria crowdsourced data. Data Sci. Eng. **2**(3), 100 209 (2017). https://doi.org/10.1007/s41019-017-0045 1
33. Leal, F., Veloso, B.M., Malheiro, B., Gonzlez-Vlez, H., Burguillo, J.C.: Scalable modelling and recommendation using Wiki-based crowdsourced repositories. Electron. Commer. Res. Appl. **33**, 100817 (2019). https://doi.org/10.1016/j.elerap.2018.11.004
34. Leng, Y., Noriega, A., Pentland, A., Winder, I., Lutz, N., Alonso, L.: Analysis of tourism dynamics and special events through mobile phone metadata. arXiv preprint arXiv:1610.08342 (2016)
35. Lepri, B., Oliver, N., Letouzé, E., Pentland, A., Vinck, P.: Fair, transparent, and accountable algorithmic decision-making processes. Philos. Technol. **31**, 611–627 (2018)
36. Lima, A., De Domenico, M., Pejovic, V., Musolesi, M.: Disease containment strategies based on mobility and information dissemination. Sci. Rep. **5** (2015). https://doi.org/10.1038/srep10650
37. Louail, T., et al.: From mobile phone data to the spatial structure of cities. Sci. Rep. **4**, 5276 (2014)
38. Lu, X., et al.: Detecting climate adaptation with mobile network data in Bangladesh: anomalies in communication, mobility and consumption patterns during cyclone Mahasen. Climatic Change **138**(3–4), 505–519 (2016)
39. Mari, L., et al.: Big-data-driven modeling unveils country-wide drivers of endemic schistosomiasis. Sci. Rep. **7**(1), 489 (2017)
40. Marz, N., Warren, J.: Big Data Principles and Best Practices of Scalable Realtime Data Systems. Manning, New York City (2006)
41. de Montjoye, Y.A., et al.: On the privacy-conscientious use of mobile phone data. Sci. Data **5**, 180286 EP– (2018). https://doi.org/10.1038/sdata.2018.286
42. Noghabi, S.A., Paramasivam, K., Pan, Y., Ramesh, N., Bringhurst, J., Gupta, I., Campbell, R.H.: Samza: stateful scalable stream processing at linkedin. Proc. VLDB Endow. **10**(12), 1634–1645 (2017)

43. Novović, O., Brdar, S., Crnojević, V.: Evolving connectivity graphs in mobile phone data. In: NetMob, The Main Conference on the Scientific Analysis of Mobile Phone Datasets, pp. 73–75. Vodafone (2015)
44. Oliver, N., Matic, A., Frias-Martinez, E.: Mobile network data for public health: opportunities and challenges. Front. Publ. Health **3**, 189 (2015)
45. Pappalardo, L., Pedreschi, D., Smoreda, Z., Giannotti, F.: Using big data to study the link between human mobility and socio-economic development. In: 2015 IEEE International Conference on Big Data (Big Data), pp. 871–878 (2015). https://doi.org/10.1109/BigData.2015.7363835
46. Pastor-Escuredo, D., et al.: Flooding through the lens of mobile phone activity. In: 2014 IEEE Global Humanitarian Technology Conference (GHTC), pp. 279–286. IEEE, October 2014. https://doi.org/10.1109/GHTC.2014.6970293
47. Peak, C.M., et al.: Population mobility reductions associated with travel restrictions during the Ebola epidemic in Sierra Leone: use of mobile phone data. Int. J. Epidemiol. **47**(5), 1562–1570 (2018)
48. Pei, T., Sobolevsky, S., Ratti, C., Shaw, S.L., Li, T., Zhou, C.: A new insight into land use classification based on aggregated mobile phone data. Int. J. Geogr. Inf. Sci. **28**(9), 1988–2007 (2014)
49. Phithakkitnukoon, S., Leong, T.W., Smoreda, Z., Olivier, P.: Weather effects on mobile social interactions: a case study of mobile phone users in Lisbon, Portugal. PloS ONE **7**(10), e45745 (2012)
50. Pons, P., Latapy, M.: Computing communities in large networks using random walks. J. Graph Algorithms Appl. **10**(2), 191–218 (2006)
51. Ramraj, T., Prabhakar, R.: Frequent subgraph mining algorithms - a survey. Procedia Comput. Sci. **47**, 197–204 (2015). https://doi.org/10.1016/j.procs.2015.03.198
52. Rehman, S.U., Khan, A.U., Fong, S.: Graph mining: a survey of graph mining techniques. In: International Conference on Digital Information Management (ICDIM 2012), pp. 88–92 (2012). https://doi.org/10.1109/ICDIM.2012.6360146
53. Ríos, S.A., Muñoz, R.: Land use detection with cell phone data using topic models: Case Santiago, Chile. Comput. Environ. Urban Syst. **61**, 39–48 (2017)
54. Rosvall, M., Bergstrom, C.T.: Maps of random walks on complex networks reveal community structure. Proc. Natl. Acad. Sci. **105**(4), 1118–1123 (2008). https://doi.org/10.1073/pnas.0706851105
55. Sen, P., Namata, G., Bilgic, M., Getoor, L., Galligher, B., Eliassi-Rad, T.: Collective classification in network data. AI Mag. **29**(3), 93 (2008)
56. Senanayake, R., Jean, N., Ramos, F., Chowdhary, G.: Modeling and decision-making in the spatiotemporal domain. In: Conference on Neural Information Processing Systems (2018)
57. Steele, J.E., et al.: Mapping poverty using mobile phone and satellite data. J. Roy. Soc. Interface **14**(127) (2017). https://doi.org/10.1098/rsif.2016.0690
58. Truică, C.-O., Novović, O., Brdar, S., Papadopoulos, A.N.: Community detection in who-calls-whom social networks. In: Ordonez, C., Bellatreche, L. (eds.) DaWaK 2018. LNCS, vol. 11031, pp. 19–33. Springer, Cham (2018). https://doi.org/10.1007/978-3-319-98539-8_2
59. Veloso, B., Leal, F., González-Vélez, H., Malheiro, B., Burguillo, J.: Scalable data analytics using crowdsourced repositories and streams. J. Parallel Distrib. Comput. **122**, 1–10 (2018). https://doi.org/10.1016/j.jpdc.2018.06.013
60. Wang, G., et al.: Building a replicated logging system with Apache Kafka. Proc. VLDB Endow. **8**(12), 1654–1655 (2015). https://doi.org/10.14778/2824032.2824063

61. Wesolowski, A., et al.: Quantifying the impact of human mobility on Malaria. Science **338**(6104), 267–270 (2012)
62. Wesolowski, A., et al.: Impact of human mobility on the emergence of dengue epidemics in Pakistan. Proc. Natl. Acad. Sci. **112**(38), 11887–11892 (2015). https://doi.org/10.1073/pnas.1504964112
63. White, T.: Hadoop: The Definitive Guide, 4th edn. O'Reilly, Newton (2015)
64. Wilson, R., et al.: Rapid and near real-time assessments of population displacement using mobile phone data following disasters: the 2015 Nepal Earthquake. PLoS Curr. **8** (2016).https://doi.org/10.1371/currents.dis.d073fbece328e4c39087bc086d694b5c
65. Zaharia, M., et al.: Resilient distributed datasets: a fault-tolerant abstraction for in-memory cluster computing. In: Proceedings of the 9th USENIX Conference on Networked Systems Design and Implementation, NSDI 2012, p. 2. USENIX Association, Berkeley (2012). http://dl.acm.org/citation.cfm?id=2228298.2228301
66. Zaharia, M., et al.: Apache spark: a unified engine for big dataprocessing. Commun. ACM **59**(11), 56–65 (2016). https://doi.org/10.1145/2934664
67. Zhu, X., Ghahramani, Z.: Learning from labeled and unlabeled data with label propagation. Technical report CMU-CALD-02-107, Carnegie Mellon University, June 2002
68. Zufiria, P.J., et al.: Identifying seasonal mobility profiles from anonymized and aggregated mobile phone data. Application in food security. PloS ONE **13**(4), e0195714 (2018)

Medical Data Processing and Analysis for Remote Health and Activities Monitoring

Salvatore Vitabile[1]([✉]) [iD], Michal Marks[2] [iD], Dragan Stojanovic[3] [iD],
Sabri Pllana[4] [iD], Jose M. Molina[5] [iD], Mateusz Krzyszton[2] [iD], Andrzej Sikora[2] [iD],
Andrzej Jarynowski[6] [iD], Farhoud Hosseinpour[7] [iD], Agnieszka Jakobik[8] [iD],
Aleksandra Stojnev Ilic[3] [iD], Ana Respicio[9] [iD], Dorin Moldovan[10] [iD],
Cristina Pop[10] [iD], and Ioan Salomie[10] [iD]

[1] University of Palermo, Palermo, Italy
salvatore.vitabile@unipa.it
[2] Research and Academic Computer Network, Warsaw, Poland
{michal.marks,mateusz.krzyszton,andrzej.sikora}@nask.pl
[3] University of Nis, Niš, Serbia
{dragan.stojanovic,aleksandra.stojnev}@elfak.ni.ac.rs
[4] Linnaeus University, Växjö, Sweden
sabri.pllana@lnu.se
[5] Universidad Carlos III de Madrid, Madrid, Spain
molina@ia.uc3m.es
[6] Interdisciplinary Research Institute in Wroclaw, Wrocław, Poland
andrzej.jarynowski@doctoral.uj.edu.pl
[7] University of Turku, Turku, Finland
farhoud.hosseinpour@utu.fi
[8] Cracow University of Technology, Kraków, Poland
ajakobik@pk.edu.pl
[9] Universidade de Lisboa, Lisbon, Portugal
alrespicio@ciencias.ulisboa.pt
[10] Technical University of Cluj-Napoca, Cluj-Napoca, Romania
Ioan.Salomie@cs.utcluj.ro

Abstract. Recent developments in sensor technology, wearable computing, Internet of Things (IoT), and wireless communication have given rise to research in ubiquitous healthcare and remote monitoring of human's health and activities. Health monitoring systems involve processing and analysis of data retrieved from smartphones, smart watches, smart bracelets, as well as various sensors and wearable devices. Such systems enable continuous monitoring of patients psychological and health conditions by sensing and transmitting measurements such as heart rate, electrocardiogram, body temperature, respiratory rate, chest sounds, or blood pressure. Pervasive healthcare, as a relevant application domain in this context, aims at revolutionizing the delivery of medical services through a medical assistive environment and facilitates the independent living of patients. In this chapter, we discuss (1) data collection, fusion, ownership and privacy issues; (2) models, technologies and solutions for

© The Author(s) 2019
J. Kołodziej and H. González-Vélez (Eds.): cHiPSet, LNCS 11400, pp. 186–220, 2019.
https://doi.org/10.1007/978-3-030-16272-6_7

medical data processing and analysis; (3) big medical data analytics for remote health monitoring; (4) research challenges and opportunities in medical data analytics; (5) examples of case studies and practical solutions.

Keywords: e-Health · Internet of Things (IoT) ·
Remote health monitoring · Pervasive healthcare (PH)

1 Introduction

Recent developments in sensor technologies, wearable computing, Internet of Things (IoT), and wireless communications have given rise to research on mobile and ubiquitous health-care and remote monitoring of peoples health and activities [61]. Health monitoring systems include processing and analysis of data retrieved from smart-phones, smart watches, smart bracelets (that is, wristbands), as well as various connected sensors and wearable devices [69]. Such systems enable continuous monitoring of patients psychological and health conditions by sensing and transmitting measurements such as heart rate, electrocardiogram (ECG), body temperature, respiratory rate, chest sounds, and blood pressure. Collected, fused, and analyzed sensor data are important for diagnosis and treatment of patients with chronic diseases (such as, hypertension and diabetes) or for monitoring and assistance of elderly people. The area of health informatics is explored by researchers with different academic backgrounds: computer scientists, physicians, mathematicians, statisticians, and sociologists. All of them have something to contribute: from medical knowledge, though computer science (that is, simulations and data analysis), to sociological and marketing know-how (such as, apps dissemination and social interventions). There are mathematical/computational models (for instance, differential equations or system dynamics) that can be involved in understanding of health-relevant processes. For example, infectious disease models can use sensoric data that are collected from human contacts; these models can be useful in risk assessment of patients.

This chapter addresses major challenges and opportunities related to the medical data collection, modelling and processing in the context of monitoring of human's health and behavior. To illustrate the use of discussed concepts and technologies we present three case studies. The first case study describes a Big Data solution for remote health monitoring that considers challenges pertaining to monitoring the health and activities of patients. We present the design and implementation of a remote health monitoring system architecture that may be employed in a public, private or hybrid cloud. The second case study describes a system designed to support distributed monitoring of human health during a trip. It is assumed that a travel agency that organizes a trip to high mountains equips the guide and tourists with sensors that monitor health parameters. The third case study describes the use of machine learning in the context of monitoring daily living activities of people with dementia. Detected anomalies in the daily living activities of people with dementia may help medical experts to distinguish between health decline symptoms caused by dementia and health decline symptoms incurred by the side effects of the prescribed medications.

The rest of this chapter is structured as follows. Section 2 discusses data collection, fusion, ownership and privacy issues. Models, technologies and solutions for medical data processing and analysis are addressed in Sect. 3. Section 4 discusses big medical data analytics for remote health monitoring. Research challenges and opportunities in medical data analytics are addressed in Sect. 5. Section 6 describes examples of case studies and practical scenarios. The chapter is concluded in Sect. 7.

2   Medical Data Collection, Fusion, Ownership and Privacy

2.1   Medical Data Collection

Medicine has always been trying to measure properties of patients (such as, clinical picture) and how to understand their health and disease. Computer science would then incorporate the results of these measurements, experiments and observation into models. Recently, the utilisation of IT tools for medicine (such as, machine learning) has undergone an accelerating growth, however all models of such system are incomplete without real data, especially register-based. For example with patient Electronic Health Record/Documentation (EHR/D) data can be provided with reasonably accuracy on clinical picture, procedures, or co-morbidity. International standard - HL7 (Health Level Seven) allows interoperability between IT providers and solutions. However, still in many countries most of medical data is analog and must be digitized (e.g. image and sound processing). Moreover, powerful computer facilities and ubiquitous wearable devices with multiple sensors have made possible the collection, processing and storage of data on individual or group of patients. Individual data can be used for risk assessment for a particular health disorder. For example the risk of being affected by an infectious disease can be calculated based on sensor data and questionnaires [36]. Data collected from group of patients potentially being in contact can be used for infectious disease risk assessment in given community. There is concern about Data Protection Act in EU from legal perspective about providing such kind of data analysis, which will be described in detail in this chapter. The consent of each patient should be requested, which could be very difficult to obtain.

2.2   Blockchain for Privacy and Security

The main application of Blockchain in medicine is traceability of drugs in many actors setup. Such a technique has been already applied in Sub-Saharian Africa and South-East Asia for verifying originality of drugs (fake drugs are big problem there). Blockchain technology can also help in investigating food-borne outbreaks, where tractability of items in supply chain with storage/transport characteristics is crucial.

2.3   Data Fusion

Data fusion (DF) is a multi-domain growing field aiming to provide data for situation understanding. Globally, threat detection and facility protection are some of the vital areas in DF research [49]. Fusion systems aim to integrate sensor data and information in databases, knowledge bases, contextual information, user mission, etc., in order to describe dynamically-changing situations [32]. In a sense, the goal of information fusion is to attain a real-time simulation of a subset of the world based on partial observations of it [50].

The ability to fuse digital data into useful information is hampered by the fact that the inputs, whether device-derived or text-based, are generated in different formats, some of them unstructured. Whether the information is unstructured by nature or the fact that information exchange (metadata) standards are lacking (or not adhered to) all of this hinders automatic processing by computers. Furthermore, the data to be fused may be inaccurate, incomplete, ambiguous, or contradictory; it may be false or corrupted by hostile measures. Moreover, much information may be hard to formalize, i.e., imaging information. Consequently, information exchange is often overly complex. In many instances, there is a lack of communication between the various information sources, simply because there is no mechanism to support this exchange.

The high data flow, either device-based or text-based, is unable to process and leads to time delays, extra costs, and even inappropriate decisions due to missing or incomplete information [13, 63].

The key aspect in modern DF applications is the appropriate integration of all types of information or knowledge: observational data, knowledge models (a priori or inductively learned), and contextual information [28, 73]. Each of these categories has a distinctive nature and potential support to the result of the fusion process.

- Observational Data: Observational data are the fundamental data about the individual, as collected from some observational capability (sensors of any type). These data are about the observable characteristic of a person that are of interest [40].
- Contextual Information: Context and the elements of what could be called Contextual Information could be defined as "the set of circumstances surrounding the acquired data that are potentially of relevance to its completion." Because of its data-relevance, fusion implies the development of a best-possible estimate taking into account this lateral knowledge [29]. We can see the context as background, i.e., not the specific entity, event, or behaviour of prime interest but that information which is influential to the formation of a best estimate of these items [27].
- Learned Knowledge: In those cases where a priori knowledge for DF process development cannot be formed, one possibility is to try and excise the knowledge through online machine learning processes operating on the observational and other data [59]. These are procedural and algorithmic methods for discovering relationships among concepts of interest that being captured by the system (sensor data and contextual information). There is a tradeoff

involved in trying to develop fully-automated algorithmic DF processes for complex problems where the insertion of human intelligence at some point in the process may be a much more judicious choice [23].

At this time, there are a multitude of problem-specific solutions to fusion, most of which are centred in specific applications, producing problem-specific results [26]. The ability to automatically combine the results of smaller problems into a larger context is still missing.

2.4   Medical Data Security Requirements Enforced by the Law and Related Ownership and Privacy Issues

All organizations that are collecting, processing and storing medical are obliged by the international and local law regulations and standards to improve their data protection strategies. The example of data protection laws required by USA is the The Health Insurance Portability and Accountability Act (HIPAA)[1], used for compliance and secure adoption of electronic health records (EHR).

HIPAA sets the rules for sensitive patient data protection with its Privacy and Security Rules. According to HIPA, a company that processes protected health information must store it in a system that is secure as far as physical, network, and process security is concerned. Security Rule of HIPAA defines requirements for health information that is held or transferred in electronic form. It requires that HIPAA-covered entities implement the following protections:

- Ensure the confidentiality, integrity, and availability of all e-PHI they create, receive, maintain or transmit;
- Identify and protect against reasonably anticipated threats to the security or integrity of the information;
- Protect against reasonably anticipated, impermissible uses or disclosures; and
- Ensure compliance by their workforce.

Additionally, it regulates technical safeguards when hosting sensitive patient data, including facility access in place, as well as policies for using workstations, electronic media, and all processes of transferring, removing, disposing, and re-using electronic media or electronic information. It enforces authorized unique user IDs, emergency access procedures, automatic log off, encryption of data, and audit reports. Also, activity tracking logs of all activity on hardware and software are necessary.

Health-care organizations must ensure the security and availability of patients data for both health-care professionals and patients.

The complete suite of HIPAA Administrative Simplification Regulations can be found at 45 CFR Part 160, Part 162, and Part 164, and includes:

- Transactions and Code Set Standards;
- Identifier Standards;

---

[1] https://www.hhs.gov/hipaa.

- Privacy Rule;
- Security Rule;
- Enforcement Rule;
- Breach Notification Rule.

General Data Protection Regulation (GDPR)[2] is a regulation in EU law on data protection and privacy within the European Union (EU) and the European Economic Area (EEA). It also specifies the conditions for exporting of personal data outside the EU and EEA areas. It specifies:

- Rights of the data subject
- Controller role
- Transfers of personal data to third countries or international organizations
- Independent supervisory authorities
- Cooperation and consistency
- Remedies, liability and penalties
- Delegated acts and implementing acts

It specifies actions to be taken that enforces the processing on systems that are processing medical data. Several examples may be:

- Data holders must notify the authorities in case of breach;
- Subjects have a right to access their data;
- The right to be forgotten that gives individuals the power to request the removal of their personal data;
- Privacy must be designed in;
- Privacy is included by default, not by unticking a box;
- Right to rectification, the data shall have the right to obtain from the controller without undue delay. The data subject have the right to have incomplete personal data completed, including by means of providing a supplementary statement.
- Every organization holding personal third party data must have a data protection officer.

The GDPR imposes stiff fines on data controllers and processors for non-compliance, up to 20 million, or 4% of the worldwide annual revenue of the prior financial year, in case of braking the basic principles for processing medical data.

To obtain the HIPAA required security level, the company may follow two paths:

1. choose a reputable HIPAA training company that offers certification credentials, and analyze the company procedures and systems by itself;
2. obtain evaluation by an independent, third party auditor, like for instance, Coalfire Systems[3] or ComplySmart[4].

[2] https://eur-lex.europa.eu/eli/reg/2016/679/oj.
[3] http://www.coalfire.com.
[4] http://www.complysmart.com.

For ensuring GRPD standards, the company may:

1. obtain the customized GDPR certificate for protection officers[5];
2. hire authorized experts[6];

For both HIPAA and GDPR compliance there is no one main central independent party that may certify the company.

GDPR specific challenges rises inside remote systems. First of all, under the GDPR personal data may not be stored longer then needed. This is why, retention procedures have to be implemented and when the data expired they have to be removed from systems. Data can be stored on multiple locations, under multiple vendors, processed by many services. The deletion of data completely have to consider also backups and copies of data stored on the remote equipment. Additionally, breaching response may also be the issue. Breach notification have to be shared among data holders. A breach event have to be well defined.

Processing of personal data outside the European Economic Area (EEA) is the next problem due to multiple location. Controllers will need to define a multi-country data strategy taking into account localization laws.

The transparency of security procedures of medical systems or third party certificates are necessary to ensure security controllers about the quality of security services.

Medical service providers must be subject of an audit to perform a control framework with privacy and privacy by design control measures.

Medical services should be monitored to address any changes in technology and recommended updates to the system. It includes newly introduced equipment, and sensors.

During processing large set of data, visibility regarding metadata and data anonymization is a big challenge. The level of protection of metadata, the respective ownership rights, rights to process the collections of metadata, intended uses of metadata should be examined carefully.

2.5 Publicly Available Medical Datasets and Reuse of Already Collected Data

Comprehensive and real-world personal health and activities datasets have a very important role in data processing and analysis; therefore several attempts have been made to create big and representative examples of real-world datasets [67].

Examples of such datasets are UbiqLog [68] and CrowdSignals [82], which contains both the data from the smartphones, and from wearable devices, smart watch/bracelet.

Biomedical signals datasets can be found at PhysioNet[7] which offers free Web access to large collections of recorded physiologic signals (PhysioBank) and related open-source software for collecting them (PhysioToolkit).

---

[5] https://www.eugdpr.institute/gdpr-certification/.
[6] https://www.forcepoint.com.
[7] www.physionet.org.

The ExtraSensory dataset contains data from 60 users and more than 300K labeled examples (minutes) originated from smartphone and smartwatch sensors. The dataset is publicly available for context recognition research [77].

Within already implemented Hospital Information System (HIS) framework a lot of data is collected (e.g. for administrative purposes), but not have been analysed from patients health perspective. Organizational structure as dedicating staff to patients, transport paths rerouting, shift distributions, geo-localizing isolated/cohorted patients, etc. can be used for example in infectious disease field. There are models and tools describing the possible spread of pathogens and could indicate an effective strategy in the fight against infectious diseases[8], however available solutions are not using HPC as it would be possible.

3   Models, Technologies and Solutions for Medical Data Processing and Analysis

Usability of e-health can rely on collecting techniques and data analysis. Various data sets (survey, diagnosis and tests, time series, spatial, panel, longitudinal data, etc.) shall be analysed by different methods (regressions, decision trees, structural equation modelling, social network analysis, agent-based modelling, machine learning, etc.).

3.1   Innovative Use of Commercial Electronic Devices (Smartphones and Watches, Bracelets, Wearables,...) for Remote Monitoring

Low-power and low cost electronic devices can be easily purchased and used. Some properties as body temperature and blood pulse can be measured with high accuracy, but developer are trying to target more and more features. FDA (Federal Drug Agency) as well as EMA (European Medicines Agency) certify digital Health Software and Devices. Most of devices on the market do not satisfy minimum conditions for certification and accreditation. Some of them as air quality monitoring devices (e.g. PM2.5 laser dust sensor for less than 5$) have been massively used in heavily polluted cities. However no medical organization recommends using home devices due to very low data quality and data provided from certified official stations should be enough. More data is not always better as it is shown in this example.

Some issues come with digital health apps and software (mhealth). Nowadays an app can be found for almost everything. Let's consider advances in image recognition using deep learning by a smartphone for measuring blood pressure by photoplethysmography. The biggest advantage of this method is simplicity, so nothing more than smartphone is needed. However, even it works well after calibration for most users, there are patients for whom the error of this procedure can reach 30%. So apps offering this feature (like icare and HDCH) were taken away from Google Play and App Store, but their equivalents are still very popular, for example in China.

---

[8] www.sirsz.pl.

Another type of sensors are bluetooth beacons to track social interactions that can be used for infectious disease control and psychological health (one of certified suppliers for these beacons is kontakt.io). Smartphone or wearable sensors can communicate between each other and collect contact data.

3.2   IoT Platforms for e-Health Applications

Thinger.io. The IoT platform is an open source alternative. Thinger.io is relatively new to the IoT ecosystem but is being used extensively in different research projects [25,43,48], or even for education [38]. It provides a ready to use cloud service for connecting devices to the Internet to perform any remote sensing or actuation over the Internet. It offers a free tier for connecting a limited number of devices, but it is also possible to install the software outside the cloud for a private management of the data and devices connected to the platform, without any limitation.

Fig. 1. Thinger.io platform

This platform is hardware agnostic, so it is possible to connect any device with Internet connectivity, from Arduino devices, Raspberry Pi, Sigfox devices, Lora solutions over gateways, or ARM devices, to mention a few. The platform provides some out of the box features like device registry; bi-directional communication in real-time, both for sensing or actuation; data and configuration storage, so it is possible to store time series data; identity and access management (IAM), to allow third party entities to access the platform and device resources over REST/Websocket APIs; third party Webhooks, so the devices can easily call other Web services, send emails, SMS, push data to other clouds, etc. It also provides a web interface to manage all the resources and generate dashboards for remote monitoring. The general overview of this platform is available at Fig. 1. The main benefit of using this platform, aside that it is open source, is the possibility to obtain a bi-directional communication with the devices, in real-time, by using standard REST-API interfaces. This way, it is possible to develop any application, i.e., desktop, mobile, Web service, that interacts with devices by using a well-known and proven interface based on REST [62]. Meanwhile, the devices can use more efficient (in terms of bandwidth, or memory footprint) binary protocols to communicate with the cloud. In the other way, this platform provides client libraries for connecting several state of the art IoT devices like Arduino-based, ESP8266, ESP32, LinkitOne, Texas Instruments CC3200, Libellium Waspmotes, Raspberry Pi, etc. The client libraries provide a comprehensive way of connecting devices and sending information to the cloud, without having to deal with complex IoT protocols.

Libelium MySignals. This is a development platform for medical devices and eHealth applications. The platform can be used to develop eHealth web applications and to test own sensors for medical applications. MySignals is an example of commercial product which is offered and supported by a Spanish company called Libelium[9]. It allows measurement of more than 20 biometric parameters such as pulse, breath rate, oxygen in blood, electrocardiogram signals, blood pressure, muscle electromyography signals, glucose levels, galvanic skin response, lung capacity, snore waves, patient position, airflow and body scale parameters. Data gathered by sensors can be stored in the MySignals or third party Cloud to be visualized in external Web and mobile app's. Libelium offers an API for developers to access the information as well as Open source HW version which is based on Arduino. One of the drawbacks is the restriction for sending the information coming from MySignals to a third party cloud server using directly WiFi radio which is limited only for HW version – option is not available for SW version running on libelium Atmega 2560 node.

FIWARE. FIWARE[10] is an open source IoT platform "combining components that enable the connection to IoT with Context Information Management and Big Data services in the cloud" [8]. FIWARE uses rather simple standard APIs for data management and exchange that can be used to develop smart applications. It provides enhanced OpenStack-based cloud hosting capabilities

---

[9] www.libelium.com/product/mysignals.
[10] https://www.fiware.org/.

and a number of components for functions offered as a Service. The adoption of FIWARE technology by the eHealth market is promoted by the industrial accelerator FICHe project [9] launched by European Commission and several industrial projects that have been developed in the FICHe context. CardioWeel [6] is an advanced driver assistance system that provides information about drivers health status using the human electrocardiogram (ECG) acquired from the drivers hands. This system is hosted on FIWARE cloud using the available virtual machines. The development of healthcare applications using FIWARE components is described in [75] and in [19].

4 Big Medical Data Analytics for Remote Health Monitoring

With the advance of remote health monitoring and pervasive healthcare concepts, an increased research work has been published to cover the topics ranging from theory, concepts, and systems, to applications of Big medical data systems for ubiquitous healthcare services.

4.1 Big Medical Data System Architecture

The analysis and health problem detection can be performed on a mobile device (phone, watch, bracelet, etc.) leveraging edge computing principles, or at a nearby computing infrastructure, e.g. IoT gateway, or a home/hospital server [22].

Physiological, health and social media data, providing insight into people activities and health conditions, could be enriched and correlated with external and environmental data collected within Smart City infrastructure (weather conditions, environment pollution/noise, temperature, city events, traffic conditions, etc.). As such, fusion, analysis and mining of IoT medical data and external/environmental data could better detect potential health problems and their cause-effect relationships with the environment.

The fusion, processing and analytics of sensor data, collected from personal mobile and health devices, as well as Smart city infrastructure are performed at the edge/fog computing components providing efficiency and minimal latency in detection of critical medical conditions that requires prompt actions. Also, this can provide a personalized health system for general well-being where individuals can be provided with healthcare tailored to their needs.

Moreover, such system should support efficient collection and analysis of massive quantities of heterogeneous and continuous health and activities data (Big Data) from a group, or a crowd of users. The storage, aggregation, processing and analysis of Big health data could be performed within public, private or hybrid cloud infrastructure. The results of data analysis and mining are provided to physicians, healthcare professionals, medical organisations, pharmaceutical companies, etc. through tailored visual analytics, dashboard applications. There is a number of research and development challenges that must be addressed

Fig. 2. A system for remote monitoring of people health and activities - general architecture

prior to wider application of such personalized healthcare systems that continuously monitor peoples health and activities and respond appropriately on critical events and conditions. These include, but are not limited to security, privacy and data ownership, sensor data fusion, scalable algorithms and systems for analytics and data mining, and edge-cloud models for processing and analytics.

The general architecture of a large-scale distributed system based on medical IoT devices and Big Data processing and analytics for remote monitoring of peoples health and activities is given in Fig. 2.

Remote monitoring systems can operate at multiple scales, providing personal and global sensing. As illustrated in [44], there are three distinct scales for sensing: personal, group and community sensing.

Personal or individual monitoring systems are designed for single individual, and are often focused on personal data collection and analysis. Typical scenarios include tracking the users exercise routines, measuring activity levels or identification of symptoms connected with psychological disorders. Although collected data might be for sole consumption of the user, sharing with medical professional is common. Popular personal monitoring technologies are Google Glass™, FitBit™ and The Nike+ FuelBand™.

If individuals share a common interest, concern or goal while participating in monitoring applications they form a group. Group monitoring systems can be popular in social networks or connected groups, where data can be shared freely, or with privacy protection. Common examples are health monitoring applications including contests related to specific goals: running distance, weight loss, calorie intake, etc.

If a number of people participating in health and activities monitoring is very large, it is called community or crowd monitoring. Crowd modeling and monitoring implies collective data analytics for the good of the community. However, it involves cooperation of persons who will not trust each other, highlighting the need for strong privacy protection and possibly low commitment levels from users. Examples of community monitoring involve tracking the spread of diseases across area, finding patterns for specific medical conditions etc. The impact of scaling to monitoring applications is to be explored, but many research issues related to information sharing, data ownership, data fusion, security and privacy, algorithms used for data mining, providing useful feedback, etc. remain open.

Khan et al. in [41] presented the latest research and development efforts and achievements in the field of smart healthcare regarding high performance computing (HPC) and large-scale healthcare architectures, data quality and large-scale machine learning models for smart healthcare, Internet-of-Things, fog computing, and m-Health, as well as wearable computing, Quality of Service (QoS), and context-awareness for smart healthcare.

The challenges in designing algorithms, methods and systems for healthcare analytics and applications have been examined in [45], along with a survey on smart healthcare technologies and solutions. The next-generation healthcare applications, services and systems related to Big healthcare data analytics are reviewed and challenges in developing such systems are discussed.

The current state and projected future directions for integration of remote health monitoring technologies into clinical and medicine practice have been presented in [31]. Several of the challenges in sensing, analytics, and visualization that need to be addressed before systems can be designed for seamless integration into clinical practice are highlighted and described.

4.2   Big IoT Data for Remote Health Monitoring

With the development of Internet of Things (IoT) concepts, the idea of IoT healthcare systems has been an interesting topic for large number of researchers. Baker et al. in [16] have presented state-of-the-art research related to wearable IoT healthcare system. A standard model for application in future IoT healthcare system was proposed, along with an overview of existing challenges including security, privacy, wearability and low-power operation. Also, the authors reviewed several research works that address IoT healthcare challenges related to rehabilitation, diabetes management, disease monitoring, heart-attack detection and general activity and health monitoring purposes. Furthermore, a four-part model was proposed as an aid in the development of future IoT healthcare systems, and it includes:

- wearable sensor and central nodes,
- short range communications,
- long range communications,
- secure cloud storage architecture and machine learning.

Islam et al. in [34] have given an overview of existing IoT–based healthcare network studies, and state-of-the-art network architectures, platforms, applications, and industrial trends in this area. Furthermore, they highlighted security and privacy issues and proposed a security model aiming to minimize security risk related to health care. Specifically, they presented an extensive overview of IoT healthcare systems, one of them being the Internet of m-Health Things (m-IoT): an operating symbiosis of mobile computing, medical sensors, and communications technologies for healthcare services.

An important part of IoT healthcare is obtaining insights from large data generated by IoT devices. The focus of [53] was on IoT architecture, opportunities and challenges, but from the data analysis point of view. In this paper a brief overview of research efforts directed toward IoT data analytics, as well as the relationship between Big Data analytics and IoT were given. Furthermore, analytic types, methods and technologies for big IoT data mining are discussed.

In [77], authors have used smartphone and smartwatch sensors to recognize detailed situations of people in their natural behavior. Initial tests were conducted over labeled data from over 300k minutes from 60 subjects. A dedicated application for data retrieval was implemented and presented. As stated in the paper, the main contribution is the emphasis on in-the-wild conditions, namely naturally used devices, unconstrained device placement, natural environment and natural behavioral content. The main challenge when recognizing context in non-controlled conditions is high diversity and variance of the data. However, it was shown that everyday devices, in their natural usage, can capture information about a wide range of behavioral attributes.

In [57] a distributed framework based on the IoT paradigm has been proposed for monitoring human biomedical signals in activities involving physical exertion. Also, a validation use case study was presented which includes monitoring footballers heart rates during a football match, and it was shown that data from BAN devices can be used to predict not only situations of sudden death but also possible injuries.

Ma et al. in [52] have presented a Big health application system based on health IoT devices and Big Data. The authors presented the architecture of health care application leveraging IoT and Big Data and introduced technology challenges and possible m-health applications based on this architecture.

One important subset of the data used for healthcare and improved quality of life are the data retrieved from healthcare services running on smarthphones such as Endomondo, Nike+, RunKeeper, and Runtastic. These applications can provide data about different lifestyles, such as sleep, diet and exercise habits all of which can be correlated with various medical conditions. In such manner, physicians can calculate risk for conditions or in cases of diagnosed ones, can adapt treatments or provide emergency responses when needed. Cortes et al. in [21] have provided an extensive analysis of traces gathered from Endomondo sport tracker service. The main Big Data challenges associated with analysis of the data retrieved from this type of applications were discussed. They include data acquisition (data redundancy, workload, flow rate), data cleaning (invalid and uncertain data from sensors), data integration, aggregation and representation (define common data representation across various applications, spatio-temporal properties of the data), query processing, data modeling and analysis (queries are important aspect of knowledge discovery), and interpretation (online and offline analysis).

The concept of smart health (s-Health), which integrates context-aware mobile health principles with sensors and information originated in smart cities, has been introduced in [74]. The authors provided a detailed overview of the smart health principles and discussed the main research challenges and opportunities in augmentation of smart healthcare with smart city concepts.

4.3 Processing and Analysis of Big Health and Mobility Data Streams

The healthcare industry generates large amounts of data, driven by record keeping, compliance and regulatory requirements and patient care [65]. The current trend is toward rapid digitalization of these massive amounts of data, and their fusion with data retrieved from personal and mobility sensors. When it comes to health care in terms of patient records, treatment plans, prescription information etc., everything needs to be done quickly, accurately and in some cases transparently enough to satisfy stringent industry regulations. However, with extended datasets, effective data processing and analysis can uncover hidden insights that improve patient care. If the data is collected out of the medical offices, they can model a patient's behavior more accurately. Furthermore, the results can be used to provide better real-time healthcare at lower cost. Real-time component requires that systems for analysis and processing must deal not only with huge amounts of data, but also with Big Data streams. This requirement has led to a proliferation of studies related to processing and analysis of big, heterogeneous streams for healthcare purposes. These streams have all main characteristics of Big Data:

- Volume: in order to create a complete overview of person's or group health, it is necessary to take into account data collected from related sources, obtained not only from medical instruments and BAN sensors, but also from social media, mobile devices or machine-to-machine data. This data can be from terabytes to exabytes, does not need to be stored, but must be effectively and analyzed and processed in timely manner.
- Velocity: Data streams with unparalleled rate and speed are generated and must be processed and analysed accordingly. In order to be effective, and to

provide responses in emergency situations, healthcare systems must process and analyze torrents of data in real time, but also be capable to perform long-term batch operations.

- Variety: Data comes in all varieties, from structured, numeric data obtained from sensors and medical devices to unstructured text documents, email, video, audio and mobility data. Systems must be capable of processing all varieties of data from text to graph data.

In order to effectively process and analyze Big health data streams, techniques for Big Data must be taken into account and adapted for data streams. Big Data in health informatics is a pool of technologies, tools, and techniques that manage, manipulate, and organize enormous, varied, and intricate datasets in order to improve the quality of patients' status. Fang et al. in [24] have given a comprehensive overview of challenges and techniques for big computational health informatics, both historical and state-of-the art. Several techniques and algorithms in machine learning were characterized and compared. Identified challenges were summarized into four categories, depending on Big Data characteristics they tackle (i.e., volume, velocity, variety, and veracity). Furthermore, a general pipeline for healthcare data processing was proposed. This pipeline includes data capturing, storing, sharing, analyzing, searching, and decision support.

Wang et al. in [81] have presented strategic implications of Big Data in healthcare, including but not limited to historical development, architectural design and component functionalities of Big Data analytics. Different capabilities of healthcare data analytics were recognized from different implementation cases, and various benefits were identified. Recognized capabilities include:

- Analytical capability for patterns of care - analytical techniques typically used in a Big Data analytics system to process data with an immense volume, variety, and velocity via unique data storage, management, analysis, and visualization technologies.
- Unstructured data analytical capability - unstructured and semi-structured data in healthcare refer to information that can neither be stored in a traditional relational database nor fit into predefined data models.
- Decision support capability - the ability to produce reports about daily healthcare services to aid managers' decisions and actions.
- Predictive capability - ability to build and assess a model aimed at generating accurate predictions of new observations, where new can be interpreted temporally and or cross-sectionally.
- Traceability - ability to track output data from all the system's IT components throughout the organization's service units.

As a result, the best practice for Big Data analytics architecture has been proposed. This architecture loosely consists of five main architectural layers: data, data aggregation, analytics, information exploration, and data governance. Ma et al. in [51] have underlined the importance of data fusion based approach to provide more valuable personal and group services, such as personalized health guidance and public health warnings. Various technologies and areas that are related to this topic were covered, including mobile, wearable and cloud computing, Big Data, IoT and Cyber Physical systems. Authors proposed cloud- and big-data-assisted layered architecture, and described each layer along with tools and technologies that can be used. Also, different applications were identified related to medical recommendations and wearable healthcare systems.

4.4   High Performance Data Analytics

Efficient analytics of large amounts of data in health care (such as, patient genomic data or X-ray images) demands computational, communication and memory resources of High Performance Computing (HPC) architectures.

HPC involves the use of many interconnected processing elements to reduce the time to solution of given a problem. Many powerful HPC systems are heterogeneous, in the sense that they combine general-purpose CPUs with *accelerators* such as, Graphics Processing Units (GPUs), or Field Programmable Gates Arrays (FPGAs). For instance ORNL's Summit—which is currently credited as the leading HPC system in the TOP500 list of most powerful computer systems [76]—is equipped with 4608 computing nodes and each node comprises two IBM Power9 22-core CPUs and six NVIDIA V100 GPUs, for a theoretical peak power of approximately 200 petaflops.

Many approaches have proposed for using HPC systems [18,39,56,60]. While multi-core CPUs are suitable for general-purpose tasks, many-core processors (such as the Intel Xeon Phi [20] or GPU [58]) comprise a larger number of lower frequency cores and perform well on scalable applications [54] (such as, DNA sequence analysis [55] or deep learning [79]).

5   Medical Data Analytics: Research Challenges and Opportunities

5.1   Adaptive Edge/Cloud Processing and Analytics

In the context of medical IoT, the particular benefits could arise from the fog and edge computing paradigms. They represent the model where sensitive data generated by body worn medical devices and smart phone sensors are processed, analyzed and mined close to where it is generated, on these devices themselves, instead of sending vast amounts of sensor data to the cloud, that could exhaust network, processing or storage resources and violate user privacy. Only aggregated, context enriched data/events are sent to the cloud for further processing and analytics. The right balance between Edge-Cloud should provide fast response to detected events, as well as conservation of network bandwidth, minimization of latency, security and preservation of privacy.

Typically, Internet of Things (IoT) is composed of small, resource constrained devices that are connected to the Internet. In essence, they are dedicated to perform specific tasks without the need of providing a general means for performing complicated, resource-consuming computations. This means that most of the data is transmitted to the cloud without prepossessing or analysis. This implies that the amount of data that is transmitted to the cloud is increasing even more rapidly than the number of IoT devices itself. Indeed, cloud computing is being recognized as a success factor for IoT, providing ubiquity, reliability, high-performance and scalability. However, IoT solutions based on cloud computing fail in applications that require very low and predictable latency or are implemented in a geographically distributed manner with a lot of wireless links. A promising technology to tackle the low-latency and geographical distribution required by IoT devices is fog computing.

The fog computing layer is an intermediate layer between the edge of the network and the cloud layer. The fog computing layer extends the computation paradigm geographically providing local computing and storage for local services. Fog computing does not outsource cloud computing. It aims to provide a computing and storage platform physically closer to the end nodes provisioning new breed of applications and services with an efficient interplay with the cloud layer. The expected benefit is a better quality of service for applications that require low latency. Lower latency is obtained by performing data analysis already at the fog computing layer. Data analysis at the fog computing layer is lightweight, and therefore more advanced analyses and processing should be done at the cloud layer. Naturally, some applications do not require real-time computation, or they need high processing power, and therefore they are performed at the cloud layer. For example, in the case of a smart community, where homes in a neighborhood are connected to provide community services, low latency is expected for making urgent decisions, and thus computation is performed within the neighborhood, instead of a cloud layer which can be located on another continent [33].

5.2 Virtualisation Technologies in e-Health

To support multi-tenancy of different applications and to achieve elasticity in large-scale shared resources, fog computing takes advantages of virtualization technologies. Virtualization and application partitioning techniques are the two key technology solutions that are employed in a fog computing platform. Virtualization includes the process of abstracting and slicing the heterogeneous computing nodes into virtual machines (VMs), hiding the details about the heterogeneity of hardware devices from the applications that are running on the fog layer. Among different virtualization technologies, Linux containers, i.e., containerization, has advantages in short implementation time, efficient resource utilization and low management cost. Application partitioning divides each task into smaller sub-tasks to be executed concurrently on distributed grids, which can improve the task offloading efficiency of applications when the node is overloaded by computationally intensive applications.

Containers provide OS level virtualization without a need for deployment of a virtual OS. Hence, they are lightweight and significantly smaller in size than VMs. Containers provide a self-contained and isolated computing environment for applications and facilitate lightweight portability and interoperability for IoT applications. Moreover, data and resource isolation in containers offers improved security for the applications running in fog nodes [17].

Recently, researchers have shown increased interest in studying and deploying container-based healthcare applications. Kačeniauskas et al. [37] have developed a software to simulate blood flows through aortic valves, as a cloud service. They have experimentally evaluated the performance of XEN VMs, KVM VMs and Docker containers and have found that Docker containers outperform KVM and XEN VMs. In [35] a framework to monitor patients symptoms has been proposed. This solution employs a Raspberry Pi that read the medical data through the sensors attached and sent it to a server. The server is running Docker containers.

A home-based healthcare framework has been proposed by Li et al. [47]. Different sensors send streams of medical data to docker containers for processing. Koliogeorgi et al. [42] has presented the cloud infrastructure of the AEGLE project, which integrates cloud technologies and heterogeneous reconfigurable computing in large scale healthcare system for Big Bio-Data analytics. AEGLE runs each service and library in different Docker containers. It also uses Kubernetes for fault tolerant, management and scaling of the containerized applications.

A conceptual model and minimal viable product implementation, that enables the analyses of genomic data, harvested by a portable genome sequencer using mobile devices, has been proposed by Araújo et al. [14]. They have used Docker to process the data and to ensure that their system will work across different devices and operating systems. Moreover they would like to prepare the Docker image available for mobile phones. In this way, it will be possible to run their system containers on mobile phones. Rassias et al. [66] has introduced a web-based platform for real-time teleconsultation services on medical imaging. Their platform consists of a client application and an ecosystem of microservices. Each system's service is running in Docker container.

Bahrami et al. [15] has proposed a method to better protect sensitive data. Their method provides real-time resource recommendation for a container scheduler according to HIPAA's (Health Insurance Portability and Accountability Act) regulations. Finally, a recent paper by Sahoo et al. [70] presents a fault tolerant scheduling framework for distribution of healthcare jobs based on their types. They have evaluated the framework with both hypervisor-based virtualization and container-based virtualization. Containers achieved faster start-up time and less response time for both CPU-intensive and data-intensive task.

6   Case Studies and Practical Solutions

6.1   Big Data Solution for Remote Health Monitoring

Taking into account all the challenges related to health/activities monitoring data and control flows that should be employed in a public, private or hybrid cloud, we have designed Remote Health Monitoring system architecture and have implemented the system tailored to analysis of mobility data for the purposes

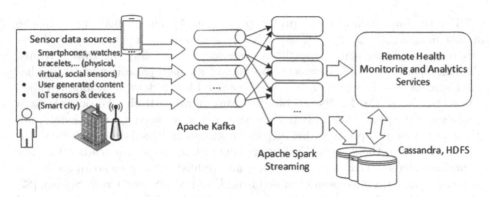

Fig. 3. The general architecture of remote health monitoring cloud infrastructure

of healthcare. The general architecture of Remote Health Monitoring system is given in Fig. 3.

To provide collection of massive and fast sensor data streams, a distributed message broker is employed that maintain a set of topics, for different users or medical conditions, where different sensor data and events will be streamed. These topics would be monitored by number of processing and analytics jobs within Big Data stream engine. Each job acquires only the data from the topics of interest, so different jobs are used to identify specific medical condition and patient behaviour. This architecture could be applied to both personalized and group healthcare systems. The main advantages are:

- Data decoupling: every measurement is streamed as a separate record to a predefined topic, so occurrence of missing data in records is easily detectable: they are absent from the topic; if data from certain sensors is missing, it can be easily left out.
- The separation at jobs level: jobs can monitor only a subset of topics; provides a perfect ground for implementation of different privacy protocols for each job.
- The user level separation: this model allows both personal and collective analysis as jobs can monitor data on individual, or a group level.
- Comprehensive visualization: the results from each jobs can be visualized separately, which can simplify the visualization itself; however, alerts and notifications from different jobs can be combined and visualized to provide an insight to general state.

Big health data stream processing and analysis currently relies on systems for massive stream analytics. A comparative analysis of the existing state-of-the art stream processing solutions is presented in [72], including both open source solutions such as Storm, Spark Streaming and S4, and commercial streaming solutions such as Amazon Kinesis and IBM Infosphere Stream. Comparison includes processing model and latency, data pipeline, fault tolerance and data guarantees. These and similar solutions can be used in healthcare use cases.

For the implementation of prototype system Apache Kafka[11] and Apache Spark Streaming[12] have been used. Kafka is chosen as it can support different topics, and messaging capabilities necessary for handling Big Data streams. Apache Spark Streaming is selected because of its main paradigm which implies that stream data is treated as series of bounded batch data, a technique called micro batching, and for its machine learning library MLlib. We do not use a mobile health application for data collection, but we created a simulation of multiple users based on pre-recorded personal health/activities data used for streaming such data to the system. Each users simulation component reads a file that contains different records in csv format, and publishes them to adequate Kafka topic. Actual data have been obtained from UbiqLog [68] and CrowdSignals [82] datasets. These datasets contain information retrieved from smartphones and smart bracelets, such as a heart rate, step count, accelerometer and gyroscope data, location, application usage and WiFi. A distinct record is generated for every measurement or event, and it contains user id, topic, and value. Id is used to separate different users, topic to identify type of measurement or event, and value to hold actual data. For each type of record there is a predefined Kafka topic. These topic streams are monitored by a number of Apache Spark Streaming jobs. Each job acquires the data from monitored topics, and performs specific health and activities related analysis. We implemented a demo job for prediction of skin temperature based on heart rate and step count values. Firstly, in offline mode we created a regression model for these parameters. Then, in Spark Streaming job, we loaded that model, and generated alert in the form of console notification if predicted temperature is higher than the predefined threshold. This illustrates that the system can be used for complex event processing. Our vision is to create jobs that can detect complex events, extrapolate valuable information, and run spatio-temporal mining algorithms on available data. Furthermore, visualization and alert generating component of the system will be implemented.

6.2   Smartphone Ad Hoc Network (SPAN) for e-Health Application

Practical Scenario. In this section, we propose a system designed to support distributed monitoring of trip participants' health. Let's assume that there is a travel agency which organizes the climbing in a high mountains, e.g. Kilimanjaro. As the agency makes reasonable policy, they equip the guide and the participants with sensors that measure health parameters (heart rate, pressure, body temperature, etc.) in order to monitor the people's health.

The guide-leader is equipped with a satellite mobile phone and can exchange information with the agency and rescue teams. The communication between the guide and the participants is organized in ad hoc manner using Bluetooth. Each participant is equipped with a smartphone and the health sensor. The sensor is connected to the smartphone by Bluetooth Low Energy.

---

[11] kafka.apache.org.

[12] spark.apache.org/streaming/.

Technology. One of the trends observed recently in the global telecommunications is a constant growth of the number of smart devices. Mobile devices are getting richer in functionality thanks to more and more computing resources, better batteries and more advanced embedded equipment (e.g. sensors, cameras, localization modules). An important parts of each mobile device are the wireless communication interfaces (e.g. WiFi, Bluetooth), which are used to exchange data between the mobile device and peripheral devices (e.g. headphones, hands-free system, etc.) or other mobile devices. Thanks to the wireless communication it is also possible to integrate smartphones with external sensors.

Thus Sikora et al. [71] decided to create the SmartGroup@Net (SGN) mobile application which allows on direct communication between people without the necessity to be in a range of cellular network infrastructure. The communication is realized over Bluetooth Low Energy (BLE) to create mobile network allowing local exchange of messages, which contain selected information about the state of the network nodes. This is an example of Smart Phone Ad hoc Network (SPAN) solution[13]. In the considered test study the Polar H7 Bluctooth Smart 4.0 heart rate sensor and Wiko Sunny phones are used – see Fig. 4.

Fig. 4. A smartphone with SGN application running together with Polar H7 heart rate sensor.

Mobile Application. SmartGroup@Net (SGN) is the mobile application, which allows on supporting outdoor search actions performed by group of people. The application is useful for different public services, that could be supported during rescue action by civilian volunteers equipped with mobile phones. Other potential applications of SGN include: increasing safety of people moving in

---

[13] SPAN network can be formed by portable devices (e.g. smartphones, tablets, etc.) which communicate over WiFi or Bluetooth and operate in ad-hoc mode. The main advantage of the SPAN network is independence not only from the network operator, but also from the tariff plan – the communication in an ad-hoc mode is free of charges.

Fig. 5. An example of the SGN application user screen with buttons and fields description

groups in areas with limited access to the mobile network – like high mountains climbing, coordination and management of rescue actions in a crisis situation area (e.g. earthquake, plane crash etc.) and other coordinated actions involving sensors carried by people or self-propelled devices. In all mentioned scenarios it is important to maintain a proper group formation and topology.

An exemplary screen of the SGN application is shown in Fig. 5. Information about the current location and the destination of the mobile phone user as well as the locations of other participants of the action are presented on the map downloaded online from the Open Street Map service[14] and stored in the cache or installed in the offline mode as image file.

The presented application uses the BLE protocol for local exchange of information between the participants of the action. The information sent by each participant include his identification data (action number, user's name and id), location (geographical coordinates), status (normal or emergency), heart rate. These data are saved in the broadcast packet, encrypted and sent to other users depending on the radio transmission range. Each of the participants of the action can simultaneously broadcast messages with their own data and listen to messages from the other group members. Thus the leader (guide) can obtain the information about health status of the participants. Depending on the situation appropriate preventive measures can be taken.

---

[14] http://www.openstreetmap.org.

6.3   Machine Learning for Monitoring Daily Living Activities of People with Dementia

Dementia is a very complex condition affecting the mental health of people and having a negative impact upon their daily life, independence and abilities. The current statistics show that dementia has a rapid spread worldwide as each year around 10 million new cases are reported [7]. Moreover, it is estimated that since 2016, dementia has become the 5th cause of deaths worldwide [12]. Even if there is no cure for dementia, the lives of people with dementia could be improved by detecting and treating challenging behavioural and psychological symptoms [7]. In this context, our vision is to leverage on novel Big Data ICT technologies and Machine Learning (ML) algorithms to analyze the daily living activities of the people with dementia aiming to determine anomalies in the pattern of their daily living activities. Such patterns might be analyzed by medical experts or professional caregivers to take actions to improve patients overall health. For example, the anomalies found in the daily living activities of people with dementia could help medical experts in differentiating between health decline symptoms introduced by dementia and health decline symptoms generated by the side effects of the prescribed medications and their interactions (i.e. polypharmacy side-effects). This would allow medical experts to better evaluate the health status of a patient and better adjust its medication plan.

This section proposes a system designed based on the Lambda architecture for the real-time analysis of daily living activities of people with dementia using machine learning algorithms. The system collects data about the daily living activities patterns of the monitored persons using a set of Raspberry Pi's that are installed in the house of the monitored person. The collected data is sent to a Big Data platform where machine learning algorithms are applied to identify anomalies in the behavior of people with dementia. The proposed system has been implemented in the context of the MEDGUIDE project [10] which is an innovative Ambient Assisted Living (AAL) project that aims to provide solutions for supporting the well-being of people with dementia and their caregivers.

Challenges of ML for Heterogeneous Data Streams. ML for data streams is a subclass of the machine learning domain in which the analyzed data is generated in real-time. In [46] several challenges that might appear when ML is applied on heterogeneous distributed data streams are identified: (a) the input data is generated by many sources, (b) the data formats are both structured and unstructured, (c) the streaming data has a high speed, (d) the data is not completely available for processing (in some cases), (e) the data might be noisy, characterized by missing values and of poor quality. Moreover several ML algorithms must be adapted to larger datasets because they were designed for smaller sets of data and the samples usually have many features because the data is monitored by a big number of sensors. According to [64] several critical issues that must be considered when analyzing real time data streams are: data incompleteness, data streams heterogeneity, high speed of data streams and data large scale.

In [78] two major approaches for data streams processing are presented. In the first approach the in-memory persists only a small part of the elements which characterize the entire data stream while in the second approach fixed length windows are used. In the second approach a selection of fixed parts of data are loaded temporarily into a memory buffer and the ML algorithms take as input the data from that memory buffer.

The authors of [30] identify another major challenge that might exist when the ML algorithms are applied on data streams: in many cases the speed of the underlying ML algorithm is much slower than the speed of the coming data. A possible solution for this challenge is to skip some of the instances from the data stream. However, in that case the outcome might be negative if the instances that are skipped contain insightful information. In [80] two steps that are typically applied for predictive analytics and for prescriptive analytics are presented. The first step is the analytic model building – in which the analytic model is generated by trying out different approaches iteratively. The second step is dedicated to the analytic model validation – when the model is tested on different datasets and improved either by changing the configurable parameters or the complete algorithm.

The Experimental Platform. Our system design is based on Lambda architecture and that can be used for the real-time analysis of the daily living activities of the people that have dementia using different ML algorithms.

Fig. 6. System for analyzing daily living activities of people with dementia using ML algorithms

Figure 6 presents the high-level architecture of a system that is used for the analysis of the daily living activities of people with dementia. The system applies ML algorithms to detect anomalies in the daily living activities patterns of the monitored patients that might require special attention from a specialized healthcare professional.

The system collects data about the daily living activities patterns of the monitored persons using a set of Raspberry Pi's that are installed in the house of the monitored person. The Raspberry Pi's collect information about different types of activities such as sleeping, feeding, hygiene, indoor activities and out-door activities. The number of times that the elder goes to the toilet and the wandering behavior during night can be used as indicatives of different stages of dementia. The caregiver being notified that the monitored patient presents anomalous behavior with respect to the regular pattern of activities may take preventive actions as to minimize the effects of dementia.

The data collected by the Raspberry Pi's is sent in the form of AVRO mes-sages to a Big Data platform created using the following technologies: Apache Zookeeper [5], Apache Kafka [3], Apache Spark [4] and Apache Cassandra [2]. Zookeeper is a server that manages the coordination of tasks for the nodes of the distributed system that is used for the processing of the streaming data. Kafka is a streaming platform that handles the real-time data. The data comes in the form of AVRO messages and is inserted in the system through the Kafka REST server. The Kafka REST server uses an AVRO schema that is persisted in the Schema Registry server to get the information from the messages. The AVRO schema imposes a set of restrictions on the messages such as the number of fields and the data types of the fields. The data is then processed in an implementation of a Lambda architecture.

Kafka Connect is a server that takes the messages from the Kafka topics and inserts them in Cassandra. In the case of batch processing the entire data stored in the database is used as training data for the classification algorithms that are used for the prediction of the daily living activities of the people with dementia, while in the case of stream processing only the last streaming information is considered. The function in the case of Lambda architecture is represented by the ML algorithm that is used for the prediction of the daily living activities. In the case of stream processing, it is unfeasible to retrain the ML algorithm each time new streaming data comes into the system because this process would take too much time compared to the time in which the prediction should be made. Considering this time restriction, depending on the size of the streaming data, the ML algorithms should be retrained at a frequency of several minutes or several hours.

The predicted data can then be sent to the caregivers or to the healthcare professionals using a healthcare application created with Spring and Angular. Spring is used for back-end and for the communication with Apache Cassandra and also for retrieving the data generated by the monitoring sensors and the results obtained after the application of the ML algorithms. Spring is also used for sending notifications to the caregivers if corrective measures must be taken. Angular is a JavaScript framework that is used for the creation of the front-end side. By using the healthcare system the caregivers should be able to see data analytics, to detect anomalies in the daily living activities of the monitored persons and should also be able to take immediate actions when they are notified.

Detecting the Side-Effects of Polypharmacy upon the Daily Life Activities of People with Dementia Using Machine Learning Algorithms. This section presents how we have used the previously described experimental platform in the context of detecting the deviations in the daily life activities, and their polypharmacy-related causes, of people with dementia using ML algorithms. We have chosen to focus on polypharmacy as it represents one of the main challenges in the treatment of dementia affecting over 21% of the elders with dementia. In particular, the Random Forest Classification algorithm has been used for detecting the deviations of the daily life activities from the patients' baseline routine, while the k-Means clustering algorithm has been used for correlating these deviations with the side-effects of drug-drug interactions. The two ML algorithms have been implemented using two Spark jobs.

Concepts Definitions. In our approach, a day containing monitored activities is defined as:

$$day = (duration(a_1), duration(a_2), \ldots duration(a_n)) \qquad (1)$$

where $duration(a_i)$ represents the total duration in hours of the activity a_i while n is the number of total activities considered. In our approach, we have considered the following five types of daily life activities as significant enough for allowing the detection of polypharmacy side effects: a_1 = sleeping, a_2 = feeding, a_3 = toilet hygiene, a_4 = functional mobility and a_5 = community mobility. Table 1 presents an example with information provided by sensors regarding the activities performed by a patient with dementia during January 2nd, 2018.

Table 1. Information provided from sensors regarding the activities performed by a patient with dementia during a day

Start time	End time	Activity
2018.01.02 00:00:00	2018.01.02 7:00:00	Sleeping
2018.01.02 7:00:00	2018.01.02 7:30:00	Toilet hygiene
2018.01.02 7:30:00	2018.01.02 8:00:00	Feeding
2018.01.02 8:00:00	2018.01.02 12:00:00	Functional mobility
2018.01.02 12:00:00	2018.01.02 13:30:00	Sleeping
2018.01.02 13:30:00	2018.01.02 14:00:00	Feeding
2018.01.02 14:00:00	2018.01.02 16:00:00	Community mobility
2018.01.02 16:00:00	2018.01.02 18:00:00	Functional mobility
2018.01.02 18:00:00	2018.01.02 18:30:00	Feeding
2018.01.02 18:30:00	2018.01.02 19:00:00	Toilet hygiene
2018.01.02 19:00:00	2018.01.02 21:00:00	Functional mobility
2018.01.02 21:00:00	2018.01.02 23:59:59	Sleeping

The representation of the day January 2nd, 2018 according to (1) is day $= (10.5, 1.5, 1, 8, 2)$.

The *baseline* for a patient with dementia is a day when the patient has a typical behavior and it is represented similar to the representation of a day (see (1)). In our approach, the baseline for each monitored patient is defined by the doctor based on discussions with the patient, its family and caregivers.

We consider that a monitored day is a *deviated day* if it contains at least one activity which has the total duration higher or lower than a pre-defined threshold compared to the same activity type in the baseline. A deviated day may be associated with a semantic annotation consisting of a drug-drug interaction and an associated side-effect. The information regarding dementia drugs, drug-drug interactions and associated side-effects are stored as instances in a Polypharmacy Management Ontology we have designed. This ontology is a simplified version of the Drug-Drug Interactions Ontology (DINTO) [83] enhanced with drugs side effects taken from [1].

Classifying a Day as Normal or as Having Significant Deviations from the Baseline Using the Random Forest Classification Algorithm. To classify a day as normal or as having significant deviations from the baseline we have used the Random Forest algorithm suitable for Big Data classification provided by Apache Spark [11]. We have trained the Random Forest classification algorithm using a data set consisting of days labeled as having or not having a significant deviation from the normal baseline.

In the testing phase, a set of new monitored days is classified, based on the data set used in the training phase, as having/not having a deviation from the baseline.

Identifying the Causes that Produced the Deviation of a Day from the Baseline. To identify the causes which led to a deviation in the daily life activities of a patient with dementia we have defined a k-Means clustering method consisting of two steps:

1. *Cluster the deviated days.* The Spark MLlib implementation of the K-Means clustering algorithm [11] has been applied on a set of deviated days, each day being annotated with a drug-drug interaction and a side-effect causing the deviation. Each cluster will contain similar annotated days and will be labeled with the annotation (i.e. drug-drug interaction and its adverse effect) of the cluster's centroid.
2. *Assign a new deviated day to a cluster resulted in the previous step.* A new deviated day will be assigned to the cluster for which the Euclidean distance between that day and the cluster's centroid is minimum. Consequently, the deviated day will be annotated with the drug-drug interaction and its adverse effect corresponding to the assigned cluster's centroid.

Figure 7 presents the resources and the data flows for detecting the side-effects of polypharmacy upon the daily life activities of people with dementia using the Random Forrest Classifier and the k-Means Clustering Method.

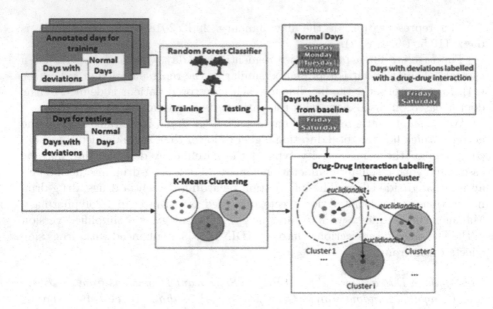

Fig. 7. The resources and the data flows for detecting the side-effects of polypharmacy upon the daily life activities of people with dementia

7   Summary

Health informatics is already an established scientific field and advances of e-health and m-health are already part of clinical practices of the XXI century medicine. Digital medicine enables optimization of decision-making processes and precise/personal medicine through the possibility of analyzing a huge amount of data at low cost. The computer assisted decision-making tools may be more efficient and safer than "analog" approaches that involve a physician.

In this chapter we have described (1) data collection, fusion, ownership and privacy issues; (2) models, technologies and solutions for medical data processing and analysis; (3) big medical data analytics for remote health monitoring; (4) research challenges and opportunities in medical data analytics; (5) three case studies. The first case study described a Big Data solution for remote health monitoring that considers challenges pertaining to monitoring the health and activities of patients. The second case study described a system designed to support distributed monitoring of human health during a trip. The third case study described the use of machine learning in the context of monitoring daily living activities of people with dementia.

References

1. https://www.drugs.com/
2. Apache Cassandra. http://cassandra.apache.org/
3. Apache Kafka: A distributed streaming platform. https://kafka.apache.org/

4. Apache Spark: Lightning-fast cluster computing. http://spark.apache.org/
5. Apache Zookeeper. https://zookeeper.apache.org/
6. CardioWheel. https://www.cardio-id.com/cardiowheel
7. Dementia. https://www.who.int/en/news-room/fact-sheets/detail/dementia
8. FIWARE. https://www.fiware.org/
9. FIWARE Accelerator Programme: FICHe project. https://www.f6s.com/fiche
10. ICT integrated system for coordinated polypharmacy management in elders with dementia. https://dsrl.coned.utcluj.ro/medguide/
11. Machine learning library (MLlib) guide. https://spark.apache.org/docs/latest/ml-guide.html
12. The top 10 causes of death. https://www.who.int/news-room/fact-sheets/detail/the-top-10-causes-of-death
13. Akbar, A., et al.: Real-time probabilistic data fusion for large-scale IoT applications. IEEE Access **6**, 10015–10027 (2018). https://doi.org/10.1109/ACCESS.2018.2804623
14. Araújo, R., Kim, A., Crisan, A.: EpiMobile: pathogen point of care diagnosis and global surveillance using mobile devices (2017)
15. Bahrami, M., Malvankar, A., Budhraja, K.K., Kundu, C., Singhal, M., Kundu, A.: Compliance-aware provisioning of containers on cloud. In: 2017 IEEE 10th International Conference on Cloud Computing (CLOUD), pp. 696–700. IEEE (2017)
16. Baker, S.D., Xiang, W., Atkinson, I.: Internet of Things for smart healthcare: technologies, challenges, and opportunities. IEEE Access **5**, 26521–26544 (2017). https://doi.org/10.1109/ACCESS.2017.2775180
17. Bellavista, P., Zanni, A.: Feasibility of fog computing deployment based on Docker containerization over RaspberryPi. In: Proceedings of the 18th International Conference on Distributed Computing and Networking, ICDCN 2017, pp. 16:1–16:10. ACM, New York (2017)
18. Benkner, S., et al.: PEPPHER: efficient and productive usage of hybrid computing systems. IEEE Micro **31**(5), 28–41 (2011). https://doi.org/10.1109/MM.2011.67
19. Celesti, A., et al.: How to develop IoT cloud e-health systems based on FIWARE: a lesson learnt. J. Sens. Actuator Netw. **8**(1), 7 (2019)
20. Chrysos, G.: Intel® Xeon Phi Coprocessor-the Architecture. Intel Whitepaper (2014)
21. Cortés, R., Bonnaire, X., Marin, O., Sens, P.: Stream processing of healthcare sensor data: studying user traces to identify challenges from a big data perspective. Procedia Comput. Sci. **52**, 1004–1009 (2015)
22. Dubey, H., et al.: Fog computing in medical Internet-of-Things: architecture, implementation, and applications. In: Khan, S.U., Zomaya, A.Y., Abbas, A. (eds.) Handbook of Large-Scale Distributed Computing in Smart Healthcare. SCC, pp. 281–321. Springer, Cham (2017). https://doi.org/10.1007/978-3-319-58280-1_11
23. Esteban, A.P., Patricio, M.A., García, J., Molina, J.M.: A feature selection approach to the group behavior recognition issue using static context information. IJDSN **9** (2013). https://doi.org/10.1155/2013/383906
24. Fang, R., Pouyanfar, S., Yang, Y., Chen, S.C., Iyengar, S.S.: Computational health informatics in the big data age: a survey. ACM Comput. Surv. **49**(1), 12:1–12:36 (2016). https://doi.org/10.1145/2932707. http://doi.acm.org/10.1145/2932707
25. Fisher, D.K., Fletcher, R.S., Anapalli, S.S., Pringle III, H.: Development of an open-source cloud-connected sensor-monitoring platform. Adv. Internet Things **8**(01), 1 (2017)

26. Garcia, A.C.B., Vivacqua, A.S., Pi, N.S., Martí, L., Molina, J.M.: Crowd-based ambient assisted living to monitor the elderly's health outdoors. IEEE Softw. **34**(6), 53–57 (2017). https://doi.org/10.1109/MS.2017.4121217
27. Gil, G.B., de Jesús, A.B., Molina, J.M.: InContexto: multisensor architecture to obtain people context from smartphones. IJDSN **8** (2012). https://doi.org/10.1155/2012/758789
28. Gómez-Romero, J., Serrano, M.A., García, J., Molina, J.M., Rogova, G.L.: Context-based multi-level information fusion for harbor surveillance. Inf. Fusion **21**, 173–186 (2015). https://doi.org/10.1016/j.inffus.2014.01.011
29. Gómez-Romero, J., Serrano, M.A., Patricio, M.A., García, J., Molina, J.M.: Context-based scene recognition from visual data in smarthomes: an information fusion approach. Pers. Ubiquit. Comput. **16**(7), 835–857 (2012). https://doi.org/10.1007/s00779-011-0450-9
30. Hapfelmeier, A., Mertes, C., Schmidt, J., Kramer, S.: Towards real-time machine learning. In: Proceedings of the ECML PKDD 2012 Workshop on Instant Interactive Data Mining (2012)
31. Hassanalieragh, M., et al.: Health monitoring and management using Internet-of-Things (IoT) sensing with cloud-based processing: opportunities and challenges. In: 2015 IEEE International Conference on Services Computing, pp. 285–292, June 2015. https://doi.org/10.1109/SCC.2015.47
32. Herrero, J.G., Patricio, M.A., Molina, J.M., Cardoso, L.A.: Contextual and human factors in information fusion. In: Human Systems Integration to Enhance Maritime Domain Awareness for Port/Harbour Security, pp. 79–92 (2010). https://doi.org/10.3233/978-1-60750-621-8-79
33. Hosseinpour, F., Meng, Y., Westerlund, T., Plosila, J., Liu, R., Tenhunen, H.: A review on fog computing systems. Int. J. Adv. Comput. Technol. **8**, 48–61 (2016)
34. Islam, S.M.R., Kwak, D., Kabir, M.H., Hossain, M., Kwak, K.: The Internet of Things for health care: a comprehensive survey. IEEE Access **3**, 678–708 (2015). https://doi.org/10.1109/ACCESS.2015.2437951
35. Jaiswal, K., Sobhanayak, S., Mohanta, B.K., Jena, D.: IoT-cloud based framework for patient's data collection in smart healthcare system using Raspberry-Pi. In: 2017 International Conference on Electrical and Computing Technologies and Applications (ICECTA), pp. 1–4, November 2017
36. Jarynowski, A., Marchewka, D., Buda, A.: Internet-assisted risk assessment of infectious diseases in women sexual and reproductive health. E-methodology, pp. 135–144 (2017)
37. Kačeniauskas, A., Pacevič, R., Starikovičius, V., Maknickas, A., Staškūnienė, M., Davidavičius, G.: Development of cloud services for patient-specific simulations of blood flows through aortic valves. Adv. Eng. Softw. **103**, 57–64 (2017)
38. Kamar, I., Chatterjee, P., Hamie, A.: Internet of Things in learning systems-a perspective of platforms. Int. J. Adv. Res. Comput. Sci. **7**(2), 52–59 (2016)
39. Kessler, C., et al.: Programmability and performance portability aspects of heterogeneous multi-/manycore systems. In: Design, Automation and Test in Europe Conference and Exhibition (DATE), pp. 1403–1408. IEEE (2012)
40. Khaleghi, B., Khamis, A.M., Karray, F., Razavi, S.N.: Multisensor data fusion: a review of the state-of-the-art. Inf. Fusion **14**(1), 28–44 (2013). https://doi.org/10.1016/j.inffus.2011.08.001
41. Khan, S.U., Zomaya, A.Y., Abbas, A. (eds.): Handbook of Large-Scale Distributed Computing in Smart Healthcare. SCC. Springer, Cham (2017). https://doi.org/10.1007/978-3-319-58280-1

42. Koliogeorgi, K., et al.: AEGLE's cloud infrastructure for resource monitoring and containerized accelerated analytics. In: 2017 IEEE Computer Society Annual Symposium on VLSI (ISVLSI), pp. 362–367. IEEE (2017)
43. La Ode Hasnuddin, S.S., Abidin, M.S.: Internet of Things for early detection of lanslides. In: Prosiding Seminar Nasional Riset Kuantitatif Terapan 2017, vol. 1 (2018)
44. Lane, N.D., Miluzzo, E., Lu, H., Peebles, D., Choudhury, T., Campbell, A.T.: A survey of mobile phone sensing. IEEE Commun. Mag. **48**(9), 140–150 (2010). https://doi.org/10.1109/MCOM.2010.5560598
45. Lee, C., et al.: Big healthcare data analytics: challenges and applications. In: Khan, S.U., Zomaya, A.Y., Abbas, A. (eds.) Handbook of Large-Scale Distributed Computing in Smart Healthcare. SCC, pp. 11–41. Springer, Cham (2017). https://doi.org/10.1007/978-3-319-58280-1_2
46. L'Heureux, A., Grolinger, K., Elyamany, H.F., Capretz, M.A.M.: Machine learning with big data: challenges and approaches. IEEE Access **5**, 7776–7797 (2017). https://doi.org/10.1109/ACCESS.2017.2696365. https://ieeexplore.ieee.org/document/7906512
47. Li, P., Xu, C., Luo, Y., Cao, Y., Mathew, J., Ma, Y.: CareNet: building a secure software-defined infrastructure for home-based healthcare. In: Proceedings of the ACM International Workshop on Security in Software Defined Networks & #38; Network Function Virtualization, SDN-NFVSec 2017, pp. 69–72. ACM, New York (2017)
48. Likotiko, E., Petrov, D., Mwangoka, J., Hilleringmann, U.: Real time solid waste monitoring using cloud and sensors technologies. Online J. Sci. Technol. **8**(1), 106–116 (2018)
49. Llinas, J.: Information fusion process design issues for hard and soft information: developing an initial prototype. In: Yager, R.R., Reformat, M.Z., Alajlan, N. (eds.) Intelligent Methods for Cyber Warfare. SCI, vol. 563, pp. 129–149. Springer, Cham (2015). https://doi.org/10.1007/978-3-319-08624-8_6
50. López, J.M.M., Herrero, J.G., Rodríguez, F.J.J., Corredera, J.R.C.: Cooperative management of a net of intelligent surveillance agent sensor. Int. J. Intell. Syst. **18**(3), 279–307 (2003). https://doi.org/10.1002/int.10089
51. Ma, X., Wang, Z., Zhou, S., Wen, H., Zhang, Y.: Intelligent healthcare systems assisted by data analytics and mobile computing. Wirel. Commun. Mob. Comput. **2018**, 16 (2018). Article ID 3928080
52. Ma, Y., Wang, Y., Yang, J., Miao, Y., Li, W.: Big health application system based on health Internet of Things and big data. IEEE Access **5**, 7885–7897 (2017). https://doi.org/10.1109/ACCESS.2016.2638449
53. Marjani, M., et al.: Big IoT data analytics: architecture, opportunities, and open research challenges. IEEE Access **5**, 5247–5261 (2017). https://doi.org/10.1109/ACCESS.2017.2689040
54. Memeti, S., Li, L., Pllana, S., Kolodziej, J., Kessler, C.: Benchmarking OpenCL, OpenACC, OpenMP, and CUDA: programming productivity, performance, and energy consumption. In: Proceedings of the 2017 Workshop on Adaptive Resource Management and Scheduling for Cloud Computing, ARMS-CC 2017, pp. 1–6. ACM, New York (2017). https://doi.org/10.1145/3110355.3110356
55. Memeti, S., Pllana, S.: Accelerating DNA sequence analysis using Intel® Xeon Phi™. In: 2015 IEEE Trustcom/BigDataSE/ISPA, vol. 3, pp. 222–227, August 2015

56. Memeti, S., Pllana, S.: HSTREAM: a directive-based language extension for heterogeneous stream computing. In: 2018 IEEE International Conference on Computational Science and Engineering (CSE), pp. 138–145, October 2018. https://doi.org/10.1109/CSE.2018.00026

57. Mora, H.M., Gil, D., Terol, R.M., López, J.A., Szymanski, J.: An IoT-based computational framework for healthcare monitoring in mobile environments. Sensors **17**, 2302 (2017)

58. NVIDIA: What is GPU-Accelerated Computing? April 2017. http://www.nvidia.com/object/what-is-gpu-computing.html. Accessed 03 Nov 2018

59. Padilla, W.R., García, J., Molina, J.M.: Information fusion and machine learning in spatial prediction for local agricultural markets. In: Bajo, J., et al. (eds.) PAAMS 2018. CCIS, vol. 887, pp. 235–246. Springer, Cham (2018). https://doi.org/10.1007/978-3-319-94779-2_21

60. Padua, D. (ed.): Encyclopedia of Parallel Computing. Springer, Boston (2011). https://doi.org/10.1007/978-0-387-09766-4

61. Perez, D., Memeti, S., Pllana, S.: A simulation study of a smart living IoT solution for remote elderly care. In: 2018 Third International Conference on Fog and Mobile Edge Computing (FMEC), pp. 227–232, April 2018. https://doi.org/10.1109/FMEC.2018.8364069

62. Sanchez-Pi, N., Martí, L., Bustamante, Á.L., Molina, J.M.: How machine learning could detect anomalies on thinger.io platform? In: Bajo, J., et al. (eds.) PAAMS 2018. CCIS, vol. 887, pp. 259–269. Springer, Cham (2018). https://doi.org/10.1007/978-3-319-94779-2_23

63. Sanchez-Pi, N., Martí, L., Molina, J.M., Bicharra García, A.C.: Information fusion for improving decision-making in big data applications. In: Pop, F., Kołodziej, J., Di Martino, B. (eds.) Resource Management for Big Data Platforms. CCN, pp. 171–188. Springer, Cham (2016). https://doi.org/10.1007/978-3-319-44881-7_9

64. Qiu, J., Wu, Q., Ding, G., Xu, Y., Feng, S.: A survey of machine learning for big data processing. EURASIP J. Adv. Sig. Proces. (1) (2016). https://doi.org/10.1186/s13634-016-0355-x. https://link.springer.com/article/10.1186/s13634-016-0355-x

65. Raghupathi, W., Raghupathi, V.: Big data analytics in healthcare: promise and potential. Health Inf. Sci. Syst. **2**(1), 3 (2014)

66. Rassias, G., Andrikos, C.O., Tsanakas, P., Maglogiannis, I.: Versatile cloud collaboration services for device-transparent medical imaging teleconsultations. In: 2017 IEEE 30th International Symposium on Computer-Based Medical Systems (CBMS), pp. 306–311. IEEE (2017)

67. Rawassizadeh, R., Kotz, D.: Datasets for mobile, wearable and IoT research. GetMobile: Mob. Comput. Commun. **20**(4), 5–7 (2017). https://doi.org/10.1145/3081016.3081018. http://doi.acm.org/10.1145/3081016.3081018

68. Rawassizadeh, R., Momeni, E., Dobbins, C., Mirza-Babaei, P., Rahnamoun, R.: Lesson learned from collecting quantified self information via mobile and wearable devices. J. Sens. Actuator Netw. **4**(4), 315–335 (2015). https://doi.org/10.3390/jsan4040315

69. Rodgers, M.M., Pai, V.M., Conroy, R.S.: Recent advances in wearable sensors for health monitoring. IEEE Sens. J. **15**(6), 3119–3126 (2015). https://doi.org/10.1109/JSEN.2014.2357257

70. Sahoo, P.K., Dehury, C.K.: Efficient data and CPU-intensive job scheduling algorithms for healthcare cloud. Comput. Electr. Eng. **68**, 119–139 (2018)

71. Sikora, A., Krzyszto, M., Marks, M.: Application of bluetooth low energy proto-col for communication in mobile networks. In: 2018 International Conference on Military Communications and Information Systems (ICMCIS), pp. 1–6, May 2018. https://doi.org/10.1109/ICMCIS.2018.8398689

72. Singh, M.P., Hoque, M.A., Tarkoma, S.: A survey of systems for massive stream analytics. arXiv preprint arXiv:1605.09021 (2016)

73. Snidaro, L., García, J., Llinas, J.: Context-based information fusion: a survey and discussion. Inf. Fusion **25**, 16–31 (2015). https://doi.org/10.1016/j.inffus.2015.01.002

74. Solanas, A., et al.: Smart health: a context-aware health paradigm within smart cities. IEEE Commun. Mag. **52**(8), 74–81 (2014). https://doi.org/10.1109/MCOM.2014.6871673

75. Sotiriadis, S., Vakanas, L., Petrakis, E., Zampognaro, P., Bessis, N.: Automatic migration and deployment of cloud services for healthcare application development in FIWARE. In: 2016 30th International Conference on Advanced Information Networking and Applications Workshops (WAINA), pp. 416–419. IEEE (2016)

76. TOP500: The TOP500 List of Most Powerful Computer Systems (2018). http://www.top500.org/. Accessed 24 Dec 2018

77. Vaizman, Y., Ellis, K., Lanckriet, G.: Recognizing detailed human context in the wild from smartphones and smartwatches. IEEE Pervasive Comput. **16**(4), 62–74 (2017). https://doi.org/10.1109/MPRV.2017.3971131

78. Valsamis, A., Tserpes, K., Zissis, D., Anagnostopoulos, D., Varvarigou, T.: Employ-ing traditional machine learning algorithms for big data stream analysis: the case of object trajectory prediction. J. Syst. Softw. **127**, 249–257 (2017). https://doi.org/10.1016/j.jss.2016.06.016. https://dl.acm.org/citation.cfm?id=3066671

79. Viebke, A., Pllana, S.: The potential of the Intel (R) Xeon Phi for supervised deep learning. In: 2015 IEEE 17th International Conference on High Performance Computing and Communications, pp. 758–765, August 2015. https://doi.org/10.1109/HPCC-CSS-ICESS.2015.45

80. Waehner, K.: How to apply machine learning to event processing (2016). https://www.rtinsights.com/big-data-machine-learning-software-event-processing-analytics/

81. Wang, Y., Kung, L., Byrd, T.A.: Big data analytics: understanding its capa-bilities and potential benefits for healthcare organizations. Technol. Forecast. Soc. Change **126**, 3–13 (2018). https://doi.org/10.1016/j.techfore.2015.12.019. http://www.sciencedirect.com/science/article/pii/S0040162516000500

82. Welbourne, E., Tapia, E.M.: CrowdSignals: a call to crowdfund the community's largest mobile dataset. In: Proceedings of the 2014 ACM International Joint Con-ference on Pervasive and Ubiquitous Computing: Adjunct Publication, UbiComp 2014 Adjunct, pp. 873–877. ACM, New York (2014). https://doi.org/10.1145/2638728.2641309

83. Zazo, M.H., Hastings, J., Segura-Bedmar, I., Croset, S., Martinez, P., Steinbeck, C.: An ontology for drug-drug interactions. In: Proceedings of the 6th Interna-tional Workshop on Semantic Web Applications and Tools for Life Sciences (2014). http://ceur-ws.org/Vol-1114/Session3_Herrero-Zazo.pdf

Towards Human Cell Simulation

Simone Spolaor[1,5], Marco Gribaudo[2], Mauro Iacono[3], Tomas Kadavy[4],
Zuzana Komínková Oplatková[4], Giancarlo Mauri[1,5], Sabri Pllana[6],
Roman Senkerik[4], Natalija Stojanovic[7], Esko Turunen[8], Adam Viktorin[4],
Salvatore Vitabile[9], Aleš Zamuda[10], and Marco S. Nobile[1,5(✉)]

[1] Department of Informatics, Systems and Communication,
University of Milano-Bicocca, Milan, Italy
nobile@disco.unimib.it
[2] Dipartimento di Elettronica, Informazione e Bioingegneria,
Politecnico di Milano, Milan, Italy
[3] Dipartimento di Matematica e Fisica,
Università degli Studi della Campania "Luigi Vanvitelli", Caserta, Italy
[4] Faculty of Applied Informatics, Tomas Bata University in Zlin,
Zlin, Czech Republic
[5] SYSBIO.IT Centre for Systems Biology, Milan, Italy
[6] Department of Computer Science, Linnaeus University, Växjö, Sweden
[7] Department of Computer Science, University of Niš, Niš, Serbia
[8] Department of Mathematics, Tampere University of Technology, Tampere, Finland
[9] Department of Biopathology and Medical Biotechnologies,
University of Palermo, Palermo, Italy
[10] Faculty of Electrical Engineering and Computer Science,
University of Maribor, Maribor, Slovenia

Abstract. The faithful reproduction and accurate prediction of the phenotypes and emergent behaviors of complex cellular systems are among
the most challenging goals in Systems Biology. Although mathematical
models that describe the interactions among all biochemical processes in
a cell are theoretically feasible, their simulation is generally hard because
of a variety of reasons. For instance, many quantitative data (e.g., kinetic
rates) are usually not available, a problem that hinders the execution of
simulation algorithms as long as some parameter estimation methods are
used. Though, even with a candidate parameterization, the simulation
of mechanistic models could be challenging due to the extreme computational effort required. In this context, model reduction techniques and
High-Performance Computing infrastructures could be leveraged to mitigate these issues. In addition, as cellular processes are characterized by
multiple scales of temporal and spatial organization, novel hybrid simulators able to harmonize different modeling approaches (e.g., logic-based,
constraint-based, continuous deterministic, discrete stochastic, spatial)
should be designed. This chapter describes a putative unified approach
to tackle these challenging tasks, hopefully paving the way to the definition of large-scale comprehensive models that aim at the comprehension
of the cell behavior by means of computational tools.

© The Author(s) 2019
J. Kołodziej and H. González-Vélez (Eds.): cHiPSet, LNCS 11400, pp. 221–249, 2019.
https://doi.org/10.1007/978-3-030-16272-6_8

Keywords: Agent-based simulation · Big data ·
Biochemical simulation · Computational intelligence ·
Constraint-based modeling · Fuzzy logic ·
High-performance computing · Model reduction ·
Multi-scale modeling · Parameter estimation ·
Reaction-based modeling · Systems biology

1   Introduction

Cells are inherently complex systems, composed by a wide variety of molecule types, whose functioning is finely regulated by an intricate network of interactions. In order for cells to respond to environmental cues, surviving and reproducing, all of their components have to act together in a orchestrated manner. This wealth of complexity is the main reason for the richness of cellular behaviours that can be found in nature, but is also a major issue in advancing to a complete understanding of these systems.

In the last decades, mathematical modeling and simulation proved to be essential tools to understand and describe how biological functions emerge from the complex network of interactions existing between cellular components [139]. However, even though modeling and simulation proved successful in describing single processes or a limited amount of interacting pathways, extending this approach to define and simulate a whole-cell turned out to be an unfeasible task (besides the notable exception reported in [58], as it will be mentioned below), especially in the case of human cells. As a matter of fact, the definition and simulation of whole-cell models is challenging for several reasons. In particular, the problem is exacerbated by the complex organization of cell systems; the difficulties encountered in integrating different data sources and mathematical formalisms in a single modeling framework; the huge demand of computational power needed to perform the simulation. Although some of these challenges were already discussed and highlighted before (see for example [67]), we hereby provide a brief summary of the main challenges in the definition and simulation of whole-cell models:

- biomolecular systems are composed of a wide variety of heterogeneous components, ranging from small molecules, complex polymers (including proteins, sugars and ribonucleic acids) and protein complexes. All these components are further organized in functionally coherent pathways and organized in specialized compartments (e.g. the organelles in eukaryotic cells), ultimately giving rise to complex (observable) phenotypes;
- cells display a complex spatial and functional hierarchical organization, that results in phenomena occurring at a wide range of spatial and temporal scales [30]. Moreover, this organization often gives rise to complex non-linear dynamics;
- cellular systems are inherently stochastic, that is, the dynamics of cellular processes is characterized by biological noise [39], which is exploited by the cell to obtain specific responses that would be impossible in its absence [37].

Thus, some cellular pathways (e.g., gene expression) must be modeled and simulated as stochastic processes;

- the different nature of the cell components entails that they are measured with different experimental techniques. Some of these components can be measured with a high accuracy and with a high throughput (e.g., genomic or RNA sequencing, mass spectrometry), while others are very difficult or impossible to measure (e.g., kinetic information on the reaction rates). Thus, modelers have to take into account the presence of vast amounts of data, often in qualitative, or semi-quantitative form, together with limited quantitative information;

- the availability of multiple types of data, and the need to model different layers of organization, led to the definition of multiple modelling frameworks [118]. Because of this, models of biochemical systems are usually focused on one of the three main layers in which cellular processes are generally divided, namely: signalling (perceive environmental changes, process information and regulation of behaviour); gene regulation (control of expression levels of gene products); metabolism, i.e., the production and consumption, driven by enzymes, of small molecules essential for the life of cells. Even though attempts to define a single framework were made before [23], the integration of multiple modelling approaches is still challenging. However, a unified modeling framework for these three layers would provide a reliable means to capture their peculiarities [45], as was shown in [58].

- the availability of large amounts of experimental data, combined with the massive complexity of cells components, leads to huge computational requirements, even when considering the simulation of a single cell. Thus, dynamic mechanistic whole-cell models—encompassing all knowledge about biochemical reactions—are basically impossible to simulate on any existing computing architecture. However, we will see that by means of some assumptions about the system, such complexity can be mitigated using hybrid modeling, and model reduction techniques.

Considering all these challenges together, it comes to no surprise that, up to date, the only available example of whole-cell model is the one presented in the pioneering work of Karr *et al.* [58]. In this seminal work, the authors succeeded in simulating a whole-cell of one of the simplest known organisms, the *Mycoplasma genitalium*, adopting for each cellular process a suitable mathematical formalism. In particular, the authors showed the feasibility of predicting different cell phenotypes from a genotype, by relying on computational approaches. To the best of our knowledge, this results was not achieved again for any more complex organism. However, the integration of multiple formalism into a single modeling framework was already explored to smaller extents also in human cell models, for example in [41]. It is out of question that the simulation of whole-cell models will prove to be a challenge for modelers and computer scientists in the coming decades, and this is especially true in the case of human cells. Here, we propose a set of modeling approaches and techniques that would allow us to advance towards the simulation of human whole-cell models.

A dynamic whole-cell model would prove useful to understand how phenotypes emerge from the complex interactions existing between cellular components. Achieving dynamic simulation of a *human* cell *in silico* would have an even more considerable impact in the fields of molecular and systems biology, bioengineering and medicine [67]. Such a model, once validated, could allow to uncover new and potential unknown processes inside human cells, providing a reliable platform to generate new hypothesis to be tested in laboratory. In this regard, *in silico* tests would guide the experimental design, greatly reducing the costs, both in term of time and resources, of a "wet" laboratory. Moreover, human cell models could be exploited to automatically assess the effects of a vast number of perturbations in physiological or pathological conditions, in order to unveil potentially new drug targets or test known drugs in a high-throughput manner. We envision that human cell models could lead to breakthroughs in many fields of application, including medicine and personalized medicine, pharmacology and drug discovery, biotechnology and synthetic biology.

Regardless of the methodology used to create a whole-cell model, there are some aspects that will always characterize this kind of approach: High-Performance Computing (HPC) is necessary to mitigate the huge computational effort, in particular by distributing the computations over massively parallel machines and co-processors; dynamics modelling requires a proper kinetic parameterization to perform predictive simulations, and such parameters are often difficult—or even impossible—to measure by means of laboratory experiments, leading to a problem of parameter estimation; biological models are often characterized by multiple scales (temporal and spatial) which are not easy to handle; to reduce the huge computational effort due to large-scale models, both model reduction techniques or phenomenological simplifications can be leveraged. All these topics will be introduced and discussed in this paper.

This manuscript is organized as follows: in Sect. 2 we describe how HPC can mitigate the exceptional computational demand required by the simulation of whole-cell models; in Sect. 3 we propose modeling approaches for the definition of whole-cell models, while in Sect. 4 we suggest some techniques that could be employed to tackle the problems mentioned above in order to create a unified modeling approach; finally, in Sect. 5 we give some final remarks and highlight potential future directions.

2   High Performance Computing and Big Data

As it was highlighted in the previous section, High Performance Computing (HPC) architectures and handling of huge amounts of data will be necessary and enabling tools for the simulation of a human cell model. HPC involves the use of many interconnected processing elements to reduce the time to solution of given a problem. Many powerful HPC systems are *heterogeneous*, in the sense that they combine general-purpose CPUs with *accelerators* such as, Graphics Processing Units (GPUs), or Field Programmable Gates Arrays (FPGAs).

There exist several HPC approaches [11,60,89] developed to improve the performance of advanced and data intensive modeling and simulation applications.

Parallel computing paradigm may be used on multi-core CPUs, many-core processing units (such as, GPUs [77]), re-configurable hardware platforms (such as, FPGAs), or over distributed infrastructure (such as, cluster, Grid, or Cloud). While multi-core CPUs are suitable for general-purpose tasks, many-core processors (such as the Intel Xeon Phi [24] or GPU [85]) comprise a larger number of lower frequency cores and perform well on scalable applications (such as, DNA sequence analysis [71], biochemical simulation [53,76,81,123] or deep learning [129]).

Widely used parallel programming frameworks [70] for heterogeneous systems include OpenACC [138], OpenCL [115], OpenMP [88], and NVIDIA CUDA [84]. OpenMP is a set of compiler directives, library routines, and environment variables for programming shared-memory parallel computing systems. Furthermore, OpenMP has been extended to support programming of heterogeneous systems that contain CPUs and accelerators. OpenCL supports portable programming of hardware provided by various vendors, while CUDA runs only on NVIDIA hardware. CUDA C/C++ compiler, libraries, and run-time software enable programmers to develop and accelerate data-intensive applications on GPU.

As concerns distributed parallel computing, the available frameworks include the Message Passing Interface (MPI) [48], MapReduce/Hadoop [51] or Apache Spark [112]. MPI is a specification of library routines helpful for users that write portable message-passing programs in C/C++, Fortran or Python. Basic assumption behind MPI is that multiple processes work concurrently using messages to communicate and collaborate with each other. The MapReduce framework, and its open source implementation Hadoop software stack, hides the details about data distribution, data availability and fault-tolerance, and allows to scale up to thousands of nodes inside cluster or Cloud computing systems. Lastly, Apache Spark [112] is a large-scale parallel computing platform that provides a wide variety of tools for structured data processing, including SQL queries (SparkSQL), streaming applications (Spark Streaming), machine learning (MLlib) and graph operations (GraphX), by means of various programming interfaces in Java, Scala, Python and R.

The data size in Bioinformatics, Computational Biology, and Systems Biology is increasing dramatically in the recent years. The European Bioinformatics Institute (EBI), one of the largest biology-data repositories, had approximately 40 petabytes of data about genes, proteins, and small molecules in 2014, in comparison to 18 petabytes in 2013 [56]. Big data problems in these fields are not only characterized by Velocity, Volume, Value, Variety, and Veracity, but also by incremental and geographically distributed data. While part of these data may be transferred over the Internet, the remaining are not transferable due to their size, cost, privacy, and other ethical issues [69]. Moreover, the computational time required by algorithms designed for the simulation of detailed mechanistic models (see Sect. 3.1) scales poorly when the models are characterized by a huge number of components. Thus, in recent years, research in Bioinformatics,

Computational Biology and Systems Biology started to adopt different HPC approaches to deal with Big Data.

In [86] Hadoop Blast (Basic Local Alignment Search Tool), in short HBlast, a parallelized BLAST algorithm is presented. HBlast exploits the MapReduce programming framework, adopting a hybrid "virtual partitioning" approach that automatically adjusts the database partition size depending on the Hadoop cluster size, as well as the number of input query sequences.

Sadasivam et al. considered in [100] a time efficient approach to multiple sequence alignment, as essential tool in molecular biology. They proposed a novel approach that combines the dynamic programming algorithm with the computational parallelism of Hadoop data grids to improve accuracy and to accelerate of multiple sequence alignment.

Li et al. developed in [65] ClustaWMPI, an accelerated version of ClustalW tool for aligning multiple protein or nucleotide sequences. In ClustalWMPI adopts MPI and runs on distributed workstation clusters as well as on traditional parallel computers.

The work presented in [15] describes a new Molecular Dynamics approach, named Desmond, that achieves unusually high parallel scalability and overall simulation throughput on commodity clusters by using new distributed-memory parallel algorithms. Desmond adopts a novel parallel decomposition method that greatly reduces the requirement for inter-processor communication, a novel message-passing technique that reduces the number of inter-processor messages, and novel highly efficient communication primitives that further reduce communication time.

The estimation of kinetic parameters, mandatory to perform cellular simulations, can be performed using population-based global optimization methods (see Sect. 4.2 for additional information). These algorithms are intrinsically parallel and can be accelerated using GPUs [78,79]. In [124] acceleration of the Differential Evolution algorithm is considered. In this work, a parallel implementation of an enhanced DE using Spark is proposed. Two different platforms have been used for the evaluation, a local cluster and the Microsoft Azure public cloud. The proposal drastically reduces the execution time, by means of including a selected local search and exploiting the available distributed resources. The performance of the proposal has been thoroughly assessed using challenging parameter estimation problems from the domain of computational systems biology. Additionally, it has been also compared with other parallel approaches, a MapReduce implementation and MPI implementation.

Coulier et al. presented in [29] a new framework, named Orchestral, for constructing and simulating high-fidelity models of multicellular systems from existing frameworks for single-cell simulation. They combined the many existing frameworks for single-cell resolution reaction-diffusion models with the diverse landscape of models of cell mechanics. They decoupled the simulation of reaction-diffusion kinetics inside the cells from the simulation of molecular cell-cell interactions occurring on the boundaries between cells. Orchestral provides a model for simulating the resulting model massively in parallel over a wide range of distributed computing environments. They proved the flexibility and scalability of the framework by using the popular single-cell simulation software eGFRD to construct and simulate a multicellular model of Notch-Delta signaling over the OpenStack cloud infrastructure.

Finally, HPC is exploited to accelerate the simulation of biochemical models that are defined according to mechanistic formalisms [118] (refer also to Sect. 3.1 for some examples). In this context, GPUs [77] were already successfully employed to achieve a considerable reduction in the computational times required by the simulation of both deterministic [53,76,123] and stochastic models [81,150]. Besides accelerating single simulations of such models, these methods prove to be particularly useful when there is a need of running multiple independent simulations of the same model. Hundreds (or even thousands) of simulations are often necessary to perform a wide variety of analysis on validated models (e.g., sensitivity analysis of kinetic parameters, or parameter sweep analysis), but also to perform parameter estimation (PE) during the definition of such models (please, refer to Sect. 4.2 for an extensive description). This kind of tasks leverages at most the availability of the many cores of the GPUs, greatly reducing the overall running time that is required to perform them [82,83].

3 Modeling Approach

In the field of Systems Biology, several modeling approaches have been defined [114,118]. Each approach exploits a different mathematical formalism and was developed to address the challenges posed by a specific (subset of) biochemical processes (e.g. metabolism [117], gene regulation, or signaling). The definition of a single, homogeneous mathematical framework to model and simulate a whole-cell seems currently unfeasible, while the integration of multiple formalisms has already proved to be able to achieve outstanding results [58]. Following this principle, we decided to define our human cell modeling framework by integrating multiple modeling approaches, namely: *(i)* mechanism-based models (in particular reaction-based and agent-based models); *(ii)* constraint-based models; *(iii)* logic-based models (in particular boolean and fuzzy logic-based models). These approaches, together with their peculiarities and limitations, will be briefly described in the following subsections.

3.1 Reaction-Based Modeling

Biochemical systems are traditionally formalized as mechanistic and fully parameterized reaction-based models (RBMs) [12]. A RBM is defined by specifying the following sets:

- the set $\mathcal{S} = \{S_1, \ldots, S_N\}$ of molecular species;
- the set $\mathcal{R} = \{R_1, \ldots, R_M\}$ of biochemical reactions that describe the interactions among the species in $\mathcal{S}$;
- the set $\mathcal{K} = \{k_1, \ldots, k_M\}$ of kinetic constants associated with the reactions in $\mathcal{R}$;

– the set of the initial concentration $Y_i \in \mathbb{R}_0^+$, with $i = 1, \ldots, N$, for each species $S_i \in \mathcal{S}$.

Any RBM can be represented in a compact matrix-vector form $\mathbf{AS} \xrightarrow{\mathbf{K}} \mathbf{BS}$, where $\mathbf{S} = (S_1, \ldots, S_N)^\top$, $\mathbf{K} = (k_1, \ldots, k_M)^\top$, and $\mathbf{A}, \mathbf{B} \in \mathbb{N}^{M \times N}$ are the stoichiometric matrices whose elements $[A]_{i,j}$ and $[B]_{i,j}$ represent the number of reactants and products occurring in the reactions, respectively. Given an RBM and assuming the law of mass-action [22], the system of coupled Ordinary Differential Equations (ODEs) describing the variation in time of the species concentrations is obtained as follows:

$$\frac{d\mathbf{Y}}{dt} = (\mathbf{B} - \mathbf{A})^\top [\mathbf{K} \odot \mathbf{Y^A}], \tag{1}$$

where $\mathbf{Y} = (Y_1, \ldots, Y_N)$ represents the state of the system at time t, $\mathbf{Y^A}$ denotes the vector-matrix exponentiation form [22], while the symbol $\odot$ denotes the Hadamard product. The system can then be simulated using a numerical method, which is usually based on implicit integration (e.g., Backward Differentiation Formulae [19]) due to the stiffness that characterizes these models.

When the chemical species have a low concentration, the dynamics of the system becomes instrinsically stochastic and the biochemical system should be simulated using specific approaches like Gillespie's Stochastic Simulation Algorithm (SSA) [43]. In SSA, the simulation proceeds one reaction at a time. Both the reaction to be fired and the time interval τ before the reactions occur are determined in a probabilistic fashion. Thus, the simulated trajectory of the system can radically diverge from the one predicted by a deterministic simulation, allowing the investigation of the emergent effects due to the intrinsic noise and providing a deeper knowledge of the system's behavior. In the case of stochastic modeling, the state of the system represents the exact number of molecules; $\mathbf{K}$ denotes the vector of the stochastic constants, encompassing all the physical and chemical properties of the reactions. These parameters are used to calculate the propensity functions, ultimately determining the probability of each reaction R_m to occur. Propensity functions are defined as:

$$a_m(\mathbf{Y}) = k_m \cdot d_m(\mathbf{Y}), \tag{2}$$

where $d_m(\mathbf{Y})$ is the number of distinct combinations of reactant molecules occurring in R_m. The delay time τ before the next reaction will occur is calculated according to the following equation:

$$\tau = \frac{1}{a_0(\mathbf{Y})} \cdot \ln \frac{1}{rnd}, \tag{3}$$

where $a_0(\mathbf{Y}) = \sum_{m=1}^M a_m(\mathbf{Y})$ and rnd is random number sampled with uniform distribution in $[0, 1)$.

Mechanistic modeling is considered the most likely candidate to achieve a detailed comprehension of biological systems [20], since it can lead to quantitative predictions of cellular dynamics, thanks to its capability to reproduce the temporal evolution of all molecular species occurring in the model. Nonetheless, the computational complexity of the simulation and analysis of such models increases with the size (in terms of components and interactions) of the systems, limiting the feasibility of this approach. Moreover the usual lack of quantitative parameters (e.g., kinetic constants, initial molecular concentrations of the species) and the partial lack of knowledge about the molecular mechanisms, sometimes due to the difficulty or impossibility to perform *ad hoc* experiments, represent further limits to a wide applicability of this modeling approach. The problems of simulation performances and parameter estimation are discussed in the next Sections.

3.2   Constraint-Based Modeling

Constraint-Based Modeling (CBM) is based on the idea that phenotypes of a given biological system must satisfy a number of constraints. Hence, by restricting the space of all possible systems states, it is possible to determine the functional states that a biochemical (in particular, metabolic) network can or cannot achieve. The fundamental assumption of constraint-based modeling is that the organism will reach a quasi-steady state that satisfies the given constraints [20].

The starting point of CBM is the transposed stoichiometric matrix $\mathbf{S} = (\mathbf{B} - \mathbf{A})^{\mathrm{T}}$, i.e., a matrix in which each row corresponds to a chemical species (e.g., metabolites), while columns correspond to reactions involving those species. Since metabolic networks typically include more reactions ("fluxes") than metabolites, the stoichiometric constraints and the steady assumption alone lead to an under-determined system in which a bounded solution space of all feasible flux distributions can be identified. Additional constraints should be incorporated to further restrict the solution space; this is usually performed by specifying linear bounds to minimum and maximum values of fluxes. Additioanl capacity constraints are generally set according to experimental data.

On top of CBM, Flux Balance Analysis (FBA) can be used to identify optimal distribution of fluxes with respect to a given objective function. Thanks to the linear definitions of fluxes, constraints and objective function, the solution space is a multi-dimensional convex polytope. FBA exploits a simplex method to efficiently identify the optimal fluxes that maximize, or minimize, the objective function (e.g., the maximization of ATP [128] in the context of mithocondria energy metabolism). CBM methods do not perform an actual simulation of the biochemical system, but can be used—under a quasi-steady state assumption—to investigate the distribution of fluxes. Interestingly, FBA has a very limited computational complexity, so that it can be leveraged to study the behavior of a metabolic systems on a whole-cell level.

3.3   Markovian Agents

Markovian agents [13] are a modeling tool that is specially suitable for large scale phenomena composed of groups of single entities that behave as Markov chains. Such entities, said *agents*, are individuals belonging to *classes* that are characterized by a common description of their dynamics. Agents may influence each other by means of a technique called *induction*, which accounts for their position in a logic map that represents the space in which they can move or be positioned in the system. The system is described by considering for each class the density of agents in each state and the probability of transition between states, so that, thanks to a *mean-field* approach, the evolution in time of the density in states may be approximately described by differential equations and a closed form solution may be obtained, with the significant advantage that the higher is the number of agents in a class, the best the approximation describes the system. The communication mechanism acts by enabling or disabling transitions, thus influencing the probability of transitions between states. This analytical description is suitable to study both transient and regime behavior of the system.

Markovian agents may be used to describe the interactions of reactions that happen in a cell in a large number of independent instances, including the effects of inhibiting factors, as well as for describing the expression of cells in tissues and organs. The technique has been applied to study biological pathways [27], cancer cells [28], whole ecosystems, such as forestry landscape [142], and other complex real-world systems [7,21,47]. The Markovian property make them suitable to describe processes that are characterized by exponentially distributed interarrival time in their evolution.

From the formal point of view, let a Markovian agents model be composed by different classes, with each class c characterized by a Markov chain with n_c states: the space Σ in which agents are located and can move is finite and can be continuous or discrete. The distribution of agents in the space can be represented by a density function $\delta : \Sigma \rightarrow \mathbb{R}^+$ so that, considering any subspace $U \subset \Sigma$, the number of agents in U is described by a Poisson distribution with mean $\int \int_U \delta(x) dx$. The model evolves by accounting for state changes of agents in their class and induction effects, birth of agents and death of agents: its evaluation can be obtained as a counting process per each class that counts the number of agents in each state of its Markov chain, in each position in space and in each instant.

Let $\chi_c(l,t) = |\chi_i^{[c]}(l,t)|$ be a vector of size $n^{[c]}$, with each element $\chi_i^{[c]}(l,t)$ representing the average number of agents of class c in state i at time t and in location l. If the space is discrete, the evolution of the counting process is thus described by a set of ordinary differential Equations 4 for each class c and in location l:

$$\frac{d\chi_c(l,t)}{dt} = b_c([\chi], l, t) + \chi_c(l,t) \cdot K_c([\chi], l, t) \tag{4}$$

where $[\chi]$ denotes the dependency on all the state of all agents in the model in any time instant, matrix K_c is the main transition kernel that accounts for spontaneous and induced actions contribution and b_c is the birth vector of new agents for the class in a state.

If the space is continuous, movement of agents is described by a diagonal velocity matrix ω_c, described in Eq. 5, that can be obtained by summing the contributions for each direction:

$$\frac{\partial(\omega_c([\chi], l, t) \cdot \chi_c(l, t))}{\partial l} = \frac{\partial(\omega_{xc}([\chi], l, t) \cdot \chi_c(l, t))}{\partial l_x} + \frac{\partial(\omega_{yc}([\chi], l, t) \cdot \chi_c(l, t))}{\partial l_y} + \cdots$$
$$(5)$$

and Eq. 4 is modified accordingly and becomes Eq. 6:

$$\frac{\partial \chi_c(l, t)}{\partial t} + \frac{\partial(\omega_c([\chi], l, t) \cdot \chi_c(l, t))}{\partial l} = b_c([\chi], l, t) + \chi_c(l, t) \cdot K_c([\chi], l, t) \quad (6)$$

in which the second term accounts for the effects of agents movement by v_c.

3.4 Logic-Based Modeling

In contrast with mechanism- and constraint-based models, logic-based model do not require kinetic or stoichiometric information to be defined. Although these models can describe the system under consideration only in qualitative terms, they provide an efficient way to simulate the dynamic evolution of complex systems, even when precise kinetic information is not available. Thanks to their closeness to human language, logic-based models are able to leverage qualitative and semi-quantitative data and they are generally regarded as more intepretable by human experts. Moreover, their flexibility allow modelers to represent in the same model highly heterogeneous components and the interactions existing among them.

Logic-based models are defined by a set of v variables $\mathcal{V}$ and a set of ϕ IF-THEN logic rules $\mathcal{F}$, describing the interactions existing between the components. Evaluation of the rules in discrete time steps drives the system's dynamics: this can be achieved by either a synchronous (deterministic) or asynchronous (stochastic) update policy [141]. Logic-based models are commonly employed in systems biology to model gene regulatory networks and signal processing [74]. Among them, Boolean models are the most simple and widely used: in this kind of models, variables can assume only two discrete states, often represented as 0 and 1, active or inactive, present or not present. Different Boolean logic models were successful in predicting cellular behaviours [141], however these assumptions often limit their ability of representing biomolecular processes.

In order to overcome these limitations, more recently fuzzy logic was proposed as an alternative to the modeling of complex biochemical systems [3]. Fuzzy logic is a powerful, multi-valued extension of boolean logic, which allows variables to assume multiple states in a continuous manner (i.e., between [0,1]) and deal with any uncertainty related to the system. More in particular, fuzzy IF-THEN inference systems are composed of ϕ rules of type:

IF v_1 is in $V_{1,1}$ and v_2 is in $V_{1,2}$ and ... and v_v is in $V_{1,v}$ THEN o is in O_1
IF v_1 is in $V_{2,1}$ and v_2 is in $V_{2,2}$ and ... and v_v is in $V_{2,v}$ THEN o is in O_2

$\cdots$

IF v_1 is in $V_{\sigma,1}$ and v_2 is in $V_{\sigma,2}$ and ... and v_v is in $V_{\sigma,v}$ THEN o is in O_σ, where $v_j, o \in \mathcal{V}$, with $i = 1, \ldots, \upsilon$, while the sets $V_{i,j}$ and O_i, with $i = 1, \ldots, \sigma$, and $j = 1, \ldots, \upsilon$ are *fuzzy (sub-)sets*, that is, the membership of the value assumed by a generic variable $v \in \mathcal{V}$ for the fuzzy subset V is equal to a degree $\alpha \in [0, 1]$. This is denoted by $\mu_V(v) = \alpha$. If all the considered sets are classical sets (i.e. always holds $\mu_V(v) \in \{0, 1\}$), then the inference system is boolean.

An advantage of fuzzy reasoning is that, thanks to the fuzzy sets, it can handle uncertainty and conflicting conclusions drawn from the logic rules [126]. Thus, it can allow for the dynamic simulation of qualitative and semiquantitative models, even when precise kinetic information is missing. Fuzzy logic has been applied to vastly different fields of research, ranging from automatic control [36] to medicine [99], but it was successfully applied also in the field of cellular biology, for example, to model signaling pathways [3] and gene regulatory networks [63].

We plan to exploit fuzzy logic in our hybrid framework to overcome the lack of kinetic parameters [14,66] and model those cellular processes that still are not understood in mechanistic detail, or whose components cannot be represented by crisp, real-valued variables (e.g., complex phenotype as apoptosis/survival, microscopy imaging data, etc.).

4   A Unified Modeling Approach

In principle, the SSA algorithm described in Sect. 3.1 can be used to simulate a stochastic trajectory of any biological model, including a whole-cell model, and such dynamics would be exact with respect to the Chemical Master Equation (CME) underlying the corresponding set of biochemical reactions. This approach could be even extended to consider the diffusion of molecules inside the cell, like in the case of the Next Subvolume Method (NSM) [38]). However, both SSA and NSM perform the simulations by applying a single reaction at a time, proceeding with time steps that are inversely proportional to the sum of the propensities (see Eq. 3) which, in turn, is proportional to the amount of reactants in the system. These circumstances generally cause an explosion of the computational effort due to exact stochastic simulation, making it unfeasible for whole-cell simulation.

An approximate but faster version of SSA, called tau-leaping [44], was proposed by Gillespie to reduce the computational burden typical of SSA: by assuming that the propensities do not change during a given time-interval (the so-called *leap condition*) the number of reactions firing can be approximated by Poisson random variables.

When the number of estimated reaction firings for all reactions increases, the Poisson processes can be approximated by a normal distribution with same mean and variance [44]. In this case, Stochastic Differential Equations (SDEs) like the Langevin equations can be exploited to model the system, which is then simulated using numeric solvers like the Euler-Maruyama method [119], strongly reducing the overall computational effort. Finally, when the propensities become extremely large, the noise term in the SDEs becomes negligible and can be removed, so that the system can be modeled using simple ODEs [44].

The proper modeling approach must be carefully selected according to the characteristics of the chemical system. Unfortunately, cellular mechanisms are controlled by reactions and pathways spanning over multiple scales, so that none of these modeling methods is really adequate. By partitioning the reactions set $\mathcal{R}$ into multiple regimes, according to their characteristics (e.g., their propensity values), it is possible to simulate each subsystem using the optimal modeling approach. It is clear that the firing of reactions in one regime can have a huge impact to the others, so that the synchronization phase—necessary to propagate the information across the regimes—becomes a mandatory and very delicate phases of multi-scale hybrid simulators, like in the case of the Partitioned Leaping Algorithm (PLA) [52].

By extending PLA by considering the additional modeling approaches described in Sect. 3.1, it is possible to achieve whole-cell models [58]. In this project, we pursue the integration of these modeling approaches, pushing the limits of human cells simulation. In order to mitigate the huge computational requirements, we plan to exploit model reduction and automatic simplification algorithms. We also plan to perform an automatic inference of some missing parts of the model (e.g., reactions, rules, parameters), exploiting state-of-the-art evolutionary and statistical methods. Finally, we will test multi-agent approaches to work on multiple scales (e.g., multiple cells or tissue simulation). All these approaches will be described in the next subsections.

4.1   Model Reduction and Simplification

The complexity of cellular systems poses some limitations on the scale of the models that can be simulated. In this context, model reduction techniques can be used to tame the complexity before the execution of simulation algorithms is performed.

The theory of complex networks has raised a great development over the recent years. The empirical and theoretical results analyzing several real systems show that complex networks can be classified using its probability distribution function $P(k)$, i.e. the probability that a node is connected to k nodes of a network. A scale-free network has the grades distribution function fitting the power-law function [57]. Several studies examining the cellular metabolism of different organisms have been conducted for determining the topological structure of a metabolic network [57]. In this direction, studies of Barabási and Albert have also analyzed many issues in scale-free networks [2].

In many organism, the metabolic networks are composed of interconnected functional modules and follow the scale-free model [49,61]. Three statistical measures can be considered in a scale-free network: the connectivity degree, the diameter of the graph, and the clustering coefficient [2]. The connectivity degree of a node is the number of incident arcs and it allows also for calculating the distribution function of the connectivity degree. The diameter provides an estimation of the average number of hops between any pair of nodes in the network. It is also linked to the shortest paths between each node pair as well as to the number of paths in the network. Finally, the clustering coefficient gives a measure of the properties of nodes to form agglomerates. In addition, metabolic network nodes can be classified into distinct groups considering the following parameters

[49]: the within-module degree, i.e., the membership degree of a node into its functional module, and the participation coefficient, i.e., a measure of the node interaction with network functional modules. The above parameters can be used to define non-hub and hub nodes as well as peripheral, provincial, connector, and kinless nodes [49,64]. These metrics pave the way to the topological analysis of a network, providing information on the connectivity and the participation degrees of each node within the network.

The topological analysis of a network can be completed by functional analysis. A cellular network is hierarchically organized with several functional modules [5,57]. Methods for a rational decomposition of the network into independent functional subsets are essential to understand their modularity and organization principles.

Using the modularization approach commonly used in the area of control theory, a cellular network can be viewed as an assembly of basic building blocks with its specific structures, characteristics, and interactions [103,135]. Modularization reduces the difficulty in investigating a complex network. Network decomposition is also needed for cellular functional analysis through pathway analysis methods that are often troubled by the problem of combinatorial explosion due to the complexity of those networks.

Two main methods can be used for network functional analysis and, as a consequence, for network model reduction and simplification: Flux Balance Analysis (FBA) and Extreme Pathways Analysis (ExPA) [59,103,137].

FBA is a mathematical technique based on fundamental physical and chemical laws that quantitatively describe the metabolisms of living cells. FBA is a constraint-based modeling approach [96]: it assumes that an organism reaches a steady-state (under any given environmental condition) that satisfies the physicochemical constraints and uses the mass and energy balance to describe the potential cellular behavior. FBA model has been developed considering the mass and energy conservation law: for each node/metabolite, the sum of incoming fluxes must be equal to the sum of the outgoing ones. The space of all feasible solutions of a linear equation constrained system lies within a three-dimensional convex polyhedron, in which each point of this space satisfies the constraints of the system [96]. When the system has an optimal and limited solution, this is unique and it is located on a polyhedron vertex. However, the system can have multiple optimal solutions (axis or plan) that are used to detect network redundancies [96].

ExPA analysis detects the vital pathways in a network. They are the unique set of vectors that completely characterize the steady-state capabilities of a network. A network steady-state operation is constrained to the region within a cone, defined as the feasible set. In some special cases, under certain constraints, this feasible set collapse in a single point inside the cone. The algorithm detects the extreme rays/generating vectors of convex polyhedral cones. Algorithm time execution is proportional to the number of nodes and pathways [137].

Many software frameworks for cellular networks analysis and simulation have been developed. Some solutions, such as Pajek [34], allows for either large complex networks analysis and visualization or network structural properties and quantities analysis. CellNetAnalyzer [62] is a MATLAB package for performing biochemical networks functional and structural analysis.

The BIAM framework implements an integrated analysis methodology based on topological analysis, FBA analysis, and Extreme Pathways analysis [26,134]. The framework supplies the needed tools for drawing a network and analyzing its structural and functional properties. Several scale-free network architectures, dealing with different application domains, have been simulated and validated [26,136]. Topological and functional analysis can be combined to select the main functional nodes and paths of a cellular network. Redundant nodes and non-vital paths could be ignored before the execution of time-constrained simulation algorithms, reducing the overall computational complexity of large scale simulation.

4.2 Parameter Estimation

Mechanistic models are characterized by a kinetic parameterization (i.e., the **K** vector described in Sect. 3.1). A precise estimation of such parameters is mandatory to perform faithful simulations of the system's dynamics. The problem of Parameter Estimation (PE) can be formulated as a minimization problem: the goal is to reduce to zero a distance between the target experimental discrete-time time-series and a simulated dynamics performed with the optimal vector of parameters [83]. Due to the characteristics of the fitness landscapes defined by the PE problem (i.e., multi-modal, non-linear, non-convex, noisy), classic optimization methods cannot be employed efficiently. On the contrary, Computational Intelligence (CI) methods based on evolutionary computation or swarm intelligence were shown to be effective for this problem [35,83], in particular the settings-free variant of PSO named Fuzzy Self-Tuning PSO [80]. Moreover, CI methods can be combined with probabilistic frameworks (e.g. expectation-maximization methods [55]) to efficiently tackle the PE of stochastic models (see for example [95]). However, when the number of missing parameters in the model becomes extremely large, like in the case of whole-cell models, conventional CI methods can show some limitations and large-scale methods must be employed.

Among the existing CI algorithms for large number of parameters, Differential Evolution (DE) [116] variants like the recent DISH [132] algorithm could be exploited. DE algorithm was introduced in 1995 by Storn and Price [116] and since then formed a basis for a set of successful algorithms for optimization domains, such as continuous, discrete, mixed-integer, or other search spaces and features [146]. The whole encompassing research field around DE was surveyed most recently in [32] and even since then, several other domain- and feature-specific surveys, studies, and comparisons have also followed [1,90,92,93]. Theoretical insight and insights to inner workings and behaviors of DE during consecutive generations has been studied in the works like [87,122,133,144].

As the continuing research in DE enhancements and insight supports a much vigorous research community, the DE algorithm variants have also steadily placed top in competitions held annually at Congress on Evolutionary Computation (CEC) [16,17,31,68,73,97,98,140]. For this reason, we expect these advanced versions of DE to be effective for the PE problem and outperform classic algorithms, especially on high dimensional problem.

The most recent variants' strain of DE is the Success-History based Adaptive Differential Evolution (SHADE) [120], which has a line of recent improvements following a taxonomy [1] stemming from JADE [149] that is based on jDE [16,144], upgraded as L-SHADE [121], SPS-L-SHADE-EIG [50], LSHADE-cnEpSin [4], jSO [18], aL-SHADE [91], and most recently, DISH [132]. These algorithms include different mechanisms and to describe the basic outline working principle to apply DE, from the following paragraph on, the basic canonical 1995 DE is described.

The canonical 1995 DE is based on parameter estimation through evolution from a randomly generated set of solutions using population P, which has a preset size of NP. Each individual (a set of estimated parameter values) in this population P consists of a vector x with a of length D. Each vector x component corresponds to one attribute of the optimized task for which parameters are being estimated. The objective function value $f(x)$ evaluates quality of the solution. The individuals in the population create improved offspring for the next generation. This process is repeated until the stopping criterion is met (either the maximum number of generations, or the maximum number of objective function evaluations, or the population diversity lower limit, or overall computational time), creating a chain of subsequent generations, where each following generation consists of eventually better solutions than those in previous generations.

Some of most used computational operators operating on population P over each generation and its vectors, are parameter adaptation, mutation [149], crossover [121], selection [132], and population restructuring including adaptation of population size [144]. First, all vectors in the initial population are uniformly generated at random between bounds $[x_{\text{lower},j}, x_{\text{upper},j}]$, $\forall j = 1, \ldots, D$:

$$x_i = \{\mathcal{U}\left[x_{\text{lower},j}, \ x_{\text{upper},j}\right]\}; \forall j = 1, \ \ldots, \ D; \forall i = 1, \ \ldots, \ NP, \tag{7}$$

then, three mutually and from current vector index i different, indices r_1, r_2, and r_3, are used to computing a differential vector (hence the name DE for algorithm) and combine it in a scaled difference manner:

$$v_i = x_{r1} + F\left(x_{r2} - x_{r3}\right), \tag{8}$$

which is then taken into crossover with the current vector at index i:

$$u_{j,i} = \begin{cases} v_{j,i} \text{ if } \mathcal{U}\left[0,1\right] \leq CR_i \text{ or } j = \ j_{\text{rand}} \\ x_{j,i} \qquad\qquad \text{otherwise} \end{cases}, \tag{9}$$

finally through selection yielding a new vector $x_{i,G+1}$ at this location i for next generation $G + 1$:

$$x_{i,G+1} = \begin{cases} u_{i,G} \text{ if } f\left(u_{i,G}\right) \leq f\left(x_{i,G}\right) \\ x_{i,G} \qquad\qquad \text{otherwise} \end{cases}. \tag{10}$$

As mentioned in the beginning of this subsection, the work on DE is ongoing and still challenging. To apply DE most efficiently on a new challenge for parameter estimation like the discussed simulation in this chapter, one of effective DE variants should be taken and adapted for the domain challenge at hand, following recent experiences on DE applications in e.g. image processing [143], energy scheduling [145], and autonomous vehicle navigation [147,148].

To assess the feasibility of DISH for the large-scale PE problem, we plan to compare its performances against state-of-the-art methods, in particular the aforementioned variants of DE and those algorithms that were shown effective for the PE in previous studies (i.e., PSO [35] and FST-PSO [83]).

Another approach for DE that may be beneficial for the given application is through unconventional synergy of the DE with several different research fields belonging to the computational intelligence paradigm, which are the stochastics processes, complex chaotic dynamics, and complex networks (CN).

As the key operation in metaheuristic algorithms is the randomness, the popularity of hybridizing them with deterministic chaos is growing every year, due to its unique features. Recent research in chaotic approach for metaheuristics mostly uses straightforwardly various chaotic maps in the place of pseudorandom number generators. The observed performance of enhanced optimizer is (significantly) different, mostly the chaotic maps secured very fast progress towards function extreme, but often followed by premature convergence, thus overall statistics has given mixed results. Nevertheless, as reported in [106], the the chaos driven heuristics is performing very well [104,107], especially for some instances in the discrete domain [33,72].

The CN approach is utilized to show the linkage between different individuals in the population. Interactions in a swarm/evolutionary algorithms during the optimization process can be considered like user interactions in social networks or just people in society. The population is visualized as an evolving CN that exhibits non-trivial features - e.g., degree distribution, clustering, and centralities. These features can be then utilized for the adaptive population control as well as parameter control during the metaheuristic run. Analysis of CNs from DE algorithm can be found in [105,108,109,130,131]; and also in a comprehensive study discussing the usability of network types [110].

4.3 Automatic Inference of Fuzzy Rules

Fuzzy IF–THEN inference systems are typically constructed by consulting human experts, who give the related fuzzy rules, shapes of the corresponding fuzzy sets and all the other required information. However, when human experts are not available or in the presence of numerous system components and/or rules, the definition of the inference system results to be particularly time consuming and laborious. An alternative approach is exploiting data mining methods, in order to automatically build inference systems by leveraging available data.

In particular, here we focus on GUHA (General Unary Hypotheses Automaton), a method of automatic generation of hypotheses based on empirical data. GUHA is based on a particular first order logic language, which allows to treat symbolically sentences such as α appears often simultaneously with β, in most cases α implies β, α makes β very probable, etc. The GUHA method is implemented in the LISpMiner software [127], which is freely downloadable from https://lispminer.vse.cz/. Once the user provides relevant *analytic questions* regarding the data, the LISpMiner software outputs the dependencies between the variables that are supported by the data. In practice, LISpMiner runs through millions of fourfold contingency tables, from which it outputs those which support the dependence provided by the user. From these findings, the IF-THEN inference system can then be constructed.

GUHA and LISpMiner were already successfully employed in different fields [127]: in the context of human cell modeling, this approach could be exploited in order to automatically build large fuzzy inference systems. In particular, this data mining method could leverage the vast availability of transcriptomic data [54], which nowadays can be generated in short time, for a reasonable cost and at single-cell resolution [113]. In such a way, we envision that the automatic generation of large-scale dynamic fuzzy models of cellular processes would be feasible. Such models would represent a significant step forward towards the integration of cellular processes that are not known in full mechanistic detail, or necessitate of a qualitative or semi-quantitative representation, inside a unified framework for human cell modelling and simulation.

4.4   Multiformalism Approaches

Given the complexity and the heterogeneity of the sub-problems that characterize the challenge posed by whole-cell modeling, a promising approach can be provided by *multiformalism modeling* [46]. Multiformalism modeling offers the possibility of obtaining complex models by allowing the coexistence of different modeling formalisms in the same model, using model composition, model generation, model abstraction on the basis of different supporting mechanisms. Multiformalism approaches allow the representation of each subsystem with the most appropriate representation, or with the description that is more familiar for the developer of that submodel, easing the interaction between experts from different domains without forcing any of them to relinquish established modeling practices: this allows to preserve existing know how and minimizes the effort needed to integrate the overall model, that is a process that is supported by a proper specialist in formalism design. Multiformalism models may be supported by closed frameworks [25,102,125], that support a predefined set of formalisms, or by open frameworks [6,42], that are designed to allow the definition of new formalisms.

The solution, or analysis, of multiformalism models may be performed by generating a specific solvable model, by generating or instantiating a simulation tool, by orchestrating specific solvers for different submodels, by producing executable code. Solution can be obtained by means of simulation, analytical techniques or by applying *multisolution*, that is the possibility of using alternate tools, explicitly decided by the modeler or automatically chosen according to the characteristics of the model, to perform the analysis. This approach also preserves, in general, tracking of numerical results back to logical elements in the model, and can provide model-wide or submodel-wide results, such as properties of parts of the system that emerge from element-related results, and may also be used to interface existing tools with new solvers, extending their applicability [10]. Multiformalism modeling approaches may support combinatorial formalisms [125], logic modeling [25], discrete state space based formalisms [6,42], continuous state space based formalisms [6], and hybrid formalisms [8] (that may use specialized solution techniques [9]). More details about multiformalism modeling concepts and principles are available for the reader in [46] and [101]. For a similar and wider concept, namely *multiparadigm modeling*, the reader can refer to [75].

5 Future Developments

In this chapter we described a putative hybrid modeling and simulation framework—exploiting several different approaches (e.g., RMBs, CBMs, boolean and fuzzy rules) and leveraging High-Performance Computing—designed to perform large-scale cell simulations. In this context, we highlighted some issues that prevent the simulation of whole-cell models, proposing some approaches in order to achieve this challenging task.

In particular, we propose the use of population-based metaheuristics for global optimization to estimate the large number of missing kinetic parameters. The emphasis in future research will be on modifying and testing robust algorithms based on DE/DISH inspired by techniques successfully adopted for solving highly constrained, large-scale and multi-objective problems. We will compare this class of algorithms against swarm intelligence techniques (e.g., PSO [94] and FST-PSO [80]) that were shown to be the most effective in previous empirical studies [35,83].

Furthermore, a thorough analysis of the relatively good results of genetic algorithms can help to develop powerful metaheuristics. Moreover, it is necessary to emphasize the fact that, like most of the above mentioned metaheuristic methods, they are inspired by natural evolution, and their development can be considered as a form of evolution. Such a fact is mentioned in the paper [93] that even incremental steps in algorithm development, including failures, may be the inspiration for the development of robust and powerful metaheuristics. Future directions in DE can be discussed not only in the journals like Swarm and Evolutionary Computation, IEEE Transactions on Evolutionary Computation, or Evolutionary Computation, but also at forthcoming conferences like Swarm, Evolutionary and Memetic Computing Conference (SEMCCO), IEEE Congress on Evolutionary Computation (CEC), and The Genetic and Evolutionary Computation Conference (GECCO), all forthcoming also for year 2019.

A lot of work still needs to be done, in order to achieve a faithful representation of a human cell *in silico*. The unified approach that we propose in this work, although challenging to achieve and possibly able to capture a wide variety of cellular behaviors, must be considered just as a starting point. As a matter of fact, many additional layers of complexity can still be considered. We assume that the biochemical systems is well-stirred, but this is often not the case. Spatial modeling and simulation can be leveraged to capture the organization in space of molecules (e.g., membrane receptors), cell organelles and cell shape itself. The combinatorial complexity of the formation of huge protein complexes or bio-polymers can also be tackled by means of specific modeling [40] and simulation frameworks [111]. Moreover, cells are not closed systems: they respond to environmental cues and they continuously interact with with other cells by exchanging chemical signals. Furthermore, cell's life cycle is coordinated by a complex cell cycle program, that allows them to grow and divide, and they are constantly subjected to the evolutionary pressure posed by the environment. External signals and cell cycle both require additional complex modeling approaches that are currently not considered in our approach. Whilst we envision that human cell simulation will remain a challenging task for the coming decades, we are working in that direction as it carries the promise of elucidating the very basic mechanisms governing the functioning of our bodies and life itself.

Acknowledgements. This chapter is based upon work from the COST Action IC1406 cHiPSet, supported by COST (European Cooperation in Science and Technology). The author AZ acknowledges the financial support from the Slovenian Research Agency (research core funding No. P2-0041). AZ also acknowledges EU support under project no. 5442-24/2017/6 (HPC – RIVR). This chapter is also based upon work from COST Action CA15140 "Improving Applicability of Nature-Inspired Optimisation by Joining Theory and Practice (ImAppNIO)" supported by COST. The authors RS and ZKO also acknowledges that work was supported by the Ministry of Education, Youth and Sports of the Czech Republic within the National Sustainability Programme Project No. LO1303 (MSMT-7778/2014), further supported by the European Regional Development Fund under the Project CEBIA-Tech no. CZ.1.05/2.1.00/03.0089. Further authors TK and AV acknowledges the support of Internal Grant Agency of Tomas Bata University under the Projects no. IGA/CebiaTech/2019/002.

References

1. Al-Dabbagh, R.D., Neri, F., Idris, N., Baba, M.S.: Algorithmic design issues in adaptive differential evolution schemes: review and taxonomy. Swarm Evol. Comput. (2018). https://doi.org/10.1016/j.swevo.2018.03.008
2. Albert, R., Barabási, A.L.: Statistical mechanics of complex networks. Rev. Mod. Phys. **74**(1), 47 (2002)
3. Aldridge, B.B., Saez-Rodriguez, J., Muhlich, J.L., Sorger, P.K., Lauffenburger, D.A.: Fuzzy logic analysis of kinase pathway crosstalk in TNF/EGF/insulin-induced signaling. PLoS Comput. Biol. **5**(4), e1000340 (2009)
4. Awad, N.H., Ali, M.Z., Suganthan, P.N., Reynolds, R.G.: An ensemble sinusoidal parameter adaptation incorporated with L-SHADE for solving CEC2014 benchmark problems. In: 2016 IEEE Congress on Evolutionary Computation (CEC), pp. 2958–2965. IEEE (2016)
5. Barabási, A.L., Oltvai, Z.N.: Network biology: understanding the cell's functional organization. Nat. Rev. Genet. **5**(2), 101 (2004)
6. Barbierato, E., Bobbio, A., Gribaudo, M., Iacono, M.: Multiformalism to support software rejuvenation modeling, pp. 271–276 (2012)

7. Barbierato, E., Gribaudo, M., Iacono, M.: Modeling and evaluating the effects of Big Data storage resource allocation in global scale cloud architectures. Int. J. Data Warehous. Min. **12**(2), 1–20 (2016). https://doi.org/10.4018/IJDWM. 2016040101

8. Barbierato, E., Gribaudo, M., Iacono, M.: Modeling hybrid systems in SIMTHESys. Electron. Notes Theor. Comput. Sci. **327**, 5–25 (2016)

9. Barbierato, E., Gribaudo, M., Iacono, M.: Simulating hybrid systems within SIMTHESys multi-formalism models. In: Fiems, D., Paolieri, M., Platis, A.N. (eds.) EPEW 2016. LNCS, vol. 9951, pp. 189–203. Springer, Cham (2016). https://doi.org/10.1007/978-3-319-46433-6_13

10. Barbierato, E., Gribaudo, M., Iacono, M., Jakóbik, A.: Exploiting CloudSim in a multiformalism modeling approach for cloud based systems. Simul. Model. Pract. Theory (2018)

11. Benkner, S., et al.: PEPPHER: Efficient and productive usage of hybrid computing systems. IEEE Micro **31**(5), 28–41 (2011). https://doi.org/10.1109/MM. 2011.67

12. Besozzi, D.: Reaction-based models of biochemical networks. In: Beckmann, A., Bienvenu, L., Jonoska, N. (eds.) CiE 2016. LNCS, vol. 9709, pp. 24–34. Springer, Cham (2016). https://doi.org/10.1007/978-3-319-40189-8_3

13. Bobbio, A., Cerotti, D., Gribaudo, M., Iacono, M., Manini, D.: Markovian agent models: a dynamic population of interdependent Markovian agents. In: Al Begain, K., Bargiela, A. (eds.) Seminal Contributions to Modelling and Simulation. SFMA, pp. 185–203. Springer, Cham (2016). https://doi.org/10.1007/978-3-319-33786-9_13

14. Bordon, J., Moškon, M., Zimic, N., Mraz, M.: Fuzzy logic as a computational tool for quantitative modelling of biological systems with uncertain kinetic data. IEEE/ACM Trans. Comput. Biol. Bioinform. **12**(5), 1199–1205 (2015)

15. Bowers, K.J., et al.: Scalable algorithms for molecular dynamics simulations on commodity clusters. In: Proceedings of the ACM/IEEE SC 2006 Conference, p. 43. IEEE (2006)

16. Brest, J., Greiner, S., Bošković, B., Mernik, M., Bošković, V.: Self-adapting control parameters in differential evolution: a comparative study on numerical benchmark problems. IEEE Trans. Evol. Comput. **10**(6), 646–657 (2006)

17. Brest, J., Korošec, P., Šilc, J., Zamuda, A., Bošković, B., Maučec, M.S.: Differential evolution and differential ant-stigmergy on dynamic optimisation problems. Int. J. Syst. Sci. **44**(4), 663–679 (2013)

18. Brest, J., Maučec, M.S., Bošković, B.: Single objective real-parameter optimization: algorithm jSO. In: 2017 IEEE Congress on Evolutionary Computation (CEC), pp. 1311–1318. IEEE (2017)

19. Cash, J.R.: Backward differentiation formulae. In: Engquist, B. (ed.) Encyclopedia of Applied and Computational Mathematics, pp. 97–101. Springer, Heidelberg (2015). https://doi.org/10.1007/978-3-540-70529-1_94. Computational Science & Engineering, 1 (edn.) Springer, Heidelberg

20. Cazzaniga, P., et al.: Computational strategies for a system-level understanding of metabolism. Metabolites **4**(4), 1034–1087 (2014)

21. Cerotti, D., Gribaudo, M., Bobbio, A., Calafate, C.T., Manzoni, P.: A Markovian agent model for fire propagation in outdoor environments. In: Aldini, A., Bernardo, M., Bononi, L., Cortellessa, V. (eds.) EPEW 2010. LNCS, vol. 6342, pp. 131–146. Springer, Heidelberg (2010). https://doi.org/10.1007/978-3-642-15784-4_9

22. Chellaboina, V., Bhat, S., Haddad, W., Bernstein, D.: Modeling and analysis of mass-action kinetics. IEEE Control Syst. Mag. **29**(4), 60–78 (2009). https://doi.org/10.1109/MCS.2009.932926
23. Chiappino-Pepe, A., Pandey, V., Ataman, M., Hatzimanikatis, V.: Integration of metabolic, regulatory and signaling networks towards analysis of perturbation and dynamic responses. Curr. Opin. Syst. Biol. **2**, 59–66 (2017)
24. Chrysos, G.: Intel® Xeon Phi™ Coprocessor-the Architecture. Intel Whitepaper (2014)
25. Ciardo, G., Jones III, R.L., Miner, A.S., Siminiceanu, R.I.: Logic and stochastic modeling with smart. Perform. Eval. **63**(6), 578–608 (2006)
26. Conti, V., Ruffo, S.S., Vitabile, S., Barolli, L.: BIAM: a new bio-inspired analysis methodology for digital ecosystems based on a scale-free architecture. Soft Comput. **23**, 1–18 (2017)
27. Cordero, F., Manini, D., Gribaudo, M.: Modeling biological pathways: an object-oriented like methodology based on mean field analysis. In: 2009 Third International Conference on Advanced Engineering Computing and Applications in Sciences, pp. 117–122, October 2009. https://doi.org/10.1109/ADVCOMP.2009.25
28. Cordero, F., Fornari, C., Gribaudo, M., Manini, D.: Markovian agents population models to study cancer evolution. In: Sericola, B., Telek, M., Horváth, G. (eds.) Analytical and Stochastic Modeling Techniques and Applications, pp. 16–32. Springer, Cham (2014). https://doi.org/10.1007/978-3-319-08219-6_2
29. Coulier, A., Hellander, A.: Orchestral: a lightweight framework for parallel simulations of cell-cell communication. arXiv preprint arXiv:1806.10889 (2018)
30. Dada, J.O., Mendes, P.: Multi-scale modelling and simulation in systems biology. Integr. Biol. **3**(2), 86–96 (2011)
31. Das, S., Abraham, A., Chakraborty, U.K., Konar, A.: Differential evolution using a neighborhood-based mutation operator. IEEE Trans. Evol. Comput. **13**(3), 526–553 (2009)
32. Das, S., Mullick, S.S., Suganthan, P.N.: Recent advances in differential evolution – an updated survey. Swarm Evol. Comput. **27**, 1–30 (2016)
33. Davendra, D., Bialic-Davendra, M., Senkerik, R.: Scheduling the lot-streaming flowshop scheduling problem with setup time with the chaos-induced enhanced differential evolution. In: 2013 IEEE Symposium on Differential Evolution (SDE), pp. 119–126. IEEE (2013)
34. De Nooy, W., Mrvar, A., Batagelj, V.: Exploratory Social Network Analysis with Pajek. Cambridge University Press, Cambridge (2018)
35. Dräger, A., Kronfeld, M., Ziller, M.J., Supper, J., Planatscher, H., Magnus, J.B.: Modeling metabolic networks in *C. glutamicum*: a comparison of rate laws in combination with various parameter optimization strategies. BMC Syst. Biol. **3**(1), 5 (2009)
36. Dubrovin, T., Jolma, A., Turunen, E.: Fuzzy model for real-time reservoir operation. J. Water Resour. Plan. Manag. **128**(1), 66–73 (2002)
37. Eldar, A., Elowitz, M.B.: Functional roles for noise in genetic circuits. Nature **467**(7312), 167 (2010)
38. Elf, J., Ehrenberg, M.: Spontaneous separation of bi-stable biochemical systems into spatial domains of opposite phases. IEE Proc.-Syst. Biol. **1**(2), 230–236 (2004)
39. Elowitz, M.B., Levine, A.J., Siggia, E.D., Swain, P.S.: Stochastic gene expression in a single cell. Science **297**(5584), 1183–1186 (2002)
40. Faeder, J.R., Blinov, M.L., Hlavacek, W.S.: Rule-based modeling of biochemical systems with BioNetGen. In: Maly, I. (ed.) Systems Biology, pp. 113–167. Springer, Heidelberg (2009). https://doi.org/10.1007/978-1-59745-525-1_5

41. Fisher, C.P., Plant, N.J., Moore, J.B., Kierzek, A.M.: QSSPN: dynamic simulation of molecular interaction networks describing gene regulation, signalling and whole-cell metabolism in human cells. Bioinformatics **29**(24), 3181–3190 (2013)
42. Franceschinis, G., Gribaudo, M., Iacono, M., Marrone, S., Mazzocca, N., Vittorini, V.: Compositional modeling of complex systems: contact center scenarios in OsMoSys. In: ICATPN 2004, pp. 177–196 (2004)
43. Gillespie, D.T.: A general method for numerically simulating the stochastic time evolution of coupled chemical reactions. J. Comput. Phys. **22**(4), 403–434 (1976)
44. Gillespie, D.T.: Approximate accelerated stochastic simulation of chemically reacting systems. J. Chem. Phys. **115**(4), 1716–1733 (2001)
45. Gonçalves, E., et al.: Bridging the layers: towards integration of signal transduction, regulation and metabolism into mathematical models. Mol. BioSyst. **9**(7), 1576–1583 (2013)
46. Gribaudo, M., Iacono, M.: An introduction to multiformalism modeling (2013)
47. Gribaudo, M., Iacono, M., Levis, A.H.: An IoT-based monitoring approach for cultural heritage sites: the Matera case. Concurr. Comput.: Pract. Exp. **29**, e4153 (2017). https://doi.org/10.1002/cpe.4153
48. Gropp, W., Lusk, E., Skjellum, A.: Using MPI: Portable Parallel Programming with the Message-Passing Interface, vol. 1. MIT Press, Cambridge (1999)
49. Guimera, R., Amaral, L.A.N.: Functional cartography of complex metabolic networks. Nature **433**(7028), 895 (2005)
50. Guo, S.M., Tsai, J.S.H., Yang, C.C., Hsu, P.H.: A self-optimization approach for L-SHADE incorporated with eigenvector-based crossover and successful-parent-selecting framework on CEC 2015 benchmark set. In: 2015 IEEE Congress on Evolutionary Computation (CEC), pp. 1003–1010. IEEE (2015)
51. Hadoop, A.: Apache Hadoop project. https://hadoop.apache.org/. Accessed 03 Nov 2018
52. Harris, L.A., Clancy, P.: A "partitioned leaping" approach for multiscale modeling of chemical reaction dynamics. J. Chem. Phys. **125**(14), 144107 (2006)
53. Harris, L.A., et al.: GPU-powered model analysis with PySB/cupSODA. Bioinformatics **33**(21), 3492–3494 (2017)
54. Hecker, M., Lambeck, S., Toepfer, S., Van Someren, E., Guthke, R.: Gene regulatory network inference: data integration in dynamic models review. Biosystems **96**(1), 86–103 (2009)
55. Horváth, A., Manini, D.: Parameter estimation of kinetic rates in stochastic reaction networks by the EM method. In: International Conference on BioMedical Engineering and Informatics, BMEI 2008, vol. 1, pp. 713–717. IEEE (2008)
56. European Bioinformatics Institute: EMBL-EBI annual scientific report 2013. https://www.embl.fr/aboutus/communication_outreach/publications/ebi_ar/ebi_ar_2013.pdf. Accessed 07 Dec 2018
57. Jeong, H., Tombor, B., Albert, R., Oltvai, Z.N., Barabási, A.L.: The large-scale organization of metabolic networks. Nature **407**(6804), 651 (2000)
58. Karr, J.R., et al.: A whole-cell computational model predicts phenotype from genotype. Cell **150**(2), 389–401 (2012)
59. Kauffman, K.J., Prakash, P., Edwards, J.S.: Advances in flux balance analysis. Curr. Opin. Biotechnol. **14**(5), 491–496 (2003)
60. Kessler, C., et al.: Programmability and performance portability aspects of heterogeneous multi-/manycore systems. In: Design, Automation & Test in Europe Conference & Exhibition (DATE), pp. 1403–1408. IEEE (2012)
61. Kitano, H.: Systems biology: a brief overview. Science **295**(5560), 1662–1664 (2002)

62. Klamt, S., Saez-Rodriguez, J., Gilles, E.D.: Structural and functional analysis of cellular networks with CellNetAnalyzer. BMC Syst. Biol. **1**(1), 2 (2007)

63. Küffner, R., Petri, T., Windhager, L., Zimmer, R.: Petri nets with fuzzy logic (PNFL): reverse engineering and parametrization. PLoS ONE **5**(9), e12807 (2010)

64. Lacroix, V., Cottret, L., Thébault, P., Sagot, M.F.: An introduction to metabolic networks and their structural analysis. IEEE/ACM Trans. Comput. Biol. Bioinform. (TCBB) **5**(4), 594–617 (2008)

65. Li, K.B.: ClustalW-MPI: ClustalW analysis using distributed and parallel computing. Bioinformatics **19**(12), 1585–1586 (2003). https://doi.org/10.1093/bioinformatics/btg192

66. Liu, F., Heiner, M., Yang, M.: Fuzzy stochastic Petri nets for modeling biological systems with uncertain kinetic parameters. PloS ONE **11**(2), e0149674 (2016)

67. Macklin, D.N., Ruggero, N.A., Covert, M.W.: The future of whole-cell modeling. Curr. Opin. Biotechnol. **28**, 111–115 (2014)

68. Mallipeddi, R., Suganthan, P.N., Pan, Q.K., Tasgetiren, M.F.: Differential evolution algorithm with ensemble of parameters and mutation strategies. Appl. Soft Comput. **11**(2), 1679–1696 (2011)

69. Marx, V.: Biology: the big challenges of big data. Nature **498**, 255–260 (2013)

70. Memeti, S., Li, L., Pllana, S., Kolodziej, J., Kessler, C.: Benchmarking OpenCL, OpenACC, OpenMP, and CUDA: programming productivity, performance, and energy consumption. In: Proceedings of the 2017 Workshop on Adaptive Resource Management and Scheduling for Cloud Computing, ARMS-CC 2017, pp. 1–6. ACM, New York (2017). https://doi.org/10.1145/3110355.3110356

71. Memeti, S., Pllana, S.: Accelerating DNA sequence analysis using Intel® Xeon Phi™. In: 2015 IEEE Trustcom/BigDataSE/ISPA, vol. 3, pp. 222–227, August 2015

72. Metlicka, M., Davendra, D.: Chaos driven discrete artificial bee algorithm for location and assignment optimisation problems. Swarm Evol. Comput. **25**, 15–28 (2015)

73. Mininno, E., Neri, F., Cupertino, F., Naso, D.: Compact differential evolution. IEEE Trans. Evol. Comput. **15**(1), 32–54 (2011)

74. Morris, M.K., Saez-Rodriguez, J., Sorger, P.K., Lauffenburger, D.A.: Logic-based models for the analysis of cell signaling networks. Biochemistry **49**(15), 3216–3224 (2010)

75. Mosterman, P.J., Vangheluwe, H.: Computer automated multi-paradigm modeling: an introduction. Simulation **80**(9), 433–450 (2004). https://doi.org/10.1177/0037549704050532

76. Nobile, M.S., Besozzi, D., Cazzaniga, P., Mauri, G.: GPU-accelerated simulations of mass-action kinetics models with cupSODA. J. Supercomput. **69**(1), 17–24 (2014)

77. Nobile, M.S., Cazzaniga, P., Tangherloni, A., Besozzi, D.: Graphics processing units in bioinformatics, computational biology and systems biology. Brief. Bioinform. **18**(5), 870–885 (2017). https://doi.org/10.1093/bib/bbw058

78. Nobile, M.S., Besozzi, D., Cazzaniga, P., Mauri, G., Pescini, D.: A GPU-based multi-swarm PSO method for parameter estimation in stochastic biological systems exploiting discrete-time target series. In: Giacobini, M., Vanneschi, L., Bush, W.S. (eds.) EvoBIO 2012. LNCS, vol. 7246, pp. 74–85. Springer, Heidelberg (2012). https://doi.org/10.1007/978-3-642-29066-4_7

79. Nobile, M.S., Besozzi, D., Cazzaniga, P., Mauri, G., Pescini, D.: Estimating reaction constants in stochastic biological systems with a multi-swarm PSO running on GPUs. In: Proceedings of the 14th Annual Conference Companion on Genetic and Evolutionary Computation, pp. 1421–1422. ACM (2012)

80. Nobile, M.S., Cazzaniga, P., Besozzi, D., Colombo, R., Mauri, G., Pasi, G.: Fuzzy self-tuning PSO: a settings-free algorithm for global optimization. Swarm Evol. Comput. **39**, 70–85 (2018)

81. Nobile, M.S., Cazzaniga, P., Besozzi, D., Pescini, D., Mauri, G.: cuTauLeaping: a GPU-powered tau-leaping stochastic simulator for massive parallel analyses of biological systems. PLoS ONE **9**(3), e91963 (2014)

82. Nobile, M.S., Mauri, G.: Accelerated analysis of biological parameters space using GPUs. In: Malyshkin, V. (ed.) PaCT 2017. LNCS, vol. 10421, pp. 70–81. Springer, Cham (2017). https://doi.org/10.1007/978-3-319-62932-2_6

83. Nobile, M.S., et al.: Computational intelligence for parameter estimation of biochemical systems. In: 2018 IEEE Congress on Evolutionary Computation (CEC), pp. 1–8. IEEE (2018)

84. NVIDIA: CUDA C Programming Guide, September 2016. http://docs.nvidia.com/cuda/cuda-c-programming-guide/. Accessed 06 Nov 2018

85. NVIDIA: What is GPU-Accelerated Computing? April 2017. http://www.nvidia.com/object/what-is-gpu-computing.html. Accessed 03 Nov 2018

86. O'Driscoll, A., et al.: HBLAST: parallelised sequence similarity–a Hadoop MapReducable basic local alignment search tool. J. Biomed. Inform. **54**, 58–64 (2015). https://doi.org/10.1016/j.jbi.2015.01.008, http://www.sciencedirect.com/science/article/pii/S1532046415000106

87. Opara, K.R., Arabas, J.: Differential evolution: a survey of theoretical analyses. Swarm Evol. Comput. (2018). https://doi.org/10.1016/j.swevo.2018.06.010

88. OpenMP: OpenMP 4.0 Specifications, July 2013. http://www.openmp.org/specifications/. Accessed 10 Mar 2018

89. Padua, D.: Encyclopedia of Parallel Computing. Springer, Heidelberg (2011)

90. Piotrowski, A.P.: Review of differential evolution population size. Swarm Evol. Comput. **32**, 1–24 (2017)

91. Piotrowski, A.P.: aL-SHADE optimization algorithms with population-wide inertia. Inf. Sci. **468**, 117–141 (2018)

92. Piotrowski, A.P., Napiorkowski, J.J.: Some metaheuristics should be simplified. Inf. Sci. **427**, 32–62 (2018)

93. Piotrowski, A.P., Napiorkowski, J.J.: Step-by-step improvement of JADE and SHADE-based algorithms: success or failure? Swarm Evol. Comput. (2018). https://doi.org/10.1016/j.swevo.2018.03.007

94. Poli, R., Kennedy, J., Blackwell, T.: Particle swarm optimization. Swarm Intell. **1**(1), 33–57 (2007)

95. Poovathingal, S.K., Gunawan, R.: Global parameter estimation methods for stochastic biochemical systems. BMC Bioinform. **11**(1), 414 (2010)

96. Provost, A., Bastin, G.: Metabolic flux analysis: an approach for solving non-stationary underdetermined systems. In: CD-Rom Proceedings 5th MATHMOD Conference, Paper, vol. 207. Citeseer (2006)

97. Qin, A.K., Huang, V.L., Suganthan, P.N.: Differential evolution algorithm with strategy adaptation for global numerical optimization. IEEE Trans. Evol. Comput. **13**(2), 398–417 (2009)

98. Qu, B.Y., Suganthan, P.N., Liang, J.J.: Differential evolution with neighborhood mutation for multimodal optimization. IEEE Trans. Evol. Comput. **16**(5), 601–614 (2012)

99. Saastamoinen, K., Ketola, J., Turunen, E.: Defining athlete's anaerobic and aerobic thresholds by using similarity measures and differential evolution. In: 2004 IEEE International Conference on Systems, Man and Cybernetics, vol. 2, pp. 1331–1335. IEEE (2004)
100. Sadasivam, G.S., Baktavatchalam, G.: A novel approach to multiple sequence alignment using Hadoop data grids. In: Proceedings of the 2010 Workshop on Massive Data Analytics on the Cloud, MDAC 2010, pp. 2:1–2:7. ACM, New York (2010). https://doi.org/10.1145/1779599.1779601
101. Sanders, W.H.: Integrated frameworks for multi-level and multi-formalism modeling. In: Proceedings 8th International Workshop on Petri Nets and Performance Models (Cat. No. PR00331), pp. 2–9, September 1999. https://doi.org/10.1109/PNPM.1999.796527
102. Sanders, W.H., Courtney, T., Deavours, D.D., Daly, D., Derisavi, S., Lam, V.V.: Multi-formalism and multi-solution-method modeling frameworks: the Möbius approach (2003)
103. Schilling, C.H., Letscher, D., Palsson, B.Ø.: Theory for the systemic definition of metabolic pathways and their use in interpreting metabolic function from a pathway-oriented perspective. J. Theor. Biol. 203(3), 229–248 (2000)
104. Senkerik, R., Pluhacek, M., Oplatkova, Z.K., Davendra, D., Zelinka, I.: Investigation on the differential evolution driven by selected six chaotic systems in the task of reactor geometry optimization. In: 2013 IEEE Congress on Evolutionary Computation (CEC), pp. 3087–3094. IEEE (2013)
105. Senkerik, R., Viktorin, A., Pluhacek, M., Janostik, J., Davendra, D.: On the influence of different randomization and complex network analysis for differential evolution. In: 2016 IEEE Congress on Evolutionary Computation (CEC), pp. 3346–3353. IEEE (2016)
106. Senkerik, R., Viktorin, A., Pluhacek, M., Kadavy, T., Oplatkova, Z.K.: Differential evolution and chaotic series. In: 2018 25th International Conference on Systems, Signals and Image Processing (IWSSIP), pp. 1–5. IEEE (2018)
107. Senkerik, R., Zelinka, I., Pluhacek, M., Davendra, D., Oplatková Kominkova, Z.: Chaos enhanced differential evolution in the task of evolutionary control of selected set of discrete chaotic systems. Sci. World J. 2014, 1–12 (2014)
108. Skanderova, L., Fabian, T.: Differential evolution dynamics analysis by complex networks. Soft Comput. 21(7), 1817–1831 (2017)
109. Skanderova, L., Fabian, T., Zelinka, I.: Differential evolution dynamics modeled by longitudinal social network. J. Intell. Syst. 26(3), 523–529 (2017)
110. Skanderova, L., Fabian, T., Zelinka, I.: Analysis of causality-driven changes of diffusion speed in non-Markovian temporal networks generated on the basis of differential evolution dynamics. Swarm Evol. Comput. 44, 212–227 (2018)
111. Sneddon, M.W., Faeder, J.R., Emonet, T.: Efficient modeling, simulation and coarse-graining of biological complexity with NFsim. Nat. Methods 8(2), 177 (2011)
112. Spark, A.: Apache Spark project. https://spark.apache.org/. Accessed 03 Nov 2018
113. Stegle, O., Teichmann, S.A., Marioni, J.C.: Computational and analytical challenges in single-cell transcriptomics. Nat. Rev. Genet. 16(3), 133 (2015)
114. Stelling, J.: Mathematical models in microbial systems biology. Curr. Opin. Microbiol. 7(5), 513–518 (2004)
115. Stone, J.E., Gohara, D., Shi, G.: OpenCL: a parallel programming standard for heterogeneous computing systems. Comput. Sci. Eng. 12(1–3), 66–73 (2010)

116. Storn, R., Price, K.: Differential evolution–a simple and efficient heuristic for global optimization over continuous spaces. J. Glob. Optim. **11**, 341–359 (1997)
117. Swainston, N., et al.: Recon 2.2: from reconstruction to model of human metabolism. Metabolomics **12**(7), 109 (2016)
118. Szallasi, Z., Stelling, J., Periwal, V.: System Modeling in Cellular Biology: From Concepts to Nuts and Bolts. The MIT Press, Cambridge (2006)
119. Talay, D.: Numerical Solution of Stochastic Differential Equations. Taylor & Francis, Milton Park (1994)
120. Tanabe, R., Fukunaga, A.: Success-history based parameter adaptation for differential evolution. In: 2013 IEEE Congress on Evolutionary Computation (CEC), pp. 71–78. IEEE (2013)
121. Tanabe, R., Fukunaga, A.S.: Improving the search performance of SHADE using linear population size reduction. In: 2014 IEEE Congress on Evolutionary Computation (CEC), pp. 1658–1665. IEEE (2014)
122. Tanabe, R., Fukunaga, A.S.: How far are we from an optimal, adaptive DE? In: 14th International Conference on Parallel Problem Solving from Nature (PPSN XIV). IEEE (2016, accepted)
123. Tangherloni, A., Nobile, M.S., Besozzi, D., Mauri, G., Cazzaniga, P.: LASSIE: simulating large-scale models of biochemical systems on GPUs. BMC Bioinform. **18**(1), 246 (2017)
124. Teijeiro, D., Pardo, X.C., Penas, D.R., González, P., Banga, J.R., Doallo, R.: A cloud-based enhanced differential evolution algorithm for parameter estimation problems in computational systems biology. Clust. Comput. **20**(3), 1937–1950 (2017)
125. Trivedi, K.S.: SHARPE 2002: symbolic hierarchical automated reliability and performance evaluator. In: Proceedings International Conference on Dependable Systems and Networks, p. 544, June 2002. https://doi.org/10.1109/DSN.2002.1028975
126. Turunen, E.: Mathematics Behind Fuzzy Logic. Physica-Verlag, Heidelberg (1999)
127. Turunen, E.: Using GUHA data mining method in analyzing road traffic accidents occurred in the years 2004–2008 in Finland. Data Sci. Eng. **2**(3), 224–231 (2017)
128. Vazquez, A., Liu, J., Zhou, Y., Oltvai, Z.N.: Catabolic efficiency of aerobic glycolysis: the Warburg effect revisited. BMC Syst. Biol. **4**(1), 58 (2010)
129. Viebke, A., Pllana, S.: The potential of the Intel (R) Xeon Phi for supervised deep learning. In: 2015 IEEE 17th International Conference on High Performance Computing and Communications, pp. 758–765, August 2015. https://doi.org/10.1109/HPCC-CSS-ICESS.2015.45
130. Viktorin, A., Pluhacek, M., Senkerik, R.: Network based linear population size reduction in shade. In: 2016 International Conference on Intelligent Networking and Collaborative Systems (INCoS), pp. 86–93. IEEE (2016)
131. Viktorin, A., Senkerik, R., Pluhacek, M., Kadavy, T.: Towards better population sizing for differential evolution through active population analysis with complex network. In: Barolli, L., Terzo, O. (eds.) CISIS 2017. AISC, vol. 611, pp. 225–235. Springer, Cham (2018). https://doi.org/10.1007/978-3-319-61566-0_22
132. Viktorin, A., Senkerik, R., Pluhacek, M., Kadavy, T., Zamuda, A.: Distance based parameter adaptation for success-history based differential evolution. Swarm Evol. Comput. https://doi.org/10.1016/j.swevo.2018.10.013. Accessed 12 Nov 2018
133. Viktorin, A., Senkerik, R., Pluhacek, M., Zamuda, A.: Steady success clusters in differential evolution. In: 2016 IEEE Symposium Series on Computational Intelligence (SSCI), pp. 1–8. IEEE (2016)

134. Vitabile, S., Conti, V., Lanza, B., Cusumano, D., Sorbello, F.: Metabolic networks robustness: theory, simulations and results. J. Interconnect. Netw. **12**(03), 221–240 (2011)

135. Vitabile, S., Conti, V., Lanza, L., Cusumano, D., Sorbello, F.: Topological information, flux balance analysis, and extreme pathways extraction for metabolic networks behaviour investigation. In: Workshop on Italian Neural Network, vol. 234, pp. 66–73. IOS Press (2011)

136. Vitello, G., Alongi, A., Conti, V., Vitabile, S.: A bio-inspired cognitive agent for autonomous urban vehicles routing optimization. IEEE Trans. Cogn. Dev. Syst. **9**(1), 5–15 (2017)

137. Wiback, S.J., Palsson, B.O.: Extreme pathway analysis of human red blood cell metabolism. Biophys. J. **83**(2), 808–818 (2002)

138. Wienke, S., Springer, P., Terboven, C., an Mey, D.: OpenACC—first experiences with real-world applications. In: Kaklamanis, C., Papatheodorou, T., Spirakis, P.G. (eds.) Euro-Par 2012. LNCS, vol. 7484, pp. 859–870. Springer, Heidelberg (2012). https://doi.org/10.1007/978-3-642-32820-6_85

139. Wolkenhauer, O.: Why model? Front. Physiol. **5**, 21 (2014)

140. Wu, G., Shen, X., Li, H., Chen, H., Lin, A., Suganthan, P.N.: Ensemble of differential evolution variants. Inf. Sci. **423**, 172–186 (2018)

141. Wynn, M.L., Consul, N., Merajver, S.D., Schnell, S.: Logic-based models in systems biology: a predictive and parameter-free network analysis method. Integr. Biol. 4(11), 1323–1337 (2012)

142. Zamuda, A., Brest, J.: Environmental framework to visualize emergent artificial forest ecosystems. Inf. Sci. **220**, 522–540 (2013). https://doi.org/10.1016/j.ins.2012.07.031

143. Zamuda, A., Brest, J.: Vectorized procedural models for animated trees reconstruction using differential evolution. Inf. Sci. **278**, 1–21 (2014)

144. Zamuda, A., Brest, J.: Self-adaptive control parameters' randomization frequency and propagations in differential evolution. Swarm Evol. Comput. **25**, 72–99 (2015)

145. Zamuda, A., Hernández Sosa, J.D.: Differential evolution and underwater glider path planning applied to the short-term opportunistic sampling of dynamic mesoscale ocean structures. Appl. Soft Comput. **24**, 95–108 (2014)

146. Zamuda, A., Nicolau, M., Zarges, C.: A black-box discrete optimization benchmarking (BB-DOB) pipeline survey: taxonomy, evaluation, and ranking. In: Proceedings of the Genetic and Evolutionary Computation Conference Companion (GECCO 2018), pp. 1777–1782 (2018)

147. Zamuda, A., Sosa, J.D.H., Adler, L.: Constrained differential evolution optimization for underwater glider path planning in sub-mesoscale eddy sampling. Appl. Soft Comput. **42**, 93–118 (2016)

148. Zamuda, A., Sosa, J.D.H.: Success history applied to expert system for underwater glider path planning using differential evolution. Expert. Syst. Appl. **119**, 155–170 (2019)

149. Zhang, J., Sanderson, A.C.: JADE: adaptive differential evolution with optional external archive. IEEE Trans. Evol. Comput. **13**(5), 945–958 (2009)

150. Zhou, Y., Liepe, J., Sheng, X., Stumpf, M.P., Barnes, C.: GPU accelerated biochemical network simulation. Bioinformatics **27**(6), 874–876 (2011)

Cloud-Based High Throughput Virtual Screening in Novel Drug Discovery

Abdurrahman Olğaç[1,2(✉)] [ID], Aslı Türe[3] [ID], Simla Olğaç[4] [ID],
and Steffen Möller[5] [ID]

[1] Laboratory of Molecular Modeling, Evias Pharmaceutical R&D Ltd.,
06830 Ankara, Turkey
aolgac@evias.com.tr
[2] Department of Pharmaceutical Chemistry, Faculty of Pharmacy,
Gazi University, 06330 Ankara, Turkey
abdurrahman.olgac@gazi.edu.tr
[3] Department of Pharmaceutical Chemistry, Faculty of Pharmacy,
Marmara University, 34668 Istanbul, Turkey
asli.demirci@marmara.edu.tr
[4] Department of Biochemistry, Faculty of Pharmacy,
Gazi University, 06330 Ankara, Turkey
csimla@gazi.edu.tr
[5] Institute for Biostatistics and Informatics in Medicine and Ageing Research
(IBIMA), Rostock University Medical Center, 18057 Rostock, Germany
steffen.moeller@uni-rostock.de

Abstract. Drug discovery and development requires the integration of multiple
scientific and technological disciplines in chemistry, biology and extensive use
of information technology. Computer Aided Drug Discovery (CADD) methods
are being used in this work area with several different workflows. Virtual
screening (VS) is one of the most often applied CADD methods used in rational
drug design, which may be applied in early stages of drug discovery pipeline.
The increasing number of modular and scalable cloud-based computational
platforms can assist the needs in VS studies. Such platforms are being developed
to try to help researchers with various types of applications to prepare and guide
the drug discovery and development pipeline. They are designed to perform VS
efficiently, aimed to identify commercially available lead-like and drug-like
compounds to be acquired and tested. Chemical datasets can be built, libraries
can be analyzed, and structure-based or ligand-based VS studies can be performed with cloud technologies. Such platforms could also be adapted to be
included in different stages of the pharmaceutical R&D process to rationalize the
needs, e.g. to repurpose drugs, with various computational scalability options.
This chapter introduces basic concepts and tools by outlining the general
workflows of VS, and their integration to the cloud platforms. This may be a
seed for further inter-disciplinary development of VS to be applied by drug
hunters.

Keywords: Drug discovery · Virtual screening ·
High performance computing · Cloud computing

J. Kołodziej and H. González-Vélez (Eds.): cHiPSet, LNCS 11400, pp. 250–278, 2019.
https://doi.org/10.1007/978-3-030-16272-6_9

1 Introduction

Pharmaceutical drug discovery is a long-lasting and costly process, spanning over 12 to 15 years and costing about 1–2 billion US Dollars [1]. The process to identify new active pharmaceutical ingredients (API) [2] starts with target identification and validation steps and follows hit identification, lead discovery and lead optimization to acquire safe and effective new drug molecules at the preclinical stage [3]. Biological screening is used to identify possible target of a hit molecule as a developable drug-candidate as the first step in drug discovery. Advances in systematic biological screening have generated automated parallel biological screening technologies, called high throughput screening (HTS) [4]. Virtual screening (VS) is a widely applied computational approach, which is performed as a hit identification method in early stages of drug discovery pipeline. VS protocols involve searching chemical libraries to identify hit compounds with a putative affinity for a specific biological target (enzyme or a receptor) for further development.

CADD methods in conjunction with VS studies emerged as valuable tools to speed up this long process and limit the cost expansion of R&D. Such studies demand a strong combination of computational resources and skills, biochemical understanding and medicinal motivation.

Effects of drugs in the human body are investigated with two main parameters, namely pharmacokinetics and pharmacodynamics [5]. While pharmacokinetic studies investigate the fate of drug substances during absorption, distribution, metabolism and elimination (ADME) processes, pharmacodynamics determines the required concentration of drug to be delivered at the site of action and the biochemical and physiological effect, which may be responsible for the targeted biological response.

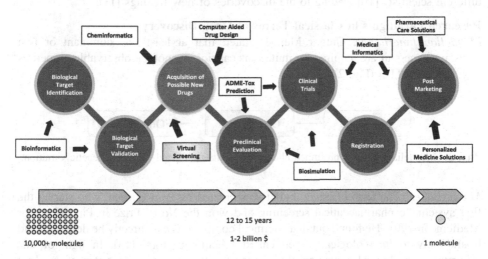

Fig. 1. Drug discovery pipeline presented together with some of the computational approaches which are used to rationalize the process.

CADD implementations deal with computational calculations of both pharma-cokinetics and pharmacodynamics parameters. Therefore, ADME and even toxicity (Tox) properties of a given compound can be predicted with computational chemistry programs prior to any experimental studies. Furthermore, *in silico* approaches can also be applied to determine the putative interactions between a ligand and a receptor (Fig. 1).

In this chapter, we briefly address challenges and applications of biochemical - and computational-drug discovery and development approaches, and their transformation in VS to be applied in cloud platforms.

2   Background

2.1   Drug Discovery and Development

Until the 19th century, the drug discovery and development process was based on the trial and error learning approach for diagnosis and curing the diseases. The therapeutic effect was completely produced with natural products (NPs) [6]. These drugs were obtained from the whole or a fraction of the NPs that contain the active pharmaceutical ingredient [7]. Natural compounds are an important source for drugs, helped with improved sensitivity and better means for their biochemical separation [8].

Starting with the first successful *in vitro* organic synthesis in laboratory by Wöhler [9], it was clear that organic compounds could be produced out of the bodies of the living organisms. However, to synthesize chemically different organic compounds, structural information had to be explained in a more efficient way. In 1858, Kekulé proposed structural theories which successfully followed by different theories from the different scientists [10] leading to the discoveries of new findings [11].

Research Paradigms in Classical Terms of Drug Discovery
Mendelian Inheritance. Gregor Mendel stated that at least one dominant or two recessive gene pair are required for mutations causing phenotype-observable properties (e.g. diseases) [12] (Fig. 2).

Fig. 2. Mendelian genetics presumed phenotypic traits to depend on single genetic variation.

Magic Bullet. The term of magic bullet was created by Paul Ehrlich, who started the first systematic pharmaceutical screening and won the Nobel Prize in Physiology or Medicine in 1908. He found out that chemical compounds can directly be delivered and bound only to its biological target, called 'chemoreceptors' [13]. In light of this information, biological targets are determined to play role in the first step of the drug discovery depending on the developing technologies and knowledge [14] (Fig. 3).

Fig. 3. Summary of the biological understanding after the "magic bullet" approach.

Research Paradigms in Modern Terms of Drug Discovery

Polygenicity. It has been shown that many common diseases can occur as a result of mutations on multiple genes, such as diabetes, asthma and heart disease. Such diseases may develop as a result of an interplay of genetical inheritance, mutations on multiple genes or contribution of environmental factors [15] (Fig. 4).

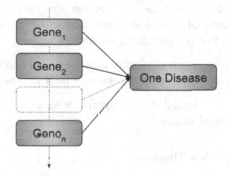

Fig. 4. Common diseases are polygenic, and this is one of the biggest challenges in the field.

Magic Shotgun. The term of magic shotgun has emerged as a result of the detection of secondary effect properties, such as adverse effects associated with the ability of the drug to affect multiple targets. This concept is related to the development of drugs with high selectivity, and to predict the potential adverse effects prior to clinical trials [16] (Fig. 5).

Fig. 5. Single compound may affect multiple targets. Such side-effects may be positive or undesired.

Several *in silico* approaches have been developed to predict side-effects and to repurpose drugs that are already on the market.

Individualized Medicine. The genetic polymorphisms of drug targets, metabolizing enzymes, or transporters may explain differences in the molecular pathophysiology of patients, even of those who are assigned with the same diagnosis [17]. The aim is to find drugs to compensate genetic deficiencies, i.e. to fight the disease at its roots. As of today, with the transcriptome and the genetic parameters obtained from a patient's tissue or blood, one can be informed about their contributions to disorders [18]. For instance, pharmacogenetics investigates how a genetic variation affects the binding site of a drug. That may suggest a higher dosage because of a disturbed molecular recognition.

Target Fishing. It can be regarded as the inverse screening wherein the ligand is profiled against a wide array of biological targets to elucidate its molecular mechanism of action by experimental or computational means.

Drug Repositioning. An approach to identify new medicinal applications for approved drugs to treat other diseases because the drugs may bind to other receptors.

Polypharmacology. Special ligand design approach to exert an effect on multiple disease-associated biological targets.

2.2   Molecular Recognition Theories

Key and Lock. In 1894, Emil Fischer proposed the model of key and lock for the molecules bearing potential effects on biological systems. According to this model, it is assumed that a ligand binds to the active site of its target which behaves like a key that fits its lock [19, 20] (Fig. 6).

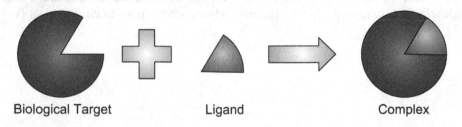

Biological Target   Ligand   Complex

Fig. 6. Key and lock model.

Induced Fit. In 1958, it was proposed by Daniel Koshland to consider the conformational changes during the interaction between the ligand and its biological target, which wasn't considered in the lock-and-key theory of Fischer. In this model, optimum-compatible binding is occurred by small but expected conformational changes during the interaction between the ligand and the biological target [36, 37]. Later, this specific conformation of the ligand has been referenced as the bioactive conformation (Fig. 7).

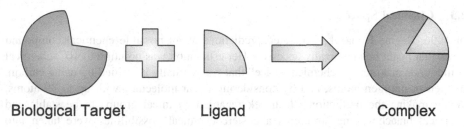

Biological Target   **Ligand**   **Complex**

Fig. 7. Induced fit model.

Thermodynamics in Ligand-Protein Binding. During the binding process of ligands to their biological targets, it is known that conformational arrangements and desolvation occur, with the help of specific physicochemical interactions [38] (Fig. 8).

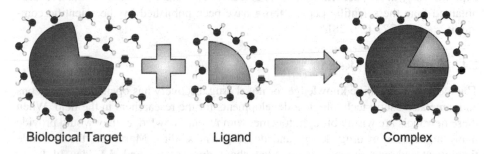

Biological Target   **Ligand**   **Complex**

Fig. 8. Desolvation effect and thermodynamics in ligand-protein binding.

The most important strategy in the process of developing novel drug candidates is to increase the affinity of binding of the ligand to its target. The energy change after the binding process is quantitatively expressed by logarithm of K_d or K_i values. These values are related to Gibbs free energy of binding [21].

$$\Delta G_{binding} = RTlnK_d \sim RTlnK_i \qquad (1)$$

In this equation, R is the gas constant, T is the absolute temperature, K_d is the equilibrium constant and K_i is the inhibitory constant that exist in the Cheng-Prusoff equation [40].

In non-covalent thermodynamic binding process, ligand-protein binding energy change is occurred and two thermodynamic quantities, the enthalpy change (ΔH) and entropy change (-TΔS), determine the sign and magnitude of the binding free energy [33, 39].

$$\Delta G_{binding} = \Delta H_{binding} - T\Delta S_{binding} \qquad (2)$$

2.3 Chemical Space

In 1996, Regine Bohacek, generated predictions about possible chemical compound types that might be chemically accessed. Her estimation was pointing to 10^{60} chemical compounds making up "chemical space" that was virtually identified by using carbon, oxygen or nitrogen atoms, and by considering linear molecules with up to 30 atoms. While making the predictions, Bohacek regarded chemical groups to be stable and chemical branches, ring structures and stereochemical possibilities were taken into account [22].

In later studies, "the limits of the chemical space" was drawn to be between 10^{18}–10^{200}, according to the results of the analyses by different methods and descriptors. Although there are many reports about this range to be accepted as Bohacek defined. But it is expected that this number will continuously increase by the discovery of new chemical skeletons [23–26]. Additionally, the number of organic compounds accessed experimentally is 10^8, according to CAS and Beilstein databases which contain records obtained from the scientific papers, those have been published by the scientific community, since 1771 [27, 28].

2.4 Rational Drug Design

The increasing scientific knowledge for novel drug discovery has opened new horizons and generated useful technological developments for the researchers in the field. When these new tools are wisely brought together with recent knowledge, they would provide many advantages in drug design and development studies. Moreover, the available theoretical and experimental knowledge about drug safety and the idea of being appropriate for human use generate extra difficulties for drug design and development [29]. It is known that not all candidate molecules with high potency can reach to a drug status due to several reasons such as inefficient systemic exposure, unwanted side effects and off-target effects. Also, a drug may not be right for every patient due to the genetic variations and off-target binding. This also effects drugs that are already on the market (Table 1).

However, molecular reasoning may give second chances for drugs that once failed in late clinical studies (at great expense) or that have been retracted from clinical use. With an improved molecular understanding, and with hindsight from the now feasible pharmacogenetics and –genomics, these compounds have a chance to find their niche for a reentry.

Conventional drug design and development approaches are associated with high affinity binding of a ligand to its target. In rational drug discovery studies, evaluating the ligands by only trial-and-error approach has lost its validity and assessing their binding to the target related diseases is insufficient [30]. By taking control of some parameters like off-target binding, ADME-Tox and bioavailability properties of the molecules that have appropriate binding properties should also be discovered for the drug candidates [49]. Therefore, revising the classical strategies with "rational" approaches has become substantial. This process is called *reverse pharmacology* or *target-based drug discovery*. In this recent approach, the questions about "Which chemotypes will be worked on?" and "Why?" should also be considered during drug design and development studies, before directly evaluating the target binding properties of the molecules [29, 30].

Table 1. Definition of the key terms related with informatic approaches used in early stage drug discovery.

Bioinformatics. The discipline responsible for biological data recording and interpretation using information technologies. Some of its applications on drug discovery include the detection of protein binding pocket, prediction of protein-protein interactions, occurrence of mutations, analysis of the biological sequences of macromolecules (e.g. similarity searches and fingerprint matches), estimation of 3D structures of biological macromolecules [31].

Cheminformatics. The discipline which accumulates and processes the chemistry related data, using information technologies. Some of its applications on drug discovery include construction of the 2D and 3D structures, storing and searching the chemical data, building chemical compound databases and datasets, QSAR / QSPR, estimation of ADME-Tox properties [31]. It can also be used to map the chemical space of compound libraries.

Pharmacoinformatics. The discipline which combines the cheminformatics and bioinformatics tools for pharma-related processes [32, 33].

---

3   Computer Aided Drug Design (CADD)

Development of mathematical formulas to calculate the potential and kinetic energies of biomolecular systems has made possible the implementation of such complex calculations with computers [34]. CADD is applicable for hit molecule discovery for new different chemotypes and for designing new derivatives.

CADD processes may be divided into molecular mechanical methods and quantum mechanical methods. In both techniques, the results are obtained through energy-based calculations. Molecular mechanics deals with the calculations at the molecular level that can be performed on an atomic basis, while quantum mechanics involves electron related complex calculations performed at the quantum level [34].

During existence of the obscurity in drug discovery studies, it is hard to reach the desired target. But, the physicochemical parameter as a factor can be useful about this topic by measuring the ADME properties [30, 35]. Also, the drug-candidate should be bound to its target with high affinity [30]. In relation to that, drug design processes are carried out within the framework of selected strategies, with the acquisition of three-dimensional bioactive conformation of the ligands. CADD is used for identifying and designing biologically active compounds and this field can be synergistically integrated with all other medicinal chemistry related fields like pharmacology, biology and chemistry [36].

3.1   Ligand-Based Drug Discovery

It is possible to store the chemical and biological information in special databases to preserve the molecular features and their biological effects obtained from a series of assays. If there is no molecular level structural data about the biological target, previously obtained structure-activity data can be used in CADD studies to find and analyze the trend between the known compounds and their activity retrospectively, then to design and discover new chemical entities prospectively [37]. A main workflow of ligand-based studies addresses the generation of a model by training on a series of compounds and subsequent testing stage of the model with test series of compounds. Later, the generated model(s) can be validated with an external series of compounds which were not used during model generation. Then the model can be used to virtually screen chemical databases within the applicability domain of the model (Fig. 9).

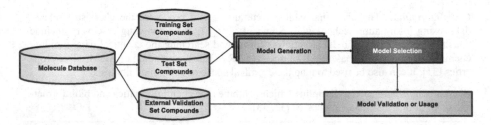

Fig. 9. Basic workflow of ligand-based modeling applications.

Quantitative Structure Activity/Property Relationships (QSAR/QSPR). In 1863, an approach about the relationship between chemical structure and biological activity was proposed by Cros [38]. After that, in 1868 Crum-Brown and Fraser evaluated this correlation in molecular level and described following equation to computationally predict the biological response (Φ) to be identified as the function of the chemical compound (C) [38, 39].

$$\Phi = f(C) \tag{3}$$

In the course of the history, many researchers have conducted studies to relate physicochemical properties and biological effects of compounds with different approaches. Through these studies, the necessity to consider molecular substitutions has emerged to try to explain biological effect or physicochemical property of a chemical structure. In 1937, Louis Hammett compared ionization rates of benzene derivatives substituted in various positions [40]. The first quantitative parameter was determined as sigma (σ), the potential electronic contribution value, which is defined by calculating electronic substituent constant values. This was the first identified quantitative parameter [38]. Then the first steric parameter for ester hydrolysis was determined by Taft as E_s constant [41]. Many other two-dimensional parameters have been continued to be developed for being used in QSAR studies [38]. Later, a multi-parametric formula was presented by Corwin Hansch that brought these parameters together. The formula was designed to calculate minimal concentration needed to mathematically formulate the biological activity, as logarithm of concentration and was measured with several independent factors in different cases; such as partition coefficient (log P), aromatic substituent constant (π), electronic substituent constant (σ), steric parameter (E_s). Free-Wilson [42], Fujita-Ban [43], A Mixed Approach - Based on Hansch and Free-Wilson Analysis [44], and Kubinyi Bilinear Analysis Method [45] are some of the first generated models used in QSAR analysis.

When all the steps are evaluated, it can be observed that QSAR has different applications. Structural activity or physicochemical property studies performed with one independent variable are named 0D-QSAR calculations and the studies with multivariate equations are called 1D-QSAR. In such equations, log P and Hammett constant can be used as independent variables. Studies that take into account the molecular descriptors and fingerprints containing information about structural and bonding characteristics resulting from the two-dimensional molecular presentation are called 2D-QSAR, if extra structural information (e.g. chirality) is included in studies these studies are named as 2.5D QSAR [46].

The efforts to explain the binding orientations of the ligands have emerged 3D-QSAR, together with the help of the developments in 3D molecular understanding through the experimental methods, force-field methods and improved molecular visualization technologies. Implementation of this approach is accomplished by forming equally divided grids in the 3D coordinate system and the surface interaction areas of the chemical compounds are determined by the following analysis methods [47] (Table 2).

Table 2. Summary of some of the 3D-QSAR approaches.

Comparative Molecular Field Analysis (CoMFA). CoMFA is a subtype of the 3D-QSAR study, which includes steric and electronic fields (Lennard-Jones and Coulomb potentials) generated on the bioactive conformation of the compounds in the training set. In CoMFA studies, it is only possible to analyze the effects of enthalpic properties on ligand-protein binding [47].
Comparative Molecular Similarity Index Analysis (CoMSIA). To explain the structure activity relationships by considering major contributions obtained by steric, electrostatic, hydrophobic, and hydrogen bond donors (HBD) or hydrogen bond acceptors (HBA) properties are added into CoMFA and this generated CoMSIA analysis [48].
Receptor-based QSAR. In this study model, which is carried out using a combination of ligand-based and structure-based approaches, bioactive conformation of the ligands is obtained by structure-based methods. Afterwards, 3D-QSAR studies are conducted through this bioactive conformation [47].

Pharmacophore Modeling. A pharmacophore aggregates functional groups of chemical compounds which are responsible for the biological response and which exhibit appropriate interaction with biological target. The term pharmacophore modeling refers to the identification and 3D display of important pharmacophore groups to illustrate the basic interactions between the ligand and the receptor. Pharmacophore modeling is generally applied to determine common structural features within a series of similar or diverse molecules by subtracting 3D maps. Once determined, the generated pharmacophore hypotheses may be used to virtually screen and to predict the biological activity of other molecules [37]. The model is generally obtained from the information belonging to the ligands. However, it is also possible to generate a pharmacophore model from the receptor itself or with a combined approach as well.

After the formation of possible bioactive conformers of the compounds, pharmacophore model can be generated in 3D by aligning the structures and mapping the 3D binding properties. More than one pharmacophore hypothesis can be generated and the most suitable one(s) can be identified by enrichment factor within their applicability domain. While generating the model(s), the optimum volume of each pharmacophore property takes the major interest.

The aim of pharmacophore modeling is to determine the optimum volume for the identified properties. If identified volumes are larger than required, the selectivity of active compounds by this model decreases and active and inactive compounds can be found together by using this model. Conversely, if the fields are smaller than they need to be, the active compounds cannot be identified by pharmacophore screening. While creating a pharmacophore model; HBA and HBD features, hydrophobic (aliphatic or aromatic) properties and negative/positive charges can be used. Besides, it is possible to identify the desirable/undesirable regions or features without any specificity [37]. Most pharmacophore modeling programs create these properties according to optimized ligand-receptor interactions. The ideas behind pharmacophores are also applied to specify new compounds that aggregate as many pharmacophores, e.g. from a series of *in silico* ligand docking experiments or after a first *in vitro* validation. The assembly of new compounds can be iterative, i.e. growing from existing binders, or starting a *de novo* design of novel drugs.

Machine Learning (ML). Relations between ligand/receptor structural properties and biochemical effects are found by statistical models. With the advent of computational chemistry and advances in structural biology, an increasing number of features may be identified *in silico* for any given ligand and receptor, which may affect virtual screening. The integration of all these data sources and tools allows for the formulation of many models.

ML covers the computer-aided development of models (or rules) and their evaluation. The use of ML techniques for drug discovery has been increasing recently both in ligand-based and structure-based studies to find rules from a set of molecular features and to predict a specific property [49]. Estimation of ADME-Tox properties by the use of physicochemical descriptors, generation of hit or lead molecules with the studies on prediction of biological activity, development of homology models, determination of bioactive conformation by the help of docking studies or pharmacophore modeling are some of the examples of ML applications in drug discovery [49].

ML can be applied as regression or classification models [49]. In the regression model, quantitative models are formed automatically. Statistically the most appropriate model is selected from the generated ones. Classifiers utilize such models to cluster the data. The learning process is carried out by known characteristics of the molecules to predict their activities/properties. In the classification model, the branches are formed on a classification tree. Biological and chemical data are placed on the leaves of the branches of the tree. It can be generated and used for various statistical decision-making scenarios. Artificial neural networks, support vector machines, decision trees and random forest techniques are some of the most applied ML techniques used in drug discovery studies [49].

3.2   Structure-Based Drug Design

Experimental studies on elucidation of the 3D structures of biological macromolecules are generally performed by x-ray crystallography and NMR methods [50] (Fig. 10). Obtained structural information about the macromolecules is stored in regional protein databases. There are three major regional databases (Protein Data Bank, PDB) for storing 3D the crystal structures of these macromolecules such as RCSB PDB [51–54] (USA), PDBe [54, 55] (Europe), PDBj [54, 56] (Japan). Likewise, the 3D structures of relatively small biological macromolecules obtained by NMR techniques are stored in the Biological Magnetic Resonance Data Bank [54, 57] (BMRB). Records stored in these databases are synchronized via the Worldwide PDB [54] (wwPDB) organization.

Fig. 10. Obtaining the 3D protein structure.

Homology Modeling. Homology modeling techniques are used to predict 3D representations of biomolecular structures. The model generation is done with the sequence of monomers (nucleotides or amino acids). The applied algorithm transfers spatial arrangements from high-resolution crystal structures of other phylogenetically sequence-similar biological structures [58].

Protein sequence information is stored in reference databases such as UniProt [59], where the information on the protein sequence and its functions are collected in one place. The UniProt database offers other web services such as BLAST [60, 61] and Clustal Omega [62] where sequence similarity and alignment can be retrieved. Consensus annotation across protein families across species is aggregated in PFAM [63] with functional annotation (Fig. 11).

Fig. 11. Basic workflow for homology model generation.

Docking. A structure-based simulation method which is used to predict the 3D binding modes and molecular interactions between ligands and their biological targets (Table 3). This technique is based on the thermodynamic calculations by following the determination of the possible binding orientation of the ligands and the proteins with appropriate interactions in the active site. The docking scores are determined based on these interactions and conformational rearrangement costs which help evaluating the generated results [58, 64, 65] (Fig. 12).

Table 3. Docking concepts, and their limitations.

Technology	Limitations
Rigid Docking. Receptor structure is treated as a rigid body and the ligands are prepared with conformational sample(s), then fit into the active site of the protein	The overall protein structure and its active site residues are flexible, this affects the binding orientations of the ligands in docking results
Induced-fit Docking. Flexibility of the active site residues is considered for the protein and these flexible active site residues flexibly adapt to accommodate the ligand	It is a computationally expensive approach that requires careful arrangement of the docking parameters and cuts off the values prior to docking simulation
Covalent Docking. In this method, binding region of the receptor that ligands bind covalently is identified and the docking procedure is performed in this specific condition	This method may generate chemically wrong binding pattern and incorrect binding pose but lowers the computational search costs of docking
Peptide Docking. Peptide docking method is used to determine binding modes of peptide structures in the active site of its biological target	Peptides, or fractions of proteins, are large and flexible ligands and hence difficult to parameterize and computationally expensive compared to the small molecules
Protein-Protein Docking. It is the general name of the docking method that is used to predict protein-protein or protein-DNA interactions those are taking place biologically	This is the most computationally demanding approach to simulate the interactions, due to the size and complexity of the macromolecules
Reverse Docking. It can be applied for target fishing the drugs or active substances, or to become aware of side-effects	Conceptionally, this approach requires a catalog of configurations for screening many targets by docking [66]

Fig. 12. Basic workflow for docking simulations.

Molecular Dynamics (MD). MD is a technique to simulate the dynamics of connected atoms in a joint molecular system of ligands and their biological targets by considering environmental factors (temperature, solvents, ions, membrane, pressure, temperature, etc.). The simulation may be run within a specified time interval, all depending on the ambient conditions set by the force-field [64, 67]. The most preferred binding orientation of the conformational samples that emerge during the simulation can be obtained by analysing the energy of the whole or a portion of the simulation and by visualizing and analyzing the inter/intra-molecular interactions (Fig. 13).

Fig. 13. General workflow for MD simulations.

4   Application of Virtual Screening

VS is a chemical search to match ligands with their biological targets. The process can be applied by either ligand-based or structure-based approaches. Related to the principles of the method used to find a hit molecule, VS covers various concepts. Regardless of the CADD approach, the process starts with a chemical database to be prepared for each molecular entry. This can be followed with *in silico* predictions of the pharmacokinetic and pharmacodynamic profiles of the molecules and a filtering of molecules within the database to obtain statistically significant and manageable sub-clusters of the chemical space [6] (Fig. 14).

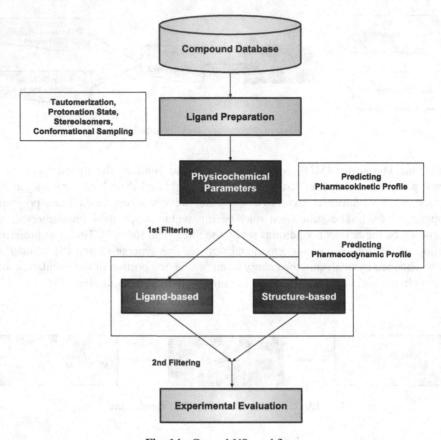

Fig. 14. General VS workflow.

4.1 Accessing Compound Databases

Chemical compound databases represent significant chemical catalogues for the discovery of hit molecules with biological activity, which compile large numbers of chemically different entities from either synthetic or natural origin [68]. They can be generated with in-house data, a combination of compound databases (previously tested or untested screening compound series) or *in silico* synthesis with building blocks. Compound databases of curated biological activity data, commercial sources of the molecules and pharmaceutical reference databases of the marketed drugs can be seen in Table 4.

Table 4. Compound databases.

Database/URL	Comment
BindingDB [69] www.bindingdb.org	Around 1.5 million binding affinity data points are available which are obtained from patents and scientific articles
chEMBL [70] www.ebi.ac.uk/chembl	More than 15 million biological activity results are available curated from scientific papers and patents
ChemSpider [71] www.chemspider.com	Contains over 67 million structural data, obtained from different data sources
DrugBank [72–76] www.drugbank.ca	Database of drug entries linked to their biological targets
DrugPort www.ebi.ac.uk/thornton-srv/databases/drugport	Structural representation of drugs with their receptors with data from DrugBank and PDB
eMolecules www.emolecules.com	Database comprises over 7 million screening compounds and 1.5 million building blocks, which are ready to order
Molport www.molport.com	Comprising around 20 million ready to be synthetized molecules, over 7 million screening compounds and around 0.5 million building blocks, which are ready to order
MMsINC [77] mms.dsfarm.unipd.it/MMsINC/search	Helps to search subsets of the database, containing over 4 million unique compounds with tautomeric and ionic states at physiological conditions as well as possible stable conformer for each molecular entry
Open PHACTS [78] www.openphacts.org	Large knowledge-base of data integration for compounds, their receptors, and pathways
PubChem [79] pubchem.ncbi.nlm.nih.gov	Contains around 100 million compounds and 250 million bioactivity data records
ZINC [80] zinc.docking.org	Contains around 740 million purchasable molecules in 2D and 220 million purchasable lead-like molecules in 3D

4.2 Preparing Ligands for Virtual Screening

It is important to assign the correct stereoisomeric or tautomeric forms and protonation states of each ligand at a specified pH to avoid changing physicochemical and conformational behavior of the molecules. Parameterization during this stage must be done very carefully for a VS study, because the molecules are generally stored in 1D or 2D within the databases. For example, a chiral entry within the database may be in a single enantiomer or a racemic mixture or a molecule may not be neutral as it is stored in the database and may be at different protonation states at different pH values.

Conformational flexibility of ligands is also important and computationally more expensive. Every additional rotation increases the number of conformations that needs to be generated and this results with a computationally more expensive VS process.

4.3   Compound Filtering

The main idea of compound filtering is to exclude the molecules which are not carrying suitable pharmacokinetic or pharmacodynamic properties. The aim is to prevent possible risks in preclinical or clinical phases of the studies. This also helps to keep down computational costs in VS studies.

Clustering by Chemical Diversity. It is possible to estimate the chemical similarities of the compounds by computer-based calculations. This lets identification of similar or diverse subsets of the libraries. Many different techniques are used for this purpose. The basic approach is to use similarity algorithms based on mathematical parameters obtained from chemical descriptors [81, 82]. Such calculations are generally done by calculating molecular fingerprints, which are a way of encoding the structure of a molecule, usually as binary digits used to symbolize the presence or absence of a chemical substructure within the molecule allowing for a similarity search in a chemical database. The most common similarity and classification algorithm is Tanimoto's similarity estimation and classification practice that regulate mathematical classification studies [82].

Filtering with Physicochemical Parameters. One of the major examples of filtering by pharmacokinetics related approaches is based on the scientific analysis of the drugs. Most drugs in the market can be used orally and it is found that there is a generally applicable rule to determine whether a biologically active compound has physicochemical properties that would make it an orally administrable drug in humans. In 1997, it is formulated by Christopher Lipinski [83, 84] and called Lipinski's rule of five (RO5). It is designed to evaluate drug-likeness of a compound, to be used in drug discovery and development studies. The properties of RO5 depend on; a molecular weight less than 500 Dalton, an octanol-water partition coefficient (log P) less than 5, equal or less than 5 HBD groups, equal or less than 10 HBA. Drug candidates which have properties of the RO5 tend to have more success in clinical trials, so have more chance to reach to the market. Such approaches let the identification of drug-like chemical space to fall within the biologically relevant subspace with a better pharmacokinetic profile of a vast unbounded chemical space.

Filtering with Ligand-Based or Receptor-Based Screening of Chemical Libraries. Ligand-based approaches focus on model generation with pre-established binding affinity data of small molecules against biological targets. These approaches are used with calculated descriptors to predict the characteristics within the molecular database. Though, structure-based approaches don't necessarily rely on existing data and try to place the molecules in the binding sites of the target and evaluate their potential affinity by binding scores within the complex biomolecular structures. Such computationally expensive calculations are preferred to run on distributed compute platforms to speed up the *in silico* screening process.

Ties with Pre-clinical Research. The search for new biologically relevant compounds is not possible without a laboratory result in which theories are confirmed, refined or disproved. Considerable time and effort are needed to be invested into the development of such tests. Eventually, it is needed to transfer the findings to human tissues.

VS may support the selection of the ligands for testing once a drug target is identified. This process is long and demands deep insights into the molecular understanding of the pathology of a disease. The selection of a target is likely to be supported from genetic studies, i.e. an observed association of DNA variation with disease phenotypes, hints the gene to target. Knock-down/out experiments are performed in the laboratories to confirm the molecular mechanism that trigger the disease.

Many researchers on rare diseases do not have industrial partners, and no drugs may be marketed for such "orphan" diseases. There are many rare diseases and consequentially many patients. To find new drugs, the availability of *in silico* approaches may be a significant guidance for the researchers, e.g. for repositioning drugs already on the market. The same approach can be applied to identify the biological targets of traditional medicines obtained from NPs [6].

Ties with Individualized Medicine. Individualized medicine identifies genetic variations that are causative for a disorder for every patient and adjusts therapy accordingly. Once a compound binds to its receptor, this yields a detailed molecular understanding how the drug works.

Such insights are of interest whenever a genetic variation may affect the binding of a drug to its receptor. Some drugs address cells with a high mutation rate, like a virus or a tumor cell. Mutations appear at random, but when the pathogen/cell benefits from it because of a lower binding affinity to the drug, it will continue to divide and pass that genetic information on. Thus, the pathogen or tumor evades the therapy. For that reason, The FightAIDS@Home project has searched for compounds with strong binding affinities to many sequence variations of the viral protein target [85].

Today, cancer patients are monitored by DNA sequencing to learn the changes in relative frequencies of genetic variations of the disease-tissue [86]. The adoption of next-generation sequencing technologies is a recent development. It will indicate the frequency of "escape routes" that may be closed with new drugs for the same target, possibly in the same binding pocket. It is with the same modeling technology that is at the root of *in silico* screening that this data can be interpreted. Without a molecular interpretation, clinicians would need to wait for insights from observations of how nuclear variation and subsequent therapy decisions affect the clinical outcome. A molecular reasoning, in contrast, is possible for every patient individually.

Automation. Several tools are available to prepare receptors and ligands. Glue language can be used to integrate different processes of such calculations [87]. In addition, there are workflow environments for CADD in particular like OPAL [88] or KNIME [89]. The users can easily develop any integration of CADD workflow that needs to be automated. Recent works integrate formal descriptions in databases (like bio.tools) [90] for content-dependent semantics-driven execution of the tools [91].

4.4 Experimental Evaluation and Validation

For biological research, *in silico* produced findings are needed to be evaluated with *in vitro* or *in vivo* biological assays. It is preferable to know the statistical strength of the model to evaluate the functionality of the model with retrospective studies, prior to biological testing. That test is likely to be performed in several stages and can be exemplified as given below. It should be noted that this stage of the work strictly depends on the nature of the target:

(a) Test of binding affinities (calorimetry, SPR)
(b) Induced structural changes (co-crystallization, NMR)
(c) Gene/Protein-function inhibition/induction (cell line, tissue sample)
(d) Effect on disease models (animal trials)

These tests are expensive, may cost the lives of animals. If the wrong compounds are chosen for testing, then this delays the treatment of humans. Testing diverse sets of compounds is preferred with respect to their binding mode and chemical structure.

5   Infrastructures and Computational Needs

Virtual screening is a data parallel process. The throughput of ligands tested in the computer almost linearly scales with the number of processors contributing. A second concern is the number of applications contributing – to the screening itself. The availability of high-performance computing (HPC) infrastructure is needed to speed up the *in silico* screening studies. In addition, accessing stronger HPC facilities has direct impact on covering bigger chemical and conformational space of compounds in VS studies or testing higher numbers of druggable targets to identify biomolecular targets of the compounds in target fishing studies.

When it is applied on thousands or millions of a series of chemical compounds, the total VS simulation time exceeds the limits of single workstations. For example, a molecular docking-based VS run, covering chemical space of millions of compounds, may take years of computation time on a single workstation. The overall compute time is fixed, also with multiple machines contributing. But by distributing the load, the effective wall-clock time can be lowered. The same VS run can be taken to months-scale by accessing hundreds of central processing unit (CPU) cores with an in-house small or medium scale HPC infrastructure or hours/days-scale by accessing thousands of CPU cores with supercomputers or on-demand cloud resources. Recent technical advancements to employ graphical processing unit (GPU) for parallel computing have fostered the concept to apply on data, i.e. deep learning or molecular dynamics.

We here discuss alternative sources for computational infrastructures and single out unique properties of the cloud environments.

5.1   Local Compute Cluster

Many computers are integrated in a local network and combined with a grid software to distribute compute jobs. The concept of a batch system is familiar to IT specialists who maintain such hardware. Larger clusters with special hardware to allow for fast I/O are referred to as HPC environments. The VS is mostly compute-intensive, data parallel computation with individual compute nodes which do not need to communicate with each other during the computations.

5.2 Volunteer Computing

Volunteer computing refers to the concept of having a program running in the background addressing a scientific problem. If several thousand individuals contribute, then one has a compute power or storage resource that can compete with the large computational clusters. It should be noted that one needs to interact with the community to keep the momentum.

Several *in silico* screening runs have been performed voluntarily. One of the most well-known was the search for an HIV protease inhibitor in FightAIDS@Home [85] with the underlying BOINC technology [92]. Because of the enormous compute power acquired by devices that are not operated by humans, the decentralization of computing is a strategically important route. Tapping into these resources for computing and to generally support the interaction of devices at the periphery is called as *edge computing*.

5.3 Cloud Computing

Cloud technologies are a means to integrate different workflows and tools on dynamically allocated resources. These instances share respective services in their specification of CADD studies, and cloud computing is an emerging solution for VS needs. The infancy of cloud solutions was in "IaaS", i.e. dynamically configured and started machines that were paid on use. Today, IaaS services are provided by many compute centers at very competitive price levels. Setups are easy to use for individuals familiar with remote access with command line interface (CLI) or graphical user interfaces (GUI).

Researchers in both academia and industry are likely to have access to a local compute cluster. But this is costly when the expenses of hardware upgrades, electricity and maintenance are added. Remote sources are highly competitive in pricing. This is meant for IT-savvy individuals who could use local resources if they had them. There is technology allowing these remote resources to behave much like an extension of a local cluster.

The most known cloud service providers are Amazon Web Services [93] and Google Cloud [94] but there are increasing numbers of open source cloud solutions that may be of interest. The OpenStack middleware [95] has evolved into a de facto standard to set up public or private cloud environment. When a software is accessed via a web interface, the server-side implementation becomes hidden. A look to the side, e.g. how payments are performed online with an interplay of many service providers, tell what clouds also mean: An interplay of services that scale.

Anticipating variants of VS principles to be employed in different and barely predictable ways are outlined in the next section. One may expect a cloud-based glue-layer of molecular modeling and genomics to emerge. But there are no CADD-Microservices/Functions as a Service, yet (Table 5).

Table 5. Classification of cloud services.

IaaS: Infrastructure as a Service is a service model which to provide remote access on de-mand to client-specified compute environments. Besides the typical virtualized setups with multiple users sharing a single processor, for HPC also "bare metal" setups are available. CADD tools may be readily usable deployed as a cloud image or be installed posteriori to a running image.

PaaS: Platform as a Service is a technical concept for an aggregation of services to facilitate software running in support of IaaS to scale in multi-user, multi-project environments.

SaaS: Software as a Service runs remotely, and stars copies of itself on multiple nodes in an IaaS environment to scale to whatever size of a problem or to as many users as there may be. The software is typically presented as a web interface, but the concept has found broad adoption from business applications to the gaming industry.

FaaS: Function as a Service. Element of a SaaS that may be invoked without context. Of-fered by all major cloud vendors, an open source implementation is Open Whisk [96]. This technology offers a route for VS-associated services to integrate into larger workflows.

5.4 Cloud-Based Solutions

Recent reviews [97, 98] and the "Click2Drug" catalog [99] give a vivid expression on describing many different sources for many partial solutions – available as semi-automated web services or as instances that may be started at one's independent disposal. How exactly a transfer of information between these tools should be per-formed, or how these tools should be run to generate redundant findings with then higher confidence – all this is yet to be clarified – both semantically and technically.

In silico approaches have been integrated in drug discovery pipeline and big pharmaceutical companies are likely to perform these often. Cloud environments are used for their advantages to reduce setup costs for professionals. Also, for creative new approaches in tackling a disease, the information on which selected target is already crucial not to lose competitive advantage. This may not be acceptable to be computed in extra mural facilities. However, for common targets, the interception of individual VS results, e.g. from a volunteer computing project, may not be considered critical.

Table 6 shows remote services that may use cloud services internally or that are offered for integration with a self-implemented workflow. Most services are agnostic with respect to the source of a request. However, some may fall back to the cloud provider's infrastructure for monetary compensation. Thus, the cloud becomes an integral part of the VS tool's deployment.

Table 6. Cloud-based solutions for virtual screening and target fishing. The table lists services that describe features of ligands or their receptors, receptor-based and ligand-based services. Services integrating multiple tools are tagged as a workflow. F stands for "Feature", R for "Receptor-based", L for "Ligand-based" and W for "Workflows".

Service	F	R	L	W	URL	Comment
3decision	X	X		X	3decision.discngine.com	Collaboration environment for researchers to exchange opinions on ligand receptor interactions
AceCloud [100]	X				www.acellera.com/ products/acecloud-molecular-dynamics-cloud-computing	Cloud image to run MD simulations with CLI on Amazon Cloud, can be used for high-throughput MD [101]
Achilles [102]	X			X	bio-hpc.ucam.edu/ achilles	Blind docking server with web interface
BindScope [103]	X	X	X	X	playmolecule.com/ BindScope	Structure-based binding prediction tool
DINC WebServer [104]	X				dinc.kavrakilab.org	A meta-docking web service for large ligands
DOCK Blaster [105]	X				blaster.docking.org	Automated molecular docking-based VS web service
DockingServer [106]	X				www.dockingserver.com	Molecular docking and VS service
Evias Cloud Virtual Screening Tool [107]	X		X		www.evias.com.tr/vst	Integrated with chemical library management system as a scalable HPC platform for structure-based VS service as a web service
HDOCK [108]	X				hdock.phys.hust.edu.cn	Protein-protein and protein-nucleic acid docking server
HADDOCK Web Server [109]	X				milou.science.uu.nl/ services/HADDOCK2.2/ haddock.php	Web-based biomolecular structure docking service
idock [110]	X				istar.cse.cuhk.edu.hk/ idock	Flexible docking-based VS tool with web interface
iScreen [111]	X		X		iscreen.cmu.edu.tw/ intro.php	A web server which started with docking of traditional Chinese medicine
LigandScout Remote [112]	X	X	X	X	www.inteligand.com	A desktop application, letting access to the cloud-based HPC for VS studies
mCule [113]	X	X	X	X	mcule.com	Integrates structure-based VS tools with purchasable chemical space

(continued)

Table 6. (*continued*)

Service	Properties				URL	Comment
	F	R	L	W		
MEDock [114]	X	X			medock.ee.ncku.edu.tw	A web server for predicting binding site and generating docking calculations
MTiOpenScreen [115]		X		X	bioserv.rpbs.univ-paris-diderot.fr/services/MTiOpenScreen	Integration of AutoDock and MTiOpenScreen in bioinformatics Mobyle environment
ParDOCK [116]		X			www.scfbio-iitd.res.in/dock/pardock.jsp	Fully automated rigid docking server, based on Monte Carlo search technique
PatchDock [117, 118]		X			bioinfo3d.cs.tau.ac.il/PatchDock	A web-server for generating docking simulations with geometry and shape complementarity principles
Polypharmacology Browser 2 (PPB2) [119]		X			ppb2.gdb.tools	A web server letting target prediction for the ligands
ProBiS [120]	X	X	X		probis.cmm.ki.si	A web-based analysis tool for binding site identification
ProBiS-CHARMMing [121]					probis.nih.gov	In addition to ProBis, it is possible to do energy minimization on ligand-protein complexes
Py-CoMFA			X	X	www.3d-qsar.com	Web-based platform that allows generation and validation of 3D-QSAR models
SwissDock [122]		X		X	www.swissdock.ch	Web-based docking service to predict ligand-protein binding
USR-VS [123]		X			usr.marseille.inserm.fr	Ligand-based VS web server using shape recognition techniques
ZincPharmer [124]	X		X		zincpharmer.csb.pitt.edu	Online pharmacophore-based VS tool for screening the purchasable subset of the ZINC or Molport databases

6 Conclusions

The goal of VS is to identify novel hit molecules within the vast chemical space to ameliorate symptoms of a disease. Hereto, the compound interacts with a target protein and changes its action in a pathological condition. None of the *in silico* molecular modeling techniques can generate perfect models for all kinds of biochemical processes. However, a large variety of tools is provided by the scientific community.

Alone or in combination, there are available VS technologies which suite the problem at hand. With clouds as HPC resources, complete workflows have been established to directly address the needs of medicinal chemists. The same technology also supports collaborative efforts with computational chemists to adjust workflows to emerging preclinical demands.

Another problem to address is the demand for HPC facilities for VS projects. These are indirect costs when using workflows already prepared as a cloud service. Clouds are attractive both for scaling with computational demands and for the enormous diversity of tools one can integrate. To minimize the costs and to complete the computation as quickly as possible, workflows should be well considered to select which tool to use while performing VS studies.

VS projects demand the investment of considerable time prior to the computation for their preparation and afterwards for *in vitro* analyses. For any isolated project it is likely to be more cost effective to share the compute facilities and expertise by using cloud-based solutions.

The authors of this text hope to have helped with an initial team building for interdisciplinary projects: There is a lot of good work to be done, algorithmically or on pre-clinical data at hand, but few groups can develop and use these techniques all on their own.

Acknowledgement. This work was partially supported by the Scientific and Technological Research Council of Turkey (Technology and Innovation Funding Programmes Directorate Grant No. 7141231 and Academic Research Funding Program Directorate Grant No. 112S596) and EU financial support, received through the cHiPSet COST Action IC1406.

References

1. U.S. Food and Drug Administration (FDA) - The Drug Development Process. https://www.fda.gov/ForPatients/Approvals/Drugs. Accessed 31 Dec 2018
2. Kopp, S.: Definition of active pharmaceutical ingredient revised, pp. 1–4 (2011)
3. Hughes, J.P., Rees, S.S., Kalindjian, S.B., Philpott, K.L.: Principles of early drug discovery. Br. J. Pharmacol. **162**, 1239–1249 (2011)
4. Cronk, D.: High-throughput screening. In: Drug Discovery and Development, pp. 95–117. Elsevier, Amsterdam (2013)
5. Introduction to pharmacokinetics and pharmacodynamics. In: Concepts in Clinical Pharmacokinetics, pp. 1–18. ASHP (2014)
6. Olğaç, A., Orhan, I.E., Banoglu, E.: The potential role of in silico approaches to identify novel bioactive molecules from natural resources. Future Med. Chem. **9**, 1663–1684 (2017)
7. Kinghorn, A.D., Pan, L., Fletcher, J.N., Chai, H.: The relevance of higher plants in lead compound discovery. J. Nat. Prod. **74**, 1539–1555 (2011)
8. Taylor, P., Mueller-Kuhrt, L.: Successful, but often unconventional: the continued and long-term contribution of natural products to healthcare (2015)
9. Wöhler, F.: Ueber künstliche Bildung des Harnstoffs. Ann. Phys. **88**, 253–256 (1828)
10. Hafner, V.K.: Gmewue 91. Angewandte Chemie **91**, 685–695 (1979)
11. Hoffmann, R.W.: Natural product synthesis: changes over time. Angewandte Chemie - Int. Ed. **52**, 123–130 (2013)
12. Mendel, G.: Versuche über Pflanzenhybriden. Verhand-lungen des naturforschenden Vereines Brünn, Bd. IV für das Jahr 1865, Abhandlungen, pp. 3–47 (1866)

13. Kaufmann, S.H.E.: Paul Ehrlich: founder of chemotherapy. Nat. Rev. Drug Discov. **7**, 373 (2008)
14. Strebhardt, K., Ullrich, A.: Paul Ehrlich's magic bullet concept: 100 years of progress. Nat. Rev. Cancer **8**, 473–480 (2008)
15. Burghes, A.H.M., Vaessin, H.E.F., de la Chapelle, A.: The land between mendelian and multifactorial inheritance. Science **293**, 2213–2214 (2001)
16. Roth, B.L., Sheggler, D.J., Kroeze, W.K.: Magic shotguns versus magic bullets: selectively non-selective drugs for mood disorders and schizophrenia. Nat. Rev. Drug Discov. **3**, 353–359 (2004)
17. Ma, Q., Lu, A.Y.H.: Pharmacogenetics, pharmacogenomics, and individualized medicine. Pharmacol. Rev. **63**, 437–459 (2011)
18. Cariaso, M., Lennon, G.: SNPedia: a wiki supporting personal genome annotation, interpretation and analysis. Nucleic Acids Res. **40**, 1308–1312 (2012)
19. Fischer, E.: Ueber die optischen Isomeren des Traubenzuckers, der Gluconsaure und der Zuckersaure. Berichte der Dtsch. Chem. Gesellschaft. **23**, 2611–2624 (1890)
20. Fischer, E.: Einfluss der Configuration auf die Wirkung der Enzyme. Berichte der Dtsch. Chem. Gesellschaft. **27**, 2985–2993 (1894)
21. Ferenczy, G.G., Keseru, G.M.: Thermodynamics guided lead discovery and optimization. Drug Discov. Today **15**(21–22), 919–932 (2010)
22. Bohacek, R.S., McMartin, C., Guida, W.C.: The art and practice of structure-based drug design: a molecular modeling perspective. Med. Res. Rev. **16**, 3–50 (1996)
23. Kirkpatrick, P.: New horizons in chemical space. Nat. Rev. Drug Discov. **3**, 375 (2004)
24. Kirkpatrick, P., Ellis, C.: Chemical space. Nature **432**, 823 (2004)
25. Dobson, C.M.: Chemical space and biology. Nature **432**, 824–828 (2004)
26. Lipinski, C., Hopkins, A.: Navigating chemical space for biology and medicine. Nature **432**, 855–861 (2004)
27. Chemical Abstracts Service (CAS) - CAS Databases. https://www.cas.org/content/cas-databases
28. Heller, S.R.: The Beilstein online database. In: ACS Symposium Series, vol. 436, pp. 1–9 (1990)
29. Huggins, D.J., Sherman, W., Tidor, B.: Rational approaches to improve selectivity in drug design. J. Med. Chem. **55**, 1424–1444 (2012)
30. Oprea, T.I., Davis, A.M., Teague, S.J., Leeson, P.D.: Is there a difference between leads and drugs? A historical perspective. J. Chem. Inf. Comput. Sci. **41**, 1308–1315 (2001)
31. Villoutreix, B.O., Lagorce, D., Labbe, C.M., Sperandio, O., Miteva, M.A.: One hundred thousand mouse clicks down the road: selected online resources supporting drug discovery collected over a decade. Drug Discov. Today **18**, 1081–1089 (2013)
32. Jelliffe, R.W., Tahani, B.: Pharmacoinformatics: equations for serum drug assay error patterns; implications for therapeutic drug monitoring and dosage. In: Proceedings of the Annual Symposium on Computer Application in Medical Care, pp. 517–521 (1993)
33. Olgaç, A., Carotti, A.: Pharmacoinformatics in drug R&D process. In: GPSS, p. 45 (2015)
34. Levitt, M.: The birth of computational structural biology. Nat. Struct. Biol. **8**, 392–393 (2001)
35. Hopkins, A.L., Groom, C.R., Alex, A.: Ligand efficiency: a useful metric for lead selection. Drug Discov. Today **9**, 430–431 (2004)
36. Guedes, R., Serra, P., Salvador, J., Guedes, R.: Computational approaches for the discovery of human proteasome inhibitors: an overview. Molecules **21**, 1–27 (2016)
37. Petterson, I., Balle, T., Liljefors, T.: Ligand based drug design. In: Textbook of Drug Design and Discovery, pp. 43–57 (2010)
38. Aki-Yalcin, E., Yalcin, I.: Kantitatif Yapı-Etki İlişkileri Analizleri (QSAR). Ankara Üniversitesi Eczacılık Fakültesi Yayınları (2003)

39. Crum-Brown, A., Fraser, T.R.: On the connection between chemical constitution and physiological action. Part II - on the physiological action of the ammonium bases derived from Atropia and Conia. Trans. R. Soc. Edinburgh **25**, 693 (1869)
40. Hammett, L.P.: Effect of structure upon the reactions of organic compounds. Benzene derivatives. J. Am. Chem. Soc. **59**, 96–103 (1937)
41. Taft, R.W.: Steric Effects in Organic Chemistry (1956)
42. Free, S.M., Wilson, J.W.: A mathematical contribution to structure-activity studies. J. Med. Chem. **7**, 395–399 (1964)
43. Fujita, T., Ban, T.: Structure-activity study of phenethylamines as substrates of biosynthetic enzymes of sympathetic transmitters. J. Med. Chem. **14**, 148–152 (1971)
44. Kubinyi, H.: Quantitative structure-activity relationships. 2. A mixed approach, based on Hansch and Free-Wilson analysis. J. Med. Chem. **19**, 587–600 (1976)
45. Kubinyi, H.: Quantitative structure-activity relationships. 7. The bilinear model, a new model for nonlinear dependence of biological activity on hydrophobic character. J. Med. Chem. **20**, 625–629 (1977)
46. Polanski, J.: Receptor dependent multidimensional QSAR for modeling drug - receptor interactions. Curr. Med. Chem. **16**, 3243–3257 (2009)
47. Sippl, W.: 3D-QSAR - Applications, recent advances, and limitations. In: Recent Advances in QSAR Studies, pp. 103–126 (2010)
48. Klebe, G., Abraham, U., Mietzner, T.: Molecular similarity indices in a comparative analysis (CoMSIA) of drug molecules to correlate and predict their biological activity. J. Med. Chem. **37**, 4130–4146 (1994)
49. Lima, A.N., Philot, E.A., Trossini, G.H.G., Scott, L.P.B., Maltarollo, V.G., Honorio, K.M.: Use of machine learning approaches for novel drug discovery. Expert Opin. Drug Discov. **11**, 225–239 (2016)
50. van der Kamp, M.W., Shaw, K.E., Woods, C.J., Mulholland, A.J.: Biomolecular simulation and modelling: status, progress and prospects. J. R. Soc. Interface 5(Suppl. 3), S173–S190 (2008)
51. Berman, H.M., et al.: The Protein Data Bank. Nucleic Acids Res. **28**, 235–242 (2000)
52. Rose, P.W., et al.: The RCSB Protein Data Bank: views of structural biology for basic and applied research and education. Nucleic Acids Res. **43**, D345–D356 (2015)
53. RCSB Protein Data Bank. http://www.rcsb.org. Accessed 31 Dec 2018
54. Berman, H., Henrick, K., Nakamura, H., Markley, J.L.: The worldwide Protein Data Bank (wwPDB): ensuring a single, uniform archive of PDB data. Nucleic Acids Res. **35**, 2006–2008 (2007)
55. Protein Data Bank in Europe. http://www.ebi.ac.uk/pdbe. Accessed 31 Dec 2018
56. Protein Data Bank Japan. https://pdbj.org. Accessed 31 Dec 2018
57. Biological Magnetic Resonance Data Bank. http://www.bmrb.wisc.edu
58. Jorgensen, F.S., Kastrup, J.S.: Biostructure based modeling. In: Textbook of Drug Design and Discovery, pp. 29–42 (2010)
59. Bateman, A., et al.: UniProt: A hub for protein information. Nucleic Acids Res. **43**, D204–D212 (2015)
60. Lopez, R., Silventoinen, V., Robinson, S., Kibria, A., Gish, W.: WU-Blast2 server at the European Bioinformatics Institute. Nucleic Acids Res. **31**, 3795–3798 (2003)
61. Altschul, S.: Gapped BLAST and PSI-BLAST: a new generation of protein database search programs. Nucleic Acids Res. **25**, 3389–3402 (1997)
62. Goujon, M., et al.: A new bioinformatics analysis tools framework at EMBL-EBI. Nucleic Acids Res. **38**, 695–699 (2010)
63. Finn, R.D., et al.: Pfam: the protein families database. Nucleic Acids Res. **42**, 222–230 (2014)

64. Fenu, L.A., Lewis, R.A., Good, A.C., Bodkin, M., Essex, J.W.: Scoring functions. In: Jhoti, H., Leach, A.R. (eds.) Structure-Based Drug Discovery, pp. 223–245. Springer, Dordrecht (2007). https://doi.org/10.1007/1-4020-4407-0_9

65. Forli, S., Huey, R., Pique, M.E., Sanner, M.F., Goodsell, D.S., Olson, A.J.: Computational protein–ligand docking and virtual drug screening with the AutoDock suite. Nat. Protoc. 11, 905–919 (2016)

66. Schomburg, K.T., Bietz, S., Briem, H., Henzler, A.M., Urbaczek, S., Rarey, M.: Facing the challenges of structure-based target prediction by inverse virtual screening. J. Chem. Inf. Model. 54, 1676–1686 (2014)

67. Rognan, D.: Structure-based approaches to target fishing and ligand profiling. Mol. Inform. 29, 176–187 (2010)

68. Moura Barbosa, A.J., Del Rio, A.: Freely accessible databases of commercial compounds for high-throughput virtual screenings. Curr. Top. Med. Chem. 12, 866–877 (2012)

69. Liu, T., Lin, Y., Wen, X., Jorissen, R.N., Gilson, M.K.: BindingDB: a web-accessible database of experimentally determined protein – ligand binding affinities. Nucleic Acids Res. 35, 198–201 (2007)

70. Gaulton, A., et al.: The ChEMBL database in 2017. Nucleic Acids Res. 45, 1–10 (2016)

71. Pence, H.E., Williams, A.: ChemSpider: an online chemical information resource. J. Chem. Educ. 87, 1123–1124 (2010)

72. Wishart, D.S., et al.: DrugBank: a comprehensive resource for in silico drug discovery and exploration. Nucleic Acids Res. 34, D668–D672 (2006)

73. Wishart, D.S., et al.: DrugBank: a knowledgebase for drugs, drug actions and drug targets. Nucleic Acids Res. 36, 901–906 (2008)

74. Knox, C., et al.: DrugBank 3.0: a comprehensive resource for "Omics" research on drugs. Nucleic Acids Res. 39, 1035–1041 (2011)

75. Law, V., et al.: DrugBank 40: shedding new light on drug metabolism. Nucleic Acids Res. 42, 1091–1097 (2014)

76. Xue, R., Fang, Z., Zhang, M., Yi, Z., Wen, C., Shi, T.: TCMID: traditional Chinese medicine integrative database for herb molecular mechanism analysis. Nucleic Acids Res. 41, 1089–1095 (2013)

77. Masciocchi, J., et al.: MMsINC: a large-scale chemoinformatics database. Nucleic Acids Res. 37, 284–290 (2009)

78. Williams, A.J., et al.: Open PHACTS: Semantic interoperability for drug discovery. Drug Discov. Today. 17, 1188–1198 (2012)

79. Kim, S., et al.: PubChem substance and compound databases. Nucleic Acids Res. 44, D1202–D1213 (2016)

80. Irwin, J.J., Sterling, T., Mysinger, M.M., Bolstad, E.S., Coleman, R.G.: ZINC: a free tool to discover chemistry for biology. J. Chem. Inf. Model. 52, 1757–1768 (2012)

81. Koutsoukas, A., et al.: From in silico target prediction to multi-target drug design: current databases, methods and applications (2011)

82. Tanimoto, T.T.: An elementary mathematical theory of classification and prediction. International Business Machines Corporation (1958)

83. Lipinski, C.A., Lombardo, F., Dominy, B.W., Feeney, P.J.: Experimental and computational approaches to estimate solubility and permeability in drug discovery and development settings. Adv. Drug Deliv. Rev. 23, 3–25 (1997)

84. Lipinski, C.A.: Lead- and drug-like compounds: the rule-of-five revolution (2004)

85. Chang, M.W., Lindstrom, W., Olson, A.J., Belew, R.K.: Analysis of HIV wild-type and mutant structures via in silico docking against diverse ligand libraries. J. Chem. Inf. Model. 47, 1258–1262 (2007)

86. Xue, Y., Wilcox, W.R.: Changing paradigm of cancer therapy: precision medicine by next-generation sequencing. Cancer Biol. Med. 13, 12–18 (2016)

87. Möller, S., et al.: Robust cross-platform workflows: how technical and scientific communities collaborate to develop, test and share best practices for data analysis. Data Sci. Eng. **2**, 232–244 (2017)
88. Ren, J., Williams, N., Clementi, L., Krishnan, S., Li, W.W.: Opal web services for biomedical applications. Nucleic Acids Res. **38**, 724–731 (2010)
89. Berthold, M.R., et al.: KNIME - the Konstanz information miner. SIGKDD Explor. **11**, 26–31 (2009)
90. Ison, J., et al.: Tools and data services registry: a community effort to document bioinformatics resources. Nucleic Acids Res. **44**, 38–47 (2016)
91. Palmblad, M., Lamprecht, A.-L., Ison, J., Schwämmle, V.: Automated workflow composition in mass spectrometry based proteomics. Bioinformatics **35**(4), 656–664 (2019). https://www.ncbi.nlm.nih.gov/pubmed/30060113
92. Balan, D.M., Malinauskas, T., Prins, P., Möller, S.: High-throughput molecular docking now in reach for a wider biochemical community. In: 20th Euromicro International Conference on Parallel, Distributed and Network-Based Processing, pp. 617–621 (2012)
93. Amazon Web Services. https://aws.amazon.com. Accessed 31 Dec 2018
94. Google Cloud. https://cloud.google.com. Accessed 31 Dec 2018
95. Open Stack. https://www.openstack.org/. Accessed 31 Dec 2018
96. Open Whisk. https://openwhisk.apache.org/. Accessed 31 Dec 2018
97. Banegas-Luna, A.J., et al.: Advances in distributed computing with modern drug discovery. Expert Opin. Drug Discov. **14**, 9–22 (2019)
98. Potemkin, V., Grishina, M., Potemkin, A.: Internet resources for drug discovery and design. Curr. Top. Med. Chem. **18**(22), 1955–1975 (2018). https://www.ncbi.nlm.nih.gov/pubmed/30499394
99. Click2Drug Catalog. https://www.click2drug.org/directory_Docking.html. Accessed 31 Dec 2018
100. Harvey, M.J., De Fabritiis, G.: AceCloud: molecular dynamics simulations in the cloud. J. Chem. Inf. Model. **55**, 909–914 (2015)
101. Doerr, S., Harvey, M.J., Noé, F., De Fabritiis, G.: HTMD: High-throughput molecular dynamics for molecular discovery. J. Chem. Theory Comput. **12**, 1845–1852 (2016)
102. Sánchez-linares, I., Pérez-sánchez, H., Cecilia, J.M., García, J.M.: High-throughput parallel blind virtual screening using BINDSURF. BMC Bioinform. **13**, S13 (2012)
103. Skalic, M., Martinez-Rosell, G., Jimenez, J., De Fabritiis, G.: PlayMolecule BindScope: large scale CNN-based virtual screening on the web. Bioinformatics 1–2 (2018)
104. Antunes, D.A., Moll, M., Devaurs, D., Jackson, K.R., Kavraki, L.E., Liz, G.: DINC 2.0: a new protein – peptide docking webserver using an incremental approach, pp. 2017–2020 (2017)
105. Irwin, J.J., et al.: Automated docking screens: a feasibility study, 5712–5720 (2009)
106. Bikadi, Z., Hazai, E.: Application of the PM6 semi-empirical method to modeling proteins enhances docking accuracy of AutoDock. J. Cheminform. **16**, 1–16 (2009)
107. Olgac, A., Budak, G., Cobanoglu, S., Nuti, R., Carotti, A., Banoglu, E.: Evias web services: cloud-based drug discovery platform. In: EuroQSAR 2016, p. 79 (2016)
108. Yan, Y., Zhang, D., Zhou, P., Li, B., Huang, S.Y.: HDOCK: a web server for protein-protein and protein-DNA/RNA docking based on a hybrid strategy. Nucleic Acids Res. **45**, W365–W373 (2017)
109. Zundert, G.C.P., et al.: The HADDOCK2.2 web server: user-friendly integrative modeling of biomolecular complexes. J. Mol. Biol. **128**, 720–725 (2016)
110. Li, H., Leung, K.S., Wong, M.H.: idock: A multithreaded virtual screening tool for flexible ligand docking. In: 2012 IEEE Symposium on Computational Intelligence in Bioinformatics and Computational Biology, CIBCB 2012, pp. 77–84 (2012)

111. Tsai, T.-Y., Chang, K.-W., Chen, C.Y.-C.: iScreen: world's first cloud-computing web server for virtual screening and de novo drug design based on TCM database@Taiwan. J. Comput. Aided Mol. Des. **25**, 525–531 (2011)
112. Kainrad, T., Hunold, S., Seidel, T., Langer, T.: LigandScout remote : a new user-friendly interface for HPC and cloud resources, 1–9 (2018)
113. Kiss, R., Sandor, M., Szalai, F.A.: http://Mcule.com: a public web service for drug discovery. J. Cheminform. **4**, P17 (2012)
114. Chang, D.T.H., Oyang, Y.J., Lin, J.H.: MEDock: a web server for efficient prediction of ligand binding sites based on a novel optimization algorithm. Nucleic Acids Res. **33**, 233–238 (2005)
115. Labbe, C.M., et al.: MTiOpenScreen: a web server for structure-based virtual screening. Nucleic Acids Res. **43**, 448–454 (2015)
116. Gupta, A., Gandhimathi, A., Sharma, P., Jayaram, B.: ParDOCK: an all atom energy based Monte Carlo docking protocol for protein-ligand complexes. Protein Pept. Lett. **14**, 632–646 (2007)
117. Schneidman-Duhovny, D., Inbar, Y., Nussinov, R., Wolfson, H.J.: PatchDock and SymmDock: servers for rigid and symmetric docking. Nucleic Acids Res. **33**, 363–367 (2005)
118. Duhovny, D., Nussinov, R., Wolfson, H.J.: Efficient unbound docking of rigid molecules, 185–200 (2002)
119. Awale, M., Reymond, J.: The polypharmacology browser PPB2: target prediction combining nearest neighbors with machine learning. J. Chem. Inf. Model. **59**(1), 10–17 (2019). https://www.ncbi.nlm.nih.gov/pubmed/30558418
120. Konc, J., Janezic, D.: ProBiS: a web server for detection of structurally similar protein binding sites. Nucleic Acids Res. **38**, 436–440 (2010)
121. Konc, J., et al.: ProBiS-CHARMMing: web interface for prediction and optimization of ligands in protein binding sites. J. Chem. Inf. Model. **55**, 2308–2314 (2015)
122. Grosdidier, A., Zoete, V., Michielin, O.: SwissDock, a protein-small molecule docking web service based on EADock DSS. Nucleic Acids Res. **39**, 270–277 (2011)
123. Li, H., Leung, K.-S., Wong, M.-H., Ballester, P.J.: USR-VS: a web server for large-scale prospective virtual screening using ultrafast shape recognition techniques. Nucleic Acids Res. **44**, W436–W441 (2016)
124. Koes, D.R., Camacho, C.J.: ZINCPharmer: pharmacophore search of the ZINC database. Nucleic Acids Res. **40**, 409–414 (2012)

Ultra Wide Band Body Area Networks: Design and Integration with Computational Clouds

Joanna Kołodziej$^{(\boxtimes)}$ (iD), Daniel Grzonka (iD), Adrian Widłak (iD),
and Paweł Kisielewicz (iD)

Department of Computer Science, Cracow University of Technology,
ul. Warszawska 24, 31-115 Cracow, Poland
jokolodziej@pk.edu.pl

Abstract. Body Area Networks (BANs) connect together nodes attached to a human body and transfer the data to an external infrastructure. The wireless communication channel and a variety of miniature sensor devices have lead to many useful applications of BANs, such as healthcare monitoring, military and emergency coordination, rescue services, sports, and entertainment. The Ultra Wide Band (UWB) communication model is widely used in wireless body area networks. UWB Radio Frequency (RF) technology provides robust and energy efficient transmission of data and signals through wireless networks. This chapter surveys recent models, applications and research challenges for future generation UWB RF technology for BANs. The chapter also discusses the state-of-the art in the cloud-based support for data storage and analysis in mobile health monitoring. Security issues for BANs in general and mobile health monitoring are addressed as a key aspect of the recent developments in the domain.

Keywords: Cloud computing · Body area networks ·
Sensor networks · Ultra wideband communication · Medical services ·
Wireless communications

1 Introduction

Based on the IEEE 802.15 standards, Body Area Network (BAN) can be defined as "a communication standard optimized for low power devices and operation on, in or around the human body (but not limited to humans) to serve a variety of applications including medical, consumer electronics/personal entertainment and others [5]". REcently, technological advancements in ultra low-power Radio Frequency (RF) technology, low-power integrated circuits, energy harvesting and storage, and wireless communications have lead to the design of lightweight, intelligent, and low-cost medical devices and sensors. With all these achievements, the thought of widespread deployment of pervasive wireless BANs for diverse

J. Kołodziej and H. González-Vélez (Eds.): cHiPSet, LNCS 11400, pp. 279–306, 2019.
https://doi.org/10.1007/978-3-030-16272-6_10

applications, such as health monitoring and military coordination, seems to be a reality of the near future [27].

Typical BAN connects self-regulating nodes (sensors, artificial skin, etc.) attached to the surface of body or implanted in the body [85]. The focus in BANs has been on medical and quality of life applications [70]. In such applications the network's nodes can be implanted medical devices, such as electrocardiogram (ECG) electrodes, activity sensors and actuators, or devices for storage of the medical data [70]. The Wireless Body Area Network (WBAN) sensors and devices may be classified based on their location into the following two main categories [3]:

– in-body nodes,
– on-body area network nodes.

Figure 1 presents the generic model of typical WBAN in-body and on-body nodes distribution with the wrist node as a local (central) base station.

Fig. 1. Generic sample model of wireless BAN [18]

The key requirements for BANs are: (i) small network scale, (ii) long battery life, (iii) short range communications and (iv) security awareness [32,85]. Many powerful sensor platforms have been developed for various applications in the past decade [75]. In the case of transceivers, decreasing the amount of energy required to transmit a bit of data means: **(a)** reducing the turn on/off times and power during transients, and **(b)** duty cycling the radio operation [41].

The Ultra Wide Band (UWB) is the key technology for data transmission in WBANs through the low-power transmission and low-power duty cycle [47]. In Ultra Wide Band Body Area Networks (UWB-BANs), the human tissues are not affected by closely placed WBAN devices. Low-power transmission and duty cycle also enable lower power consumption in the network nodes and long battery time, which is the basic requirement for such systems. UWB technology also conforms to the size and cost constraints of BAN devices [27]. From the implementation perspective, the major advantages of using UWB radios are: (a) low implementation complexity, (b) low duty cycling operation, and (c) bit rate scalability [22].

UWB BANs have been surveyed already from the different aspects [12, 47] such as communication channel models [8, 72, 73, 81], transmitter design [34, 70], antenna design [38, 72], and performance evaluation [13, 23, 73]. This chapter summarizes all the above surveys and gives the general and wider view on the design, architecture and technological issues. It addresses the main challenges related to BANs and UWB-BANs and presents the recently developed models based on the cloud computing support for the patient's health monitoring, patients' data storage, analysis and processing with the security criterion for inter and intra-cloud communication and data access.

The rest of the chapter is organized as follows. BANs application areas are discussed in Sect. 2.1. Section 2.2 presents the classification of the wireless technologies used in WBANs. In Sect. 2.3, some practical issues and relations between different requirements of BANs are discussed. Sections 2.4 and 3 define the research challenges and state-of-the art in UWB BANs. The concept of cloud-based support for WBANs is presented in Sect. 4. Security aspects related to the cloud support in mobile health applications based on UWB-BANs are discussed in Sect. 5. The chapter ends with the conclusions and highlights of the future research directions in the domain specified in Sect. 6.

2 BAN's Applications and Challenges

Various types of the main BANs components, namely, vital sign monitoring sensors, motion detectors (through accelerometers) and communication protocols for data processing and system access, make these networks very useful in providing numerous services in healthcare, research, lifestyle, emergency, sports, and military [12, 26, 32]. In this section we first discuss the major application areas for BANs, present the candidate technologies for wireless communication and data transmission, and then highlight the most important practical and research challenges regarding WBAN technologies.

2.1 Applications of BANs

The major areas of applications of BANs can be specified as follows.

Healthcare: BANs are used to connect sensor devices with remote monitoring and assistance systems for physically disabled and elderly persons. Mobile devices can be used to send and receive data to hospitals from the ambulances carrying patients to alert the concerned authorities and to get information about providing first aid to save people's lives [32]. BANs also enable a continuous monitoring of patient's condition by sensing and transmitting vital signs, such as heart rate, ECG, body temperature, respiratory rate, chest sounds, blood pressure, etc. [9,41]. It makes BANs an important tool for diagnosis and treatment of patients with chronic diseases, such as hypertension, diabetes, etc. BANs are also beneficial to hospital patients who are monitored pervasively regardless of their location. Pervasive in-patient monitoring through implanted devices enables medical staff to predict, diagnose, and start treatment before the patient reaches an adverse stage of the disease [26,77]. BANs are also highly beneficial for monitoring and assistance of elderly people, as more and more people demand a better quality of life.

Work and Emergency Services: BANs are used in emergency services like rescue systems, firefighting, etc. [47]. Using miniature sensors, the condition and location of firefighters is monitored. These sensors are also used to transfer information to a person, e.g., a commander who is not present at the site. Based on the information provided by sensors, the commander can coordinate emergencies with the team carrying out the rescue operation.

Lifestyle and Sports: BANs are also beneficial in providing quality of life and sport healthcare monitoring [83]. Such applications may include wearable entertainment systems, car navigation systems, and tour guides. In sports, BANs are used to monitor a player vital signs, such as the heart rate of a marathon runner.

Military: BANs are also used in war and combat scenarios by the military and police personnel. Wearable sensors are integrated into the uniforms of soldiers. This network can then be used to connect different devices, such as health sensors, surveillance cameras, and Personal Digital Assistants (PDAs) installed on different personnel body parts [16].

It is envisioned that wireless body area networks will become the heart of the future Internet and will play a vital role in access and exchange of information in order to provide better facilities in healthcare, education, and lifestyle [41]. Real-time patients vital signs monitoring, emergency and battlefield coordination may be read as a part of science fiction and movies. But one such ambitious project is underway at University of Washington, to display real-time information gathered from different body sensors through LEDs built in contact lenses [58].

2.2   Candidate Wireless Technologies

In this section, various wireless technologies that are leading competitors in the upcoming market of BANs are discussed. Communication between sensor devices is called intra-BAN communication while BAN communication with other networks is called extra-BAN communication [37]. Selection of appropriate technology for intra-BAN communication is a research issue where end-to-end performance of candidate wireless technologies is determined by the complete protocol stack (i.e., including Physical layer (PHY) and upper protocol layers).

Bluetooth Classic: Bluetooth is a short range wireless communication standard that defines the link and application layers to support data and voice applications. Piconet is a short range network made up of up to eight Bluetooth devices. Bluetooth Special Interest Group has developed the Bluetooth Health Device Profile (HDP) that defines the requirements for qualified Bluetooth healthcare and fitness device implementations. Bluetooth is widely adopted wireless technology for intra-BAN communication in WBANs [66].

Bluetooth Low Energy: Bluetooth Low Energy (BTLE) is another candidate wireless technology for BANs. It provides simple device discovery and reliable point-to-multipoint data transfer, with encryption, power save functionalities, and ultra low power idle mode operation. The key advantages of BTLE are the strength of the Bluetooth brand, the promise of interoperability with Bluetooth radios in mobile phones and low-power operations [66].

ZigBee: ZigBee defines a network, security, and application layer protocol suite on top of the PHY and Media Access Control (MAC) layers defined by the IEEE 802.15.4 Wireless Personal Area Network (WPAN) standard. The PHY layer exploits the direct sequence spread spectrum technique for interference tolerance and MAC layer exploits carrier sense multiple access with collision avoidance (CSMA/CA) for channel access. ZigBee also provides support for personal health devices complying with the IEEE 11073 standard, including electro-cardiographs, glucometers, pulse oximeters, blood pressure monitors, thermometers, weight scales, and respirometers [12].

ANT: ANT is a proprietary technology designed for general purpose wireless personal area network applications. ANT features low latency, simple design, ability to trade off a data rate against power consumption, and a net data rate of 20 kb/s (over-the-air data rate is 1 Mb/s) [12].

Sensium: Sensium is a proprietary ultra-low-power transceiver platform custom designed for healthcare and lifestyle management applications. The network adopts a master-slave architecture where joining and leaving the network is managed centrally and all communications are single-hop [12].

Zarlink: Zarlink has developed an ultra-low-power RF transceiver, ZL70101, for medical implantable applications. It uses a Reed-Solomon coding scheme together with cyclic redundancy check (CRC) in order to achieve a highly reliable link. The key features of Zarlink ZL70101 are extremely low power consumption, ultra-low power wakeup circuit, MedRadio compliance and security [12].

Other Technologies: Proprietary RF technologies such as BodyLAN and Z-Wave are also emerging on the horizon. Inductive coupling (IC) and body coupled communications (BCC) technologies are also promising. The data rate of IC is limited, and it cannot initiate communication from inside the body. BCC transceivers are capacitively coupled to the skin and use the human body as a channel to exchange data. BCC is energy efficient, and alleviates interference and coexistence issues. BCC can also be used for user identification and automatic formation of BANs [66].

2.3   Practical Challenges

BANs face several important challenging issues regarding their efficiency, practical deployment, and social adoption [32,54]. These issues constrain the solution space, and need to be considered carefully when designing mechanisms for data security and privacy in WBANs.

Conflict Between Security and Efficiency: High efficiency is strongly demanded for data security in WBANs because of the resource constraints. Wearable sensors are often extremely small and have insufficient power supplies, which render them inferior in computation and storage capabilities. Thus, the cryptographic primitives used by the sensor nodes should be as lightweight as possible, in terms of both fast computation and low storage overhead [41].

Conflict Between Security and Safety: Whether the data can be obtained whenever needed or not can be very crucial for patients' safety. Too strict and inflexible data access control may prevent the medical information from being accessed on time by legitimate medical staff, especially in emergency scenarios where the patient may be unconscious and unable to respond. On the other hand, a loose access control scheme opens back doors to malintent users. It is hard to ensure strong data security and privacy while allowing flexible access [20].

Conflict Between Security and Usability: The devices should be easy to use and foolproof, since the users might be non-expert patients. As the setup process of the data security procedures is patient-related, it should involve as few interactions with humans as possible. For instance, to bootstrap initial secure communication between all the nodes in a WBAN for secure data communication, device pairing techniques can be adopted [20]. The devices should offer security services during the phase of data collecting and processing by the advanced data processing centers like, Cloud or Big Data processing systems [78], but not disturbing their daily usage.

Requirement for Device Interoperability: Patients can buy sensor devices from different manufacturers, it may be difficult to pre-share any cryptographic materials among them. It would be hardly possible to establish data security procedures that require minimum settings and efforts, and can work with a wide range of devices [54].

2.4   Research Challenges

In this section we summarize different research challenges associated with BANs [12,26,66]. These issues need to be addressed for the widespread deployment of BANs. BANs brings forward a number of research issues that need to be considered in the design of RF wireless systems. Users can carry several BAN devices globally, hence, BAN radios are required to operate worldwide. There is an abundance of high power technologies in Industrial, Scientific, and Medical radio bands (ISM bands) that can cast performance degradation on the low-power BAN devices which thus makes them less appealing for high fidelity medical applications. Wireless Medical Telemetry Service (WMTS) bands are heavily used but their use is restricted to healthcare facilities in the United States. UWB can be exploited for wearable applications but it raises the issue of coexistence with high-datarate multimedia applications [12]. The rules for MedRadio wing band are very strict and limiting [21]. These issues have provoked the Federal Communication Commission (FCC) to think about opening up 2360–2400 MHz range for medical BANs. This is planned to hold up wideband entrenched micro-stimulator devices that can serve as an artificial nervous system to reinstate sensation, mobility, and function to paralyzed limbs and organs [66].

Another research issue in BANs is a channel model design. The channel model plays a vital role in the design of PHY technologies. Experimental channel modeling for embedded and wearable devices is difficult because humans and healthcare facilities are involved and both are governed by regulations [72].

An antenna design for body area networks is yet another challenging issue due to limitations on the size, stuff, and form of the antenna [84]. Only non-caustic and biocompatible material, such as titanium or platinum, can be used for implants, which results in degraded performance when compared with the antennas made of copper. Organ and location of antenna decides its shape and size which further restricts the choice of designer [66,82].

A physical layer protocol design requires reducing power consumption without affecting reliability. Flawless connectivity should be maintained in dynamic environments without the slightest possible performance degradation in terms of throughput, data loss, and latency. Rapid turnaround time from transmission to reception and speedy wakeup from sleep mode can add significance to power savings [26].

Energy efficient hardware is also an issue; existing wireless technologies draw relatively high peak current and mainly rely on duty cycling the radio between sleep and active modes to minimize the average current drawn. Researchers have been exploring several promising techniques, such as low-power listening and wake-up radios, which are intended to minimize power consumed by idle listening [47].

Coexistence of multiple BANs in crowded places, such as hospitals, needs a robust MAC protocol. The MAC protocol should be able to cope with topology changes caused by movement of nodes. Channel migration protocols need to be developed to be able to migrate to a quiet channel when serious hindrance is noticed [26].

Medical devices are subject to strict regulations to promote the safety and welfare of users. Compliance to applicable regulations set forth by the FCC, U.S. Food and Drug Administration (FDA), European Telecommunications Standards Institute (ETSI), and other regulatory agencies is essential [66].

3   UWB Solutions for BANs

Communication and efficient data transmission are the crucial issues in the design and management of modern WBANs. The Federal Communication Commission urges the use of WMTS for medical applications. However, the people

Table 1. Main properties of communication and data transmission bands for BANs and WBANs [66].

Frequency (MHz)	Acronym	Scalability to BAN applications	
		Merits	Demerits
401–406	MedRadio	Worldwide availability, good propagation characteristics, quiet channel, medical only	Secondary usage, body-worn applications not allowed in 402–405 MHz core band, large antenna size, limited bandwidth, stringent rules
433.05–434.79	General Telemetry	Good propagation characteristics	Not internationally agreed, EU/AU/NZ/SA only, crowded spectrum, large antenna, limited bandwidth
608–614 1395–1400 1427–1432	WMTS	Good propagation characteristics, medical only, antenna size reasonable	Licensed secondary use limited to healthcare providers inside healthcare facilities in US, limited spectrum, heavily used
868–870	General Telemetry	Good propagation characteristics, excellent building penetration characteristics	EU only, limited spectrum, heavily used
902–928	ISM	Good propagation characteristics	US/Canada only, crowded spectrum, used by low powered unlicensed devices, harmful interference
2400–2483.5 2400–2500	ISM	Worldwide availability, small antenna, large bandwidth	Crowded spectrum, many standards and technologies
5725–5850	ISM	Worldwide availability, small antenna, large bandwidth	Existing standards and technologies, severe attenuation
4200–4800 7250–8500	UWB	Worldwide availability, short range, low power, huge bandwidth, does not interfere largely	Coexistence with high data rate multimedia applications, severe attenuation

who are authorized to use this band are physicians and trained technicians [64]. Other technologies include unlicensed ISM, Medical Implant Communications Service (MICS), and UWB. ISM band is usually utilized to protect adjacent channel interference, and additionally it is used by other classical Wireless Sensor Network (WSN) technologies. In this context UWB technology seems to be the most promising band candidate for the future generation WBANs.

In Table 1 we compare the main properties of the communication and data transmission bands in BAN and WBAN networks.

In this section we first define the main concept of UWB technology and then present possible benefits of the deployment of this mechanism in WBANs. We focus on the aspects of the whole system and transmitter design, communication channel modeling and the project of the physical layer of WBAN. The models are presented along with a short survey of the most notable and projects proposed in the literature.

3.1 UWB Technology

UWB RF technology allows a robust and energy effective data and signals transmission through wireless networks. By using a wide bandwidth, UWB offers an effective and low-cost combination of data and energy management systems by utilizing bands within the frequency range of 3.1–10.6 GHz. UWB signals have an inherent noise-like behavior due to their extremely low maximum effective isotropically radiated power. This makes them difficult to detect, which is crucial in the medical applications, where security aspects are very important. There are various implementations of UWB technology which differ in frequency band and signal characteristics. The most common UWB model is based on a specification of the multi-layer WiMedia Alliance protocol[1] presented in Fig. 2.

Fig. 2. WiMedia UWB protocol (see also [6])

---

[1] www.wimedia.org/en/index.asp.

Two main layers of the WiMedia Alliance protocol are UWB based Physical (PHY) and Media Access Control (MAC) layer, which together form the "common radio platform" in the protocol stack. In PHY layer the frequency spectrum is divided into 14 bands and 6 band groups as shown in Fig. 3.

Fig. 3. UWB frequencies and band groups

Additional technical specifications for UWB include: **(a)** Multi-band Orthogonal Frequency Division Multiplexing with over 110 sub-carriers per channel (4.125 MHz bandwidth sub-carrier bandwidth), **(b)** a channel bandwidth of 528 MHz, and **(c)** a low broadcast power that allows same-channel coexistence with the other close band devices such as 802.11a/b/g/n and Bluetooth radios [6]. The MAC protocol defines a multi-frame (Super-frame [6]) structure with sequentially executed beacon and data periods (see Fig. 4).

Fig. 4. UWB MAC frames

Beacons are transmitted by the UWB device(s) in order to provide the timing and resource access information, which is passed on and transmitted during the data phase. The PHY and MAC layers can be additionally combined with the other wireless protocols, such as Wireless-USB or Bluetooth 3.0, as an additional option for integration into mobile devices.

3.2   UWB BAN System Model

There is no standardized architecture or system design for UWB BANs, but research is being done in this area and a number of works have been proposed with different designs for the architecture of BAN system. In [69], Roy et al. have proposed a promising architecture for body area networks, i.e., a multi-sensor multi-antenna architecture. In this approach, every sensor carries an antenna and the sink is placed in closed vicinity of a body. This sink is the central device and it supports an antenna array. Most of the computational complexity lies in the sink. Authors have proposed a complete analytical channel model for the on-body diffracted waves mechanism. IEEE 802.15.4a group has developed a low cost, low complexity, low power and low range physical layer based on UWB technology. The under discussion architecture is also built on the channel model of IEEE 802.15.4a. UWB is chosen because its low power spectral density and large bandwidth offers many advantages, such as low interference, low sensibility to fading, and accurate positioning. This architecture is expected to exploit the array gain and in turn increase the (Signal to Noise Ratio) SNR. Since power saving is a critical issue in such systems, the architecture minimizes the transmission power requirement and increases the battery lifetime of sensors. Different measurements were taken to test the proposed architecture in different scenarios. Issues like path loss, tapped delay time, and correlation aspects are discussed in detail. Tap mean amplitude decays with the delay and is described by a dual-slope power law. Parameters depend on the locations of transmitting and receiving antennas. This work only considers the first waves interfering with the human body. More research needs to be done on the delayed waves which are coming after reflection through the surroundings.

In [39], Kim et al. have proposed an UWB system employing binary zero correlation duration (ZCD) code for wireless BANs. As different devices are mounted on human body so there are chances of multiple access interference (MAI); in order to avoid this and to enhance the performance, binary ZCD is used as a spreading code for ultra wide band. This work shows that system performance can be enhanced considerably without adding much complexity by applying ZCD code.

In [68], Rajagopal et al. have proposed a chaotic based UWB system. The system meets the ultra low power requirements of body area networks while providing 100 kbps to 10 Mbps data rates, thus enabling a wide range of applications. Chaotic UWB modulation scheme is used to attain spectrum flexibility at minimum cost and power.

In [15], Chen et al. have explored the application of cooperative communications in UWB body area networks. Cooperative communications make use of available user terminals as relays that cooperate together to form a virtual antenna array. This work focuses on the system deployment scenario when the subject is in sitting posture. Vital channel parameters, such as path loss, power delay profile, power variation, and effective received power cross-correlation, are investigated. The main feature of this work is that it utilizes the directional antennas in such a way so as to minimize human exposure to electromagnetic radiation keeping health concerns in mind. This work also provides a full-bandwidth view of a body-centric channel through a time-domain apparatus. The method used calculates the system diversity levels and it is expected to serve as a standard for assessing the performance of various diversity based techniques in body centric scenarios.

3.3   UWB Transmitter Design for BANs

The power saving requirements of BANs impose some constraints on the transceiver architecture and UWB signaling strategy. Implementation of UWB transceivers is still in the phase of research and conventional trends cannot be followed because of these constraints. So, the logical alternative is to look for analog front end implementations and simplest possible transceiver architectures. Low power UWB implementation for BANs have to meet the following design guidelines:

1. Low duty cycle signaling,
2. Non-coherent architecture at the receiver,
3. Pulse generator consuming low power, and
4. In order to comply with regulations, increase spreading factor in case of short pulse waveforms. That is, the average power concentrated in a pulse duration is spread into the spreading factor.

   UWB-based systems use pulse position modulation (PPM) to transmit information with the 40 MHz clock frequency of modulator. In [70], Ryckaert et al. highlight the potential of UWB for short-range communication. Most of the UWB transmitter building blocks are switched off between the pulses, which allows to minimize the energy consumption. Authors have evaluated the overall power consumption of the transmitter through a link budget analysis in a wireless BAN context, taking into account explicit channel models. A comparison of narrow-band implementations with UWB shows great reduction in power consumption. In [34], Kohno et al. have presented an ultra low power transceiver design for BANs. Transmitters and detectors are also described. System is analyzed in terms of packet error ratio, link budget, and power consumption. This can be done by adopting the IEEE 802.15.6 standard.

   If research maintains its current momentum in this area, further enhancements are expected both at circuit and algorithmic level which will make UWB a promising and key technology for ultra-low-power communications.

3.4   WBANs Antennas for UWB Frequencies

Another important issue of WBANs is the antenna design which should meet the size limit and biocompatibility requirements. The antenna for a wireless body area network faces numerous RF challenges. Several antenna designs have been proposed in the literature, a few of them are discussed below.

   In [84], Yazdandoost et al. have presented an antenna design which operates in UWB frequency from 3.1 to 5.1 GHz. Two layers of substrate are used in the antenna to cancel the effects of human body on performance of the antenna. Performance is then analyzed in free space as well as close to the human body. Experiments in different scenarios are performed without making any changes to the antenna design. The antennas become directional when placed close to the human body as it affects the radiation patterns of antenna. Similarly, human body absorbs a large amount of output power which affects performance. The proposed antenna design provides better performance when placed close to the human body due to the second substrate layer.

In [38], Attari et al. have presented a small size ultra wide band antenna for BANs. The proposed antenna works in the range of 3.1–10.6 GHz in free space, which is then modified by using a PEC (perfect electric conducting) plane. PEC is used as a reflector to enhance performance when antenna is in close proximity to the human body. Simulation results show that the modified antenna has better performance in frequency and time domain. The proposed antenna design reduces the effect of the body on the antenna, thus, increasing the gain of antenna when placed close to the human body by using a PEC plane.

In [2], Almpanis et al. have presented an inverted truncated annular dielectric resonator antenna for BANs. The antenna operates at 3.4–5.0 GHz. The properties of antenna are discussed theoretically and practically. Performance is analyzed in free space and close to human body and demonstrates good results in frequency, as well as time domain. Although the design is presented specifically for BANs, the design concepts are general and it can be used for other applications with minor modifications.

3.5 Using UWB for Transmission Channel Modeling in WBANs

The high capacity transmission channel of the UWB systems is one of the most important advantage due to which UWB is employed in on-body and in-body medical monitoring systems. Research has been done on the study of path loss for various onbody and in-body devices. As data rate for BANs is very low and the range is limited, UWB is being considered as most suitable air-interface. A lot of work has been done on path loss model but the propagation channel has not been discussed in detail so far. When two sensors are communicating on the human body, a receiver can receive the signal in 3 ways: (a) propagating through the body, (b) diffracting around the body, and (c) reflections off nearby scatters and then back toward the body. The human body itself is a quite complex environment and no one has studied it explicitly from the perspective of wireless communication. Several channel models are presented in [8, 72, 73, 81].

In [72], Takizawa et al. have proposed stochastic channel models on power delay profile and path loss. All the models are derived from CTF (channel transfer functions) in a hospital room. Path loss model is presented for several bands while power delay profile is only presented for UWB.

In [73], Aoyagi et al. have provided channel models for BANs in UWB frequency band. The statistical model and parameters are extracted directly from measured channel CFTs. Channel models are derived on both path loss and power delay profile. In [8], Betancur et al. have proposed a similar statistical channel model.

3.6   UWB BAN Physical Layer

According to the technical requirement of the WBAN task group, many companies and research institutes have proposed physical layer architectures to provide fundamental technologies for WBAN communication systems. Since there are various service scenarios for in-body or on-body applications, the physical layer proposals include UWB and narrowband techniques [14]. The physical layer is responsible for: (a) activation and deactivation of the radio transceiver, (b) Clear Channel Assessment (CCA) within the current channel, and (c) data transmission and reception.

In [17], Choi et al. have proposed the design of a PHY simulator for wireless BAN system in IEEE 802.15.6. As there are varying scenarios for body area networks, including in-body and on-body scenarios depending on the application, the physical layer proposals include UWB, as well as narrowband techniques. In the WBAN PHY case, the modulation method is adjusted according to frequency band and data rate. Several works on performance evaluation based on different channel models for UWB BANs are present in the literature. In [13], Chang et al. have investigated the performance of UWB-MIMO for BAN channel capacity through extensive measurements for both spatial and polar antenna arrays. Channel frequency responses were measured in 3–10 GHz frequency range that covers the whole UWB band. Effects of bandwidth, array spacing, antenna polarization, and propagation conditions, from the measured channels, were analyzed on the UWB-MIMO channel capacity. MIMO channels are formed by combining a number of single input single output channel responses. It was observed that the MIMO channel capacity decreases with bandwidth and frequency; furthermore, the receiving power decreases when frequency band is increased. High frequency components have low power, so they don't contribute much to the channel capacity. Similarly, when the receiving array spacing is increased, the channel capacity and the spatial correlation co-efficient are decreased in most of cases, and the maximum value of power difference between any two sub-channels is increased. In order to achieve maximum channel capacity, array spacing of the spatial array should be lower than one wavelength. Device compactness can be achieved without sacrificing channel capacity in case of a polar array, in contrast to spatial arrays in non-line of sight (NLOS) conditions; in line of sight (LOS) conditions the maximum achievable capacity of a spatial array is higher than that of the polar array.

In [71], Sangodoyin et al. have investigate on the impact of body mass index (BMI) on the body-to-body propagation channels. They provided a detailed description of a measurement campaign for wireless body-to-body propagation channels. Measurements were done in an anechoic chamber to clearly work out the impact of the body. Channel frequency responses were measured in 2–10 GHz frequency range.

In [73], Takizawa et al. have presented performance evaluation of UWB wireless BANs, which shows that the modulation scheme has to pay much penalty if it uses a non-coherent receiver as compared to coherent detection. In [23], Domenicali et al. have analyzed the performance of BAN composed of IEEE

802.15.4a UWB sensors. The parameters used for performance evaluation are BER (bit error rate), network lifetime, and throughput. The work presents a unique case by analyzing performance in the presence of an external interfering network. BAN performance can be improved by using an optimized time hopping code assignment strategy.

In [80], and [22], performance evaluation method is presented which observes the waveform distribution along the signal path. Performance of a transceiver is evaluated in terms of BER. Results show that the human body casts more effect on performance than the environment, especially in case of NLOS path for a propagation channel. Selection of suitable pulse shape depends upon the modulation schemes used.

3.7 Optimal Locations for Sensors in UWB BANs

Knowledge of precise locations of sensors is necessary for successful data transmission in many medical applications. In WBAN these locations must be estimated with a very high (millimeter-scale) precision. Localization in WSNs has been actively studied during the last few years. Many methodologies effective in the standard wireless architectures, such as the received-signal-strength-indicator (RSSI) technique [35] and time-of flight (TOF) measurement technique [10], can be successfully applied in WBANs and other medical applications.

In [1], Abbasi et al. have investigated the optimum locations for placing sensors on human body. Experiments were performed on more than 100 transceiver locations for LOS and NLOS scenarios. Path loss models were developed and performance was evaluated for different scenarios. An orthogonal frequency-domain multiplexing (OFDM) based UWB system was used and calculations were performed on the basis of BER values (see Table 2), on selected locations. Best possible locations identified by this work are legs and arms for LOS and NLOS scenarios, respectively.

Table 2. BER values for different parts of human body [1]

Body part	On-body	
	LOS (Front side)	NLOS (Back side)
	BER	BER
Trunk (Rx23/Rx75)	3.7e−2	9.98e−4
Left arm (Rx27/Rx90)	3.89e−5	5.1e−5
Right arm (Rx38/Rx89)	4.76e−3	7.67e−5
Left leg (Rx44/Rx104)	4.83e−6	2.34e−5
Right leg (Rx47/Rx101)	1.83e−5	1.26e−4
Head (Rx54/Rx57)	9.99e−4	6.54e−4

State-of-the-art of 3D localization systems have been surveyed in [42]. In [40] the authors present a methodology of the transmission of a 300 ps Gaussian pulse, which is modulated by an 8 GHz carrier signal as a direct support to a localization system for indoor WBANs that provides accuracy in the 1–10 mm range and seems to be one of the most promising solutions for the future generation positioning techniques.

4   Cloud Support to Mobile e-Health Systems and WBANs

E-health system was considered as a solution for the presented model because it is the most powerful and it allows to interact remotely between patients and professionals. Due to providing data from WBAN to this system, these can help to solve many of the patient's medical problems. Although communication protocols and efficient data transmission between sensors, network body, local base node, and the external network base station (signal receivers) are crucial in the design of modern WBANs, data processing and replication, remote patient monitoring by medical personnel, and a fast and secure access to the data still remain challenging and complex issues in today's IT-based health care systems. Conventional medical systems are still built on workflows that consist of paper medical records, duplicated test results, handwritten notes. The U.S. Department of Health and Human Services has published in 2009 the *Health Information Technology for Economic and Clinical Health (HITECH) Act* [33] which contains a format known as an *Electronic Medical Record (EMR)* [44] for digitizing the patients' data and medical tests to make them transparent to patients together with health plan costs, covered services, and health insurance. A successful practical implementation of such U.S digitization idea (and its extension to be a global system) needs a low-cost scalable IT infrastructure that allows a fast remote access of patients and doctors to the system and data. This system must be easily adaptable to various patients' and other users' needs, departmental policies and organizational sizes, and security and data protection must be the paramount system's characteristics. Recently, cloud computing seems to be a good candidate for supporting IT-based health medical systems as it successfully offers multiple benefits for enterprise computing environments [67].

Cloud computing enables convenient and on-demand access to a shared configurable computing resources of various types, namely physical infrastructures (servers, datacenters, networks), virtual servers and web-based services to distributed users [31]. All these resources are provisioned by the service providers and local resource providers with possible minimal cost and management efforts and interactions. Major characteristics of cloud computing which are important in medical data storage, data analysis and processing, can be defined as follows [11,46]:

- **on-demand self-service:** each cloud user can deploy and configure the cloud servers and services himself, no interactions with service providers are necessary;
- **multitenancy:** the resources and costs are shared across a large community of cloud users;
- **scalability:** an efficient and low-cost configuration and assignment of system resources according to consumer demand;
- **easy system access:** cloud resources and services are accessed through standard (Internet) protocols, using standard web browsers regardless of their location and platform, e.g., smart phones.
- **meeting security demand:** dedicated services for higher security requirements, [76].

Model described above is supported by cloud-based architecture. Data from body sensors in WBANs are received by Cloud Client and then, they are sent directly to the cloud, which consist with the providers of the service such as: Software as a Service (SaaS) that is a cloud computing model in which the application is running on the service provider's computers and it is available to users via the Internet; Platform as a Service (PaaS) which provides the runtime environment and the system on which the application runs; Infrastructure as a Service (Iaas) which provides the appropriate equipment to implement the described model and allows to its scalability at any time [30]. These services collect received from Cloud Client data from sensors in a Data center with access to Cloud Storage Facilities. The general architecture of cloud-based WBAN support infrastructure is presented in Fig. 5.

Fig. 5. Cloud-based support to WBANs

In this model a patient, equipped with BAN sensors and a mobile device, such as smart phone or a tablet, communicates to the cloud system through a cloud web client or a specially designed standalone application. The base sensor module in WBAN collects the patient's data and transmits it to the mobile device (often via Bluetooth) without the patient's intervention. The cloud client (cloud platform interface), installed at the mobile device, forwards the patient's data to the appropriate web service installed at the cloud platform. The collected data is stored, analyzed, and processed by a software module. The results of this analysis (and possible diagnosis) are disseminated to the patient, his doctor, who can be another mobile cloud user, emergency services (if necessary), hospital etc., at specified time intervals or just single time period (point). Patient's historical medical reports are available for retrieval from the cloud after user authentication.

Although many popular cloud computing platforms, either free (e.g., iCloud [36] and DropBox [25]) or commercial (e.g., GoGrid [28], Amazon AWS [4], Google Cloud Platform [29]) are already available for pervasive management of large volumes of user's data, they may not be suitable for many health care applications. Moreover, cloud computing for health care needs highest level of availability, security, and privacy for the patients' data in order to gain acceptance in the marketplace. Development of high security and accessibility of cloud computing services and personalization of processed patients' data are contentious issues in the design of scalable IT-based systems supporting WBANs [37].

4.1 State-of-the Art

The integration of WBANs and cloud service providers to provide mobile health facilities has transformed from a vision of future to a nowday facility. Numerous renowned hospitals in Europe and US provide e-health services based on Electronic Health Records (EHR) with cloud integration [58]. In the following lines we discuss the state-of-the art research proposals regarding ubiquitous health based on WBAN-cloud integration.

In [46] the authors present the could-based support for the analysis of the electrocardiogram (ECG) data. The proposed system model consist of the three traditional cloud layers, that is: (a) Software, (b) Platform, and (c) Infrastructure. The software layer provides data upload, storage, and analysis facilities. The platform layer consists of three modules: (a) container scaling manager, (b) workflow engine [45], and (c) Aneka scheduling environment [79]. The workflow engine is installed inside the container and manages the execution of the workflow process in ECG analysis. The ECG data processed in this workflow can be either numerical or graphical (ECG) [7], and are calculated and compared with the patients historical data and standard values. The container scaling manager creates new containers according to the number of incoming requests (tasks). The tasks composed in the workflow module are submitted to the Aneka [79] scheduling environment. This scheduling system plays the role of a workflow distribution and management platform based on the conventional master-slave model adopted in cloud systems. The Aneka master is installed on the platform cloud layer while the slaves are task executors installed on the infrastructure entities (virtual machines) of the cloud. For the security of data communication between different layers, a third party Public Key Infrastructure (PKI) is proposed. This model is a good example of the utilization of the public cloud environment for real-time monitoring the patient's health condition.

Similar idea is presented as the *HealthCloud* project in [24]. The cloud service client is designed as a web application for the Android OS consisting of: **(a)** Patient Health Record module which retrieves patient records form the cloud, **(b)** Medical Imaging module that decodes and displays the image according to the Digital Imaging and Communications in Medicine (DICOM) [19] and JPEG2000 compression standard. The Amazon's S3 cloud service [4] has been utilized for the evaluation of the developed model in WLAN and 3G networks with different JPEG2000 compression parameters. SSL data encryption is proposed to secure data communication. A similar model based on Internet of Things (IoT) communication framework for mobile health care is described in [48].

Doherty et al. [60] have proposed a physiological lifelogged data framework that stores lifetime events of a person over a cloud. While the lifelogged data can help people remember what they were doing at a particular moment, it can also be analyzed to find out potential reasons behind a medical condition. The proposed 'SmartLogger' system provides three interfaces to view the physiological data. The query interface allows a user to search data based on temporal queries. The chart interface provides graphical images of physiological activities, such as the heart rate measured by a ECG sensor. The context interface provides additional information gathered from various bio-sensors such as the location of the user, images of the surroundings, and audio data that might be helpful in classifying a temporal event.

Research has also been done on cloud-sensor integration to build community-centric information sensing and dispensing applications that work on the basis of publication subscription model [50]. A publication-subscription broker that delivers information to users via a cloud service application consists of: **(a)** a sensor data stream monitoring and processing component, **(b)** a registry component that saves information about user subscriptions to different applications, **(c)** an analyzer component that maps data streams to corresponding applications, and **(d)** a disseminator component that sends data to a subscribed user using an event matching algorithm.

WBAN-cloud integration for mobile health care systems is a novel idea with benefits of computational and storage offloading. However, researchers have opposed cloud computing approach to ubiquitous healthcare due to the communicational overhead such a system incurs, delays experienced, and continuous connectivity requirement with the cloud [49]. Instead, a ubiquitous healthcare system based on a resource provisioning framework that harnesses the computational and storage capabilities of computing devices lying in close vicinity is proposed. The authors of [49] have proposed a wireless communication model to transmit patient data and to prioritize data streams based on severity of patient's condition. The model is a two-tier hierarchical architecture consisting of inter and intra-BAN communications. Inside each BAN, a cluster head (CH) is selected based on higher computational and communicational power to act as a gateway for all inter-BAN sensor nodes. The CH may himself act as a broker or offload the tasks to a base station. The broker of the proposed system is composed of a workflow manager and a scheduler/optimizer. The workflow manager receives service requests from sensors. The optimizer identifies the appropriate service providers in the vicinity for service distribution. The service provides volunteer themselves or they are identified by request-response messages. These messages contain the computational (CPU cycles) and storage (bytes) facility available at a service provider. In this manner ubiquitous health can be provided without the requirement of cloud connectivity.

5 Security Challenges and Solutions

BANs are meant to support medical applications mainly. Hence, privacy, security, (Quality of Service) QoS, and reliability are important factors besides energy efficiency. Traditional security and privacy techniques are not appropriate for BANs due to bounded processing power, memory, and energy, as well as the lack of a user interface, unskilled users and global roaming. Hence, novel lightweight and resource-efficient methods have to be developed for BANs [66]. Global roaming over heterogeneous infrastructure networks further complicates end-to-end security provisions. Cloud integration of mobile health applications has given rise to new security concerns such as trustworthiness of the cloud client and secure extra-BAN communication.

Security and privacy of patients' data when it is stored in and retrieved from the cloud, user authentication and authorization for access to the data, and internal management of data by the cloud provider are major concerns in the cloud-based mobile health applications. Researchers have proposed the use of TSL/SSL protocol to secure communication between the cloud and the patient [24,59]. The trust between the cloud and the patient is still a major research issue to be dwelled upon. The process of authentication between a user and a service provider for the identification of proper authorization level is based on trusted third party certification authority in many cloud based applications. The trusted third party certification authority is responsible for the implementation of the authentication and authorization system based on the PKI. Cloud support provides the opportunity to offload computationally intensive jobs form the mobile devices to the cloud. In the following lines we present state-of-the art research proposals for security challenges in WBAN and WBAN cloud integration.

Nkosi and Mekuria [43] propose a security service provision framework based on the cloud services as a solution for mobile health concerns. Security is provided as a service to the mobile devices like other services provided by the cloud. In this model, the mobile devices are cloned over the cloud infrastructure. When the mobile device faces a computationally intensive task, it transfers the task to its clone over the cloud. The task is executed in the cloud and the output is sent back to the mobile device. The only concern about Security As a Service (SasS) model is the security of the communication channel between the cloud and the mobile device. This threat is mitigated by implementation of secure communication protocols. Similar task off-loading scheme has been presented in [55]. Task offloading techniques help the resource constrained mobile devices and sensors to execute their task over the cloud, but they also incur communication overhead.

Wang et al. [57] have proposed a distributed dynamic integrity check and data storage scheme for WSNs. The data to be encrypted is divided into n blocks. Each data block is encrypted using a secret key. Each encrypted data block is distributed among n neighbors, thus providing secure data storage. When an integrity check is required for the data, each node having a share of the n blocks of the data computes and broadcasts its integrity checksum. Thus, the distributed storage and computation reduces the memory overhead on a single sensor node.

To secure medical data from a determined adversary, Pietro et al. [62] have proposed a data survivability scheme based on continuous movement of data from one sensor node to another. It is assumed that the adversary knows the origins of the target data and can compromise a subset of nodes to capture that data. The continuous data communication, replication, and encryption applied in this scheme makes it impractical for energy constrained WBANs.

Access privileges to medical data in WBANs can be maintained by implementing a Role-Based Access Control (RBAC) model [65]. The participating WBAN entities are assigned groups according to their roles, such as physicians and patients. Each user role is mapped to user-privilege set in one to many mappings. RBAC is simplistic and well suited for the requirements of WBANs. An RBAC scheme based on secret key encryption for medical WBANs is proposed in [63]. The proposed scheme utilizes the random key predistribution methods defined in [53]. By predistributing encryption keys, a user can establish a pairwise keys with all entities in the WBAN. Each pairwise key is mapped to a role, thus, access privileges are assigned to each pair of keys. The predistribution and pairwise key management make this scheme impractical for large WBANs configurations.

In [74] a secure data communication model for scalable cloud computing applications is presented. The model adds a Security Manager entity to the generic cloud model. The security manager is a trusted third extension of the cloud provider. The security manager generates public and private keys of each user, regenerates keys after expiry, generates session keys and maintains access control list for each data set.

A data re-encryption scheme proposed in [52] is used to offer confidential data storage that is even private to a cloud provider. A user encrypts the data before sending it to the cloud where the security manager re-encrypts the data before it is stored in the cloud. The authors have also provided a variation of the model in which data encryption is offloaded to the security manger while data re-encryption is performed by the cloud provider.

In [56] researchers have presented a novel cross-cloud domain based trust model. A trust value is associated with each client and domain entity. When an entity A wants to communicate with an entity B, it compares the entity B's trust value with its trust threshold. If the trust value is greater than the trust threshold, it will continue with the transaction. Otherwise it will abort the operation. Trust values are updated on the basis of completed transactions which have not violated trust relationship between two entities.

Sorber et al. [61] have proposed a novel mHealth model based on a wrist-watchlike wearable device, *Amulet*. An Amulet provides many advantages over mobile and PDA based mHealth modes such as: (a) Amulet is tightly coupled with the patient's body unlike mobile devices and PDA's, which can be out of transmission range of the sensor devices, (b) Amulet uses special-purpose hardware to support secure mHealth applications. Unlike mobile devices, the Amulet provides secure storage of encryption keys, (c) the Amulet provides interoperability between sensor and mobile devices by implementing multiple low-power radios supporting diverse wireless technologies, and (d) Amulet is able to authenticate the wearer by various physiological parameters, such as pulse and galvanic skin response (GSR).

Researchers [51] have proposed a Plug-n-Test approach to secure medical data sensing and processing in mobile phones based on plug-in smart cards that provide a trusted computing platform. The smart card provides processing and storage of encrypted data. The smart card thus exchanges keys with medical sensors and the back-end cloud for sending and receiving encrypted data. The test model includes a JavaCard applet and two Android phones with smat-card integration. The test model implementation shows 20% energy consumption overhead in worst case, 59–69% increase in latency time, and 44% communication overhead while ensuring data confidentiality and integrity.

The proposals discussed in the above section ensure data security which is critical in the context of medical health records but each proposal also incurs computational and communicational overheads while ensuring data security. A lightweight, universally accepted security framework for WBANs providing ubiquitous health facilities is an area with great research potential.

6   Conclusions and Future Directions

The WBAN is an emerging and promising technology that is expected to change people's daily life and healthcare experiences. Data security, safety, efficiency, and privacy in WBANs are the key research issues, and a number of considerable challenges still remain to overcome. The research in this area is still in its infancy, but it is believed it will draw a huge amount of interest in next few years.

This chapter has highlighted many research and practical issues related to WBANs supported by the UWB wireless technologies. UWB wireless technology for intra-BAN communications is one of the most promising methodology for the effective data transmission in today's medical applications. However, some early results on the application of the other technologies, such as Bluetooth and ZigBee, are also available, but no standard has been developed so far for WBANs.

There is a big potential in designing a physical layer for WBANs. Previous work includes some UWB and narrow band techniques. A channel modeling field is also in a research phase and the complex environment of the human body poses many challenges to researchers in this regard. There is no standard antenna design for wireless BAN devices. Antenna needs to be comfortable and compatible with the human body. The issues of directionality, antenna gain needs to be investigated in detail when working around the human body. Neither a transmitter design has not been finalized yet. Different transmitter designs have been proposed with the focus on low-power transmitters. Apart from these technical details, there are a lot more issues to be resolved for social acceptance of BANs. These include conflicts between different requirements, such as security and efficiency.

Cloud computing infrastructure provides a cost effective and easy to use data sharing and access platform which is ideal for the IT enabled healthcare systems. Requirements of such a cloud supported health system is high availability of data for healthcare personnel and security of the patients' data. Authentication and authorization solutions provided by third parties have been proposed as a solution for data confidentiality requirements.

Catering all these challenges is most likely to require new methods and protocols for MAC and PHY, and state-of-the-art antenna design, transmitter design, and lightweight security protocols. UWB is being considered as most promising candidate for BANs. The state-of-the-art in system design, channel modeling, performance evaluation, transmitter design, and antenna design of UWB BANs is also presented in this chapter. The WBAN-cloud integration and related security challenges have also been thoroughly surveyed. Researchers, engineers, and practitioners from various disciplines, must come together to overcome technical roadblocks in order to bring the vision of a ubiquitous body area network to reality.

References

1. Abbasi, Q.H., Khan, M.M., Alomainy, A., Hao, Y.: Characterization and modelling of ultra wideband radio links for optimum performance of body area network in health care applications. In: 2011 International Workshop on Antenna Technology (iWAT), pp. 206–209 (2011)
2. Almpanis, G., Fumeaux, C., Fröhlich, J., Vahldieck, R.: A truncated conical dielectric resonator antenna for body-area network applications. IEEE Antennas Wirel. Propag. Lett. **8**, 279–282 (2009)
3. Drude, S.: Requirements and application scenarios for body area networks. In: Mobile and Wireless Communications Summit (2008)
4. Amazon Web Services. aws.amazon.com
5. IEEE 802.15. www.ieee802.org/15/pub/TG6.html
6. Ayar, E.: UWB Wireless Video Transmission Technology in Medical Applications. NDS Surgical Imaging (NDSsi) White Paper-Report (2010)
7. Bahoura, M., Hassani, M., Hubin, M.: DSP implementation of wavelet transform for real time ECG wave forms detection and heart rate analysis. Comput. Methods Programs Biomed. **52**(1), 35–44 (1997)
8. Betancur, L., Cardona, N., Navarro, A., Traver, L.: A statistical channel model for on body area networks in ultra wide band communications. In: Proceedings of the IEEE Radio and Wireless Symposium, vol. 1, pp. 715–718 (2008)

9. Basu, S., Sarkar, M., Nagaraj, S., Chinara, S.: A survey on ultra wideband and ultrasonic communication for body area networks. Int. J. Ultra Wideband Commun. Syst. **3**(3), 143–154 (2016)
10. Baunach, M., Kolla, R., Mvihlberger, C.: Beyond theory: development of a real world localization application as low power WSN. In: Proceedings of IEEE Conference on Local Computer Networks, Dublin, Ireland, 15–18 October 2007, pp. 872–884 (2007)
11. Buyya, R., Broberg, J., Goscinski, A. (eds.): Cloud Computing: Principles and Paradigms. Wiley, Hoboken (2011)
12. Cao, H., Leung, V., Chow, C., Chan, H.: Enabling technologies for wireless body area networks: a survey and outlook. IEEE Commun. Mag. **47**(12), 84–93 (2009)
13. Chang, W.J., Tarng, J.-H., Peng, S.-Y.: Frequency-space-polarization on UWB MIMO performance for body area network applications. IEEE Antennas Wirel. Propag. Lett. **7**, 577–580 (2008)
14. Cwalina, K., Sławomir, A., Rajchowski, P.: An off-body narrowband and ultra-wide band channel model for body area networks in a ferry environment. In: Proceedings of the IRACON 7th MC Meeting and 7th Technical Meeting, pp. 1–20 (2018)
15. Teo, Y.J., et al.: Cooperative communications in ultra-wideband wireless body area networks: channel modeling and system diversity analysis. IEEE J. Sel. Areas Commun. **27**(1), 5–16 (2009)
16. Hoyt, R., Reifman, J., Coster, T., Buller, M.: Combat medical informatics: present and future. In: Proceedings of the AMIA 2002 Annual Symposium, San Antonio, TX, pp. 335–339 (2002)
17. Choi, B.K., Kim, B.S., Lee, S., Wang, K.Y., Kim, Y.J., Chung, D.: Narrowband physical layer design for WBAN system. In: Proceedings of the First International Conference on Pervasive Computing, Signal Processing and Applications, pp. 154–157 (2010)
18. Contaldo, M., Banerjee, B., Ruffieux, D., Chabloz, J., Le Roux, E., Enz, C.C.: A 2.4-GHz BAW-based transceiver for wireless body area networks. IEEE Trans. Biomed. Circuits Syst. **4**(6), 391–399 (2010)
19. The Digital Imaging and Communications in Medicine (DICOM) Standard. medical.nema.org
20. Mare, S., Sorber, J., Shin, M., Cornelius, C., Kotz, D.: Adaptive security and privacy for mHealth sensing. In: Proceedings of the 2nd USENIX Conference on Health Security and Privacy (HealthSec 2011), pp. 2–12. USENIX Association, Berkeley (2011)
21. Merli, F., Skrivervik, A.K.: Design and measurement considerations for implantable antennas for telemetry applications. In: Proceedings of 4th European Conference on Antennas and Propagation EuCAP, pp. 1–5 (2010)
22. De Santis, V., Feliziani, M., Maradei, F.: Safety assessment of UWB radio systems for body area network by the FD2TD method. IEEE Trans. Magn. **46**(8), 3245–3248 (2010)
23. Domenicali, D., De Nardis, L., Di Benedetto, M.-G.: UWB body area network coexistence by interference mitigation. In: Proceedings of IEEE International Conference on Ultra-Wideband, ICUWB 2009, Vancouver, Canada, 9–11 September 2009, pp. 713–717 (2009)
24. Doukas, C., Pliakas, T., Maglogiannis, I.: Mobile healthcare information management utilizing cloud computing and android OS. In: Proceedings of the 32nd Annual International Conference of the IEEE EMBS Buenos Aires, Argentina, 31 August–4 September 2010, pp. 1037–1040 (2010)

25. DropBox. www.dropbox.com
26. Drude, S.: Requirements and application scenarios for body area networks. In: 16th IST Mobile And Wireless Communications Summit, pp. 1–5 (2008)
27. Gerrits, J.F.M., Farserotu, J.R., Long, J.R.: Low-complexity Ultra-Wide-Band communications. IEEE Trans. Circuits Syst. **55**(4), 329–333 (2008)
28. GoGrid Storage Services. www.gogrid.com
29. Google Cloud Platform. cloud.google.com
30. Grzonka, D.: The analysis of OpenStack cloud computing platform: features and performance. J. Telecommun. Inf. Technol. **3**, 52–57 (2015)
31. Grzonka, D., Szczygiel, M., Bernasiewicz, A., Wilczynski, A., Liszka, M.: Short analysis of implementation and resource utilization for the OpenStack cloud computing platform. In: Proceedings of 29th European Conference on Modelling and Simulation, ECMS 2015, pp. 608–614 (2015)
32. Hanson, M.A., et al.: Body area sensor networks: challenges and opportunities. Computer **42**(1), 58–65 (2009)
33. HITECH. www.hhs.gov/ocr/privacy/hipaa/administrative/enforcementrule/hitechenforcementifr.html
34. Hernandez, M., Kohno, R.: Ultra low power UWB transceiver design for body area networks. In: 2nd International Symposium on Applied Sciences in Biomedical and Communication Technologies, Israel 2009, pp. 1–4 (2009)
35. Hjortland, H.A., Lande, T.S.: CTBV integrated impulse radio design for biomedical applications. IEEE Trans. Biomed. Circuits Syst. **3**(2), 79–88 (2009)
36. iCloud. www.icloud
37. Val, J., et al.: Mobihealth: mobile health services based on body area networks. In: Istepanian, R.S.H., Laxminarayan, S., Pattichis, C.S. (eds.) M-Health. Topics in Biomedical Engineering, pp. 219–236. Springer, Boston (2006). https://doi.org/10.1007/0-387-26559-7_16
38. Karimabadi, S.S., Attari, A.R.: Gain enhancement of small size UWB antenna for wireless body area network applications. In: IEEE Proceedings of ICEE 2010, 11–13 May 2010, pp. 50–53 (2010)
39. Kim, E.C., Park, S., Cha, J.S., Kim, J.Y.: Improved performance of UWB system for wireless body area networks. IEEE Trans. Consum. Electron. **56**(3), 1373–1379 (2010)
40. Kuhn, M., Zhang, C., Mahfouz, M., Fathy, A.E.: Real-time UWB indoor positioning system with millimeter 3-D dynamic accuracy. In: Proceedings of IEEE Antennas and Propagation Society International Symposium, Charleston, CS, 1–5 June 2009 (2009)
41. Latré, B., Braem, B., Moerman, I., Blondia, C., Demeester, P.: A survey on wireless body area networks. Wireless Netw. **17**(1), 1–18 (2011)
42. Meier, C., Terzis, A., Lindenmeier, S.: A robust 3D high precision radio location system. In: Proceedings of IEEE/MTT-S International Microwave Symposium, Honolulu, HI, 3–8 June 2007, pp. 397–400 (2007)
43. Nkosi, M.T., Mekuria, F.: Cloud computing for enhanced mobile health applications. In: Proceedings of the IEEE 2nd International Conference on Cloud Computing Technology and Science, CloudCom 2010, pp. 629–633 (2010)
44. Open Clinical Knowledge Managemnt for Medical Care. www.openclinical.org/emr.html
45. Pandey, S., Voorsluys, W., Rahman, M., Buyya, R., Dobson, J., Chiu, K.: A grid workflow environment for brain imaging analysis on distributed systems. Concurr. Comput. Pract. Exp. **21**(16), 2118–2139 (2009)

46. Pandey, S., Voorsluys, W., Niu, S., Khandoker, A., Buyya, R.: An autonomic cloud environment for hosting ECG data analysis services. Future Gener. Comput. Syst. **20**, 147–154 (2012)

47. Chen, M., Gonzalez, S., Vasilakos, A., Cao, H., Leung, V.C.: Body area networks: a survey. Mob. Netw. Appl. **16**(2), 171–193 (2011)

48. Bui, N., Zorzi, M.: Health care applications: a solution based on the Internet of Things. In: Proceedings of the 4th International Symposium on Applied Sciences in Biomedical and Communication Technologies (ISABEL 2011). ACM, New York (2011). Article 131, 5 p

49. Viswanathan, H., Chen, B., Pompili, D.: Research challenges in computation, communication, and context awareness for ubiquitous healthcare. IEEE Commun. Mag. **50**(5), 92–99 (2012)

50. Hassan, M.M., Song, B., Huh, E.-N.: A framework of sensor-cloud integration opportunities and challenges. In: Proceedings of the 3rd International Conference on Ubiquitous Information Management and Communication (ICUIMC 2009), pp. 618–626. ACM, New York (2009)

51. Sorber, J.M., Shin, M., Peterson, R., Kotz, D.: Plug-n-trust: practical trusted sensing for mhealth. In: Proceedings of the 10th International Conference on Mobile Systems, Applications, and Services (MobiSys 2012), pp. 309–322. ACM, New York (2012)

52. Ateniese, G., Fu, K., Green, M., Hohenberger, S.: Improved proxy re-encryption schemes with applications to secure distributed storage. ACM Trans. Inf. Syst. Secur. **9**, 1–30 (2006)

53. Wenliang, D., Deng, J., Han, Y.S., Varshney, P.K., Katz, J., Khalili, A.: A pairwise key predistribution scheme for wireless sensor networks. ACM Trans. Inf. Syst. Secur. **8**, 2 (2005)

54. Li, M., Lou, W., Ren, K.: Data security and privacy in wireless body area networks. Wireless Commun. **17**, 1 (2010)

55. Chun, B.-G., Maniatis, P.: Augmented smartphone applications through clone cloud execution. In: Proceedings of the 12th Conference on Hot Topics in Operating Systems (HotOS 2009), p. 8-8. USENIX Association, Berkeley (2009)

56. Li, W., Ping, L.: Trust model to enhance security and interoperability of cloud environment. In: Jaatun, M.G., Zhao, G., Rong, C. (eds.) CloudCom 2009. LNCS, vol. 5931, pp. 69–79. Springer, Heidelberg (2009). https://doi.org/10.1007/978-3-642-10665-1_7

57. Wang, Q., et al.: Dependable and secure sensor data storage with dynamic integrity assurance. In: Proceedings of the IEEE INFOCOM, pp. 954–962 (2009)

58. Weiss, A.: Health and biomedical informatics. netWorker **13**(4), 18–25 (2009)

59. Kurschl, W., Beer, W.: Combining cloud computing and wireless sensor networks. In: Proceedings of the 11th International Conference on Information Integration and Web-based Applications and Services (iiWAS 2009), pp. 512–518. ACM, New York (2009)

60. Doherty, A.R., Tolle, K.M., Smeaton, A.F.: Utilising contextual memory retrieval cues and the ubiquity of the cell phone to review lifelogged physiological activities. In: Proceedings of the 1st International Workshop on Interactive Multimedia for Consumer Electronics (IMCE 2009), pp. 19–26. ACM, New York (2009)

61. Sorber, J., et al.: An amulet for trustworthy wearable mHealth. In: Proceedings of the Twelfth Workshop on Mobile Computing Systems and Applications (HotMobile 2012). ACM, New York (2012). Article 7

62. Di Pietro, R., et al.: Catch me (if you can): data survival in unattended sensor networks. In: 2008 Sixth Annual IEEE International Conference on Pervasive Computing and Communications (PerCom), pp. 185–194 (2008)
63. Morchon, O.G., Baldus, H.: Efficient distributed security for wireless medical sensor networks. In: 2008 International Conference on Intelligent Sensors, Sensor Networks and Information Processing, pp. 249–254 (2008)
64. Istepanian, R.S.H., Laxminarayan, S., Pattichis, C.S.: M-Health: Emerging Mobile Health Systems. Springer, New York (2005). https://doi.org/10.1007/b137697
65. Venkatasubramanian, K.K., Gupta, S.K.S.: Security solutions for pervasive healthcare. In: Xiao, Y. (ed.) Security in Distributed Grid Mobile and Pervasive Computing, pp. 443–464. Auerbach, Boston (2007)
66. Patel, M., Wang, J.: Applications, challenges, and prospective in emerging body area networking technologies. IEEE Wirel. Commun. 17(1), 80–88 (2010)
67. Qiu, X., et al.: Cloud technologies for bioinformatics applications. In: Proceedings of the 2nd Workshop on Many-Task Computing on Grids and Supercomputers, pp. 1–10. ACM (2009)
68. Rajagopal, S., Kang, N.-G., Park, S.-H., Bynam, K., Cho, C., Won, E.T.: Chaotic UWB based system design for ultra low power body area networks. IEEE Trans. Microw. Theory Tech. 56(10), 15–18 (2008)
69. Roy, S., Oestges, C., Horlin, F., De Doncker, P.: A comprehensive channel model for UWB multisensor multiantenna body area networks. IEEE Trans Antennas Propag. 58(1), 163–170 (2010)
70. Ryckaert, J., et al.: Ultra-WideBand transmitter for wireless body area networks. IEEE Trans. Circuits Syst. I 52(12), 2515–2525 (2005)
71. Sangodoyin, S., Molisch, A.F.: Experimental investigation of the impact of BMI on ultrawideband MIMO body-to-body networks. In: Proceedings of the IEEE 87th Vehicular Technology Conference (VTC Spring), pp. 1–5 (2018)
72. Takizawa, K., et al.: Channel models for wireless body area networks. In: Proceedings of the 30th Annual Conference of IEEE Engineering in Medicine and Biology Society, pp. 1549–1552 (2008)
73. Takizawa, K., Aoyagi, T., Kohno, R.: Channel modeling and performance evaluation of UWB-based wireless body area networks. In: IEEE ICC 2009 (2009)
74. Tysowski, P.K., Hasan, M.A.: Re-encryption-based key management towards secure and scalable mobile applications in clouds. In: IACR Cryptology ePrint Archive, pp. 668–668 (2011)
75. Lorincz, K., et al.: Mercury: a wearable sensor network platform for high-fidelity motion analysis. In: Proceedings of the 7th ACM Conference on Embedded Networked Sensor Systems (SenSys 2009), pp. 183–196. ACM, New York (2009)
76. Jakóbik, A., Grzonka, D., Palmieri, F.: Non-deterministic security driven meta scheduler for distributed cloud organizations. Simul. Model. Pract. Theory 76, 67–81 (2017)
77. Varshney, U.: Pervasive healthcare and wireless health monitoring. Mob. Netw. Appl. 12, 113–127 (2007)
78. Jakóbik, A.: Big data security. In: Pop, F., Kołodziej, J., Di Martino, B. (eds.) Resource Management for Big Data Platforms: Algorithms, Modelling, and High-Performance Computing Techniques. CCN, pp. 241–261. Springer, Cham (2016). https://doi.org/10.1007/978-3-319-44881-7_12
79. Vecchiola, C., Chu, X., Buyya, R.: Aneka: a software platform for .NET-based could computing. In: High Speed and Large Scale Scientific Computing, pp. 267–295. IOS Press (2009)

80. Wang, S., Park, J.-T.: Modeling and analysis of multi-type failures in wireless body area networks with semi-Markov model. IEEE Commun. Lett. **14**(1), 6–8 (2010)
81. Xia, L., Redfield, S., Chiang, P.: Experimental characterization of a UWB channel for body area networks. EURASIP J. Wirel. Commun. Netw. **2011**, Article ID 703239, 11 p. (2011). https://doi.org/10.1155/2011/703239
82. Yan, S., Soh, P.J., Vandenbosch, G.A.E.: Wearable ultrawideband technology-a review of ultrawideband antennas, propagation channels, and applications in wireless body area networks. IEEE Access **6**, 42177–42185 (2018)
83. Yang, G.-Z. (ed.): Body Sensor Networks. Springer, London (2006). https://doi.org/10.1007/1-84628-484-8
84. Yazdandoost, K.Y., Kohno, R.: UWB antenna for wireless body area network. In: Proceedings of the Asia-Pacific Microwave Conference, APMC 2006, pp. 1647–1652 (2006)
85. Zasowski, T., Wittneben, A.: Performance of UWB receivers with partial CSI using a simple body area network channel model. IEEE J. Sel. Areas Commun. **27**(1), 10 (2009)

Survey on AI-Based Multimodal Methods for Emotion Detection

Catherine Marechal[1] (ID), Dariusz Mikołajewski[2,3] (ID),
Krzysztof Tyburek[2] (ID), Piotr Prokopowicz[2] (ID),
Lamine Bougueroua[1] (ID), Corinne Ancourt[4] (ID),
and Katarzyna Węgrzyn-Wolska[1(✉)] (ID)

[1] Allianstic Rescarch Laboratory, Efrei Paris, Villejuif, France
{catherine.marechal,lamine.bougueroua,
katarzyna.wegrzyn-wolska}@efrei.fr
[2] Institute of Mechanics and Applied Computer Science,
Kazimierz Wielki University, Bydgoszcz, Poland
{dmikolaj,krzysiekkt,piotrek}@ukw.edu.pl
[3] Neurocognitive Laboratory, Centre for Modern Interdisciplinary Technologies,
Nicolaus Copernicus University, Toruń, Poland
darek.mikolajewski@wp.pl
[4] MINES ParisTech, PSL University, CRI, Paris, France
corinne.ancourt@mines-paristech.fr

Abstract. Automatic emotion recognition constitutes one of the great challenges providing new tools for more objective and quicker diagnosis, communication and research. Quick and accurate emotion recognition may increase possibilities of computers, robots, and integrated environments to recognize human emotions, and response accordingly to them a social rules. The purpose of this paper is to investigate the possibility of automated emotion representation, recognition and prediction its state-of-the-art and main directions for further research. We focus on the impact of emotion analysis and state of the arts of multimodal emotion detection. We present existing works, possibilities and existing methods to analyze emotion in text, sound, image, video and physiological signals. We also emphasize the most important features for all available emotion recognition modes. Finally, we present the available platform and outlines the existing projects, which deal with multimodal emotion analysis.

Keywords: Affective computing · Emotion detection ·
Automatic data processing · Data collection · Expressed emotion · Big data ·
Artificial intelligence

1 Introduction

Affective Computing (AC) has been a popular area of research for several years. Many research has been conducted to enable machines detect and understand human affective states, such as emotions, interests and the behavior. It attempts to bridge the communication gap between human users and computers with "soulless" and "emotionless"

© The Author(s) 2019
J. Kołodziej and H. González-Vélez (Eds.): cHiPSet, LNCS 11400, pp. 307–324, 2019.
https://doi.org/10.1007/978-3-030-16272-6_11

feeling. The inability of today's systems to recognize, express and feel emotions limits their ability to act intelligently and interact naturally with humans.

To become more user-friendly and effective, systems need to become sensitive to human emotions. Verbal and nonverbal information is very important because it complements the verbal message and provides a better interpretation of the message. It is very useful to design and develop systems that can measure the emotional state of a person based on, for example, gestures (body movements and postures), facial expression, acoustic characteristics and emotions expressed in the text. In the practical case, body signals and facial expressions recorded in real-time by sensors and cameras can be associated with predetermined emotions.

It is interesting to merge the multimodal information retrieved by these devices with information from analysis of emotions and intensity in text. For example, the ultimate goal may be to improve the system's decisions so that they can react accordingly to recognized emotions, which will allow better human-machine interaction.

Conventional wisdom says that 70–90% of communication between humans is nonverbal. The studies conducted by Albert Mehrabian in 1967 established the 7%–38%–55% rule, also known as the "3V rule": 7% of the communication is verbal, 38% of the communication is vocal and 55% of the communication is visual [1]. This justifies the interest and importance of nonverbal communication.

The first study in the field of emotion detection was born during the sixties/seventies. The most prominent example is that of mood rings [2]. The principle is simple; rings contain thermotropic liquid crystals that react with body temperature. When a person has stressed, his mood ring take on a darker color.

The scientific publications of Rosalind Picard (MIT) have introduced a great progress in this field since the nineties [3, 4]. He is one of the pioneers of affective computing. In his book "Affective Computing", Picard proposed that emotion can be modeled using the nonlinear sigmoid function. Over the last 20 years, the development of technology has allowed the implementation of relatively good system market and efficient such as ambient intelligence (AMI), virtual reality (VR) and augmented reality (AR).

Nowadays, in the automotive field for example, an on-board computer that is able to detect confusion, interest or fatigue can increase safety. The AutoEmotive (MIT Media Lab) is a prototype equipped with sensors and a camera placed on the steering wheel [5]. This vehicle measures the level of stress and fatigue of the driver. When the need arises, he puts a background music, changes the temperature and light in the vehicle interior, or still proposes to follow a less stressful journey.

We have structured the remainder of the paper as follows. Section 2 describes in general existing works dealing with the emotion detection and multimodal emotion analysis problem. Section 3 presents the basic modalities and methods used for emotion analysis. We have presented the related existing projects dealt with this problem in Sect. 4. We summarize the survey and introduce some directions for future research in Sect. 5.

2 Multimodal Emotion Analysis

Traditional emotion recognition and classification associate the "value" to at least several basic emotions such as happiness, joy, neutrality, surprise, sadness, disgust, anger, or fear.

Multimodal emotion analysis becomes very popular research domain. Started from the classic language-based definition of sentiment analysis was extended to a multimodal with other relevant modalities (video, audio, sensor data, etc.). Different techniques and methods are combined to achieve it; very often, they are based on big data methods; semantic rules and machine learning.

A novel multimodal implicit emotion recognition system can be built upon an AI-based model designed to extract information on the emotion from different devices. To feed such a model, a video data captured by the camera embedded in the user's device (laptop, desktop, tablet, etc.), an audio signals collected from microphones embedded in mobile devices, and motion signals generated by sensors in wearable devices can be used.

Several multimodal datasets include sentiment annotations. Zadeh et al. introduced the first multimodal dataset (MOSI) with opinion-level sentiment intensity annotations and studying the prototypical interaction patterns between facial gestures and spoken words when inferring sentiment intensity. They proposed a new computational representation, called multimodal dictionary, based on a language-gesture study and evaluated the proposed approach in a speaker-independent model for sentiment intensity prediction [6]. For other examples of data sets we can cite ICT-MMMO [7] and MOUD [8] datasets.

One of the most challenges in multimodal emotion analysis is to model the interactions between language, visual and acoustic behaviors that change the observation of the expressed emotion (named the inter-modality dynamics). A second challenge in multimodal emotion analysis (named intra-modality dynamics) is to efficiently explore emotion, not only on one but on highly expressive nature modality (ex. spoken language where proper language structure is often ignored, video and acoustic modalities which are expressed through both space and time. To solve this problem, Zadeh introduced the Tensor Fusion Network (TFN), which combine the intra-modality and inter-modality models. Inter-modality dynamics is modeled with a new multimodal fusion approach, named Tensor Fusion, which explicitly aggregates unimodal, bimodal and trimodal interactions. Intra-modality dynamics is modeled through three Modality Embedding Subnetworks, for language, visual and acoustic modalities, respectively [9]. Interesting work is realized by Poria et al., who developed a LTSM-based network to extract contextual features from the video for multimodal sentiment analysis [10].

Additionally, they presented a multimodal sentiment analysis framework, which includes sets of relevant features for text and visual data, as well as a simple technique for fusing the features extracted from different modalities [11].

The previous presented methods combine and analyze data from various types of modality, the basis for all these analyzes is appropriate detection of emotion on each modality input. At the same time, we must point out that for each modality individually we can also perform emotion analysis. In the next chapter, we will describe the methods of emotion analysis for each modality separately.

3 Basic Modalities for Emotion Analysis

3.1 Emotion in Text

Opinion Mining (OM) and Sentiments Analysis (SA) consists in identifying orientation or intensity of sentiments and opinion in pieces of texts (blogs, forums, user comments, review websites, community websites, etc.). It enables determining whether a sentence or a document expresses positive, negative or neutral sentiment towards some object or more. In addition, it allows for classification of opinions/sentiments according to intensity degrees.

Definition. An opinion is a quadruple (O, F, H, S) where O is a target object, F is a set of features of the object O, H is a set of opinion's holders, S is the set of sentiment/opinion value of the opinion's holder on feature $f_i \in F$ of the object O.

According to Liu [12] "sentiment analysis is the field of study that analyses people's opinions, sentiments, evaluations, appraisals, attitudes, and emotions toward entities such as products, services, organizations, and their attributes. It represents a large problem space. There are also many names and slightly different tasks, e.g., sentiment analysis, opinion mining, opinion extraction, sentiment mining, subjectivity analysis, affect analysis, emotion analysis, review mining, etc."

Sentiments analysis is a complex technique. Sentiments and opinions can often be expressed in a subtle manner that creates difficulty in the identification of their emotional value. Moreover, opinions and sentiments are highly sensitive to the context and the field in which they are used: the same string might be positive in one context and negative in another. In addition, on the Internet, everyone uses his or her own style and vocabulary, what adds extra difficulty to the task. It is not yet possible to find out an ideal case to marking the opinion in a text written by different users, because the text does not follow the rules. Therefore, it is impossible to schedule every possible case. Moreover, very often the same phrase can be considered as positive for one person and negative for another one.

Text analysis and social network analysis have gained importance with growing interest in Big Data. Both deal with large amounts of data, largely unstructured, and the Big Data benefit comes from the application of these two methods of data analysis. We will begin by examining some of the ways in which text analysis can be applied to sentiment analysis before moving on to social network analysis.

Text Analysis

Sentiment Analysis (SA) [13] is a computational study of how opinions, attitudes, emoticons and perspectives are expressed in language. Sentiment Detection, or in its simplified form – Polarity Classification, is a tedious and complex task. Contextual changes of polarity indicating words, such as negation, sarcasm as well as weak syntactic structures make it troublesome for both machines and humans to safely determine polarity of messages.

Sentiment analysis methods involve building a system to collect and categorize opinions about a product. This consists in examining natural language conversations happening around a certain product for tracking the mood of the public. The analysis is performed on large collections of texts, including web pages, online news, Internet discussion groups, online reviews, web blogs, and social media. Opinion Mining aims to determine polarity and intensity of a given text, i.e., whether it is positive, negative, or neutral and to what extent. To classify the intensity of opinions, we can use methods introduced in [14–16].

Social Networks
Social Networks are indisputably popular nowadays and show no sign of slowdown. According to the Kepios study [17], the number of active users of social networks increased by 13% in 2017 to reach 3.3 billion users in April 2018. For example, Facebook attracts more than 2.2 billion users a month. Penetrating ever more aspects of our daily life, they become not only a considerable threat to our privacy, but also an encompassing tool for analyzing opinions, habits, trends and some would even say – thoughts.

In the current growth of artificial intelligence, machine learning and natural language processing, driven by new technological possibilities, it is possible to automate the analysis of vast amounts of publicly published data

Text Mining and Social Network Analysis have become a necessity for analyzing not only information but also the connections across them. The main objective is to identify the necessary information as efficiently as possible, finding the relationships between available information by applying algorithmic, statistical, and data management methods on the knowledge. The automation of sentiment detection on these social networks has gained attention for various purposes [18–20].

Twitter is a social network that allows the user to freely publish short messages, called Tweets via the Internet, instant messaging or SMS. These messages are limited to 140 characters (more exactly, NFC normalized code points [21]). With about 330 million monthly active users (as of 2018, Twitter Inc.), Twitter is a leading social network, which is known for its ease of use for mobile devices (90% of users access the social network via mobile devices). Twitter known by the diversity of content, as well as its comprehensive list of APIs offered to developers. With an average of 500 million messages sent per day, the platform seems ideal for tracking opinions on various subjects. Furthermore, the very short format messages facilitate classification since short messages rarely discuss more than one topic.

However, automated interpretation is complicated by embedded links, abbreviations and misspellings. Facing these challenges is becoming increasingly important for Economic and Market Intelligence in order to successfully recognize trends and threats.

The frequent expression of negative emotion words on social media has been linked to depression. The aim of [22] was to report on the associations between depression severity and the variability (time-unstructured) and instability (time-structured) in emotion word expression on Facebook and Twitter across status updates. Several works on depression have emerged. They are based on social networks: Twitter [23, 24] and Facebook [25, 26].

Several authors have been interested in the use of emoticons to complete the sentiment analysis. Authors in [27] utilize Twitter API to get training data that contain emoticons like :) and :(. They use these emoticons as noisy labels. Tweets with :) are thought to be positive training data and tweets with :(are thought to be negative training data. In [28], authors present the ESLAM (Emoticon Smoothed LAnguage Models) which combine fully supervised methods and distantly supervised methods. Although many TSA (Twitter Sentiment Analysis) methods have been presented. The authors in [29] explored the influence of emoticons on TSA.

3.2   Emotion Detection in the Sound

Automatic emotion recognition based on utterance level prosodic features may play an important role within speaker-independent emotion recognition [30]. The recognition of emotions based on the voice has been studied for decades [31–34]. However, most of the work-concerned data collected in a controlled environment in which the data are clean without significant noise and directly well segmented. In addition, the majority of such a system are speech-oriented. In the real world, the process is much more complex. There are many factors such as background noise and not speech voice like a laugh, a whimper, a cry, a sigh, etc., which greatly aggravate the results obtained in a controlled environment. These factors will make the real emotion recognition trained on the data from the controlled environment unsuccessful.

The author in [35] focused on mono-modal systems with speech as only input channel. He proposed FAU Aibo Emotion Corpus, which is a speech corpus with naturally occurring emotion-related states. FAU Aibo is a corpus of spontaneous, emotionally colored speech of German children at the age of 10 to 13 years interacting with the Sony Robot Aibo. Eleven emotion-related states are labeled on the word level. Best results have been obtained on the chunk level where a classwise averaged recognition rate of almost 70% for the 4-class problem anger, emphatic, neutral and motherese has been achieved.

Voice-based emotion recognition system relying on audio input has low requirements for hardware. Especially the recent emerging of speech-based artificial assistant, e.g. Google Home, Amazon Alexa, etc., provides the ready-to-employ platform for voice-based emotion recognition system.

Audio Analysis: Background

Nowadays human speech recognition (HSR) and automatic speech recognition (ASR) systems have a very wide application. This aspect is also referred to the recognition of emotion state. Emotion recognition by research human speech is connected with two research areas. First is related to synthetic approach, which allows generating artificial speech samples filled specific emotions. The second issue concerns machine recognition of the speaker's emotions. In order to possible, a machine (IT system) has to learn human emotions expressed out of speech like speech intonation, articulation, etc. By the recognizing emotions from human speech, we can notice which kind of emotion is dominant during conversation. Possible to recognize emotions state like sadness, fear, embarrassment, terror, etc. Connected with this, machines could help people in making right decisions by recognizing emotions, especially in irrational situations where decisions have to be made faster than a rational performing mind. Sometimes it is valuable to artificially influence mental and emotional states to get a better individual performance in stress-related occupations and prevent mental disorders from happening [36]. Recent research has shown that under certain circumstances multimodal emotion recognition is possible even in real time [37].

Feature Extraction
Sound signals (including human speech) is one of the main mediums of communication and it can be processed to recognize the speaker or even emotion. This diagnosis is possible through signal decomposition and time-frequency analysis. During this analysis, key physical features are found which are clearly able to describe the emotional background of the speaker. Analyzing speech as a sound and not the meaning of spoken words is possible eliminate the language barrier by focusing only on the emotional message. This can be obtained by calculating the values of descriptors be able to describe such features as the ratio of amplitudes in particular parts of the signal, the shape of the signal waveform, the frequency distribution, etc. The basic principle behind emotion recognition lies with analyzing the acoustic difference that occurs when talking about the same thing under different emotional situations [38].

The accurate selection of descriptors and their combination, allows to determine which emotions are dominant in conversation - that is, their worth is very important for classification. It is therefore necessary to index the speech signal to evaluate the speaker's emotions. Acquiring features is possible by investigating time domain and frequency domain speech signals. This way, it is practicable to obtain feature vector which can be able to automatic objects classification - it means, automatic classification of emotion state too. During research is necessary concentrate on insightful research frequency domain, not forgetting the time domain descriptors either. There are some physical features applied for indexing speech, like: spectrum irregularity, wide and narrow band spectrograms, speech signals filtering and processing, enhancement and manipulation of specific frequency regions, segmentation and labeling of words, syllables and individual phonemes [37]. Moreover, the Mel-Frequency Cepstral Coefficients (MFCC) is widely used in speech classification experiments due to its good performance. It extracts and represents features of speech signal - including kinds of emotions. The Mel-Cepstral takes short-time spectral shape with important data about the quality of voice and production effects. To calculate these coefficients the inverse cosine transform of decimal logarithm of the Mel filtered short-term spectrum of energy must be done. The purpose of improving results of experiment and searching effective spectral feature vector, constant spectral resolution is used [39]. For the reduction of leakage effect, the Hamming window is implemented. This is necessary for increasing the efficiency of frequency in human speech [38].

There is MPEG 7 standard, which gives many descriptors definitions for the physical features of sound (including human speech). These descriptors are defined on the base of analysis of digital signals and index of most important their factors. The MPEG 7 Audio standard contains descriptors and description schemes that can be divided into two classes: generic low-level tools and application-specific tools [40]. MPEG 7 descriptors are being very helpful for assessment features of human speech in a general sense. They can be used to assess the emotions because each emotional state expressed in speech contains specific numeric values of MPEG 7 descriptors.

After the extraction of features, the machine learning part of the generic system should analyze features and find statistical relationships between particular features and emotional states. This part of the system is also called "classifier". Most commonly used classification algorithms are Artificial Neural Networks (ANN), k-Nearest Neighbor (k-NN) and Support Vector Machines (SVM), decision trees. Furthermore, probabilistic models such as the Gaussian mixture model (GMM) or stochastic models such as Hidden Markov Model (HMM) can be applied [36].

Accuracy

Emotion analysis of speech is possible; however, it highly depends of the language. Automatic and universal emotion analysis is very challenging. Analyze of emotion is more efficient when perform for one dedicated language. Study by Chaspari et al. showed that emotion classification in speech (Greek language) achieved accuracy up to 75.15% [41]. Similar study by Arruti et al. showed mean accuracy of 80.05% emotion recognition rate in Basque and a 74.82% in Spanish [42].

3.3   Emotion in Image and Video

Nonverbal behavior constitutes useful means of communication in addition to spoken language. It allows to communicate even complex social concepts, in various contexts, thus may be regarded not only supplementary, but also as basic way of emotion recognition. It is possible to easily reading the affects, emotions and intentions from face expressions and gestures. Indeed, Ekman (one of the pioneers in the study of facial expressions and emotions) [43] identifies at least six characteristics from posed facial actions that enable emotion recognition: morphology, symmetry, duration, speed of onset, coordination of apexes and ballistic trajectory. They are common to all humans confirming Darwin's evolutionary thesis. Therefore, an emotional recognition tools based on facial video is universal.

However, automatic and either - automatic semi recognition of the meaning of face expressions and gesture still constitutes true challenge. We will focus on facial expressions.

3.4   Automatic Facial Emotion

The human face, as a modality for emotion detection takes a dominant position in the study of affect. It is possible to register the facial information automatically in real-time, without requiring any specialized equipment except a simple video camera. Thus, facial expressions as a noninvasive method are used in behavioral science and in clinical. Therefore, automatic recognition of facial expressions is an important component for emotion detection and modeling the natural human-machine interfaces.

The face is equipped with a large number of independent muscles, which can be activated at different levels of intensity. Consequently, the face is capable of generating a high number of complex dynamic facial expression patterns. There are three main dimensions of facial variation: morphology, complexion and dynamics. As first two dimensions, morphology and complexion, deals with static dimensions, there are very useful for facial recognition but their role for emotion analyze is not significant. The third one, the dynamics, play the most important role for emotion face analysis [44]. Although mapping of facial expressions to affective states is possible, the automatic recognizing of humans' emotion from the facial expressions, without effort or delay is still a challenge.

Automatic detection of emotions from facial expressions are not simple and their interpretation is largely context-driven. To reduce the complexity of automatic affective inference, measurement and interpretation of facial expressions, Ekman and Friesen developed in 1978 special system for objectively measuring facial movement; the Facial Action Coding System (FACS) [45]. FACS, based on a system originally developed by a Swedish anatomist named Hjortsjö [46] became the standard for identifying any movement of the face. Later, Ekman and Sejnowski studied also computer based facial measurements [47].

FACS is a common standard to systematically categorize and to index the physical expression of emotions. The basic values of FACE are Action Units (AUs). AUs are the fundamental actions of individual muscles or groups of muscles. The AUs are grouped in several categories and identified by a number: main codes, head movement codes, eye movement codes, visibility codes, and gross behavior codes. The intensities of AUs are annotated in five categories, by appending letters A–E to the AUs (A for minimal intensity-trace, B for slight intensity, C for marked, D for severe, E for maximum intensity). For example, AU1A signifies the weakest trace of AU1 and AU1E is the maximum intensity possible of AU1 for the individual person.

The eyes and mouth have high importance to emotion detection; therefore, to successfully recognize an emotion, the observations mostly rely on the eye and mouth regions. Furthermore, the actions of eyes and mouth allowed grouping the expressions in a continuous space, ranging from sadness and fear (reliance on the eyes) to disgust and happiness (mouth). Combining these observations with facial AUs increase knowledge about the areas involved in displaying each emotion. For example, "happy" denoted by AU6 + AU12, comprises AU6 (Cheek Raiser) and AU12 (Lip Corner Puller), whereas 'sad' (AU1 + AU4 + AU15) comprises AU1 (Inner Brow Raiser), AU4 (Brow Lowerer) and AU15 (Lip Corner Depressor).

The computer algorithm for facial coding extracts the main features of the face (mouth, eyebrows, etc.) and analyzes movement, shape and texture composition of these regions to identify facial action units (AUs). Therefore, it is possible to track tiny movements of facial muscles in individuals' face and translate them into universal facial expressions like happiness, surprise, sadness, anger and others.

Very important is also the way, how the emotional representation is created. Afzal et al. [48] performed studies differences between human raters' judgments of emotional expressions and three automatically generated representations in video clips. First, the point-based display was created from the output of a commercial automatic face-tracker [49] on a black background. Second one, stick figure models, which connecting the automatically tracked feature-points using straight lines and sketching eyes using typical shape. The last one, 3D XFace Animation was a 3D animated facial expressions and displays created using XFace open source toolkit. Their experiences confirmed that the human judgement is still the best one, with the highest recognition rates, followed by stick-figure models, point-light displays, and then XFace animations.

3.4.1   Existing Tools for Automatic Facial Emotion Recognition

Facial emotion recognition is one of the most important methods for nonverbal emotion detection. Several popular commercial packages offer specific facial image analysis tasks, including facial expression recognition, facial attribute analysis, and face tracking. We cite below few examples:

IntraFace (IF) [50], a publicly available software package offering:

- automated facial feature tracking,
- head pose estimation,
- facial attribute recognition,
- facial expression analysis from video,
- unsupervised synchrony detection to discover correlated facial behavior between two or more persons.

It also measure an audience reaction to a talk given or synchrony for smiling in videos of parent-infant interaction.

The Emotion API (Microsoft Azure)

Microsoft Azure proposes on-line API to recognize emotions in images and in videos [51]. The Emotion API permits input data directly as an image or as "bounding box" from Face API. In the output, it returns the confidence across a set of eight emotions: anger, contempt, disgust, fear, happiness, neutral, sadness, and surprise. Emotion API is able to track how a person or a crowd responds to your content over time.

Emotion API provide the interface for C#, cURL, Java, JavaScript, PHP, Python, Ruby. It is also possible to implement these API in R [52].

Micro Expressions Training Tool

Ekman has created several training tools [53] to enhance understanding of emotions and relationships:

- Micro Expressions Training Tool (METT and intensive MEITT) to teach how to detect and interpret micro expressions,
- Subtle Expressions Training Tool (SETT) to learn how to see emotions as they develop. SETT provides foundational knowledge of how emotions emerge in just one region on the face.
- Micro Expressions Profile Training Tool (MEPT): you to identify micro expressions from different angles.

3.5   Emotion Detected by the Physiological and Motor Signals

Recently the physiological and motor data are accessible by IoT technology. People are interested in purchasing connected objects in order to monitor their healthy like heart rate, blood pressure, number of burned calories and analyze their movements. We can find a lot work for healthcare applications but at the same time, this technology can be used to emotion detection. As an example, we can cite work done by Amira et al. [54] as a good example of using the emotion analyze for healthcare purpose. This work takes into consideration the emotional state of the peoples (stress, happiness, sadness, among) and analyze that using the appropriate AI tools to detect emotion, to categorize it and then analyze its impact on cardiovascular disease.

Physiological Signals

Automatic emotion recognition based on physiological signals is a key topic for many advanced applications (safe driving, security, mHealth, etc.). Main analyzed physiological signals useful for emotion detection and classification are:

- electromyogram (EMG) - recording of the electrical activity produced by skeletal muscles,
- galvanic skin response (GSR) - reflecting skin resistance, which varies with the state of sweat glands in the skin controlled by the sympathetic nervous system, where conductance is an indication of psychological or physiological state,
- respiratory volume (RV) - referring to the volume of air associated with different phases of the respiratory cycle,
- skin temperature (SKT) - referring to the fluctuations of normal human body temperature,
- blood volume pulse (BVP) - measures the heart rate,
- heart rate (HR),
- electrooculogram (EOG) - measuring the corneo-retinal standing potential between the front and the back of the human eye,
- photoplethysmography (PPG) - measuring blood volume pulse (BVP), which is the phasic change in blood volume with each heartbeat, etc.

The recognition of emotions based on physiological signals covers different aspects: emotional models, methods for generating emotions, common emotional data sets, characteristics used and choices of classifiers. The whole framework of emotion recognition based on physiological signals has recently been described by [55].

Decision-level weight fusion strategy for emotion recognition in multichannel physiological signals using MAHNOB-HCI database has been recently described [56]. Various classification tools may be used, including artificial neural networks (ANN), support vector machine (SVM), k-nearest neighbors (KNN), and many more. More advanced emotion representation models, including clustering of responses, are created for purposes of further studies and increased recognition accuracy.

Özerdem and Polat used EEG signal, discrete wavelet transform and machine learning techniques (multilayer perceptron neural network - MLPNN, and k-nearest neighbors - kNN algorithms) [57].

Research by Jang et al. used ECG, EDA, SKT and more sophistical machine learning (ML) algorithms [58]:

- linear discriminant analysis (LDA) - finds a linear combination of features that characterizes or separates two or more classes of objects or events,
- classification and regression trees (CART) - uses a decision tree as a predictive model to go from observations about an item represented in the branches, to conclusions about the item's target value represented in the leaves,

- self-organizing map (SOM) - a type of artificial neural network that is trained using unsupervised learning to produce a low-dimensional, discretized representation of the input space of the training samples, called a map,
- Naïve Bayes algorithm - based on applying Bayes' theorem with strong (=naive) independence assumptions between the features,
- Support Vector Machine (SVM) - supervised learning models with associated learning algorithms analyzing data used for classification and regression analysis.

Kortelainen et al. showed results of combining physiological signals (heart rate variability parameters, respiration frequency) and facial expressions were studied [59].

Motor Signals

Body posture and movement is one of the most expressive modalities for humans. Researchers have recently started to exploit the possibilities for emotion recognition based on different motor signals. Zachartos et al. present well done analyze of emerging techniques and modalities related to automated emotion recognition based on body movement and describes application areas and notation systems and explains the importance of movement segmentation [60]. At the same time, this work outlines that this field still requires further studies. To recognize the emotion different postural, kinematic and geometrical feature are used. Tsui et al. use the keystroke typing patterns (usually on a standard keyboard) for automatic recognizing of emotional state [61].

Li et al. proposed another way to solve this problem by analyzing the human pattern of movement of the limbs (gait) recorded by Microsoft Kinect [62]. The gait pattern for every subject was extracted from 3-dimensional coordinates of 14 main body joints using Fourier transformation and Principal Component Analysis (PCA). To classify signals' features four ML algorithms were trained and evaluated:

- Naive Bayes (described above),
- Random Forests - an ensemble learning method for classification, regression and other tasks, that operate by constructing a multitude of decision trees at training time and outputting the class that is the mode of the classes (classification) or mean prediction (regression) of the individual trees,
- LibSVM - an integrated software for support vector classification, regression, and distribution estimation,
- Sequential Minimal Optimization (SMO) - is an algorithm for solving the quadratic programming problem arising during the training of support vector machines.

They showed that human gait reflects the walker's emotional state.

Accuracy

Accuracy of the emotion recognition and classification based on physiological signals identification have improved significantly. Research by Goshvarpour et al. using HRV and PRV, and fusion rules (feature level, decision level) showed classification rates improved up to 92% (sensitivity: 95%, specificity: 83.33%) [63]. Previous studies have provided evidence for general recognition rate from 57,77% to 85,46% for different emotional states, that more higher set of analyzed signals and more recognized emotions provides better results [64–66]. High-observed recognition accuracy was also in research by Jang et al.: 84.7% [58].

Özerdem and Polat used EEG signal - resultant average overall accuracy was 77.14% (using MLPNN) and 72.92% (using kNN) [56]. The highest accuracy achieved by Li et al. was 80.5% [62]. Accuracy for combining heart rate variability, respiration frequency, and facial expressions was relatively low: 54.5% [59]. Results of the 2011 i2b2/VA/Cincinnati Medical Natural Language Processing Challenge showed that the best of 24 participants' teams achieved accuracy of 61.39% [67].

It should be noted that all algorithm must be personalized to each person in order to be reliable.

4   Related Project

4.1   openSMILE (Speech & Music Interpretation by Large-Space Extraction) [68]

Originally created in the scope of the European EU-FP7 research project SEMAINE (http://www.semaine-project.eu). OpenSMILE is a modular and flexible feature extractor for signal processing and machine learning applications. However, due to their high degree of abstraction, openSMILE components can also be used to analyze signals from other modalities, such as physiological signals, visual signals, and other physical sensors, given suitable input components.

4.2   openEAR (Emotion and Affect Recognition)

It consists of three major components: the core component is the SMILE (Speech and Music Interpretation by Large-Space Extraction) signal processing and feature extraction tool, which is capable generating >500 k features in real-time (Real-Time Factor (RTF) < 0.1), either from live audio input or from offline media [69]. The advantages of this solution are: open-source, multi-threaded, real-time emotion recognition framework providing an extensible, platform independent feature extractor implemented in C++, pre-trained models on six databases which are ready-to-use for on-line emotion and affect recognition, and supporting scripts for model building, evaluation, and visualization. This framework is compatible with related tool-kits, such as HTK and WEKA by supporting their data-formats.

4.3   ASC-Inclusion (Interactive Emotion Games for Children with Autism)

Understand and express emotions through facial expressions, vocal intonation and body gestures. This project aims to create an internet-based platform that will assist children with Autism Spectrum Condition (ASC) to improve their socio-emotional communication skills. The project will attend both the recognition and the expression of socio-emotional cues, aiming to provide an interactive-game where to give scores on the prototypically and on the naturalness of child's expressions. It will combine several state-of-the-art technologies in one comprehensive virtual world environment, combining voice, face and body gesture analysis, providing corrective feedback regarding the appropriateness of the child's expressions [70].

4.4   INTERSPEECH - Computational Paralinguistics ChallengE (ComParE)

In this Challenge, authors introduced four paralinguistic tasks, which are important for the realm of affective human-computer interaction, yet some of them go beyond the traditional tasks of emotion recognition. Thus, as a milestone, ComParE 2013 laid the foundation for a successful series of follow-up ComParEs to date, exploring more and more the paralinguistic facets of human speech in tomorrow's real-life information, communication and entertainment systems [71].

5   Conclusion

In this paper, we presented existing multimodal approaches and methods of emotion detection and analysis. Our study includes emotion analyze in text, in sound, in image/video and physiological signals. We showed that automated emotion analysis is possible and can be very useful for improving the exactness of the computer/machine reaction and making possible to anticipate the emotional state of the interlocutor more quickly.

Not only basic emotions can be analyzed, but also the cognitive assessment (interpretation of stimuli in the environment) and their physiological response. Such an approach may cause quicker development of more user-friendly systems and environments supporting everyday life and work.

Automatic emotion analysis requires advanced recognition and modeling, very often based on artificial intelligence systems. Presented approach may be successful, but the limitations of the current knowledge and experience still concern tools for automatic non-invasive emotion measurement and analysis.

We should be aware that among requirements on automatic emotion recognition key might constitute portability, non-intrusiveness, and low price. Novel intelligent systems may be friendlier, preventing the computers from acting inappropriately.

In this state of the arts, we have addressed, of course only some most important issues. No doubt, there is need for further effort of scientists and engineers toward more advanced AI-based automatic emotion recognition systems. Further research may constitute an important part of future technological, clinical, and scientific progress.

Acknowledgement (COST + PHC Polonium). This state of the art was published in cooperation with the COST Action IC1406 High-Performance Modelling and Simulation for Big Data Applications (cHiPSet), supported by COST (European Cooperation in Science and Technology).

This article is based upon the work done under the project PHC POLONIUM 2018 (PROJECT N° 40557VL), realized between the AlliansTIC Research Laboratory of Efrei Paris Engineering School (France) and the Institute of Mechanics and Applied Computer Science, Kazimierz Wielki University in Bydgoszcz (Poland).

References

1. Mehrabian, A., Ferris, S.R.: Inference of attitudes from nonverbal communication in two channels. J. Consult. Psychol. **31**(3), 248 (1967)
2. Mood Ring Monitors Your State of Mind, Chicago Tribune, 8 October 1975, at C1: Ring Buyers Warm Up to Quartz Jewelry That Is Said to Reflect Their Emotions. The Wall Street Journal, 14 October 1975, at p. 16; and "A Ring Around the Mood Market", The Washington Post, 24 November 1975, at B9
3. Picard, R.W.: Affective Computing. MIT Press, Cambridge (1997)
4. Picard, R.W., Vyzas, E., Healey, J.: Toward machine emotional intelligence: analysis of affective physiological state. IEEE Trans. Pattern Anal. Mach. Intell. **23**(10), 1175–1191 (2001)
5. Hernandez, J., et al.: AutoEmotive: bringing empathy to the driving experience to manage stress. In: DIS 2014, 21–25 June 2014, Vancouver, BC, Canada. ACM (2014). http://dx.doi.org/10.1145/2598784.2602780. 978-1-4503-2903-3/14/06
6. Zadeh, A., Zellers, R., Pincus, E., Morency, L.P.: Multimodal sentiment intensity analysis in videos: facial gestures and verbal messages. IEEE Intell. Syst. **31**(6), 82–88 (2016). https://doi.org/10.1109/mis.2016.94
7. Wöllmer, M., et al.: YouTube movie reviews: sentiment analysis in an audio-visual context. IEEE Intell. Syst. **28**(3), 46–53 (2013)
8. Perez-Rosas, V., Mihalcea, R., Morency, L.P.: Utterance-level multimodal sentiment analysis. In: ACL, vol. 1, pp. 973–982 (2013)
9. Zadeh, A., Chen, M., Poria, S., Cambria, E., Morency, L.P.: Tensor fusion network for multimodal sentiment analysis, arXiv:1707.07250. In: Proceedings of the 2017 Conference on Empirical Methods in Natural Language Processing, 7–11 September 2017, Copenhagen, Denmark, pp. 1103–1114. Association for Computational Linguistics
10. Poria, S., Cambria, E., Hazarika, D., Majumder, N., Zadeh, A., Morency, L.P.: Context-dependent sentiment analysis in user-generated videos. In: Proceedings of the 55th Annual Meeting of the Association for Computational Linguistics, vol. 1, pp. 873–883 (2017)
11. Poria, S., Cambria, E., Howard, N., Huang, G.B., Hussain, A.: Fusing audio, visual and textual clues for sentiment analysis from multimodal content. Neurocomputing **174**(Part A), 50–59 (2016). https://doi.org/10.1016/j.neucom.2015.01.095. ISSN 0925-2312
12. Liu, B.: Sentiment analysis and opinion mining. Synth. Lect. Hum. Lang. Technol. **5**(1), 1–167 (2012)
13. Pang, B., Lee, L.: Opinion mining and sentiment analysis. J. Found. Trends Inf. Retrieval **2**(1–2), 1–135 (2008)
14. Dziczkowski, G., Wegrzyn-Wolska, K.: RRSS - rating reviews support system purpose built for movies recommendation. In: Wegrzyn-Wolska, K.M., Szczepaniak, P.S. (eds.) Advances in Intelligent Web Mastering. Advances in Soft Computing, vol. 43, pp. 87–93. Springer, Berlin (2007). https://doi.org/10.1007/978-3-540-72575-6_14
15. Dziczkowski, G., Węgrzyn-Wolska, K.: An autonomous system designed for automatic detection and rating of film. Extraction and linguistic analysis of sentiments. In: Proceedings of WIC, Sydney (2008)
16. Dziczkowski, G., Węgrzyn-Wolska, K.: Tool of the intelligence economic: recognition function of reviews critics. In: ICSOFT 2008 Proceedings. INSTICC Press (2008)
17. Kepios: Digital in 2018, essential insights into internet, social media, mobile, and ecommerce use around the world, April 2018. https://kepios.com/data/
18. Ghiassi, M., Skinner, J., Zimbra, D.: Twitter brand sentiment analysis: a hybrid system using n-gram analysis and dynamic artificial neural network. Expert Syst. Appl. **40**(16), 6266–6282 (2013)

19. Zhou, X., Tao, X., Yong, J., Yang, Z.: Sentiment analysis on tweets for social events. In: Proceedings of the 2013 IEEE 17th International Conference on Computer Supported Cooperative Work in Design, CSCWD 2013, 27–29 June 2013, pp. 557–562 (2013)
20. Salathé, M., Vu, D.Q., Khandelwal, S., Hunter, D.R.: The dynamics of health behavior sentiments on a large online social network. EPJ Data Sci. **2**, 4 (2013). https://doi.org/10.1140/epjds16
21. Sriram, B., Fuhry, D., Demir, E., Ferhatosmanoglu, H., Demirbas, M.: Short text classification in Twitter to improve information filtering. In: Proceedings of the 33rd International ACM SIGIR Conference on Research and Development in Information Retrieval, 19–23 July 2010, pp. 841–842. http://doi.acm.org/10.1145/1835449.1835643
22. Seabrook, E.M., Kern, M.L., Fulcher, B.D., Rickard, N.S.: Predicting depression from language-based emotion dynamics: longitudinal analysis of Facebook and Twitter status updates. J. Med. Internet Res. **20**(5), e168 (2018). https://doi.org/10.2196/jmir.9267
23. Wang, W., Hernandez, I., Newman, D.A., He, J., Bian, J.: Twitter analysis: studying US weekly trends in work stress and emotion. Appl. Psychol. **65**(2), 355–378 (2016)
24. Reece, A.G., Reagan, A.J., Lix, K.L., Dodds, P.S., Danforth, C.M., Langer, E.J.: Forecasting the onset and course of mental illness with Twitter data (Unpublished manuscript). https://arxiv.org/pdf/1608.07740.pdf
25. Park, J., Lee, D.S., Shablack, H., et al.: When perceptions defy reality: the relationships between depression and actual and perceived Facebook social support. J. Affect. Disord. **200**, 37–44 (2016)
26. Burke, M., Develin, M.: Once more with feeling: supportive responses to social sharing on Facebook. In: Proceedings of the ACM 2016 Conference on Computer Supported Cooperative Work, pp. 1462–1474 (2016)
27. Go, A., Bhayani, R., Huang, L.: Twitter sentiment classification using distant supervision. J. CS224N Proj. Rep., Stanford **1**, 12 (2009)
28. Liu, K.L., Li, W.J., Guo, M.: Emoticon smoothed language models for Twitter sentiment analysis. In: AAAI (2012)
29. Węgrzyn-Wolska, K., Bougueroua, L., Yu, H., Zhong, J.: Explore the effects of emoticons on Twitter sentiment analysis. In: Proceedings of Third International Conference on Computer Science & Engineering (CSEN 2016), 27–28 August 2016, Dubai, UAE
30. Bitouk, D., Verma, R., Nenkova, A.: Class-level spectral features for emotion recognition. Speech Commun. **52**(7–8), 613–625 (2010)
31. Busso, C., et al.: Analysis of emotion recognition using facial expressions, speech and multimodal information. In: Sixth International Conference on Multimodal Interfaces, ICMI 2004, October 2004, State College, PA, pp. 205–211. ACM Press (2004)
32. Dellaert, F., Polzin, T., Waibel, A.: Recognizing emotion in speech. In: International Conference on Spoken Language (ICSLP 1996), October 1996, Philadelphia, PA, USA, vol. 3, pp. 1970–1973 (1996)
33. Lee, C.M., et al.: Emotion recognition based on phoneme classes. In: 8th International Conference on Spoken Language Processing (ICSLP 2004), October 2004, Jeju Island, Korea, pp. 889–892 (2004)
34. Deng, J., Xu, X., Zhang, Z., Frühholz, S., Grandjean, D., Schuller, B.: Fisher kernels on phase-based features for speech emotion recognition. In: Jokinen, K., Wilcock, G. (eds.) Dialogues with Social Robots. LNEE, vol. 427, pp. 195–203. Springer, Singapore (2017). https://doi.org/10.1007/978-981-10-2585-3_15
35. Steidl, S.: Automatic classification of emotion-related user states in spontaneous children's speech. Ph.D. thesis, Erlangen (2009)
36. Lugovic, S., Horvat, M., Dunder, I.: Techniques and applications of emotion recognition in speech. In: MIPRO 2016/CIS (2016)

37. Kukolja, D., Popović, S., Horvat, M., Kovač, B., Ćosić, K.: Comparative analysis of emotion estimation methods based on physiological measurements for real-time applications. Int. J. Hum.-Comput. Stud. **72**(10), 717–727 (2014)
38. Davletcharova, A., Sugathan, S., Abraham, B., James, A.P.: Detection and analysis of emotion from speech signals. Procedia Comput. Sci. **58**, 91–96 (2015)
39. Tyburek, K., Prokopowicz, P., Kotlarz, P.: Fuzzy system for the classification of sounds of birds based on the audio descriptors. In: Rutkowski, L., Korytkowski, M., Scherer, R., Tadeusiewicz, R., Zadeh, L.A., Zurada, J.M. (eds.) ICAISC 2014. LNCS (LNAI), vol. 8468, pp. 700–709. Springer, Cham (2014). https://doi.org/10.1007/978-3-319-07176-3_61
40. Tyburek, K., Prokopowicz, P., Kotlarz, P., Michal, R.: Comparison of the efficiency of time and frequency descriptors based on different classification conceptions. In: Rutkowski, L., Korytkowski, M., Scherer, R., Tadeusiewicz, R., Zadeh, L.A., Zurada, J.M. (eds.) ICAISC 2015. LNCS (LNAI), vol. 9119, pp. 491–502. Springer, Cham (2015). https://doi.org/10.1007/978-3-319-19324-3_44
41. Chaspari, T., Soldatos, C., Maragos, P.: The development of the Athens Emotional States Inventory (AESI): collection, validation and automatic processing of emotionally loaded sentences. World J. Biol. Psychiatry **16**(5), 312–322 (2015)
42. Arruti, A., Cearreta, I., Alvarez, A., Lazkano, E., Sierra, B.: Feature selection for speech emotion recognition in Spanish and Basque: on the use of machine learning to improve human-computer interaction. PLoS ONE **9**(10), e108975 (2014)
43. Ekman, P.: Facial expression and emotion. Am. Psychol. **48**, 384–392 (1993)
44. Jack, R.E., Schyns, P.G.: The human face as a dynamic tool for social communication. Curr. Biol. Rev. **25**(14), R621–R634 (2015). https://doi.org/10.1016/j.cub.2015.05.052
45. Ekman, P., Friesen, W., Hager, J.: Facial action coding system. Research Nexus. Network Research Information, Salt Lake City (2002)
46. Hjortsjö, C.H.: Man's face and mimic language (1969). https://books.google.com/books/about/Man_s_Face_and_Mimic_Laguage.html?id=BakQAQAAIAAJ
47. Ekman, P., Huang, T.S., Sejnowski, T.J., et al.: Final report to NSF of the planning workshop on facial expression understanding, vol. 378. Human Interaction Laboratory, University of California, San Francisco (1993)
48. Afzal, S., Sezgin, T.M., Gao, Y., Robinson, P.: Perception of emotional expressions in different representations using facial feature points. IEEE (2009). 978-1-4244-4799
49. http://www.nevenvision.com. Licensed from Google Inc.
50. De la Torre, F., Chu, W.S., Xiong, X., Vicente, F., Ding, X., Cohn, J.: IntraFace. In: IEEE International Conference on Automatic Face and Gesture Recognition Workshops (2015). https://doi.org/10.1109/fg.2015.7163082
51. https://azure.microsoft.com/en-us/services/cognitive-services/emotion/
52. http://thinktostart.com/analyze-face-emotions-r/
53. https://www.paulekman.com/micro-expressions-training-tools/
54. Amira, T., Dan, I., Az-Eddine, B., et al.: Monitoring chronic disease at home using connected devices. In: 2018 13th Annual Conference on System of Systems Engineering (SoSE), pp. 400–407. IEEE (2018)
55. Shu, L., et al.: A review of emotion recognition using physiological signals. Sensors (Basel) **18**(7), 2074 (2018)
56. Wei, W., Jia, Q., Feng, Y., Chen, G.: Emotion recognition based on weighted fusion strategy of multichannel physiological signals. Comput. Intell. Neurosci. **2018**, 9 (2018). 5296523
57. Özerdem, M.S., Polat, H.: Emotion recognition based on EEG features in movie clips with channel selection. Brain Inform. **4**(4), 241–252 (2017)
58. Jang, E.H., Park, B.J., Park, M.S., Kim, S.H., Sohn, J.H.: Analysis of physiological signals for recognition of boredom, pain, and surprise emotions. J. Physiol. Anthropol. **34**, 25 (2015)

59. Kortelainen, J., Tiinanen, S., Huang, X., Li, X., Laukka, S., Pietikäinen, M., Seppänen, T.: Multimodal emotion recognition by combining physiological signals and facial expressions: a preliminary study. In: Conference Proceeding of the IEEE Engineering in Medicine and Biology Society, vol. 2012, pp. 5238–5241 (2012)
60. Zacharatos, H., Gatzoulis, C., Chrysanthou, Y.L.: Automatic emotion recognition based on body movement analysis: a survey. IEEE Comput. Graph Appl. **34**(6), 35–45 (2014)
61. Tsui, W.H., Lee, P., Hsiao, T.C.: The effect of emotion on keystroke: an experimental study using facial feedback hypothesis. In: Conference Proceedings of the IEEE Engineering in Medicine and Biology Society, pp. 2870–2873 (2013)
62. Li, S., Cui, L., Zhu, C., Li, B., Zhao, N., Zhu, T.: Emotion recognition using Kinect motion capture data of human gaits. PeerJ **4**, e2364 (2016)
63. Goshvarpour, A., Abbasi, A.: Goshvarpour, A: Fusion of heart rate variability and pulse rate variability for emotion recognition using lagged poincare plots. Australas. Phys. Eng. Sci. Med. **40**(3), 617–629 (2017)
64. Khezri, M., Firoozabadi, M., Sharafat, A.R.: Reliable emotion recognition system based on dynamic adaptive fusion of forehead biopotentials and physiological signals. Comput. Methods Programs Biomed. **122**(2), 149–164 (2015)
65. Gouizi, K., Bereksi Reguig, F., Maaoui, C.: Emotion recognition from physiological signals. J. Med. Eng. Technol. **35**(6–7), 300–307 (2011)
66. Verma, G.K., Tiwary, U.S.: Multimodal fusion framework: a multiresolution approach for emotion classification and recognition from physiological signals. Neuroimage **102**(Part 1), 162–172 (2014)
67. Yang, H., Willis, A., de Roeck, A., Nuseibeh, B.: A hybrid model for automatic emotion recognition in suicide notes. Biomed. Inform. Insights **5**(Suppl. 1), 17–30 (2012)
68. Eyben, F., Weninger, F., Wöllmer, M., Shuller, B.: Open-Source Media Interpretation by Large Feature-Space Extraction, November 2016. openSMILE by audFERING
69. Eyben, F., Wöllmer, M., Shuller, B.: openEAR - introducing the munich open-source emotion and affect recognition toolkit. In: 2009 3rd International Conference on Affective Computing and Intelligent Interaction and Workshops. https://doi.org/10.1109/acii.2009.5349350
70. O'Reilly, H., et al.: The EU-emotion stimulus set: a validation study. Behav. Res. **48**, 567–576 (2016). https://doi.org/10.3758/s13428-015-0601-4. Psychonomic Society, Inc. 2015
71. Schuller, B., et al.: Affective and behavioural computing: lessons learnt from the first computational paralinguistics challenge. Comput. Speech Lang. **53**, 156–180 (2019). Elsevier, ScienceDirect

Forecasting Cryptocurrency Value by Sentiment Analysis: An HPC-Oriented Survey of the State-of-the-Art in the Cloud Era

Aleš Zamuda[1]([envelope]) [iD], Vincenzo Crescimanna[2] [iD], Juan C. Burguillo[3] [iD],
Joana Matos Dias[4] [iD], Katarzyna Wegrzyn-Wolska[5] [iD], Imen Rached[5] [iD],
Horacio González-Vélez[6] [iD], Roman Senkerik[7] [iD], Claudia Pop[8] [iD],
Tudor Cioara[8] [iD], Ioan Salomie[8] [iD], and Andrea Bracciali[2] [iD]

[1] Faculty of Electrical Engineering and Computer Science, University of Maribor,
Koroška cesta 46, 2000 Maribor, Slovenia
ales.zamuda@um.si
[2] Department of Computing Science and Mathematics, University of Stirling,
Stirling FK9 4LA, UK
vincenzo.crescimanna1@stir.ac.uk,abb@cs.stir.ac.uk
[3] Department of Telematic Engineering, University of Vigo,
Campus Universitario, 36310 Vigo, Spain
j.c.burguillo@uvigo.es
[4] Faculty of Economics, University of Coimbra,
Av. Dias da Silva 165, 3004-512 Coimbra, Portugal
joana@fe.uc.pt
[5] Allianstic Research Laboratory, EFREI Paris,
Ecole d'ingénieurs généraliste Informatique et technologies du numérique,
30-32 Avenue de la République, 94800 Villejuif, France
{katarzyna.wegrzyn-wolska,imen.rached}@efrei.fr
[6] Cloud Competency Centre, National College of Ireland,
Mayor Street Lower – IFSC, Dublin 1, Ireland
horacio@ncirl.ie
[7] Faculty of Applied Informatics, Tomas Bata University in Zlin,
T. G. Masaryka 5555, 760 01 Zlin, Czech Republic
senkerik@utb.cz
[8] Computer Science Department, Technical University of Cluj-Napoca,
26-28 Baritiu Street, 400027 Cluj-Napoca, Romania
{claudia.pop,tudor.cioara,ioan.salomie}@cs.utcluj.ro

Abstract. This chapter surveys the state-of-the-art in forecasting cryptocurrency value by Sentiment Analysis. Key compounding perspectives of current challenges are addressed, including blockchains, data collection, annotation, and filtering, and sentiment analysis metrics using data streams and cloud platforms. We have explored the domain based on this problem-solving metric perspective, i.e., as technical analysis, forecasting, and estimation using a standardized ledger-based technology. The envisioned tools based on forecasting are then suggested, i.e., ranking

© The Author(s) 2019
J. Kołodziej and H. González-Vélez (Eds.): cHiPSet, LNCS 11400, pp. 325–349, 2019.
https://doi.org/10.1007/978-3-030-16272-6_12

Initial Coin Offering (ICO) values for incoming cryptocurrencies, trading strategies employing the new Sentiment Analysis metrics, and risk aversion in cryptocurrencies trading through a multi-objective portfolio selection. Our perspective is rationalized on the perspective on elastic demand of computational resources for cloud infrastructures.

Keywords: Cryptocurrency · Blockchain · Sentiment Analysis · Forecasting · ICO · CSAI · Cloud computing

1   Introduction

This chapter presents a position survey on the overall objective and specific challenges encompassing the state of the art in forecasting cryptocurrency value by Sentiment Analysis. The compounding perspectives of current challenges are addressed, such as the blockchain technologies, underlying data collection of items from social media, the annotation, and filtering of such items, and the Sentiment Analysis as a resulting metric of the observed data streams.

We describe a Cryptocurrency Sentiment Analysis Indicator (CSAI) and identify its required inner workings compounding perspectives. Further possibilities are then explored, based on this new metric perspective, such as technical analysis, forecasting, and beyond. The envisioned tools based on forecasting are then suggested, i.e., ranking Initial Coin Offering (ICO) values for incoming cryptocurrencies, trading strategies employing the new Sentiment Analysis metrics, and risk aversion in cryptocurrencies' trading through multi-objective portfolio selection. Since the introduction of Bitcoin [94] and rise of blockchain-related algorithms [96] and technologies [10,74,98,130,137], there has been a significant increase in their recognition and analysis. In this chapter, we focus on the specific aspect of value for the blockchain projects related to cryptocurrencies.

While High-Performance Computing (HPC) and Cloud Computing are not *sine qua non* for cryptocurrencies, their use has become pervasive in their transaction verification ("mining"). Cryptocurrencies rely on powerful computational nodes to verify transactions, convert them into groups "blocks", and add them to the blockchain. Such verification is based on well-established complex cryptology algorithms [70] (ergo, the term cryptocurrencies) which assure user anonymity and payment untraceability. With the convergence of HPC and clouds [102], elastic computational resource utilization has become commonplace in different domains, including of course, Cryptocurrencies. Moreover, a recent survey on open challenges and trends in cloud computing [18] recognizes blockchain as a disruptive influencer of the field.

In the following section, related work is provided, introducing sentiment analysis, cryptocurrencies, and their value forecasting. Section 3 highlights for the interested reader, more about cryptocurrencies and blockchain, in general, and lists an example blockchain application for energy markets. After Sect. 3, specific challenges are addressed, listing the specific perspectives. Section 4 covers influence pertaining to social media, Sect. 5, social media data annotation and sentiment dictionary, Sect. 6, Filtering of Tweets, Sect. 7, the perspective on core resulting Sentiment Analysis for cryptocurrencies, Sect. 8, technical analysis, Sect. 9, ranking of ICOs, Sect. 10, portfolio selection using multi-objective optimization, and Sect. 11, investment approaches. Then, the Conclusion section summarizes the surveyed perspectives.

2   Related Work

As this chapter focuses on the objective of Sentiment Analysis for cryptocurrencies, the more recent related work leading to the formation of this objective is initially presented in this section. Namely, when analyzing the impact of cryptocurrencies, there are different possibilities on which to focus, like prediction of value or some other underlying principles and features of technologies enabling these cryptocurrencies.

We first focus on the Bitcoin cryptocurrency and the trading volumes of Bitcoin as introduced using Google Search Engine as the media feed [87]. In [126], search engine query trends are predicted for Bitcoin. A connection between Bitcoin search queries on Google Trends and Wikipedia is established in [68], where their relationship is also studied. An attempt to explain Bitcoin prices and adoption rates using Google Search is made in [109]. Returns and volatility perspective when using Bitcoin volume analysis is discussed in [9]. A text mining from an online forum which analyzes user opinions and aims to predict value fluctuations for Bitcoin is reported in [67]. A survey of methods and models for textual sentiment in finance is presented in [63]. Dynamic topic modeling for cryptocurrency community forums is introduced in [76]. A crowdsourced perspective is presented in [80], listing future directions in international financial integration research. For Bitcoin value formation, a model based on an empirical study is given in [57]. In [101], high frequency volatility is forecasted for cryptocurrencies. Some of the underlying determinants, including technology and economic factors influencing exchange rates for cryptocurrencies, are presented for the case of Bitcoin in [73]. A cryptocurrency price prediction using news and social media sentiment was first introduced in [69], followed shortly by the predicting of cryptocurrency price bubbles using social media data and epidemic modeling in [104]. The popular modern techniques from Artificial Intelligence and general softcomputing paradigms have been utilized in recent work [89], where price prediction based on historical price values was compared over machine learning with different types of neural networks, and further, in [72], where the sentiment-based prediction of alternative cryptocurrency price fluctuations using a gradient boosting tree model is given. In [105], a mutual-excitation of cryptocurrency market returns and social media topics is investigated, whereas the paper [84] reports a recent study considering the impact of social media on Bitcoin value. Finally, a study measuring the interaction between media sentiment, based on news articles as well as blog posts and the Bitcoin price, is given in [136]. Another broader time-series analysis used to study the general relationships between Bitcoin prices and fundamental economic variables, technological factors and measurements of collective mood derived from Twitter feeds was presented in [51].

An example type of media data feeds' content influencing cryptocurrency sentiment are social media channels' posts about ransomware and email-based hacker attacks, mostly influencing the sentiment as negative sentiment posts. The cybersecurity threads' (i.e., computer malware, ransomware, virus, worm, trojan horse, retrovirus, botnet, etc.) [129] development and their impact on society and financial markets are a significant topic today. Hackers enjoy anonymity under blockchain technology, that may have high social cost [82]. For example, the paper [6] shows that a substantial amount of Bitcoin blockchain operations and addresses are involved in ransomware money processing. Ransomware represents a type of software cyber-attack, where the hackers take advantage of victims' operating system vulnerabilities to deploy dedicated ransomware code. Once it has happened, the major harmful activity lies in the encryption of files with certain extensions that are expected to be highly personally important (documents, photos, etc.). The victim still can access (boot) the operating system, usually getting a message specifying the amount of ransom in cryptocurrency, the hacker's wallet address and the time left to pay the ransom in exchange to get the decryption key. On the other hand, the email-based hacker attacks are more frequent and easier to perform. The victim usually receives an email stating some mix of technical info and blackmailing based description of a situation that the hacker takes over the control of web browser, email, and social networks applications remotely, and will send some private information to all gathered contacts, unless a certain amount in cryptocurrency is paid within a given time slot. Both of the cybersecurity threads mentioned above are influencing the blockchain value and should be taken into consideration in any future developed forecasting sentiment aggregator to achieve better accuracy. The reasons and relations are given in an original work [122], where the author investigates how the cybersecurity shocks affect the demand for blockchain settlement, transaction fees, mining reward, and cryptocurrency exchanges. That paper also explores in detail the theory given in [44], and their findings show that sudden shocks to the exogenous demand for blockchain settlement are resulting in an increase in transaction fees and a reduction in the endogenous demand [122].

Following the ongoing research and published works listed in this section, the perspectives compounding the presented research topic of this chapter are identified in Sects. 4–11 as specific challenges in sentiment analysis for cryptocurrency value forecasting.

3   Background: Cryptocurrencies and Blockchain

Widely considered immutable time-stamped data structures, blockchains implement peer-to-peer networks where participants can verify interactions concurrently using decentralized peer-to-peer consensus protocols. As an emerging technology trend, different research [115] and industrial [29] perspectives are being assembled to document its potential disruptive impact [22].

Blockchains have five unique characteristics, namely:

1. Peer-to-peer communication without a central authority.
2. Transparent transaction processing with optionally-disclosed ownership.
3. Decentralized transaction history verifiable by all participants.
4. Immutability of records assuring chronological sequence and accessibility.
5. Logic-based processing to trigger algorithms and events.

The aforementioned characteristics have made blockchain particularly suitable to manage *cryptocurrencies*: Electronic cash systems administered via peer-to-peer consensus. Indeed, the most widely known for cryptocurrency, the Bitcoin [94], remains something like the gold Standard for financial blockchain applications. Nonetheless, while blockchains have been used extensively in financial entities, their decentralized immutability characteristics have made them particularly suitable for applications in other domains as diverse as Law [92], Food Traceability [50], and Open-source Software Management [42]. To highlight the importance of blockchain technologies evaluation, an example in surrounding blockchain technologies for Energy markets follows in the next subsection.

3.1 Blockchain Technologies for Energy Markets

The energy grid is moving to a new era, shifting from centralized broadcast-like energy systems to decentralized smart energy systems by incorporating a large number of small scale Distributed Energy Prosumers (DEP). The advent of intermittent decentralized renewable energy sources is completely changing the way in which electricity grids are managed, supporting the shift to more decentralized smart energy systems. Variations in energy production, either surplus or deficit, may threaten the security of supply, leading to energy distribution systems' overload, and culminating in power outages or service disruptions, forcing the DEPs to shed or shift their energy demand to deal with peak load periods [34,108,131].

The centralized energy systems take limited account of local conditions and are difficult to be optimized, and offer no incentives for consumers to manage and adjust their consumption according the generation profiles. In this context, the H2020 eDREAM project [45] contributes to the transformation of the traditional energy systems into novel decentralized and community-driven ones, by leveraging on blockchain technology to exploit local capacities and constraints fully at micro-grid level to preserve the continuity and security of supply at affordable costs at smart grid level. The grid is modeled as a collection of DEPs' resources able to coordinate through a blockchain based infrastructure to support fully decentralized management, control and stable grid operation. The eDREAM project presents a blockchain decentralized management relying on the implementation of [34]:

– A distributed ledger for storing DEPs' energy data at the micro-grid level. All monitored energy data recorded at the level of a DEP are registered and stored as immutable transactions. Therefore, the individual energy production or energy consumption values are aggregated in blocks which are then replicated in the ledger.

- A set of self-enforcing smart contracts for decentralized energy management and control. Through specific mechanisms, these contracts enable the peer-to-peer-trading of energy among DEPs and offer-demand matching and decentralized coordinated control for energy stakeholders, such as the DSO (Distribution System Operator). The contracts are able to assess and trace the share of contracted flexibility services actually activated in real-time by the aggregators (from their enrolled prosumers).
- Consensus based validation for transactions' validation and financial settlement. The project offers the solution of a novel blockchain-based validation that goes in the direction of increased reliability of the smart grid system operation, better energy incentives for DEPs, and increased usage of renewable energy.

Three types of smart management scenarios are supported with self-enforcing smart contracts [33]: (i) The provisioning of energy flexibility services by the DSO leveraging on aggregators, (ii) The implementation of a decentralized green energy market at the micro-grid level promoting the consumption of renewable energy where it is produced, and (iii) The creation of a community based coalition of prosumers, allowing them to participate in the national energy or capacity market.

The Provisioning of Flexibility Services supposes that prosumers are able to offer and trade their flexibility in terms of loads' modulation. They are involved via enabling aggregators, or directly with the DSO via direct Demand Response and control of DEP's energy assets. Using smart contracts, the DSO is able to assess and trace the share of contracted flexibility services, actually activated in real-time by the aggregators (from their enrolled prosumers) at the grid level. At the same time, the self-enforcing smart contracts act as a decentralized control mechanism used to manage the levels of energy flexibility from aggregators and enrolled prosumers on one side, and from aggregators to the DSO on the other side, associating incentive and penalties' rates. If relevant deviations between the expected energy flexibility request and the actual delivered flexibility are detected by smart contracts, specific actions are taken to rebalance the energy demand with the energy production.

The Decentralized Green Energy Market designed at the micro-grid level enacts any small-scale prosumer to participate and trade energy directly. The market acts as a management mechanism by rewarding the consumption of renewable energy when it is available, leveraging on green energy tokens, making sure that the potential energy imbalances at the micro-grid level are addressed locally and not exported to higher smart grid management levels. The non-fungible tokens are generated at a rate proportional with the forecast renewable energy production [103], transforming the energy in a transactable digital asset. The producers and consumers use the generated tokens to participate in the electricity market sessions and leverage on self-enforcing smart contracts to submit energy bids/offers and transact energy in a peer-to-peer fashion.

The Creation of Virtual Power Plants (VPP) addresses the increasing need to optimize the output from multiple local generation assets (i.e. wind-turbines, small hydro, photovoltaic, back-up generators, etc.) that serve primarily local communities and have export connections at the power distribution network. The benefits behind creating such coalitions are that a mix of different energy generation resources, which have different energy generation models and scale, may be interested to cooperate in a convenient way, with a view to achieving pre-defined smart grid sustainability objectives. The VPP aims at maximizing the utilization and revenues from RES and classic generation sources through accessing different markets as an aggregated portfolio, bringing its capacity to the optimum paying service at any time. The DEPs can ultimately participate on other higher-level energy markets, such as a flexibility service provider to a TSO (Transmission System Operator) or a wholesale capacity provider on the wholesale or capacity market.

The adoption of the above presented blockchain based management approaches will transform the smart grid into a democratic community that no longer relies on a central authority, but can take any decision through smart contracts rules, enforced and verified by each DEP of the grid. At the same time, it is in line with the European strategic vision of creating a secure and sustainable energy system by 2050, and reducing the greenhouse gas emissions by at least 80% [46].

4   Specific Challenge A: Influence on Social Media

Social networks are enabling people to interact, and are ever-changing their human relations to the virtual world. People utilize these media platforms for different activities; to express their opinions and their sentiments, to share their experiences, to react to another person. We can observe in this space different human interactions, and we can define many roles related to relations between different users.

We can observe, among others, influential, trusted, or popular individuals. These roles of users in social networks are significant and useful in various disciplines, such as Economy, Finance, Marketing, political and social campaigns, and recommendations. Defining, distinguishing, and measuring the strength of those relations becomes challenging, both in the theoretical and practical fields. The roles of trusted or influential users, users with high reputation, and popular users, can be used in various ways. An interesting work to define, classify, and present a hierarchy of all the terms was done by Rakoczy [111]. In this survey, we are interested in particular in *influence* approach, the relation which, as we suggest, has the strongest correlation between social media and the cryptocurrency tendency, and, in general, with the financial trends. The research involving influence and influential users is an important part of social network analysis.

The term *influence* is used widely and intuitively means the capacity to influence the character, development, or behavior of someone or something, or the effect itself. We name influencer the person exerting the influence action.

Although this intuitive meaning is well understood, in social network analysis, *influence* seems to be an ambiguous term that depends strictly on the presumed assumptions. For instance, Kempe et al. [64] focused on influence in the information flow and spread sense. On the other hand, other works, e.g. [56] and [140], targeted the quantity aspect of influence, targeting mainly users in central positions in a social network. The analysis of influence is an interdisciplinary domain, involving not only social network analysis, but also social sciences, e.g. Sociology, use of graph theory, statistics, and others [100].

The existing state-of-the-art methods considering influence regard this topic in two different approaches, which are: (i) Influential users' discovery and (ii) Influence diffusion information spread within the network with particular focus on the most optimized way to diffuse the information in a social network maximally.

4.1   Influential Users' Discovery

The methods for influential users discovery try to find users who have an impact on the network and the users who, in some way (structurally, by modifying the behavior, adding information to network, etc.), try to answer the following question: Which users are in such a position and are making such a difference to other users that the structure of the network, behavior, actions, or preferences of other users is changed because of this influential activity? Here, we can find two approaches: Based only on the central position of the user (topology-based approaches: Degree centrality, closeness centrality, and betweenness centrality [142]), or more complex, which takes into account more aspects, like a user's history, content, and other influence properties. Many methods which used topology criteria are based on PageRank [23,56,128,138].

Alternatively, there are also some works that have used additional information provided directly from users about the topic, namely hashtags. RetweetRank and MentionRank [140] are examples of such approaches that are using hashtag information in order to group users together via subject. There have been approaches to provision cloud resources elastically, based on social media, potentially for disaster situations [121]. These methods are similar, using as a base for the network either retweets or mentions. Additionally to the works presented above, there are obviously other works that also deal with the influence evaluation. In the famous work of Hirsh [58], the author presents a metric that aims to calculate the influence of researches, based on individual's publications.

4.2   Influence Diffusion and Influence Maximization

The issue of influence diffusion is a general problem of how the information spreads within a network, where users (nodes) are connected by edges which signify the influence. The best known methods are the *Linear Threshold* (LT) model [64], the modified LT named Delayed LT (DLT) model [93], or *Independent Cascade* (IC) model [64].

Influence maximization is a particular subproblem originating directly from the influence diffusion problem, that is particularly interesting and studied widely. Influence maximization is searching the answer to the following question: Which users to target for spreading some information in order to have maximum possible users in a social network talking/knowing about this information? Hence, such methods aim to find users who will share the information most widely (propagate it further). On the contrary to approaches for the influential users' discovery, these methods are connected strictly with diffusion of information.

4.3 General Model

A general and simple model for for evaluating the influence between a user's network platform is *Action-Reaction-Influence-Model* (ARIM). It is based on the users' proactive and reactive behaviors, that can be found on basically any social networking site, and can be used with different data sets. A few interesting approaches based on ARIM were proposed: e.g., method to calculate influence in time-dependent citation networks [113], and an algorithm to predict the reputation using the known influence value [114]. Finally, a very interesting and new approach of micro-influencer was defined [112].

5 Specific Challenge B: Social Media Feeds' Annotation and Dictionary Definition

A market sentiment dictionary for financial social media data applications is presented in [27], and then a fine-grained analysis of financial Tweets is described in [26]. The dictionary in [27] with 8,331 words, 112 hashtags, and 115 emojis is available publicly at http://nlg.csie.ntu.edu.tw/nlpresource/NTUSD-Fin/ under CC BY-NC-SA 4.0 license. It is built from posts in the StockTwits dataset [71], at that time providing 334,798 labeled posts from 13,059 users and crawled through StockTwits API (https://api.stocktwits.com/developers/docs). The dictionary stores unstemmed tokens appearing at least ten times and showning significant difference in chi-squared test (significance level 0.05) between expected and observed frequency. Also, stopwords, punctuations, digits, URLs, user ids, and tickers are removed from the input posts, while still specifically processing emojis. Input posts with less than two words are also removed. As the paper also analyses sentiment, it is discussed that based on this dictionary, the sentiment of investors may depend on the positions they hold (e.g. positive investor sentiment does not imply bullish market sentiment due to the target of the investor).

The FiQA 2018 Task 1 (https://sites.google.com/view/fiqa/home) is supported by Social Sentiment Index (SSIX) Horizon 2020 project (https://ssix-project.eu/), and it includes 675 training instances to predict continuous sentiment. In [26], utilizing the dictionary [27], the FiQA 2018 Task 1 is evaluated over different neural network models with Keras (https://github.com/keras-team/keras): Convolution Neural Network (CNN), Bidirectional Long Short-Term Memory (Bi-LSTM), and Convolution Recurrent Neural Network (CRNN).

6   Specific Challenge C: Filtering Tweets

As Sentiment Analysis (SA) usually works on top of Twitter feeds, it is necessary to pre-process the Tweets before SA, as described in the following. Pre-processing the data, as defined in [55], is the process of cleaning and preparing the text for classification. This phase has a relevant role in sentiment analysis tasks, indeed, reducing the redundancy and the noise intrinsic in the online data, allowing a better and fast classification [55]. The pre-processing method can be distinguished in two stages: *Transformation* and *filtering*. The first stage is quite standard, consisting in operations like white space removal, expanding abbreviation, stemming, stop words removal, and negation handling, while, instead, the second stage regards the choice and selection of the features, which, in Machine Learning, is called *feature selection* [145].

Such task can be described mathematically as the problem to find an optimal function $f : \mathcal{T} \to S$, where $\mathcal{T}$ is the (cleaned) text space and $S \subset \mathbf{R}^d$ the feature space; where the optimum is defined according to a certain metric that is defined a priori.

In a text mining context, the feature selection task is composed by three steps: Choice of the type of features, giving a weight to each feature, and selecting the relevant features [145]; i.e. scoring each potential feature according to a particular metric, and then taking the n best features. According to the mathematical description given above, the problem is equivalent to choosing the metric with which to evaluate the embedding map. We note that, differently from other fields like image or audio processing, when a combination of features does not have any meaning, then the type of features must be chosen by the user. In this section, we will focus on the third step: The possible methods to extract features specific for Sentiment Analysis, while the ranking of these features is addressed in Sect. 9. For a complete review of the possible type of features, we refer to [1] and [55], and for a description of the weight models and for a complete review on feature selection on text mining we refer to [25,49,54].

The most common metric in feature selection is the χ^2 (chi-squared), a measure expressing the divergence between the feature and the class. A drawback of this metric is that it works only when the dataset is big and there are no rare features. Another two popular metrics are the Accuracy, measuring the expected accuracy of a simple classifier built from the single feature, and the F_1, the harmonic mean of the precision and recall.

As observed in [49], all these metrics are equivalent, and one outperforms the others according to the dataset. In the review where twelve metrics are compared, Forman [49], proposed a new metric, the Bi-Normal Separation (BNS), an extension of the χ^2 where also the frequency of the appearance of the feature is considered. This metric is good in most common cases, but, when predictions move outside of this set, good results are not guaranteed. For example, in a highly skewed data context, the BNS does not work better and two information theoretic measures outperform it: Information Gain and $ITF \cdot IDF_2$, [77].

7 Specific Challenge D: Sentiment Analysis

Sentiment Analysis, also known as opinion mining, refers to the use of natural language, text analysis and computational linguistics to identify or extract subjective information from the attitude of a speaker/writer from a set of customer resources in order to classify the polarity. From the point of view of text mining, Sentiment Analysis is an automatic classification massive task as a function of the positive or negative emotions transmitted by the textual message.

In general, Sentiment Analysis tries to determine the opinion from a person with respect to a topic. Such opinion may involve an evaluation, the emotional state of the user at the time of writing, or the emotional communicative intention, i.e., how the customer tries to influence the reader or interlocutor.

Present approaches can be grouped into three main categories: Knowledge-based, statistical methods, and hybrid techniques [21].

- Knowledge-based techniques classify text into emotional categories based on the presence of unambiguous affective words like happy, sad, bored, etc. [97]. These methods also imply the use of lexical affinity to assign arbitrary words a certain affinity to particular emotions [125].
- Statistical methods take advantage of Machine Learning techniques like Support Vector Machines, mutual inference, semantic analysis, etc. [134]. More sophisticated methods try to detect the emotion and what is the target of such feeling [66]. Grammar dependent relations among words are usually applied to achieve such complex purpose, implying a deep grammar analysis of the message [41].
- Hybrid approaches leverage on both knowledge representation and Machine Learning techniques. These methods take advantage of knowledge represen tation models like ontologies and semantic nets, being able to extract implicit information [19].

On the one hand there are open source tools that use Machine Learning techniques, statistics, and natural language processing to automate the processing of huge amounts of data [41], including web pages, online news, discussion fora, social networks, web blogs, micro-blogging, etc. On the other hand, knowledge based systems use public access resources like SentiWordNet [7] or SenticNet [20] to extract semantic and affective information linked to natural language concepts. Sentiment Analysis can also be performed on visual content, i.e., images and videos (denoted as Multimodal sentiment analysis). One of the first approaches in this direction was SentiBank [14], utilizing an adjective noun pair representation of visual content.

In order to measure the precision and recall of a Sentiment Analysis tool, it is usually compared with human judgments about others' opinions [59]. However, humans when evaluated in the same way only show an 80% of precision on average, and this means that a program with a 75% of precision works almost as well as humans [99].

8   Specific Challenge E: Technical Analysis and Forecasting

SA has a wide range of applications [48], for example monitoring the review of consumer products, evaluating the popularity of public people or discovering a fraud; but, the SA can also be applied in prediction settings. Indeed, SA was used with good results to predict: Elections [132], football matches [110], stock prices [13,85,147], and cryptocurrency fluctuations [2,68,124]. In this survey, we are interested in the latter application, but in all the different contexts described in this paragraph, the prediction problem, from a mathematical point of view, can be described in the same way: Find a function $f : \mathcal{S} \rightarrow \mathbf{R}$, such that given the sentiment s_t (called the dependant or the explanatory variable), the associated value is the prediction (unknown a priori) of (the independent or response variable) x_{t+1}, i.e. $f(s_t) = x_{t+1}$. A simple linear regression model could be summarized by the equation:

$$x_{t+1} = \beta s_t + \epsilon,$$

where other unobserved factors determining x_{t+1} are captured by the error term ϵ. The dependent variable x_{t+1} in the textual sentiment finance literature is typically Bitcoin price and/or trade volume [2,37,51,61,67,136] or Bitcoin return and volatility, as in [30].

Logistic regression is used if the response variable is dichotomous. Here, the dependent variable is a binary variable, whose value is equal to 1 if a certain event has happened, and 0 otherwise. The idea is to examine if Sentiment Analysis is associated significantly with a certain event.

In almost all the examples listed above in this section, the models used to estimate the function f are restricted to the linear ones: Linear or logistic regression in case the features are correlated, or Naive Bayes when the dataset is relatively small [141]. The only exception is represented by [13], where the authors used Fuzzy Neural Networks, a hybrid system that combines the theories of Fuzzy Logic and Neural Networks, [95]. Before proceeding with the description of recent forecasting models for cryptocurrency, it is worth underlining two points: First, such simple models are used because the feature space S is, in general, low dimensional; indeed, more complex models like Support Vector Machines or Neural Network architectures suffer from overfitting. Second, although many works show the relationship between the market and the social sentiments [85,117,147] as highlighted by [148], if the financial instruments attract sufficient messages, in general, the sentiments do not lead financial markets in a statistically significant way. The latter observation can explain the reason why most of the work on cryptocurrency forecasting based on SA are tested with the well-known cryptocurrency Bitcoin, see e.g. [35], or with a specific cryptocurrency, like *ZClassic*, [72]. For financial time series analysis, in order to overcome the problem of the incomplete reliability of sentiments, it is usual to combine SA with auto-regressive models (see e.g. [53] and reference therein, with such approach being suggested also for cryptocurrency), indeed as shown in [12], where the traded volume is driven primarily by past returns. This idea considers multimodal architectures, and although it is suggested in many works [12,24], it is still not applied.

When forecasting cryptocurrencies' values, a key topic is to consider if they should be classed as currencies, assets, or investment vehicles. If they are traded for investment purposes, like hedging or pricing instruments, investigating the volatility of these cryptocurrencies becomes important, and could help others make better informed decisions in terms of portfolio and risk management. Specifically, cryptocurrencies' volatility levels are usually much higher than traditional currencies [39]. Volatility models were used in [139] to test the effects of sentiment or sentiment-related variables on the second moment of stock returns. GARCH-type models and the "realized volatility" approach were employed. A stock volatility prediction using Recurrent Neural Networks with SA was presented in [79]. In [62], the ability of several GARCH models to explain the Bitcoin price volatility was studied, and the optimal model was presented in terms of goodness-of-fit to the data. GARCH modeling of 7 other Cryptocurrencies was presented in [32]. A study on forecasting high frequency volatility for cryptocurrencies and traditional currencies with Support Vector Regression was presented in [101].

As another approach to forecasting, in [133], a fuzzy inference system for forecasting cryptocurrency price variation is developed, with trading rules being optimized through the use of a Genetic Algorithm (the use of Genetic Algorithms to determine trading rules has also been used before in Foreign Exchange markets, FX [90]). One of the advantages of this type of methodology compared with black box machine learning models, is its interpretability.

9 Specific Challenge F: Ranking ICOs

After the introduction of a new measurement indicator like CSAI, such introduction brings with it a challenge of how to include the new indicator within existing schemes that fuse different indicators to then support decision-making.

In fusing the different data streams together, one approach is to assign weights or ranks to indicators. The Machine Learning algorithm designs operating on Big Data, such as stability selection [145], might be used on top of indicator values when tackling the ranking of ICOs. As stability selection also highlights outliers, it might also be helpful in optimizing [144] real-world value chains like energy efficiency and sustainability [52], given a proper access to blockchain data including cryptocurrencies, as well as possible Big Data from the SA streams.

10 Specific Challenge H: Multi-objective Cryptocurrency Portfolio Selection

As cryptocurrency evaluation usually includes taking into account risk [47], several cryptocurrencies might be needed as a set to balance this risk. Namely, a portfolio selection of cryptocurrencies might increase robustness when trading. In portfolio selection, multi-objective optimization algorithms are applied, and are gaining importance [4,91,107,149], as their applicability over global optimization problems contributes towards better multiple criteria decision-making. As a perspective therefore, this is an important challenge to be listed among future directions connected to cryptocurrency analysis.

In [16] it is stated that it is possible to reduce investment risk substantially by adding several different cryptocurrencies to a portfolio, using the traditional Markowitz model. In a similar manner in [106], performance of an equally weighted portfolio and an optimal Markowitz portfolio considering four popular cryptocurrencies is compared, considering different levels of risk-aversion, and reaching the conclusion that there are no significant differences between the two portfolios. In [36], the diversification advantages of including cryptocurrencies in short-term investment portfolios is analyzed, justified by the fact that cryptocurrencies are highly connected to each other but not to other financial assets. In [78], data from ten cryptocurrencies are used, and the conclusion is reached that, through diversification, investment results can be reached.

Portfolio selection is inherently a multi-objective problem, even when using mono-objective models like the Markowitz mean-variance framework. The optimal portfolio will always be a compromise solution between risk and return. By changing parameters in the Markowitz model, it is possible to define an efficient frontier that will exhibit the existing risk-return compromises. There is evidence that cryptocurrencies can be seen more as a speculative asset than as a currency [11,17]. These findings justify the use of optimization models for determining optimal portfolios that also consider investments in cryptocurrencies. If there are metrics capable of calculating expected risk and return for cryptocurrencies' investments, then most of the available methodologies can be used in this setting.

In [88], a copula-based approach is presented considering the multiperiod portfolio optimization, using Differential Evolution (DE). DE is a metaheuristic for global optimization [38,127,135,143] that is also applied successfully to many other challenges, like [52,146], therefore improvements in DE can also have potential impact on portfolio selection and, hence, cryptocurrency analysis. In a multiperiod problem [88], investors have the possibility of changing the allocation of their investments during the considered horizon. In [88] it is stated that this flexibility of rebalancing the portfolio is advantageous, especially due to the high volatility that cryptocurrencies present. Portfolio rebalancing is also considered in [65], where information about the market psychology is included, evaluated using fuzzy reasoning processes that are able to be determined under overevaluation possibilities. The investor profile will, hence, determine the efficient solution that is most adequate to his/her risk aversion preferences.

10.1   Optimization Algorithms

Metaheuristics have long been used for portfolio optimization. In [91] a review is presented of Evolutionary Algorithms used for multi-objective portfolio management. As a recent contribution, a review of Swarm Intelligence methods applied to portfolio optimization can be found in [47].

A Genetic Algorithm that takes into consideration transaction costs is introduced in [5]. A Genetic Algorithm is also used in [120]. The authors consider cardinality constraints, floor constraints, and also round-lot constraints. The objective functions consider the maximization of return and minimization of risk, along with the maximization of the sampling distance. This last objective is only used to improve the behavior of the optimization algorithm. A multi-objective evolutionary approach that is able to produce an efficient frontier of portfolios is introduced in [31], taking into account some constraints, like lower and upper limits to the investment that can be made in each asset, or the maximum and minimum number of assets that the portfolio should consider. This type of cardinality constraints is also considered in the work of [118], where the authors describe a hybrid algorithm combining Evolutionary Algorithms, quadratic programming, and a pruning heuristic. Five different multi-objective Evolutionary Algorithms are compared in [3] for the mean-variance cardinality constrained portfolio optimization problem. The authors conclude that SPEA2 seems to be better, but all multi-objective approaches perform better than single-objective ones. A mean-semivariance framework, taking into account adverse return variations only, is described in [83]. Two different Genetic Algorithms are compared (NSGAII and SPEA2), embedding the use of technical analysis indicators. Other applications of Genetic Algorithms can be found in [75,123].

Ant Colony Optimization is the methodology chosen in [43] to tackle multi-objective portfolio selection, and the authors realize that there are some efficient portfolios that are extremely difficult to find. The authors report better results than the ones obtained with simulated annealing and NSGA. Particle Swarm Optimization is used by [40]. The method seems to be particularly well suited to be used for low-risk investment portfolios. An Artificial Bee Colony metaheuristic is described in [28] for portfolio optimization, interpreting returns as fuzzy numbers. Varying the risk tolerance parameter will lead to different efficient portfolios. The authors acknowledge that real-world constraints have an important impact on the investment strategy. Fuzzy numbers are also used by [119] to represent the uncertainty in future returns. Three objectives are considered there simultaneously: The maximization of the possibilistic expected returns, the minimization of the downside risk (absolute semi-deviation below mean), and the minimization of the skewness of every portfolio. Cardinality constraints are also included.

The multi-objective portfolio optimization is transformed into a mono-objective problem using fuzzy normalization and uniform design method in [116]. The resulting model is then solved using an invasive weed optimization algorithm. The original model considers two more objectives in addition to the Markowitz mean-variance model: the stock profit gained relative to its market price, and the representation of experts' recommendations. Fuzzy numbers are also used in [86], to describe asset returns and develop a multi-objective approach based on a genetic algorithm. In [81] an approach is presented that uses a self-organizing Fuzzy Neural Network embedded into an heuristic that explores simplex local searches. Finally, [60] use machine learning tools, namely, deep reinforcement learning, to define cryptocurrencies' portfolios based on technical aspects only (price and movement).

11 Specific Challenge G: Investment Approaches with the New ICO Sentiment Indicator

The technical analysis covered in this chapter is the SA (Sect. 7) with forecasting (Sect. 8) and indicators fusion (Sect. 9), followed by optimization algorithms' supported multi-objective portfolio selection (Sect. 10). Besides technical analysis however, investment approaches with cryptocurrencies must take into account particular characteristics, like the herding effect, as identified in [15]. Risks from these characteristics can be caused through a lack of diversification of cryptocurrencies' portfolios, making investors more exposed to investment risk, as explained in the previous section. These characteristics also include long memory, stochastic volatility, and leverage [104]. Keeping pertained characteristics in mind and together through technical analysis, a trader might then evaluate a cryptocurrency as a whole and trade the cryptocurrency as a financial asset [8].

12 Conclusion

This chapter covered the different aspects of necessary perspectives needed when preparing forecasting and investment, supported by cryptocurrency social media Sentiment Analysis. Eight specific perspectives were identified, and the current state-of-the-art was covered in separate sections of the chapter, all focusing around a new type of indicator, the CSAI. In the following work, some more specific implementations and experimental results could be presented, based on the guidelines, outlines, and integration possibilities presented in this chapter.

Acknowledgements. This chapter is based upon work from COST Action IC1406 High-Performance Modelling and Simulation for Big Data Applications (cHiPSet), supported by COST (European Cooperation in Science and Technology). The author AZ acknowledges the financial support from the Slovenian Research Agency (Research Core Funding No. P2-0041). AZ also acknowledges EU support under Project No. 5442-24/2017/6 (HPC – RIVR). This chapter is also based upon work from COST Action CA15140 "Improving Applicability of Nature-Inspired Optimisation by Joining Theory and Practice (ImAppNIO)" supported by COST. The authors CP, TC and IS also acknowledge that the work presented in this chapter is supported financially by the eDREAM Project Grant number 774478, co-funded by the European Commission as part of the H2020 Framework Programme. This work was supported by the Fundacao para a Ciencia e a Tecnologia (FCT) under Project Grant UID/Multi/00308/2019. Author RS also acknowledges that work was supported by the Ministry of Education,

Youth and Sports of the Czech Republic within the National Sustainability Programme Project No. LO1303 (MSMT-7778/2014), further supported by the European Regional Development Fund under the Project CEBIA-Tech no. CZ.1.05/2.1.00/03.0089.

References

1. Abbasi, A., Chen, H., Salem, A.: Sentiment analysis in multiple languages: feature selection for opinion classification in Web forums. ACM Trans. Inf. Syst. (TOIS) **26**(3), 12 (2008)
2. Abraham, J., Higdon, D., Nelson, J., Ibarra, J.: Cryptocurrency price prediction using tweet volumes and sentiment analysis. SMU Data Sci. Rev. **1**(3), 1 (2018)
3. Anagnostopoulos, K.P., Mamanis, G.: The mean-variance cardinality constrained portfolio optimization problem: an experimental evaluation of five multiobjective evolutionary algorithms. Expert Syst. Appl. **38**(11), 14208–14217 (2011)
4. Aouni, B., Doumpos, M., Pérez-Gladish, B., Steuer, R.E.: On the increasing importance of multiple criteria decision aid methods for portfolio selection. J. Oper. Res. Soc. **69**, 1525–1542 (2018)
5. Aranha, C., Iba, H.: Modelling cost into a genetic algorithm-based portfolio optimization system by seeding and objective sharing. In: 2007 IEEE Congress on Evolutionary Computation, pp. 106–203. IEEE, Singapore (2007)
6. Athey, S., Parashkevov, I., Sarukkai, V., Xia, J.: Bitcoin pricing, adoption, and usage: theory and evidence. Stanford University Graduate School of Business Research Paper No. 16–42 (2016). https://ssrn.com/abstract=2826074
7. Baccianella, S., Esuli, A., Sebastiani, F.: SentiWordNet 3.0: an enhanced lexical resource for sentiment analysis and opinion mining. In: Seventh International Conference on Language Resources and Evaluation (LREC), vol. 10, pp. 2200–2204 (2010)
8. Bagheri, A., Peyhani, H.M., Akbari, M.: Financial forecasting using ANFIS networks with quantum-behaved particle swarm optimization. Expert Syst. Appl. **41**(14), 6235–6250 (2014)
9. Balcilar, M., Bouri, E., Gupta, R., Roubaud, D.: Can volume predict Bitcoin returns and volatility? A quantiles-based approach. Econ. Model. **64**, 74–81 (2017)
10. Bartoletti, M., Bracciali, A., Lande, S., Pompianu, L.: A general framework for Bitcoin analytics. arXiv preprint arXiv:1707.01021 (2017)
11. Baur, D.G., Hong, K., Lee, A.D.: Bitcoin: medium of exchange or speculative assets? J. Int. Fin. Markets Inst. Money **54**, 177–189 (2018)
12. Bianchi, D.: Cryptocurrencies as an asset class? An empirical assessment (6 June, 2018). WBS Finance Group Research Paper (2017)
13. Bollen, J., Mao, H., Zeng, X.: Twitter mood predicts the stock market. J. Comput. Sci. **2**(1), 1–8 (2011)
14. Borth, D., Ji, R., Chen, T., Breuel, T., Chang, S.F.: Large-scale visual sentiment ontology and detectors using adjective noun pairs. In: Proceedings of the 21st ACM International Conference on Multimedia, pp. 223–232. ACM (2013)
15. Bouri, E., Gupta, R., Roubaud, D.: Herding behaviour in cryptocurrencies. Fin. Res. Lett. (2018). https://doi.org/10.1016/j.frl.2018.07.008
16. Brauneis, A., Mestel, R.: Cryptocurrency-portfolios in a mean-variance framework. Fin. Res. Lett. (2018). https://doi.org/10.1016/j.frl.2018.05.008
17. Brauneis, A., Mestel, R.: Price discovery of cryptocurrencies: Bitcoin and beyond. Econ. Lett. **165**, 58–61 (2018)

18. Buyya, R., et al.: A manifesto for future generation cloud computing: research directions for the next decade. ACM Comput. Surv. **51**(5), 105:1–105:38 (2018)
19. Cambria, E., Hussain, A.: Sentic Computing: Techniques, Tools, and Applications, vol. 2. Springer, Dordrecht (2012). https://doi.org/10.1007/978-94-007-5070-8
20. Cambria, E., Olsher, D., Rajagopal, D.: SenticNet 3: a common and common-sense knowledge base for cognition-driven sentiment analysis. In: Twenty-Eighth AAAI Conference on Artificial Intelligence (2014)
21. Cambria, E., Schuller, B., Xia, Y., Havasi, C.: New avenues in opinion mining and sentiment analysis. IEEE Intell. Syst. **28**(2), 15–21 (2013)
22. Casino, F., Dasaklis, T.K., Patsakis, C.: A systematic literature review of blockchain-based applications: current status, classification and open issues. Telematics Inform. (2018, in Press) https://doi.org/10.1016/j.tele.2018.11.006
23. Cataldi, M., Aufaure, M.A.: The 10 million follower fallacy: audience size does not prove domain-influence on Twitter. Knowl. Inf. Syst. **44**(3), 559–580 (2015)
24. Catania, L., Grassi, S., Ravazzolo, F.: Forecasting cryptocurrencies financial time series. CAMP Working Paper Series No. 5 (2018)
25. Chandrashekar, G., Sahin, F.: A survey on feature selection methods. Comput. Electr. Eng. **40**(1), 16–28 (2014)
26. Chen, C.C., Huang, H.H., Chen, H.H.: Fine-grained analysis of financial Tweets. In: Companion of the Web Conference 2018 on the Web Conference 2018, pp. 1943–1949. International World Wide Web Conferences Steering Committee (2018)
27. Chen, C.C., Huang, H.H., Chen, H.H.: NTUSD-Fin: a market sentiment dictionary for financial social media data applications. In: Proceedings of the 1st Financial Narrative Processing Workshop (FNP 2018) (2018)
28. Chen, W.: Artificial bee colony algorithm for constrained possibilistic portfolio optimization problem. Phys. A: Stat. Mech. Appl. **429**, 125–139 (2015)
29. Chen, Y.: Blockchain tokens and the potential democratization of entrepreneurship and innovation. Bus. Horiz. **61**(4), 567–575 (2018)
30. Cheoljun, E., Kaizoji, T., Kang, S.H., Pichl, L.: Bitcoin and investor sentiment: statistical characteristics and predictability. Physica A **514**, 511–521 (2019)
31. Chiam, S.C., Al Mamun, A., Low, Y.L.: A realistic approach to evolutionary multiobjective portfolio optimization. In: 2007 IEEE Congress on Evolutionary Computation, pp. 204–211. IEEE (2007)
32. Chu, J., Stephen, C., Saralees, N., Joerg, O.: GARCH modeling of cryptocurrencies. J. Risk Fin. Manag. **10**(4), 1–15 (2017)
33. Cioara, T., et al.: Enabling new technologies for demand response decentralized validation using blockchain. In: 2018 IEEE International Conference on Environment and Electrical Engineering and 2018 IEEE Industrial and Commercial Power Systems Europe, pp. 1–4. IEEE (2018)
34. Claudia, P., Tudor, C., Marcel, A., Ionut, A., Ioan, S., Massimo, B.: Blockchain based decentralized management of demand response programs in smart energy grids. Sensors **18**, 162 (2018)
35. Colianni, S., Rosales, S., Signorotti, M.: Algorithmic trading of cryptocurrency based on Twitter sentiment analysis. CS229 Project (2015)
36. Corbet, S., Meegan, A., Larkin, C., Lucey, B., Yarovaya, L.: Exploring the dynamic relationships between cryptocurrencies and other financial assets. Econ. Lett. **165**, 28–34 (2018)
37. Cretarola, A., Figà-Talamanca, G., Patacca, M.: A sentiment-based model for the BitCoin: theory, estimation and option pricing (2017). https://doi.org/10.2139/ssrn.3042029. https://ssrn.com/abstract=3042029

38. Das, S., Mullick, S.S., Suganthan, P.: Recent advances in differential evolution - an updated survey. Swarm Evol. Comput. **27**, 1–30 (2016)
39. David, Y.: Handbook of Digital Currency Bitcoin, Innovation, Financial Instruments, and Big Data. Elsevier, Amsterdam (2015). https://doi.org/10.1016/B978-0-12-802117-0.00002-3
40. Deng, G.F., Lin, W.T., Lo, C.C.: Markowitz-based portfolio selection with cardinality constraints using improved particle swarm optimization. Expert Syst. Appl. **39**(4), 4558–4566 (2012)
41. Dey, L., Haque, S.M.: Opinion mining from noisy text data. Int. J. Doc. Anal. Recogn. (IJDAR) **12**(3), 205–226 (2009)
42. D'mello, G., González-Vélez, H.: Distributed software dependency management using blockchain. In: 27th Euromicro International Conference on Parallel, Distributed and Network-Based Processing, PDP 2019, pp. 1–8. IEEE, Pavia (2019, to appear)
43. Doerner, K., Gutjahr, W.J., Hartl, R.F., Strauss, C., Stummer, C.: Pareto ant colony optimization: a metaheuristic approach to multiobjective portfolio selection. Ann. Oper. Res. **131**(1–4), 79–99 (2004)
44. Easley, D., O'Hara, M., Basu, S.: From Mining to Markets: The Evolution of Bitcoin Transaction Fees. SSRN 3055380 (2018)
45. eDREAM: H2020 eDREAM Project. http://edream-h2020.eu/en/
46. Energy4Europe, European Commission: Energy Strategy and Energy Union, Secure, Competitive, and sustainable Energy. https://ec.europa.eu/energy/en/topics/energy-strategy-and-energy-union
47. Ertenlice, O., Kalayci, C.B.: A survey of swarm intelligence for portfolio optimization: algorithms and applications. Swarm Evol. Comput. **39**, 36–52 (2018)
48. Feldman, R.: Techniques and applications for sentiment analysis. Commun. ACM **56**(4), 82–89 (2013)
49. Forman, G.: An extensive empirical study of feature selection metrics for text classification. J. Mach. Learn. Res. **3**(Mar), 1289–1305 (2003)
50. Galvez, J.F., Mejuto, J., Simal-Gandara, J.: Future challenges on the use of blockchain for food traceability analysis. TrAC Trends Anal. Chem. **107**, 222–232 (2018)
51. Georgoula, I., Pournarakis, D., Bilanakos, C., Sotiropoulos, D.N., Giaglis, G.M.: Using time series and sentiment analysis to detect the determinants of Bitcoin prices. In: MCIS 2015 Proceedings 20 (2015). https://aisel.aisnet.org/mcis2015/20/
52. Glotić, A., Zamuda, A.: Short-term combined economic and emission hydrothermal optimization by surrogate differential evolution. Appl. Energy **141**, 42–56 (2015)
53. Guidolin, M., Hyde, S., McMillan, D., Ono, S.: Non-linear predictability in stock and bond returns: when and where is it exploitable? Int. J. Forecast. **25**(2), 373–399 (2009)
54. Guyon, I., Elisseeff, A.: An introduction to variable and feature selection. J. Mach. Learn. Res. **3**(Mar), 1157–1182 (2003)
55. Haddi, E., Liu, X., Shi, Y.: The role of text pre-processing in sentiment analysis. Procedia Comput. Sci. **17**, 26–32 (2013)
56. Haveliwala, T.H.: Topic-sensitive PageRank. In: Proceedings of the 11th International Conference on World Wide Web, pp. 517–526. ACM (2002)
57. Hayes, A.S.: Cryptocurrency value formation: an empirical analysis leading to a cost of production model for valuing Bitcoin. Telematics Inform. **34**(7), 1308–1321 (2017)

58. Hirsch, J.E.: An index to quantify an individual's scientific research output. Proc. Nat. Acad. Sci. U.S.A. **102**(46), 16569 (2005)
59. Hussein, D.M.E.D.M.: A survey on sentiment analysis challenges. J. King Saud Univ.-Eng. Sci. **30**(4), 330–338 (2018)
60. Jiang, Z., Liang, J.: Cryptocurrency portfolio management with deep reinforcement learning. In: 2017 Intelligent Systems Conference (IntelliSys), pp. 905–913. IEEE (2017)
61. Kaminski, J.C.: Nowcasting the Bitcoin market with Twitter signals. arXiv preprint arXiv:1406.7577v3 (2016). https://arxiv.org/pdf/1406.7577v3.pdf
62. Katsiampa, P.: Volatility estimation for Bitcoin: a comparison of GARCH models. Econ. Lett. **158**, 3–6 (2017)
63. Kearney, C., Liu, S.: Textual sentiment in finance: a survey of methods and models. Int. Rev. Fin. Anal. **33**, 171–185 (2014)
64. Kempe, D., Kleinberg, J., Tardos, É.: Maximizing the spread of influence through a social network. In: Proceedings of the Ninth ACM SIGKDD International Conference on Knowledge Discovery and Data Mining, pp. 137–146. ACM (2003)
65. Khayamim, A., Mirzazadeh, A., Naderi, B.: Portfolio rebalancing with respect to market psychology in a fuzzy environment: a case study in Tehran Stock Exchange. Appl. Soft Comput. **64**, 244–259 (2018)
66. Kim, S.M., Hovy, E.: Identifying and analyzing judgment opinions. In: Proceedings of the Main Conference on Human Language Technology Conference of the North American Chapter of the Association of Computational Linguistics, pp. 200–207. Association for Computational Linguistics (2006)
67. Kim, Y.B., Lee, J., Park, N., Choo, J., Kim, J.H., Kim, C.H.: When Bitcoin encounters information in an online forum: using text mining to analyse user opinions and predict value fluctuation. PloS One **12**(5), e0177630 (2017)
68. Ladislav, K.: BitCoin meets Google Trends and Wikipedia: quantifying the relationship between phenomena of the Internet era (2013). https://www.nature.com/srep/
69. Lamon, C., Nielsen, E., Redondo, E.: Cryptocurrency Price Prediction Using News and Social Media Sentiment (2016). http://cs229.stanford.edu/proj2017/final-reports/5237280.pdf
70. Law, L., Sabett, S., Solinas, J.: How to make a mint: the cryptography of anonymous electronic cash. Technical report, National Security Agency, Office of Information Security Research and Technology, Cryptology Division, 1001 Pennsylvania Avenue, DC, USA, June 1996
71. Li, Q., Shah, S.: Learning stock market sentiment lexicon and sentiment-oriented word vector from StockTwits. In: Proceedings of the 21st Conference on Computational Natural Language Learning (CoNLL 2017), pp. 301–310 (2017)
72. Li, T.R., Chamrajnagar, A.S., Fong, X.R., Rizik, N.R., Fu, F.: Sentiment-based prediction of alternative cryptocurrency price fluctuations using gradient boosting tree model. arXiv preprint arXiv:1805.00558 (2018)
73. Li, X., Wang, C.A.: The technology and economic determinants of cryptocurrency exchange rates: the case of Bitcoin. Decis. Support Syst. **95**, 49–60 (2017)
74. Lim, S.Y., et al.: Blockchain technology the identity management and authentication service disruptor: a survey. Int. J. Adv. Sci. Eng. Inf. Technol. **8**(4–2), 1735–1745 (2018)
75. Lin, C.C., Liu, Y.T.: Genetic algorithms for portfolio selection problems with minimum transaction lots. Eur. J. Oper. Res. **185**(1), 393–404 (2008)

76. Linton, M., Teo, E.G.S., Bommes, E., Chen, C.Y., Härdle, W.K.: Dynamic topic modelling for cryptocurrency community forums. In: Härdle, W.K., Chen, C.Y.H., Overbeck, L. (eds.) Applied Quantitative Finance. SC, pp. 355–372. Springer, Heidelberg (2017). https://doi.org/10.1007/978-3-662-54486-0_18
77. Liu, C., Kübler, S., Yu, N.: Feature selection for highly skewed sentiment analysis tasks. In: Proceedings of the Second Workshop on Natural Language Processing for Social Media (SocialNLP), pp. 2–11 (2014)
78. Liu, W.: Portfolio diversification across cryptocurrencies. Fin. Res. Lett. (2018). https://doi.org/10.1016/j.frl.2018.07.010
79. Liu, Y., Qin, Z., Li, P., Wan, T.: Stock volatility prediction using recurrent neural networks with sentiment analysis. In: Benferhat, S., Tabia, K., Ali, M. (eds.) IEA/AIE 2017. LNCS (LNAI), vol. 10350, pp. 192–201. Springer, Cham (2017). https://doi.org/10.1007/978-3-319-60042-0_22
80. Lucey, B.M., et al.: Future directions in international financial integration research - A crowdsourced perspective. Int. Rev. Fin. Anal. **55**, 35–49 (2018)
81. Lumanpauw, E., Pasquier, M., Quek, C.: MNFS-FPM: a novel memetic neuro-fuzzy system based financial portfolio management. In: 2007 IEEE Congress on Evolutionary Computation, pp. 2554–2561. IEEE, Singapore (2007)
82. Ma, J., Gans, J.S., Tourky, R.: Market structure in Bitcoin mining. Technical report, National Bureau of Economic Research (2018)
83. Macedo, L.L., Godinho, P., Alves, M.J.: Mean-semivariance portfolio optimization with multiobjective evolutionary algorithms and technical analysis rules. Expert Syst. Appl. **79**, 33–43 (2017)
84. Mai, F., Shan, Z., Bai, Q., Wang, X., Chiang, R.H.: How does social media impact Bitcoin value? a test of the silent majority hypothesis. J. Manag. Inf. Syst. **35**(1), 19–52 (2018)
85. Mao, Y., Wei, W., Wang, B., Liu, B.: Correlating S&P 500 stocks with Twitter data. In: Proceedings of the First ACM International Workshop on Hot Topics on Interdisciplinary Social Networks Research, pp. 69–72. ACM (2012)
86. Mashayekhi, Z., Omrani, H.: An integrated multi-objective Markowitz-DEA cross-efficiency model with fuzzy returns for portfolio selection problem. Appl. Soft Comput. **38**, 1–9 (2016)
87. Matta, M., Lunesu, I., Marchesi, M.: The predictor impact of Web search media on Bitcoin trading volumes. In: 2015 7th International Joint Conference on Knowledge Discovery, Knowledge Engineering and Knowledge Management (IC3K), vol. 1, pp. 620–626. IEEE (2015)
88. Mba, J.C., Pindza, E., Koumba, U.: A differential evolution copula-based approach for a multi-period cryptocurrency portfolio optimization. Fin. Markets Portfolio Manag. **32**(4), 399–418 (2018)
89. McNally, S., Roche, J., Caton, S.: Predicting the price of Bitcoin using machine learning. In: 2018 26th Euromicro International Conference on Parallel, Distributed and Network-Based Processing (PDP), pp. 339–343. IEEE (2018)
90. Mendes, L., Godinho, P., Dias, J.: A forex trading system based on a genetic algorithm. J. Heuristics **18**(4), 627–656 (2012)
91. Metaxiotis, K., Liagkouras, K.: Multiobjective evolutionary algorithms for portfolio management: a comprehensive literature review. Expert Syst. Appl. **39**(14), 11685–11698 (2012)
92. Millard, C.: Blockchain and law: incompatible codes? Comput. Law Secur. Rev. **34**(4), 843–846 (2018)
93. Mohammadi, A., Saraee, M., Mirzaei, A.: Time-sensitive influence maximization in social networks. J. Inf. Sci. **41**(6), 765–778 (2015)

94. Nakamoto, S.: Bitcoin: a peer-to-peer electronic cash system. Bitcoin.org (2008)
95. Nauck, D., Klawonn, F., Kruse, R.: Foundations of Neuro-Fuzzy Systems. Wiley, Hoboken (1997)
96. Nguyen, G.T., Kim, K.: A survey about consensus algorithms used in blockchain. J. Inf. Process. Syst. **14**(1), 101–128 (2018)
97. Ortony, A., Clore, G.L., Collins, A.: The Cognitive Structure of Emotions. Cambridge University Press, Cambridge (1990)
98. Panarello, A., Tapas, N., Merlino, G., Longo, F., Puliafito, A.: Blockchain and IoT integration: a systematic survey. Sensors **18**(8), 2575 (2018)
99. Pang, B., Lee, L.: Seeing stars: exploiting class relationships for sentiment categorization with respect to rating scales. In: Proceedings of the 43rd Annual Meeting on Association for Computational Linguistics, pp. 115–124. Association for Computational Linguistics (2005)
100. Peng, S., Zhou, Y., Cao, L., Yu, S., Niu, J., Jia, W.: Influence analysis in social networks: a survey. J. Netw. Comput. Appl. **106**, 17–32 (2018)
101. Peng, Y., Albuquerque, P.H.M., de Sá, J.M.C., Padula, A.J.A., Montenegro, M.R.: The best of two worlds: forecasting high frequency volatility for cryptocurrencies and traditional currencies with Support Vector Regression. Expert Syst. Appl. **97**, 177–192 (2018)
102. Petcu, D., González–Vélez, H., Nicolae, B., García–Gómez, J.M., Fuster–Garcia, E., Sheridan, C.: Next generation HPC clouds: a view for large-scale scientific and data-intensive applications. In: Lopes, L., et al. (eds.) Euro-Par 2014. LNCS, vol. 8806, pp. 26–37. Springer, Cham (2014). https://doi.org/10.1007/978-3-319-14313-2_3
103. Petrican, T., et al.: Evaluating forecasting techniques for integrating household energy prosumers into smart grids. In: 14th International Conference on Intelligent Computer Communication and Processing, pp. 79–85. IEEE (2018)
104. Phillips, R.C., Gorse, D.: Predicting cryptocurrency price bubbles using social media data and epidemic modelling. In: 2017 IEEE Symposium Series on Computational Intelligence (SSCI), pp. 1–7. IEEE (2017)
105. Phillips, R.C., Gorse, D.: Mutual-excitation of cryptocurrency market returns and social media topics. In: Proceedings of the 4th International Conference on Frontiers of Educational Technologies, pp. 80–86. ACM (2018)
106. Platanakis, E., Sutcliffe, C., Urquhart, A.: Optimal vs naïve diversification in cryptocurrencies. Econ. Lett. **171**, 93–96 (2018)
107. Ponsich, A., Jaimes, A.L., Coello, C.A.C.: A survey on multiobjective evolutionary algorithms for the solution of the portfolio optimization problem and other finance and economics applications. IEEE Trans. Evol. Comput. **17**(3), 321–344 (2013)
108. Pop, C., et al.: Decentralizing the stock exchange using blockchain an ethereum-based implementation of the Bucharest Stock Exchange. In: 14th International Conference on Intelligent Computer Communication and Processing, pp. 459–466. IEEE (2018)
109. Puri, V.: Decrypting Bitcoin prices and adoption rates using Google search. CMC Senior Theses **1418** (2016)
110. Radosavljevic, V., Grbovic, M., Djuric, N., Bhamidipati, N.: Large-scale World Cup 2014 outcome prediction based on Tumblr posts. In: KDD Workshop on Large-Scale Sports Analytics (2014)
111. Rakoczy, M., Bouzeghoub, A., Wegrzyn-Wolska, K., Gancarski, L.A.: Users views on others - analysis of confused relation-based terms in social network. In: Debruyne, C., et al. (eds.) OTM 2016. LNCS, vol. 10033, pp. 155–174. Springer, Cham (2016). https://doi.org/10.1007/978-3-319-48472-3_9

112. Rakoczy, M.E., Bouzeghoub, A., Lopes, G.A., Wegrzyn-Wolska, K.: In the search of quality influence on a small scale – micro-influencers discovery. In: Panetto, H., Debruyne, C., Proper, H., Ardagna, C., Roman, D., Meersman, R. (eds.) OTM 2018. LNCS, vol. 11230. Springer, Cham (2018). https://doi.org/10.1007/978-3-030-02671-4_8

113. Rakoczy, M.E., Bouzeghoub, A., Gançarski, A.L., Wegrzyn-Wolska, K.: Influence in time-dependent citation networks. In: 12th International Conference on Research Challenges in Information Science, RCIS 2018, 29–31 May 2018, Nantes, France, pp. 1–11 (2018)

114. Rakoczy, M.E., Bouzeghoub, A., Gançarski, A.L., Wegrzyn-Wolska, K.: Reputation prediction using influence conversion. In: 17th IEEE International Conference on Trust, Security and Privacy in Computing and Communications/12th IEEE International Conference on Big Data Science and Engineering, Trust-Com/BigDataSE 2018, 1–3 August 2018, New York, NY, USA, pp. 43–48 (2018)

115. Reyna, A., Martín, C., Chen, J., Soler, E., Daíz, M.: On blockchain and its integration with IoT. Challenges and opportunities. Future Gener. Comput. Syst. **88**, 173–190 (2018)

116. Rezaei Pouya, A., Solimanpur, M., Jahangoshai Rezaee, M.: Solving multi-objective portfolio optimization problem using invasive weed optimization. Swarm Evol. Comput. **28**, 42–57 (2016)

117. Ruiz, E.J., Hristidis, V., Castillo, C., Gionis, A., Jaimes, A.: Correlating financial time series with micro-blogging activity. In: Proceedings of the Fifth ACM International Conference on Web Search and Data Mining, pp. 513–522. ACM (2012)

118. Ruiz-Torrubiano, R., Suarez, A.: Use of heuristic rules in evolutionary methods for the selection of optimal investment portfolios. In: 2007 IEEE Congress on Evolutionary Computation, pp. 212–219. IEEE (2007)

119. Saborido, R., Ruiz, A.B., Bermúdez, J.D., Vercher, E., Luque, M.: Evolutionary multi-objective optimization algorithms for fuzzy portfolio selection. Appl. Soft Comput. **39**, 48–63 (2016)

120. Skolpadungket, P., Dahal, K., Harnpornchai, N.: Portfolio optimization using multi-objective genetic algorithms. In: 2007 IEEE Congress on Evolutionary Computation, pp. 516–523. IEEE (2007)

121. Smith, P., González-Vélez, H., Caton, S.: Social auto-scaling. In: 26th Euromicro International Conference on Parallel, Distributed and Network-Based Processing, PDP 2018, pp. 186–195. IEEE, Cambridge (2018)

122. Sokolov, K.: Ransomware Activity, Demand for Blockchain Settlement and the Upper Bound of Congestion-Induced Mining Reward. SSRN Working Paper (2018). https://ssrn.com/abstract=3175986

123. Soleimani, H., Golmakani, H.R., Salimi, M.H.: Markowitz-based portfolio selection with minimum transaction lots, cardinality constraints and regarding sector capitalization using genetic algorithm. Expert Syst. Appl. **36**(3), 5058–5063 (2009)

124. Stenqvist, E., Lönnö, J.: Predicting Bitcoin price fluctuation with Twitter sentiment analysis (2017)

125. Stevenson, R.A., Mikels, J.A., James, T.W.: Characterization of the affective norms for english words by discrete emotional categories. Behav. Res. Methods **39**(4), 1020–1024 (2007)

126. Stocchi, M., Lunesu, I., Ibba, S., Baralla, G., Marchesi, M.: The future of Bitcoin: a synchrosqueezing wavelet transform to predict search engine query trends. In: KDWeb (2016)

127. Storn, R., Price, K.: Differential evolution - a simple and efficient heuristic for global optimization over continuous spaces. J. Global Optim. **11**, 341–359 (1997)
128. Sung, J., Moon, S., Lee, J.-G.: The influence in Twitter: are they really influenced? In: Cao, L., et al. (eds.) BSI/BSIC 2013. LNCS (LNAI), vol. 8178, pp. 95–105. Springer, Cham (2013). https://doi.org/10.1007/978-3-319-04048-6_9
129. Szor, P.: The Art of Computer Virus Research and Defense. Pearson Education, London (2005)
130. Tonelli, R., Ducasse, S., Fenu, G., Bracciali, A.: 2018 IEEE 1st International Workshop on Blockchain Oriented Software Engineering (IWBOSE), 20 March 2018, Campobasso, Italy. IEEE (2018)
131. Tudor, C., et al.: Optimized flexibility management enacting data centres participation in smart demand response programs. Future Gener. Comput. Syst. **78**, 330–342 (2018)
132. Tumasjan, A., Sprenger, T.O., Sandner, P.G., Welpe, I.M.: Predicting elections with Twitter: what 140 characters reveal about political sentiment. In: International AAAI Conference on Web and Social Media, Fourth International AAAI Conference on Weblogs and Social Media, vol. 10, no. 1, pp. 178–185 (2010)
133. Tupinambas, T.M., Leao, R.A., Lemos, A.P.: Cryptocurrencies transactions advisor using a genetic Mamdani-type fuzzy rules based system. In: IEEE International Conference on Fuzzy Systems, p. 7 (2018)
134. Turney, P.D.: Thumbs up or thumbs down?: semantic orientation applied to unsupervised classification of reviews. In: Proceedings of the 40th Annual Meeting on Association for Computational Linguistics, pp. 417–424. Association for Computational Linguistics (2002)
135. Viktorin, A., Senkerik, R., Pluhacek, M., Kadavy, T., Zamuda, A.: Distance based parameter adaptation for success-history based differential evolution. Swarm Evol. Comput., 12 November 2018. https://doi.org/10.1016/j.swevo.2018.10.013
136. Vytautas, K., Niels, D., Jochen, D.W.: Using sentiment analysis to predict interday Bitcoin price movements. J. Risk Fin. **19**(1), 56–75 (2018)
137. Wang, W., et al.: A survey on consensus mechanisms and mining management in blockchain networks. arXiv preprint arXiv:1805.02707 (2018)
138. Weng, J., Lim, E.P., Jiang, J., He, Q.: TwitterRank: finding topic-sensitive influential Twitterers. In: Proceedings of the Third ACM International Conference on Web Search and Data Mining, pp. 261–270. ACM (2010)
139. Werner, A., Murray, Z.F.: Is all that talk just noise? The information content of internet stock message boards. J. Fin. **59**, 1259–1294 (2004)
140. Xiao, F., Noro, T., Tokuda, T.: Finding news-topic oriented influential Twitter users based on topic related hashtag community detection. J. Web Eng. **13**(5&6), 405–429 (2014)
141. Yogatama, D., Dyer, C., Ling, W., Blunsom, P.: Generative and discriminative text classification with recurrent neural networks. In: Thirty-Fourth International Conference on Machine Learning (ICML 2017) (2017)
142. Zafarani, R., Abbasi, M.A., Liu, H.: Social Media Mining: An Introduction. Cambridge University Press, New York (2014)
143. Zamuda, A., Brest, J.: Self-adaptive control parameters' randomization frequency and propagations in differential evolution. Swarm Evol. Comput. **25**, 72–99 (2015)
144. Zamuda, A., Nicolau, M., Zarges, C.: A black-box discrete optimization benchmarking (BB-DOB) pipeline survey: taxonomy, evaluation, and ranking. In: Proceedings of the Genetic and Evolutionary Computation Conference Companion (GECCO 2018), pp. 1777–1782 (2018)

145. Zamuda, A., Zarges, C., Stiglic, G., Hrovat, G.: Stability selection using a genetic algorithm and logistic linear regression on healthcare records. In: Proceedings of the Genetic and Evolutionary Computation Conference Companion (GECCO 2017), pp. 143–144 (2017)
146. Zamuda, A., Sosa, J.D.H.: Success history applied to expert system for underwater glider path planning using differential evolution. Expert Syst. Appl. **119**(1 April 2019), 155–170 (2019)
147. Zhang, X., Fuehres, H., Gloor, P.A.: Predicting stock market indicators through Twitter "I hope it is not as bad as I fear". Procedia-Soc. Behav. Sci. **26**, 55–62 (2011)
148. Zheludev, I., Smith, R., Aste, T.: When can social media lead financial markets? Sci. Rep. **4**, 4213 (2014)
149. Zopounidis, C., Galariotis, E., Doumpos, M., Sarri, S., AndriosopouloS, K.: Multiple criteria decision aiding for finance: an updated bibliographic survey. Eur. J. Oper. Res. **247**(2), 339–348 (2015)

Author Index

Printed in the United States
By Bookmasters